ANALECTA BIBLICA
INVESTIGATIONES SCIENTIFICAE IN RES BIBLICAS

— 150 —

GEORGE KEERANKERI, S.J.

THE LOVE COMMANDMENT IN MARK

An Exegetico-Theological Study
of Mk 12,28-34

EDITRICE PONTIFICIO ISTITUTO BIBLICO - ROMA 2003

Vidimus et approbamus ad normam Statutorum Universitatis

Romae, ex Pontificia Universitate Gregoriana
die 26 mensis Novembri anni 2002

R.P. Prof. KLEMENS STOCK, S.J.
R. P. Prof. MASSIMO GRILLI

ISBN 88-7653-150-5
© E.P.I.B. – Roma – 2003

EDITRICE PONTIFICIO ISTITUTO BIBLICO
Piazza della Pilotta, 35 - 00187 Roma, Italia

To my beloved Parents:

Rosamma Cheruvallil
and
Varkey Kcerankeriparampil

PREFACE

This book is the improved version of my doctoral dissertation, «*The Love Commandment in Mark*», defended at the Faculty of Theology of the Pontifical Gregorian University, Rome, on 26 November, 2002. It is also the fulfillment of a long-cherished dream. Its subject, constituting the core demands of God in both the Old and the New Testaments, has fascinated me for several years. The intrinsic connection of the Markan version of the Love Commandments with the person of Jesus and his Passion, which the thesis elaborates, is also an insight that has suggested itself to me for a long time. Years of teaching, coupled with deeply pedagogic life-experiences, slowly matured my thinking. Yet, my first attempts at articulation were fledgling and imperfect. It took the sage and experienced guidance of my director, Professor Klemens Stock, S.J. of the Pontifical Biblical Institute Rome, to enable me to give adequate form and expression to my reflection on the theme. While I thank the Lord for his providential guidance throughout this process, I place on record my profound gratitude to the significant role my director has played in this work by his rigorous, demanding direction and painstaking accompaniment.

I am also deeply grateful to Professor Massimo Grilli, of the Pontifical Gregorian University, the second reader of my thesis, for his appreciative comments on my work and for his valuable suggestions for its improvement.

My heart-felt thanks are due also to the community of the Pontifical Biblical Institute of which I was part, for all the support and companionship I have received throughout the period of my doctoral studies.

Next, I must remember my family and friends. First my parents, both of whom are gone for their eternal reward some fifteen years ago, but who taught me, by word and example, the rudiments of the Christian faith. Also, my brothers and sisters and close relatives who carry the torch lit by them and live out their faith.

Then come my colleagues and students of «Vidyajyoti», the Jesuit Faculty of Theology in Delhi, India, where I teach. I must first mention Professor T. K. John who has been a true friend and guide all along my teaching career, from whom I have learnt many things and whose advise I esteem; then all my other colleagues with whom I have shared my life and teaching since several years. I also remember many batches of students, Jesuits, seminarians, other religious men, brothers, sisters and lay persons, both at the Faculty and outside, for whom I have had the privilege to interpret the word of God and spend my life. I cherish their memory and value their friendship.

Next, I remember with thanks my superiors who have been associated with this endeavor: Rev. Fr. Julian Fernandes, S.J., currently a General Assistant of the Society of Jesus, who was the Provincial of India earlier, for his wise and supportive decisions in my regard; Rev. Fr. Varkey Perekkatt, S.J., the latter's successor, for giving me the timely permission to continue my studies in Rome, thus enabling me to get the expert guidance I needed for my thesis and to have it done in a prestigious University; Rev. Fr. John Manipadam, S.J., the Provincial of Kerala, my original Jesuit Province, and Rev. Fr. Lisbert D'Souza, S.J., my current superior, for their steady support and appreciation.

Further, I thank Missionswissenschaftliches Institut Missio, Aachen, which gave me a generous scholarship for an year's research abroad in connection with the preparation of this thesis in its early stages.

I recall also my many friends who have helped me in myriad ways by their invaluable personal support and love. I can only recommend them to the Lord, as such a contribution cannot be repaid adequately but only accepted thankfully.

Finally, I thank in a special way Rev. Fr. Albert Vanhoye, S.J. for his incisive comments and helpful suggestions, and for graciously accepting to publish this work in the «Analecta Biblica» series which he directs.

TABLE OF CONTENTS

PART II: THE LOVE COMMANDMENT IN MARK

GENERAL INTRODUCTION

1. The Problem

This book studies the text of the love commandment (Mk 12,28-34) within the gospel of Mark. Formulated as a problem, the question it investigates is the following: Do the texts of the love commandment, Deut 6,4-5 and Lev 19,18, have the same meaning in the gospel of Mark (12,28-34) as in their OT contexts or do they acquire, over and above this, a specific Markan significance? If so, what is their full Markan specificity?

It is our contention that there is a specificity to the Markan interpretation of the love commandment, one intimately linked to the person of Jesus and expressed in a variety of data, both formal and thematic. This specificity can be found there in an integral reading of the gospel, one which converges to argue for such a specificity. We attempt to establish this by investigating this pericope (12,28-34) within the gospel employing modern Redaction-criticism. As no full-length study so far has been conducted on this question from this perspective, this treatment of the topic is new. It also limits itself to the gospel of Mark.

2. Status Quaestionis and the Focus of Our Study

Previous studies on the topic of the love commandment (Mk 12,28-34) consist of mostly generalized treatments in the form of certain books and articles. None of these are exclusively devoted to the study of Mk 12,28-34 but rather include it in their wider ambit.

Among the more important of the books on the topic belongs the study of Klaus Berger, *Die Gesetzesauslegung Jesu. Ihr historischer Hintergrund im Judentum und im Alten Testament. Teil I: Markus und Parallelen*[1]. It is essentially an investigation on Jesus' interpretation of the Law and its historical background in Judaism and in the OT, with special reference to Mk and its parallels and its implications and consequences for Judaism and Christianity. It deals with the love commandment as a central question in this connection, as it is understood

---

[1] WMANT 40, Neukirchen 1972.

as summarizing the Law. It is thus not a study which has the love commandment as its principal focus.

In the treatment of the love commandment itself, Berger investigates the *religionsgeschichtlich* background of the idea of this commandment as the quintessence of the Law which he holds is to be found in the Hellenistic and, more closely, Philonic understanding of εὐσέβεια and δικαιοσύνη as the basic principles of religion which made possible the combination of Deut 6,4-5 and Lev 19,18 in Hellenistic Judaism understood as the sum and substance of the Law and came into Christianity through its influence. In his study, Berger also attempts to outline the theological-historical significance of the adoption of this Hellenistic double-principle, εὐσέβεια καὶ δικαιοσύνη, through Hellenistic Judaism and early Christianity in the above manner.

Similarly, V. P. Furnish, *The Love Command in the New Testament*[2], is a study of this commandment as it occurs in different documents of the NT, a monograph which tries to bring out its specific nuances in each of these books. The love commandment text of our study, Mk 12,28-34 and parallels, which mention both the commandment to love God wholeheartedly and the commandment to love the neighbor, are considered in this study. But, since the rest of the instances of this commandment mention only love of neighbor and does not explicitly refer to the commandment to love God, most of this work focuses on the former (Lev 19,18). Furnish's study thus primarily concentrates on the commandment to love the neighbor in different NT documents and has the nature of a generalized work on the topic, as it tries to be exhaustive.

A third book, Mudiso Mba Mundla, *Jesus und die Führer Israels. Studien zu den sog. Jerusalemer Streitgesprächen*[3], is a study of the controversies of Jesus' Jerusalem ministry (11,27-33; 12,13-17; 12,18-27; 12,28-34; 12,35-37) from a Form-critical point of view. The study of the pericope of the love commandment (12,28-34) forms part of this general project[4]. It discusses its Form-critical aspects and goes on to indicate its structure and then clarifies the meaning of the citations of the love commandment in the OT and their Source-critical relationships *vis-à-vis* the versions of Mt and Lk and the possible Tradition-history of the pericope. This is followed by a discussion of the rise of the love commandment from the point of view of its possible *relig-*

---

[2] New York 1972

[3] Münster 1984.

[4] Cf. M. MUNDLA, *Jesus und die Führer*, 110-229.

ionsgeschichtlich background. An exegetical study of the two commandments in Mk follows which also clarifies the relationship between
them. The reply of the scribe (12,32f) is discussed and a certain interpretation given to the concluding remark of Jesus in 12,34b. The newness of the teaching of Jesus in the love commandment is then clarified
in relation to his Kingdom proclamation and the study also probes the
historicity of this commandment. While the pericope is seen as belonging to the group of controversies which forms part of Jesus' Jerusalem
ministry, no systematic attempt is made to study its literary and thematic relationships in regard to its wider contexts. Although the pericope is discussed in relation to the macro-text of the gospel, it is done
in very general terms and concludes with the general observation, that
its occurrence just before the Passion Narrative points to Jesus as the
historical realization of the love commandment. For all this, Mundla's
study is a brief one and not a detailed monograph on the issue.

The fourth, Heikki Sariola., *Markus und das Gesetz*[5], is a Redaction-critical study of the passages in Mk that deal with the Law which
aims at discovering the Evangelist's theological position *vis-à-vis* the
Law. It includes six studies: (1) on Ritual Purity (7,1-23); (2) on Sab-
bath (2,23-28; 3,1-6 + 1,21-39); (3) on Marriage (10,2-12); (4) on the
Decalogue (10,17-27); (5) on the Greatest Commandments (12,28-34);
(6) and on the Temple (11,15-19 + 14,55-64 and 15,29-32). Law materials on these topics are dealt with in the following way: First, it is
subjected to the traditional Redaction-critical analysis to divide the text
into tradition and redaction. Though Redaction-criticism is stressed, the
data of Literary-criticism such as suspense, narrative logic, content and
linguistic indices are also employed as also Form-criticism. Besides
these qualitative methods, quantitative Markan traits are also used,
though to a lesser extent, because these can only exercise a cumulative
effect on the division of redaction and tradition. Though the natural order of the different methods is respected, the author stresses their cumulative effect and does not speak of a clear priority of anyone of
them. In the second phase, Redaction-criticism is continued and the
Law material is analyzed according to the results obtained in the
analysis of the first phase, to decipher the particular theological perspective that each of these two types of materials manifests. Yet the
primary interest is in the Markan orientation to Law.

The order of study is based on content. The final chapter sketches
Mk's theology of the Law based on the whole material discovered. I.

---

[5] AASF. DHL 56, Helsinki 1990.

this, the character of the Law material is clarified and possible reasons for them explained. In conclusion, the important principles of Mk concerning Law are delineated and his understanding of Law outlined.

Employing this over-all methodological project, the love commandment pericope is studied in two phases. It is first subjected to the traditional Redaction-critical analysis, and the text is divided into tradition and redaction. In the second phase of Redaction-criticism, the two types of data are examined for the theology of Law each manifests, and this results in highlighting Mk's theology of the love commandment. The pericope is seen in its relationship to the preceding controversies in the Jerusalem ministry (12,13-27), which puts it into relief as the most important of Jesus' temple-teaching. It is also seen in relation to the following pericope (12,35-37), but the relationship is indicated in passing and is not systematically developed.

In a final step, the conception of the love commandment seen in its analysis is considered in relation to the previous Law-pericopes studied (cf. 10,17-27; 11,15-19; 3,1-6; 7,1-23), which reveals the second love commandment to be the summary of the second table of the Decalogue. Although the first love commandment probably was the summary of the first table of the Decalogue or of similar commandments in the OT for the traditional material, still it cannot be proved to be the case for the theology of Mk. This is because Sariola believes that, on the basis of the redactional activity of Mk in 12,28-34, the first commandment (Deut 6,4 = Mk12,29) has an independent importance beside the first great commandment (12,30)[6].

The fifth, Jarmo Kiilunen, *Das Doppelgebot der Liebe in syno ptischer Sicht. Ein redaktionskritischer Versuch über Mk 12,28-34 und die Parallelen*[7], is a specific monographic study on this topic and its Synoptic parallels. Although it is qualified as a Redaction-critical study, the aim of this work is to establish the correctness of the Two-sources theory by an analysis of this pericope, using a combination of Source-critical and Redaction-critical approaches. For this purpose, it examines all the main theories of Synoptic inter-dependence, in particular the Two-sources and Two-gospels theories, and by a minute comparison of the three parallel texts of the love commandment, attempts to establish the correctness of the Two-sources theory. The Source-critical analysis is then buttressed by a Redaction-critical one and the study concludes that, while Source-critical data alone cannot decide the question one way or the

---

[6] Cf. H. SARIOLA, *Markus und das Gesetz*, 207.
[7] STAT 250, Helsinki 1989.

other, a combination of the latter data with Redaction-critical results decides the issue clearly in favor of the Two-sources theory.

In the Redaction-critical analysis itself, only the versions of Mt and Lk are studied systematically. Mk's redaction and theology are not seriously analyzed. It is treated in general terms, with a statement that the Markan pericope has its own profile, identity and theological thrust and by naming certain salient features, but without a systematic study. This follows from the position that by clarifying the redactions of Lk and Mt on the Markan text, the latter is shown to be original which entails that, given the author's purpose, it is not necessary to dwell on it elaborately.

Finally, apart from these longer studies, there are a number of articles on the love commandment (12,28-34 + par.), some of which are by notable scholars and contribute significantly to the discussion of the topic[8] or clarify aspects of it. These micro-studies do not however affect the scope of our investigation, and hence we shall not describe them here but refer to them in the course of our discussion wherever relevant.

As a full-length, detailed doctoral dissertation on the love commandment pericope (12,28-34) using modern Redaction-critical method, our study has a focus and scope that are clearly identifiable and distinct from the foregoing studies. Not only does it investigate the question in its theoretical aspect of the gospel's interpretation of this commandment in a synchronic, integral perspective, but it also studies the practical aspect of its fulfillment in the Passion of Jesus, his teaching by example, which give it a specific identity as a detailed, systematic and wholistic study. It further differentiates itself from most of them by its first part which devotes two separate chapters to the OT meaning and background of the texts of the love commandment, Deut 6,4-5 and Lev 19,18. The further contours of this study will become clearer below as we sketch its itinerary and describe its main contents.

---

[8] Cf. The more important of these are the following: BORNKAMM, G., «Das Doppelgebot der Liebe», in *Geschichte und Glaube* I, Gesammelte Aufsätze Band III. München, 1968, 37-45; BURCHARD, C., «Das Doppelte Liebesgebot in der frühen christlichen Überlieferung», *Der Ruf Jesu und die Antwort der Gemeinde*, Fs. J. Jeremias, Göttingen, 1970, 39-62; FULLER, R.H., «The Double Commandment of Love: A Test Case for the Criteria of Authenticity», in *Essays on the Love Comm andment*, Fuller, R.H., ed. Philadelphia, 1978, 41-56; KERTELGE, K., «Das Doppelgebot der Liebe im Markusevangelium», in *À Cause de l'Évangile. Études sur les Synoptiques et les Actes*. Fs. P. J. Dupont, O.S.B, Le Div 123, Paris 1985, 304-322.

3. Methodology

The methodology we follow is modern Redaction-criticism, whose distinguishing characteristic from classical Redaction-criticism[9] is that it is synchronic[10]. The method «concentrates on the text as it now appears in written form and as a complex whole of text signals»[11] and takes this text as a structured and coherent unit in which the elements are combined in a way to create a unitary body[12]. The meaning of the text is therefore found in relationships produced by patterns of organization within this common framework. Thus, the text becomes an independent and autonomous system which creates meaning within a singular frame of reference[13]. This implies that in the application of this method our pericope will discover its meaning within its textual unit seen in the wider context of the total gospel of Mark.

More specifically, our method differs from classical Redaction-criticism in the following respects. The latter studied a particular document, for instance a gospel, in relation to its source documents and thus sought to distinguish between tradition and redaction through a process of Source-critical, Tradition-critical and Redaction-critical analyses. In determining tradition and redaction it also presupposed Source-critical hypotheses such as the Two-sources theory, the Three document hypothesis, and the like. In both cases, the procedures involved pre-suppositions that are hypothetical which, for this reason, could only produce hypothetical results. Our method prescinds from both these steps. No attempt is made to distinguish between tradition and redaction and no source-hypothesis is presupposed. The document under study is taken as a given, wholistic document to be understood in terms of itself.

Thus, we study the pericope in an integral reading. After establishing its delimitation, an essential step which determines its immediate context in which vocabulary and syntax and individual statements produce a web of meaning, it is analyzed at its grammatical, morphological, syntactical and semantic levels. However, special attention is given to the study of its vocabulary and syntax as these occur in the gospel,

---

[9] For an accurate general understanding of this latter method see, N. PERRIN, *What is Redaction Criticism?*, 1-3.

[10] Cf. W. EGGER, *Methodenlehre zum Neuen Testament*, 74-75.

[11] Cf. B.M.F. VAN IERSEL, *A Reader-Response Commentary*, 17; J. G. COOK, *The Structure and Persuasive Power*, 2, adds that it focuses on the meaning of the text as it stands without asking questions about its historical development.

[12] Cf. W. EGGER, *Methodenlehre zum Neuen Testament*, 74.

[13] Cf. E.K. BROADHEAD, *Teaching with Authority*, 26.

by analyzing their occurrences and contexts there. Since the text remains always part of the whole, the totality of their usage in their different contexts in the gospel would reveal the characteristic meaning these have in it, and hence, also their particular redactional nuances. A syntactic study, would show them in their relation to one another in constituting specific meanings and creating specific statements. These statements are then seen in their interrelationships and coherence to one another bringing about a total statement, which forms Mark's version of the love commandment. Thus, the study of the love commandment pericope as text would reveal its full meaning in the context of the gospel. This will include the literary and theological data that the gospel yields for its understanding in its macro-text which reveal its meaning within the gospel.

In this process, in some cases where it is useful and necessary to sharpen the specificity of the Markan text, a Synoptic comparison is also attempted, but this is done without presupposing any hypothetical Synoptic theory. The gospels concerned are taken as wholistic documents to be understood in terms of themselves, and are compared because of their similarities and differences *vis-à-vis* the Markan text, in order to sharpen the latter's individuality. Similarly, in certain cases, to clarify the meaning of particular motifs or statements, this comparative study has been extended to other relevant parts of the NT and the OT, which have a potential to enlighten them. The total outcome of these steps results in the articulation of the Markan redaction and reveals the Markan specificity of the love commandment.

4. The Itinerary and Principal Contents

The dissertation is divided into two parts and consists of four chapters and a final conclusion. Part I, which comprises the first two chapters, focuses on the love commandment in the OT, while Part II, which consists of the remaining two chapters, studies it in the gospel of Mk.

Thus Ch. I, after briefly clarifying the text-form of the commandment to love God, looks at the structure of Deut 6,4-5. This is followed by the exegesis of this text and a discussion of its context in Deuteronomy. Ch. II similarly, after a short discussion of the text-form of the commandment to love the neighbor, studies the formulation and structure of Lev 19,17-18 of which it is part. This is succeeded by the exegesis of the text of the commandment (v18b) and the clarification of its context in the book of Leviticus. These chapters thus give us a basis for the investigation of the gospel texts of the love commandment and enable us to see if they mean the same thing in Mk, or undergo a change or expansion of meaning there.

Part II, on the other hand, takes up the study of the love commandment in the gospel of Mark (12,28-34). Thus Ch. III, after a brief introduction of the pericope and delineation of its structure and form, investigates it exegetically, with special emphasis on the text of the love commandment, to bring out its integral meaning. For this purpose, special attention is paid to the commandment's vocabulary in its occurrence within the gospel. While this chapter thus deals with the theoretical aspect of Jesus' teaching on the love commandment in Mk, Ch. IV dwells on its practical aspect, that is, on the fulfillment of this commandment in the Passion of Jesus, his teaching by example, which thus complements the former and concludes it. Upon this, the final conclusion, after a brief summary of the findings of the research chapter by chapter, sees the Markan specificities in a global, unifying vision and closes by drawing the consequences of the Markan interpretation of the love commandment.

PART ONE

THE OLD TESTAMENT MEANING AND CONTEXT OF THE LOVE COMMANDMENT (DEUT 6,4-5 AND LEV 19,18)

INTRODUCTION

Part I is devoted to the study of the love commandment in the OT. It will consist in the clarification of the meaning of the texts of the commandment in their original OT contexts. This will give us a basis for our study of the gospel text and enable us to see if they mean the same thing in Mk or undergo a change or expansion of meaning.

CHAPTER I

The Commandment to Love God:
Deuteronomy 6,4-5

The chapter, after briefly clarifying the text form, will look at the structure of Deut 6,4-5. This will be followed by the exegesis of this text and a discussion of its context in Deuteronomy.

1. The Text Form

1.1 in Mark

The commandment to love God in Mark 12,29-30 does not present any textual problems. B. Metzger, *A Textual Commentary on the Greek New Testament,* (1994²) does not mention any serious problem concerning it. As there is scholarly consensus on the text as it stands, we shall take it as stabilized.

We shall, however, briefly discuss this text in relation to the LXX and MT to get a clear picture of it before we take up the discussion on its meaning in the Old Testament context.

1.2 in LXX

Mk 12,29-30 basically agrees with the text of Deuteronomy 6,4-5 in the LXX[1], except for the fact that in the Markan text there is the addition of καὶ ἐξ ὅλης τῆς διανοίας σου. The term διανοία here has no equivalent in the LXX[2]. Thus, in this extension of 3 terms into 4, the

---

[1] A. RAHLFS, *Septuaginta* I, gives a variant in Deut 6,5. It notes that καρδίας in this verse belongs to the original text of LXX at this point in Codex Alexandrinus (A). In Codex (Bᵛ) one finds at this place διανοίας. However, the rescriptor has so thoroughly suppressed the original text that it is no longer possible to decipher it. At any rate, the presence of διανοίας in Bᵛ in place of καρδίας is not a serious problem, since it is a rescriptor's contribution.

[2] Except for its presence in the text of LXX Bᵛ. According to A.T. FRANCE, *Jesus and the OT*, 240, this reading is most likely due to an assimilation to the Gospels.

Markan text can be said to differ from the LXX. It must be noted, however, that Mk is not alone in this. Lk has also the same 4 terms in his parallel text (cf. Lk 10,25-28) but there is difference in the word-order. In the Lukan text διανοία comes as the final term before ἰσχύς, while in Mk it is *vice versa*. In the Matthean version too the term διανοία is found, but the number of terms is reduced to 3 and διανοία occurs as the final term, neither ἰσχύς nor δύναμις being present in his list (cf. Mt 22,34-40). Thus, the presence of διανοία is a common Synoptic phenomenon, while the extension of terms from 3 to 4 is shared by both Mk and Lk. The ἰσχύς in Mk is in place of δύναμις in LXX.

The presence of διανοία in the Markan text and similarly in other Synoptics may be explained as a LXX influence since διανοία is a frequent translation of לב in it. An example for this is the variant rendering of Deut 6,5 in LXX (B*). It may also be due to a combination of two variants known to the author. It is but natural that a text in such constant liturgical use had several variant Aramaic forms[3], and Jesus or the Evangelist(s) might have combined two variants known to them in citing this well-known confession of Israel's faith[4].

1.3 in MT

The Markan text differs also from the MT version in the addition of καὶ ἐξ ὅλης τῆς διανοίας σου which has no equivalent in it. Mk also translates the MT מאד with ἰσχύς instead of the δύναμις of the LXX which also becomes the final member of the commandment in the his text. It has been suggested, that this Markan variation comes from the LXX translation of 2Kgs 23,25 where a MT מאד is translated with ἰσχύς in a similar formula. But there is little evidence to support this. It could very well be an independent translation of the MT מאד[5]. But

---

[3] Cf. A.T. FRANCE, *Jesus and the OT*, 240-241.

[4] For an evolutionary approach to the textual history of these citations see, K.J. THOMAS, «Liturgical Citations», 205-214. The author sees 4 different stages in the development of the text. He thinks that the citations originally corresponded to the LXX text most nearly equivalent to the Hebrew. The variants which arose later are accounted for as changes introduced in the history of the textual tradition for interpretational and grammatical reasons, *Ibid.*, 213. But the view seems quite hypothetical.

[5] A.T. FRANCE, *Jesus and the OT*, 240, says that the rendering of מאד with ἰσχύς makes the Markan text at this point agree with the MT against the LXX, as the latter has a different rendering of it. He rejects the suggestion that this Markan formulation may be influenced by LXX 2Kgs 23,25 and believes that it may be an independent translation of the MT מאד or of some Aramaic equivalent.

even with this change the terms κᾰρδία, ψυχή, ἰσχύς would have been sufficient to cover the MT list of לבב, נפש, מאד respectively, and hence the addition of διανοία in Mk stands out as a difference from MT and LXX.

2. The Structure of Deut 6,4-5

Deuteronomy 6,4-5 has a certain structure. There is first an address followed by a confessional formula with which is linked a commandment to love God with a single-minded devotion. The address שמע ישראל directs what follows to Israel as a community of faith, as well as to the individuals which constitute that community and share in its oneness. The confessional formula proper, יהוה אלהינו יהוה אחד, was the slogan of the deuteronomic reform that summarized the quintessence of Israel's faith in a confession[6]. The commandment that follows which enjoins total love and devotion to Yahweh, is the adequate response that Israel is to render to its unique God[7]. In its basic structure, the שמע thus involves two fundamental elements: an indicative followed by an imperative. First, there is the indicative, a basic statement in the form of a confession. Then, comes an imperative that enjoins a response to what is stated in the indicative. As the second is a response to the first, it is intimately linked with the latter and is a consequence of it.

However, the indicative involved is not any sort of statement. It concerns the nature of Yahweh, the God of Israel, a God it came to know through its historical experience of liberation from slavery in Egypt and through years of sustenance in the period of sojourn in the wilderness and of conquest and in and through the gift of the land[8]. The confessional formula when it tells Israel יהוה אלהינו יהוה אחד encapsulates in itself the revelation of Yahweh to Israel in and through its history. This fact qualifies this indicative as revelation, an all-important peculiarity. The nature of this indicative also qualifies the nature of the imperative which follows on it. It is the response of Israel to this central revelation in the form of commandment. Thus, the structure involved is better rendered as: (a) revelation; (b) response to the revelation or command-

---

6 Cf. R. ALBERTZ, *A History*, 351.

7 Cf. R. ALBERTZ, *A History*, 351. Also, S.R. DRIVER, *Deuteronomy*, 90; M. WEINFELD, *Deuteronomy*, 350. While the substance of this formulation is shared by these authors, the characterization of the שמע in terms of an indicative followed by an imperative is ours.

8 Cf. Deut 5,6; D.L. CHRISTENSEN, *Deuteronomy*, 145.

ments. The second is rooted in the first and follows from it[9]. In its entirety, שמע therefore, divides into: (a) Address: שמע ישראל; (b) Revelation: יהוה; אלהינו יהוה אחד; (c) Commandment or Response to the Revelation: ואהבת את יהוה אלהיך בכל-לבבך ובכל-נפשך ובכל-מאדך:

3. Exegesis of Deut 6,4-5

We shall here first clarify the meaning of the address form ישראל שמע and then pass on to explain the exact meaning of the monotheistic proclamation which accompanies it (v4). This will be followed by the explanation of the meaning of the commandment to love God integrally (v5).

3.1 The Address Form, (שמע ישראל)

In the section in Deut which deals with the principal commandment (Chs 5-11), the phrase שמע ישראל functions as a structure sign. This phrase, the vocative ישראל united with the imperative שמע, stands at the absolute or relative beginning of deuteronomic speeches, betraying its role as a structure sign[10]. In Chs 5-11 this combination of imperative שמע with vocative ישראל occurs 3 times: at 5,1; 6,4; 9,1. These mark the beginning of the minor didactic speeches in this part. As such, the role of this introductory formula as a structure sign in this section of the book is beyond doubt[11].

Although formally it is employed here as a structure sign, functionally it is a didactic formula which expresses an invitation to listen with a spirit of obedience. It has its roots in the Wisdom literature where formulas akin to this are employed by the wise teacher to address his pupil. The following formula שמע בני, («Listen, my son»), found in Proverbs (Prov 1,8; 4,10) and in Ps 34,12 (in plural) are typical examples[12]. An attitude of reverent obedience to what is said is in-

---

[9] Cf. S.R. DRIVER, *Deuteronomy*, 89; D.L. CHRISTENSEN, *Deuteronomy*, 142-143. The same pattern of the indicative of revelation followed by an imperative of commandments as consequence based on it, is present also in the presentation of the Decalogue in Deut Ch 5. Thus, we have the first in 5,6 and the second in 5,7-21.

[10] Cf. N. LOHFINK, *Das Hauptgebot*, 66.

[11] Cf. N. LOHFINK, *Das Hauptgebot*, 66.

[12] However, one should, as M. WEINFELD, *Deuteronomy*, 199, points out, make a minor distinction between שמע with a vocative as an opening address without an object, as in Deut 6,4; 9,1; 20,3; 27,9 and שמע with an object (the commandments), as occurs in Deut 4,1 (with אל) and 5,1 (with את) The same distinction holds good in the

volved in this address form. It is in this sense that שמע in our formula is to be understood. The appeal to listen obediently is addressed to the community of Israel. The address is made in the singular form, (שמע is imperative present second person singular), because Deut considers Israel as one cohesive entity[13].

3.2 The Confessional Formula (Deut 6,4)

In the Hebrew text of the commandment to love God, the formula שמע ישראל introduces the fundamental confessional formula: יהוה

אלהינו יהוה אחד.The LXX specifies the TM with the addition of only one ἐστιν which excludes other possible interpretations of it.

The MT text of this formula consists of the following elements: twice יהוה, in the first and the third places respectively, the substantive אלהים with the first person plural possessive suffix, and the adjective אחד. The following translations, certain of them understood in more ways than one, are possible:

1. Yahweh is our God, Yahweh is one. (RSV Footnote reading; R. Jicchaq[14]; R. Levi[15]).

2. Yahweh is our God, Yahweh alone. (Ibn Ezra, NJPS[16]; RSV Footnote reading).

3. Yahweh our God is one Yahweh. (cf. Driver 1902[17]; Also, R. Pinᵉchas b.Chama[18]; R. Acha[19]).

4. Yahweh our God, Yahweh is one. (RSV Footnote reading)[20].

The first two translations take יהוה as subject and אלהינו as predicate. While this is theoretically possible, it cannot be substantiated because in Deut the phrase יהוה אלהינו never occurs as subject and

---

book of Proverbs in the following occurrence, between 8,33; 23,20 (compare Ps 34,12) and between 1,8; 4,10; etc.

[13] Cf. M. WEINFELD, Deuteronomic School, 305.

[14] Cf. Str-B, II, 29.

[15] Cf. Str-B, II, 29.

[16] Cf. The New Jewish Publication Society of America, Translations to the Holy Scriptures, ad locum.

[17] Cf. S.R. DRIVER, Deuteronomy, 89-90.

[18] Cf. Str-B, II, 28.

[19] Cf. Str-B, II, 28-29.

[20] Cf. M. WEINFELD, Deuteronomy, 337. Also, Str-B, II, 30.

predicate but אלהינו always stands in apposition to יהוה (1,6; 5,2; 6,20.24.24 etc.), as N. Lohfink has pointed out[21]. Also against the first, is the fact that there is no sufficient reason for the resumption of the subject by the second יהוה[22]. Against the second is the lack of justification for assigning a double sense to אחד, since it takes אחד to mean «alone» when it actually means «one». In Hebrew the term for «alone» is לבד (2Kgs 19,15; Ps 86,10)[23] and אחד is not used adverbially in it[24]. The third translation looks awkward, because the first subject is discontinued[25]. Yet, G. Braulik maintains this rendering by taking אחד, «one» here as having the sense «only»[26]. In this sense, this rendering may be a possibility. However, C. Gordon's interpretation of אחד, «one» as a numeric name of God[27] must be rejected, as this position features nowhere in the OT. Israel came to know Yahweh through its historical experience of him, and not by borrowing practices like this from other cultures. Hence, the third and the fourth translations are the best options[28] and must be preferred[29].

However, M. Weinfeld contends that the «one» here connotes not only unity but also aloneness. On the basis of 1Chr 29,1: «God has chosen my son Solomon alone» (= שלמה בני אחד בחר־בו אלהים:), he argues that the word «one» = אחד here implies exclusiveness. He answers the objection, often raised against this translation, that «alone» in Hebrew is לבד and not אחד, by quoting A.B. Ehrlich who maintains that לבד is an adverb and hence inappropriate in a nominal sentence. For him, then, אחד is used here correctly[30].

---

[21] Cf. N. LOHFINK, «Gott im Buch», 108-109.

[22] Cf. S.R. DRIVER, *Deuteronomy*, 89.

[23] Cf. S.R. DRIVER, *Deuteronomy*, 89.

[24] Cf. R. ALBERTZ, *A History*, 351; n 65.

[25] Against Driver. Cf. M. WEINFELD, *Deuteronomy*, 337.

[26] Cf. G. BRAULIK, «Das Deuteronomium und die Geburt», 262.

[27] Cf. C. GORDON, «His name is "One"», *JNES* 29 (1970) 198. On the basis of the use of «one» or other numbers for God in ancient cultures of ancient Near East (known from Akkadian, Ugaritic and Egyptian texts) and Greece the author contends that אחד in the OT is the name of God. He goes on to say: «In the שמע it is quite possible that אחד means not only that there is but one God, but also that his name is אחד (One) : שמע ישראל יהוה אלהינו יהוה אחד (Deut 6:4) «Hear O Israel, Yahweh is our God, Yahweh is "One"», *Ibid.*, 98-99.

[28] Cf. R. ALBERTZ, *A History*, 351, n. 65.

[29] We may note that the fourth rendering corresponds to the Markan citation of Deut 6,4 in Mk 12,29-34.

[30] Cf. M. WEINFELD, *Deuteronomy*, 337-338; A. B. EHRLICH, *Miqra, ad locum*.

Weinfeld also cites in favor of this understanding Sumarian and Ug-aritic pagan liturgical texts, as well as texts of mystery cults where oneness implies aloneness. These pagan proclamations cannot be taken as monotheistic in themselves, as they have a hymnic liturgical nature. In this they are, in fact, similar to Deut 6,4. But what really tips the balance in favor of a monotheistic understanding of Deut 6,4, is its association with the first two commandments of the Decalogue and its connection with other proclamations in the sermons of Deut like 10,17[31].

However, the notion of exclusiveness is not explicit in this text as we find in Deut 4,35: «Yahweh alone is God: there is none beside him» or in Deutero-Isaiah 44,6; 44,5; 45,6.14.18.22; 46,9; or in 1Kgs 8,60 and 2Kgs 19,15.19. Nevertheless, the statement of unity in it seems to imply monotheism. This means that, while the monotheistic position sharpened and came to full expression during the Babylonian exile[32], it is incorrect to say that it was created there. Weinfeld finds monotheistic declarations in the Elijah traditions (יהוה הוא האלהים = Yahweh [alone] is God, 1Kgs 18,39), and in the Elisha stories («Now I know that there is no God in the whole world except in Israel», 2Kgs 5,15; cf. v17), and also in the older parts of Deut (Deut 7,9; 10,17), and he rejects attempts to interpret these phrases in a henotheistic sense (*contra* N. Lohfink *et al.*[33]). The mention of «other gods» (Deut 6,14; 13,8 etc.), does not involve the existence of Polytheism as Lohfink thought, because אלהים אחרים = «other gods» may imply idols and connote foreign worship in general. Besides, it is used as a conventional expression for deviation and apostasy. Hence, it does not tell us anything about Israel's belief in polytheism. The depiction of «other gods» as man-made, which starts with Hosea (8,6; 13,2; 14,4; cf. Is 2,8; Mic

---

[31] Cf. M. WEINFELD, *Deuteronomy*, 338.

[32] Cf. N. LOHFINK, «Gott im Buch», 107; G. BRAULIK, «Das Deuteronomium und die Geburt», 115-160.

[33] In the ancient Near East polytheism was widespread and it always left open the possibility of monolatry. While people believed in many gods, the person who worshipped one of these gods more or less consciously summed up in that god all that divinity meant for him or her. In another place and for another person, another god could be the manifestation of the whole of the divine. The term monolatry or henotheism refers to this belief.

Lohfink has maintained that in the period before Babylonian exile Israel's Yahwism had the nature of monolatry or henotheism. Israel did not deny that there were other gods but only that Yahweh was Israel's only God and is supreme for them. According to him, it is only with deutero-Isaiah during the exile that Israel arrived at real monotheism, N. LOHFINK, *Great Themes*, 135-152.

5,12) may in fact point to Israelite belief in the eighth-century that other gods are futile and devoid of any real power[34].

The phrase «Yahweh is one» (יהוה אחד), is thus a liturgical proclamation and, in view of the considerations above, connotes exclusiveness and uniqueness, and because of its special context in Deut has a monotheistic flavor.

Some scholars have maintained that the formula stresses the unicity of Yahweh, in the sense that it negates a multiplicity of attributes in Yahweh or a division in respect to localities[35] and activities in him as was common in the case of certain pagan gods[36], a problem which seems to have affected Yahwism as well, as certain texts seem to imply (cf. Jer 2,28; 11,13)[37]. While this is not impossible at some level in popular religion, it does not seem to be a concern of the text here, as the fragmentation of Yahweh is never explicitly recognized as a problem[38] nor discussed. It also does not figure as an argument to support the policy of unification and centralization of worship. Hence, the term אחד does not seem to have the connotation of unicity, as part of a polemic against the multiplying of Yahweh's manifestations.

The uniqueness of God here is understood as sole and exclusive. This is supported by the following injunction[39] which is phrased in ab-

---

[34] Cf. M. WEINFELD, *Deuteronomy*, 350; P.D. MILLER, *Deuteronomy*, 101, however, points out that in Mk 12,32 both meanings-the Lord is one and besides the Lord there is no other-are found in the Great Commandment pericope, which gives a canonical support for the claim that both meanings may be understood as legitimate. Nevertheless, whether this support is enough to decide the meaning of אחד in its original context in Deut is doubtful.

[35] Thus, P.D. MILLER, *Deuteronomy*, 98-99, claims that there is some evidence at least in popular religion, of a tendency to identify Yahweh, the Lord of Israel, with partieular places or locales. This possibility is at least suggested by references to «Yahweh of Samaria» and «Yahweh of Teman» in Hebrew inscriptions from the eighth century found at Kuntillet Ajrud, in the Negeb. He observes that, to some extent, these inscriptions point also to an incipient reverence of the *asherah* as a Yahweh symbol before becoming a separate object of worship, since the phrase «Yahweh and his *asherah*» appears in them more than once. This tendency, he thinks, had the potential to bring about a splitting and multiplying of Yahweh's manifestations.

[36] Thus Baal was thought of as having different attributes and identities depending upon the places of worship, A. PENNA, *Deuteronomio*, 118.

[37] Cf. M. WEINFELD, *Deuteronomy*, 349-351.

[38] Cf. S.D. MCBRIDE, «The Yoke of the Kingdom», 295.

[39] In so far as it gives it a more adequate basis for the demand for exclusive love made in it. For, a God who is «one» but not «unique» might not necessarily be a worthy object of human love, S.R. DRIVER, *Deuteronomy*, 90.

solute and exclusive terms, that is, to love God with one's whole being, to the exclusion of any rival to that love[40].

3.3 The Commandment to Love God exclusively (Deut 6,5)

The monotheistic proclamation of Deut 6,4 is followed by the injunction to love Yahweh exclusively. The MT text of v5 runs thus: ואהבת את יהוה אלהיך בכל־לבבך ובכל־נפשך ובכל־מאדך׃, which the LXX renders in the following way: καὶ ἀγαπήσεις κύριον τὸν θεόν σου ἐξ ὅλης τῆς καρδίας σού καὶ ἐξ ὅλης τῆς ψυχῆς σου καὶ ἐξ ὅλης τῆς δυνάμεώς σου. Syntactically, the verb ואהבת is linked with the imperative שמע in v4. The Hebrew construction of an imperative (here שמע), followed by a perfect ו-conversive, (here ואהבת), has an imperative meaning and is fitting for legal prescriptions. This makes the injunction to love God exclusively a corollary of the monotheistic declaration concerning Yahweh in v4. Vv 4 and 5, thus, form one unit[41]. The meaning, then, is that since Yahweh our God is one, you shall love him exclusively. The monotheistic proclamation of Yahweh, is thus the basis for the demand for exclusive and single-minded love of God.

3.3.1 The Nature of Love: Its Theological Character

The response demanded as a consequence of the proclamation of the uniqueness of God, is love (cf. ואהבת). We shall now turn to an examination of its exact meaning in Deuteronomy.

The verb root for love, אהב, together with its derivatives, is found 23 times in Deut. Of these 19 occur in a theological context, of which 13 have a human subject. Except for 10,19 where the «stranger» is the object of the verb «to love», all other instances have Yahweh as their object[42]. The term is used to express one's relationship to Yahweh, and this points to its theological character. Since in 12 out of 13 occurrences human love has Yahweh as its object, it is clear that in Deuteronomy the theological use of the term predominates. Even in 10,19, which enjoins love for the stranger, a theological dimension obtains because of the reference to Israel's experience in Egypt. In this use of the term, Deut has a striking closeness to the prophecy of 8th century B.C., which exhibits an almost completely exclusive theological use of

---

[40] Cf. n.34.

[41] Cf. M. WEINFELD, *Deuteronomy*, 351; A. PENNA, *Deuteronomio*, 118.

[42] Cf. K. ZOBEL, *Prophetie und Deuteronomium*, 51.

it[43]. The verb אהב, to love, in Deut is, thus, a theological concept that defines Israel's relationship to Yahweh and is a recurrent term in the book[44]. Its meaning and function can be seen in an analysis of its occurrences in Deut. According to content and grammatical standpoints, the 13 instances of אהב in theological contexts can be divided into the following three groups: The demand of love in the perfect (6,5; 11,1; 10,19); demand of love in infinitive constructions (10,12; 11,13.22; 19,9; 30,6.16.20); and motivation for love with suffixed active participles. (5,10; 7,9; 13,4)[45].

a) *Demand for Love in the Perfect*

The first instance of group 1, the demand of love in the perfect, is precisely Deut 6,5, the demand for exclusive love of Yahweh. As we saw above[46], after the fundamental statement on the unique Yahweh in v4, v5 explicitates the consequences for Israel which follow from it. V5 demands love that is undivided, and exclusively directed to Yahweh. Vv4 and 5 are also intimately connected. The general and abstract statement in v4 affirms Yahweh as «our God» and is oriented to Israel as a collectivity. But v5 speaks of Yahweh strikingly as «*thy* God» [second person singular]», and is thereby directed to each individual in the collectivity. It clarifies, how the God of Israel becomes the unique God for Israel in actual life. Only through the undivided love of each Israelite, will the idea of the one and only Yahweh become a reality for it[47].

The content of the undivided love demanded in v5, consists in a new step which becomes clear in v6. For, the commanded love is related in its concrete execution to the הדברים, «which I command you today» (v6). These words refer to the deuteronomic law announced in Deut 5,1.31 and detailed in subsequent chapters. This pointed reference to the law clearly warrants the conclusion, that to love Yahweh with all one's heart and all one's soul and all one's might means to observe his commandments with a single-minded devotion. The love for Yahweh, thus, means observance of law and expresses itself in the praxis of the law[48].

---

[43] Cf. K. ZOBEL, *Prophetie und Deuteronomium*, 75.
[44] Cf. K. ZOBEL, *Prophetie und Deuteronomium*, 75.
[45] Cf. K. ZOBEL, *Prophetie und Deuteronomium*, 51.
[46] Cf. 3.3.
[47] Cf. K. ZOBEL, *Prophetie und Deuteronomium*, 52.
[48] Cf. K. ZOBEL, *Prophetie und Deuteronomium*, 54.

As we see, the word love in Deut 6,5 emphasizes different nuances depending on whether one links it with the foregoing or the following verse. Connecting v5 with v4 brings the uniqueness of Yahweh into the fore, who, because he is unique and undivided, must be loved with an undivided love. Linking vv 5 + 6, on the other hand, emphasizes the vital connection between love towards Yahweh and observance of the law[49]. Both aspects are important, and together, give us the full meaning and implications of the love commandment in v5.

This connection between love of Yahweh and the observance of the law is confirmed and further deepened by Deut 11,1. Deut 11,1a repeats 6,5a: «And you shall love Yahweh your God». 11,1b, on the other hand, tries to ensure the love towards Yahweh with other means than 6,5b, as it immediately speaks of the practice of the law: «And you shall keep his charge, his statutes, his ordinances and his commandments always»[50]. The command to love in 11,1a is to be interpreted, with good reason, by the following ושמרת, (and you shall keep), of 11,1b. Hence, what becomes clear in 6,5b through a consideration of its immediate context, namely v6, is stated here *in expressis verbis*[51]. In this sense, Deut 11,1 not only supports, but also further clarifies and confirms the connection between exclusive love of Yahweh and observance of the commandments. Love for Yahweh is realized in the observance of his law and commandments. It also ensures the continuance of the love relationship with Yahweh[52].

b) *Demand for Love in Infinitive Constructions (10,12; 11,13.22; 19,9; 30,6.16.20)*

These 7 texts in Deut demand love for Yahweh in infinitive constructions. They can be divided into two smaller groups in the way they speak of love. Thus, four of these (Deut 11,13.22; 19,9; 30,16), speak of love of Yahweh as the task of obedience to the law, while the remaining 3 texts (Deut 30,6.20; 10,12) speak of love of Yahweh as the basis of human life; and Deut 10,12 mentions also «fear», «walking with Yahweh», and «serving him» as the basis of well-being of man. But all of them, in one way or the other, connect love of Yahweh and obedience to the law.

---

[49] Cf. K. ZOBEL, *Prophetie und Deuteronomium*, 54, n.176.
[50] Cf. K. ZOBEL, *Prophetie und Deuteronomium*, 54-55.
[51] Cf. K. ZOBEL, *Prophetie und Deuteronomium*, 58.
[52] Cf. K. ZOBEL, *Prophetie und Deuteronomium*, 54-55.

+ Deut 11,13.22; 19,9; 30,16, Love of Yahweh as the Task of Obedience to the Law. These 4 texts actually invert the sequence «love-observance of the law» we saw in 6,5f and 11,1, but they do not thereby alter the intention of those texts. The conception, in short, is: one observes the law out of love for Yahweh which is a necessary pre-condition for well-being. Thus, a logical sequence emerges here of the concepts «love»-«law»-«well-being» as a phenomenon of deuteronomistic theology. Between love and well-being there is a necessary third factor. In this conception, therefore, love for Yahweh is not a sufficient pre-condition for divine blessings. It has to be concretized, and thus tested, in the observance of the law[53].

+ Deut 30,6.20, Love of God as the Basis of Human Life. The remaining texts in infinitive constructions consider the love for Yahweh as the foundation of human life. Deut 30,6.20 is particularly significant. Though the hitherto oft-mentioned connection of love and observance of commandments is not clearly present here, it is not totally missing. This is clear from the thought movement till v8: Learning from the experience of judgment (v1f) Israel takes the first step of conversion to Yahweh. But Yahweh himself brings the movement to fulfillment by circumcising the heart of Israelites and enabling them to a fuller love of him (v6), which is proved in the obedience to his law (v8)[54].

Actually, thus, vv6 and 20 motivate and establish love towards Yahweh with a promise of life. This point is important, because these two verses are the only ones in Deut which make love for Yahweh a pre-condition for maintenance of life in the promised land[55].

+ Deut 10,12, Love of Yahweh (Fear of Yahweh, Walking in his ways and Serving him) Expressed in the Observance of the Law as the Basis of Well-being of Man. While this text, like the previous, connects love of Yahweh expressed in the observance of the law as the basis of human life, it also mentions other synonymous terms for it. It thus first speaks of the fear of Yahweh and goes on to list other synonymous phrases: «And now Israel, what does Yahweh require of you except to fear Yahweh, to walk in his ways, to love him (לאהבה אתו) and serve Yahweh with whole heart and whole soul».

The appeal addressed to Israel thus demands fear of Yahweh, walking in his ways, love, service and observance of the law. It thus requires

---

[53] Cf. K. ZOBEL, *Prophetie und Deuteronomium*, 61-63.
[54] Cf. K. ZOBEL, *Prophetie und Deuteronomium*, 63-65.
[55] Cf. K. ZOBEL, *Prophetie und Deuteronomium*, 67.

twice a certain inner orientation of the human person (אהב, ירא), which is manifested and concretized in the observance of the law. Love towards Yahweh and fear of him, are mentioned as the real motive of man for keeping the commandments of Yahweh or «walking in his ways». The goal of this is well-being. This is evident in v13b, which motivates the observance of the law by saying: «so that it goes well with you». We see here again that preferred structure which presents the observance of the commandments as the middle member in a threefold construction: (love [or fear]-observance of law-well-being)[56].

c) *Motivation for Love in Suffixed Active Participles (5,10; 7,9; 13,4)*

The Motivation to love in suffixed active participles are found in Deut in the following texts: 5,10; 7,9; 13,4. Their thought-content agrees in characteristic peculiarities, which makes it advisable to consider them together.

The block that begins in 5,6 whose theme is the safeguarding of the exclusive worship of Yahweh and formulates the first Decalogue commandment, comes to its end in v10. After v6 began with the self introduction of Yahweh as the God who brought Israel out of Egypt, vv7-9a mentions the first consequences, namely, not having any other gods and not worshipping them. The grounding of this series of prohibitions begins in v9b and extends to v10. Yahweh is a jealous God, visiting the iniquity of the fathers upon their children, but showing graciousness to thousands who love him (לאהבי) and keep his commandments. V10, thus, demands love for Yahweh alone, because he is a jealous God. The linkage of love and observance of law as pre-condition for divine blessing, typical of Deut, though found, is more distant. In a similar way, the preferred conception in Deut: love + observance of law = well-being, is found in the other two texts, Deut 7,9 and 13,4, although love here is not so much demanded as skillfully counseled. It is motivated, in so far as Yahweh's חסד is promised to all who love him[57].

In the linkage of אהב and חסד in 5,10 and 7,9 Zobel sees an influence of the prophecy of 8th century, but in a way that has transformed its thought-content. This prophecy used the active participle of אהב negatively to describe Israel's permanent falling away from Yahweh. Israel fell away from her God because of her false love.

---

56 Cf. K. ZOBEL, *Prophetie und Deuteronomium*, 69-70.
57 Cf. K. ZOBEL, *Prophetie und Deuteronomium*, 72-73.

In this prophetic thought, the observance of law is understood as the real content of חסד (Mi 6,8; Hos 12,7; Is 16,5), and the absence of חסד signals lawlessness (Hos 4,1f). But according to Deut the human attitude אהב concretizes itself in the observance of the law, which shows how love has become something positive in it, characterizing man's positive response to God. Deut's conception of חסד is also different, in that it is thought of as God's gift, following and dependent on the observance of the law. Thus, Deut gives the motivation for the praxis of the law with the promise of divine חסד. With these changes in nuance, it has gone a step further than Hosea and Micha. Yet it avoids the use of חסד in the sense of an unconditional gift. When it uses the term, Deut qualifies or conditionalizes it with love or similar words for observance of the law[58].

d) *Summary Definition of Love in Deuteronomy*

Having clarified the meaning of the concept «love of God» (אהב) in Deuteronomy, we may now define it as the inner holistic orientation of the human person to God based on his/her deliberate decision. This concretizes itself in the observance of God's commandments or the Law. Thus, the word love, originally an emotionally-charged relation-determination *vis-à-vis* human beings, things, or God, becomes in Deut a motif for observance of law[59], a theological reality. While it can be used equally beside other verbs as relation-determination towards Yahweh, it can also remain beside verbs for observance of law[60].

---

[58] Cf. K. ZOBEL, *Prophetie und Deuteronomium*, 73-75.

[59] As far as the motivation for love for Yahweh is concerned, it is interesting to note that Deut does not mention love of Yahweh as the basis of Israel's love towards him. Statistically, 5 times no basis is given for it (Deut 11,13.22; 3,6.16.20), K. ZOBEL, *Prophetie und Deuteronomium*, 76, n.261; a further 4 times the events in Egypt are mentioned as its basis (Deut 5,6-10; 10,19; 11,1-7; 13,6), *Ibid.*, 77, n.262; twice the uniqueness of Yahweh (Deut 6,4f. 10,12-15), *Ibid.*, n.263, and once his love of righteousness (Deut 19,9), *Ibid.*, n.264. In this connection Zobel also points out that in the grounding or motivating of the love commandment the theological concepts of «election» and «covenant» play hardly any role at all. The lone instance of a connecting of love, election and covenant is Deut 7,6f, *Ibid.*, n.265. For him this shows that the linkage of love, election and covenant is not a central theological motif in Deut, *Ibid.*, n.266.

[60] Cf. K. ZOBEL, *Prophetie und Deuteronomium*, 75-77. Since the love towards Yahweh concretizes itself in the observance of the Law, it can be commanded. There is, thus, no incongruity in the commandment to love, *Ibid.*, 76. But love as a motif for observance of law means also that the orientation to God and relationship with him which love of God involves, relates to fellow human beings as well, since the commandments involve God's will concerning the way his people should relate to one an-

These related terms include fear, walking in his ways, obedience and service, (Deut 10,12; cf. 11,13; 30,16.20). These phrases are synonymous and emphasize both one's inner orientation to God and its expression in the observance of the commandments[61].

3.3.2 The Modality of Love: The Meaning of the Tripartite Formula

The demand for total, exclusive love is made in the commandment by a tripartite formula created by the use of the following three terms in the MT: לבב, נפש and מאד, their LXX equivalents being, καρδία, ψυχή, and δύναμις.

לבב or καρδία means heart which in the Old Testament is understood as the seat and center of rational (cf. Jer 5,21; Hos 7,11; Job 12,24) and affective life[62]. The לב, the synonymous variant of לבב in the MT, is understood in Deut as the repository, place of ethically positive *habitus* of man and his sincere conviction[63]. In the Hebrew Anthropology, the heart is presented as the place of deliberative decision which, in this context, will be for or against Yahweh[64]. While לבב and לב are interchangeable, Deut and Deuteronomic literature have a preference for ללבב[65]. «With all your heart», thus, means with one's total inner intellectual and deliberative orientation.

נפש or ψυχή means soul or life force and, in a broader sense, it can also denote in the OT spiritual passion and action of every type[66]. It is the organ of desires or affections (Deut 12,20; 24,15; Ps 24,4; 143,8). The latter two instances, it may be noted, have God as the object of desire[67]. נפש in connection with the word «love», means «affection» or «aversion», in any case, the emotional orientation of one's own exis-

---

other. In this sense, the vertical relationship the love commandment in Deut 6,5 stresses, necessarily involves a horizontal dimension in its conception and execution, *Ibid.*

[61] In this connection see also, M. WEINFELD, *Deuteronomy*, 351.

[62] Cf. BAUMGÄRTEL., «Καρδία», *TDNT*, III, 605-607.

[63] Cf. H.J. FABRY, «לֵב», «לֵבָב», *ThWAT*, IV, 413-415; «In ihm ist die aufrichtige Gesinnung des Menschen angesiedelt (in Spr.23,19 mit der Weisheit verbunden)», 443.

[64] Cf. K. ZOBEL, *Prophetie und Deuteronomium*, 72, n.239.

[65] Cf. M. WEINFELD, *Deuteronomy*, 332.

[66] Cf. E. JACOB., «Ψυχή», *TDNT*, IX, 608-31.

[67] Cf. S.R. DRIVER, *Deuteronomy*, 73-74.

tence towards Yahweh[68]. «With all your soul», thus, means with full devotion, with one's total emotional and affectional orientation.

To love with one's «whole heart» and «whole soul» means the total inner orientation of the person, his deliberate decision for Yahweh, the undividedness of his affection-filled devotion[69].

מאד or δύναμις means strength or might, and is largely co-extensive with ἰσχύς[70]. מאד is used, in this sense, only in the שמע and in the deuteronomistic passage 2Kgs 23,25. Otherwise, it is an adverb meaning «very». מאד as «strength» or «might» implies two things: ability (power or strength), and resources or wealth. Semantically, it is similar to the nouns כח and חיל in Hebrew, which mean mainly strength but also signify wealth[71].

The three terms are preceded by the particle כל in MT and ὅλη in the LXX, and are governed by the preposition ב in MT and ἐξ in LXX. The combination of this particle with the preposition, has the effect of stressing the aspect of totality. It seems to be significant that these terms, preceded by כל / ὅλη + preposition, occur only thrice in the entire OT. Apart from its incidence in Deut 6,5, it is found in the LXX in 2Kgs 23,25 and in 2Chr 35,19[72], and in the MT at 2Kgs 23,25, the LXX parallel of 2Chr 35,19 being absent in the MT. However, Deut 6,5 is the only instance of this tripartite formula with אהב in the OT, since the text of 2Kgs 23,25 is with שוב and 2Chr 35,19 with its Greek equivalent ἐπέστρεψεν.

In the passage of 2Kgs 23,25, the terms preceded by the particle + preposition occur in a statement of evaluation on the reign of king Josiah. It says: «Before him there was no king who turned to the Lord with all his heart and with all his soul and with all his might according to the law of Moses nor did any like him arise after him». Thus, Josiah

---

[68] Cf. C. WESTERMANN, «נֶפֶשׁ», «Seele», THAT, II, 71-96. Also, K. ZOBEL, Prophetie und Deuteronomium, 72, n.239.

[69] Cf. K. ZOBEL, Prophetie und Deuteronomium, 71-72; 75.

[70] Cf. W. GRUNDMANN, «ἰσχύω», TDNT, III, 397-402.

[71] Cf. M. WEINFELD, Deuteronomy, 339.

[72] In both 2Kgs 23,25 and 2Chr 35,19 the preposition preceding the particle ὅλη is ἐν, governing the dative case, whereas in the text of Deut 6,5 the preposition before the particle is ἐξ, governing the genitive case. It may be also noted, that the MT מאד is rendered by the LXX in Deut 6,5 with δύναμις, while in 2Kgs 23,25 the term used is ἰσχύς. In the text of 2Chr 35,19, which is not found in the MT, the third term used is also ἰσχύς.

is presented here as a person who served the God of Israel as he truly deserves, as the commandments require.

2Chronicles 35,19 is a parallel passage dealing with the same subject-matter, but is found only in the LXX, the MT having left this out. Here too the reign of king Josiah is evaluated in almost identical words: «There was no one like him before him who turned to the Lord with all his heart and with all his soul and with all his might according to all the law of Moses; nor did any like him arise after him».

Thus, in both cases, the 3 terms are employed together to describe the conduct of a king who served the Lord as he really deserves, with a total and singular devotion. Judging from the three contexts where these terms preceded by particle כֹל / ὅλη + preposition appear together, this phraseology seems to have a special purpose. It seems to be employed in the OT for the unique purpose of describing with a note of insistence the total and singular character of the love and devotion with which God is to be loved. Putting it differently, it is most likely that «the three phrases expressed a totality in a climactic fashion: heart-will, the whole self, to excess or muchness»[73]. The total character of the response is emphatically underlined[74]. It indicates, as McBride puts it: «the superlative degree of total commitments»[75].

---

[73] Cf. P.D. MILLER, *Deuteronomy*, 103.

[74] Outside of the above contexts, the combination נפֹש לב / לבב (= «heart», «soul») preceded by the particle כֹל is more commonly used to express the idea of totality and single-mindedness of the devotion due to God. The distribution of this bipartite formula is wholly confined to Deut and deuteronomic literature, M. WEINFELD, *Deuteronomy*, 339. Thus, we find the bipartite formula in Deut in 4,29 with דֹרשֹ; in 11,18 with שֹים; in 26,16 with עֹשֹה + שֹמר; in 30,2 with שֹמע; in 30,10 with שֹמר + שֹמע + שֹוב. In DtrG they stand in Jos 22,5; 23,14; 1Sam 2,35; 1Kgs 2,4; 8,48; 2Kgs 23,3. In the prophets, we find it in Jer 32,41, a deuteronomic editorial strand, K. ZOBEL, *Prophetie und Deuteronomium*, 70, n.237. These data clearly reveal it to be a characteristic of deuteronomic school. The bipartite formula also strongly expresses the wholeness demanded for the love of Yahweh.

According to Zobel the shrinkage of the tripartite formula to the bipartite one, with «might» being left out, is a reflection of the impact of the exile on the love theology of Deuteronomy. This tragedy with its bitter experiences, taught Israel to put no great value in «might» namely, military power and resources, especially considering that, except for king Josiah, all its kings have been disloyal to Yahweh, but to concentrate on the «heart» and «soul», the inner core of the person and community, its inner orientation. For details see, K. ZOBEL, *Prophetie und Deuteronomium*, 71-72.

[75] Cf. S.D. MCBRIDE, «The Yoke of the Kingdom», 304.

4. The Context of Deut 6,4-5

After having seen the exegesis of Deut 6,4-5 we shall now consider this text in its context in the book of Deuteronomy.

4.1 Deut 6,4-5 vis-à-vis its Preceding Context

The most important preceding context of Deut 6,4-5, the שמע, is Ch 5 which presents the Decalogue (cf. 5,6-22) where, as we observed above[76], the revelation of God precedes the commandments which follow. The Decalogue is presented with the statement in 5,6: «I am the Lord your God, who brought you out of the land of Egypt, out of the house of bondage» (Deut 5,6). This is followed by the first commandment: «You shall have no other gods before me» (Deut 5,7), and then by the remaining commandments (5,8-22). The שמע and the rest of Ch 6 which comes after this is considered as a commentary and restatement of the first commandment of the Decalogue[77]. Its placement following the Decalogue in Ch 5 and its thematic unity with the first commandment justify this understanding.

The same connection between the revelation of God and the commandments is reflected, though perhaps less directly, in 5,23-6,3 which is the concluding section of Deut 4,44-6,3. This passage, which immediately ensues the giving of the Decalogue in 5,6-22, is arranged in a concentric pattern, from a rhythmic perspective, with seven subsections. It reviews, in the form of a reminiscence coupled with exhortation on the part of Moses, the chief elements of the event of the theophany of Sinai and the giving of the principal commandment, the statutes and the ordinances[78] and exhorts the observance of these for all time to come that the people may prosper in the land they are going to enter[79].

---

[76] Cf. n.9.

[77] Cf. P.D. MILLER, *Deuteronomy*, 79.

[78] These include: the theophany (5,23-24); people's complaint to Moses (5,25-26); people's request to him «Be our mediator» upon their fear of the divine presence (5,27-28a); Yahweh's response: «Be their mediator» (5,28b-31); Moses' request: «Do as Yahweh has commanded» (5,32-33); the reference to the giving of the principal commandment, the statutes and the ordinances (6,1-2a.); Summary: the commandments are for all time (6,2b-3). For further details see, D.L. CHRISTENSEN, *Deuteronomy*, 132-133.

[79] Cf. Deut 6,2b-3.

It contains the same sequence of revelation of God (cf. the theophany [5,23]; the statement: the Lord our God has shown his glory and greatness [5,25]) followed by giving of the commandments (cf. 5,29.31; 6,1-2a) and is intimately connected with it; the fear (= love) of God[80] as the principal commandment and the connection between love of God and keeping of the commandments (v29). 6,1-3 in particular functions as a bridge, which concludes the larger section on the Ten Commandments (4,44-6,3) and introduces the next major section (6,4-7,11), which contains the שמע and the principal commandment to love God[81].

The connection of 5,23-6,3 to the commandments, on the one hand, and the שמע (6,4-5), on the other, is highlighted, in particular, in the incidence in it of the verbal root דבר eleven times (cf. 5,24.25.27 [bis].28 [5].31; 6,3). It concretely emphasizes the fact that both the Ten Commandments, which are now concluded, and the principal commandment, which follows immediately (Deut 6,5), are indeed the word of God[82]. Thus, both 5,6-22 and 5,23-6,3 which precede Deut 6,4-5 provide its immediate context and share the above connections with it.

The understanding of שמע's link with its preceding context (cf. 5,6) enables us, in particular, to place the revelation of Yahweh and the response to that Revelation in Deut 6,4-5 in its proper perspective. The Yahweh who is revealed there as one and unique is the Yahweh who brought Israel out of the house of bondage. The revelation is thus placed in the context of Israel's experience of liberation. It is in and through this that Yahweh has revealed himself as unique and one. The self-revelation of Yahweh is part and parcel of his saving deeds, and is mediated through them[83]. It is his gift *par excellence* in and through all his other gifts to Israel. This also qualifies the response to the revelation in a particular way. It roots the commandment to love wholeheartedly in the context of unconditional gift, grace and fellowship. The commandment is to be a spontaneous and adequate

---

[80] For the synonymous character of these terms see, 3.3.1 b); 3.3.1 d). Also, Deut 10,12.

[81] Cf. D.L. CHRISTENSEN, *Deuteronomy*, 133; 135

[82] Cf. D.L. CHRISTENSEN, *Deuteronomy*, 135.

[83] Cf. D.L. CHRISTENSEN, *Deuteronomy*, 145.

response on the part of a graced people, enjoying Yahweh's fellowship out of grateful love[84].

4.2 Deut 6,4-5 vis-à-vis its Following Context

What immediately follows Deut 6,4-5 is a catechetical section of which it is part, namely 6,4-25. It is associated with the liturgical dramatization of the experience of Exodus and the entry into Canaan celebrated at Gilgal after crossing the Jordan, referred to in Exod Chs 12-13, a tradition which has influenced Deut Ch 6[85]. This connection of Deut 6,4-5 thus points to its liturgical origins. After the confession of Deut 6,4-5, this catechetical section has a didactic passage enjoining the education of children through the monotheistic creed (6,7), and a demand to remember the words of Yahweh by phylacteries and door inscriptions (6,8-9). The section ends with the command to teach successive generations the great deeds of the Exodus, thus motivating the observance of the laws (6,20-25). These two pericopes, 6,7-9 and 6,20-25, frame a homily in 6,10-19, which contains references to the Decalogue, and emphasizes the topic of complete devotion to God in the context of the new land and in the face of temptations coming from prosperity there[86].

4.3 The Wider Context of Deut 6,4-5

A wider important context for the שמע is provided by the section which follows the Decalogue in Ch 5 which centers on the exclusive loyalty to Yahweh consisting in the whole-hearted observance of his commandments[87]. In fact, it deals with המצוה, «the commandment» (5,29), as opposed to החקים והמשפטים (5,29; 6,1)[88]. The המצוה, «the commandment», which enjoins exclusive loyalty to Yahweh, opens with our citation of the שמע in this part, and is elaborated in the paranaetic sermons found in the following chapters till Ch 11. For this reason, N. Lohfink has characterized Chs 5-11 as dealing with the המצוה, «the commandment» or *das Hauptgebot* (the principal commandment). Chs 12-28, by contrast, deal with   החקים והמשפטים, «the laws and

---

84 Cf. S.R. DRIVER, *Deuteronomy*, 91.
85 Cf. M. WEINFELD, *Deuteronomy*, 328-30.
86 Cf. M. WEINFELD, *Deuteronomy*, 328.
87 Cf. 4.1.
88 Cf. M. WEINFELD, *Deuteronomy*, 328.

judgments», (cf. 5,29; 6,1) or *die Einzelgebote*, (the individual commandments) which are specifications of the principal commandment.

Within this context Deut 6,4-5 constitutes the המצוה or *das Hauptgebot* in summary form, in so far as it consists of Israel's central confession of faith and its greatest religious obligation of exclusive loyalty to Yahweh, its one and only God[89]. As the summary of the central commandment, 6,4-5 has clearly a pivotal role in the book of Deuteronomy.

5. Conclusion

Our study of the commandment to love God (Deut 6,4-5) in its OT context, has shown that it has a structure involving an address, the formula of monotheistic confession and the commandment to love God exclusively based on it. It clarified the address form שמע ישראל to be a didactic formula which expresses an invitation to listen with an attitude of obedience, and the confessional formula to be a monotheistic proclamation in a liturgical context which understands the uniqueness of God in exclusive terms. The ו-*conversive* formulation of the commandment, which follows the monotheistic proclamation (Deut 6,5), reveals it to be the consequence of it. It is because the Lord God is unique that he should be loved with a whole-hearted devotion. The exegesis of the commandment to love God clarified, that the verb love (אהב) in Deut is a theological concept which means the inner holistic orientation of the human person to God based on his/her deliberate decision and which concretizes itself in the observance of God's commandments. This is clear particularly from the connection between Deut 6,5 + 6; and also from 11,11. The tripartite formula of the modality of love underlines the holistic character of the love commanded. An understanding of love of God in this sense makes clear, that it can be commanded. Finally, a consideration of the שמע *vis-à-vis* its wider contexts showed, that it contains the principal commandment in summary form, and as such has a pivotal role in Deuteronomy.

---

[89] This division of the book of Deuteronomy, Chs 5-26 into two parts: the first dealing with the great commandment (*das Hauptgebot*) (Chs 5-11) and the second dealing with its specifications (*die Einzelgebote*) (Chs 12-26), has been made for the first time by N. Lohfink in his book, *Das Hauptgebot*. There is scholarly consensus on this division and nomenclature today. Cf. N. LOHFINK, *Das Hauptgebot*.

CHAPTER II

The Commandment to Love the Neighbor:
Leviticus 19,18

The chapter, after a concise treatment of the text form of the commandment to love the neighbor, will look at the formulation and structure of Lev 19,17-18, of which it is part. This will be followed by the exegesis of the text of the commandment (v18b), and the discussion of its context in the book of Leviticus.

1. The Text Form

Mk 12,31 does not present any textual problems or variants to be accounted for. Metzger, *A Textual Commentary on the Greek New Testament* (1994[2]) does not mention any problem concerning it. The text of this commandment: καὶ ἀγαπήσεις τὸν πλησίον σου ὡς σεαυτόν, literally corresponds to the LXX version of Leviticus, 19,18. The LXX, in its turn, translates the MT faithfully. The form in the MT appears in the following manner: ואהבת לרעך כמוך (= «And you shall love your neighbor as yourself»). The LXX rendering of it is a fair translation, and involves neither addition nor subtraction. Thus, the Markan text fully agrees with the LXX, on the one hand, and MT, on the other. The picture thus is one of perfect correspondence, and hence we may take the text as stabilized.

2. The Structure of Lev 19,17-18

The commandment occurs in Ch 19 of the book of Leviticus, which is part of the «Holiness Code» that comprises Lev Chs 17-26. Within Ch 19 itself, it forms part of vv11-18, its second section, which focuses on injunctions on the treatment of one's fellow human beings. It consists of four paragraphs, all ending with the motive clause, «I am the Lord» (vv12.14.16.18). The section has a predominant social focus in its understanding of holiness which brings to a climax the general social preoccupation that defines the laws in Ch 19, as compared to the rest of the book. The commandment to love the neighbor in 19,18 comes as a crowning conclusion of this section.

The commandment in Lev 19,18 forms an inseparable part of vv17-18 because of its formulation: ואהבת לרעך כמוך = «but you shall love your neighbor as yourself». The ו-*conversive* ואהבת, with which it starts, is intimately linked with the foregoing and has an adversative sense which we shall discuss below. Because of this formulation vv17-18 form one unit.

2.1 *The Structure of this Unit*

Structurally, we have in 19,17-18 six commands: (1) לא־תשנא את־ אחיך בלבבך = «You shall not hate your brother in your heart» (v17a); (2) הוכח תוכיח את־עמיתך = «but you shall reason with your neighbor» (v17b); (3) ולא־תשא עליו חטא: = «lest you bear sin because of him» (v17b); (4) לא־תקם = «You shall not take vengeance» (v18a); (5) ולא־ תטר את־בני עמך = «or bear any grudge against the sons of your own people» (v18α); (6) ואהבת לרעך כמוך = «but you shall love your neighbor as yourself» (v18β). אני יהוה: = «I am Yahweh». These include four prohibitions and two positive commands which are distributed three per verse, that is, two prohibitions and one positive command per verse. The arrangement shows an alternation of general commands (vv17a.18aβ) and particular prescriptions (vv17b.18aα). The commands show a chiastic arrangement. The passage, thus, presents an ABB'A' pattern[1].

Besides, as G. Barbiero points out, the strophe is constructed antithetically, in the form of «don't do this, do that». To the initial prohibition (לא־תשנא) a positive alternative is contrasted (הוכח תוכיח). V18aα resumes in clear parallelism with v17a, the prohibition (לא־תקם ולא־ תטר): v18aβ again contrasts the positive command to it (ואהבת). We have, therefore, twice the sequence «prohibition + commandment»[2]. The way the prohibition against hatred of the brother in Lev 19,17 is formulated is also significant, in that it is phrased in general terms. This makes it an evident antithetic parallel to the commandment on brotherly love in 19,18aβ, which is also formulated in general terms[3]. The text of vv17-18, thus, presents a solid formal unity in its formulation and has to be taken as a unit.

---

[1] Cf. G. BARBIERO, *L'asino del nemico*, 265.

[2] Cf. G. BARBIERO, *L'asino del nemico*, 265.

[3] Cf. G. BARBIERO, *L'asino del nemico*, 270.

2.2 *The Content of this Unit*

The Verses deal with situations of dispute or offense involving fellow-Israelites. V17 proscribes keeping of hatred in one's heart against an adversary, and instead commands «reasoning with him» or open, frank confrontation or fraternal correction, in which the matter is sorted out. To the violent solution condemned in v17a, v17b offers, in contrast, another path to resolve the problem: fraternal correction (הוכח תוכיח) Similarly, in v18(a.α) two forms of hatred are condemned, revenge and resentment, and in its place the positive attitude of love is commanded (v18β)[4]. The relation of v18aβ with what precedes is expressed in MT by the conjunction ו (cf. ואהבת). Coming after two prohibitions (cf. לא־תקם ולא־תטר את־בני עמך), and introducing a positive command, this ו acquires an adversative character. «You shall not take vengeance or bear any grudge *but* you shall love»[5]. Thus, the final commandment contrasts the positive sentiment of love to the negative attitude of revenge and resentment. This shows, as Barbiero rightly contends, that the love commandment involved here is the commandment to love the enemy[6]. Putting it inversely, the thought process is: If you love, you will not take revenge nor nurse resentment against an adversary in case of offenses or disputes, but take the path of fraternal correction to resolve them (הוכח תוכיח). Thus, both its contrast-structure and its content, which proscribe a hateful and negative option and command in its place the positive step of caring fraternal correction, which is a concrete expression of love of the adversary, clearly points to the commandment involved here as love of enemy (among one's own people) expressed in deeds[7].

---

[4] Cf. G. BARBIERO, *L'asino del nemico*, 266.

[5] Cf. G. BARBIERO, *L'asino del nemico*, 282.

[6] Cf. G. BARBIERO, *L'asino del nemico*, 266, n.3. However, it must be admitted that the enemy involved is a member of one's own people and hence the love of enemy in question here is limited to such inimical members within one's own people.

[7] It is interesting to note, that both these perspectives of taking Lev 19,17-18 as one unit, thus, interpreting v18b, the commandment to love, in the context of vv17-18a and of seeing the whole unit as involving a prohibition of vengeance against an offending brother followed by the commandment to love him instead, find an echo, though sparsely, in traditional Jewish interpretations, as R. NEUDECKER, «Jewish Interpretation», 509-511, points out. One such passage is found in the *Talmud Jerushalmi*, (cf. yNed 9,4 (41c), which explains the reason for the commandment of Lev 19,18a («You shall not take vengeance nor bear a grudge against the children of your people») with the following telling metaphor: «If someone is chopping meat and in doing so cuts one hand, does he then avenge himself on the hand which held the knife by cutting that hand too? Since all Israelites form one single body, anyone who takes

3. Exegesis of Lev 19,18

We shall now turn to the exegesis of this commandment, in which we shall clarify the nature of the love commanded, the object of love (רע), the modality of love (כמוך), and finally the commandment's grounding by its concluding divine self-introductory formula.

3.1 *The Nature of Love*

The commandment to love the neighbor (19,18β) is phrased positively unlike the prohibitions which precede it. It is formulated with (ואהבת), which is a ו-*conversive* perfect second person singular. The Hebrew construction of a particle of negation (לא) + an imperative (here expressed in the *Yiqtol* verb forms of the prohibitions which precede (cf. לא־תקם ולא־תטר את־בני עמך, v18aα)[8], followed by a perfect ו-*conversive,* here (ואהבת), has an imperative meaning and is appropriate for legal prescriptions. Its adversative structure noted above, strongly commands the positive attitude of love in place of the prohibited attitudes of hatred and bearing of grudge against an inimical brother.

The love commanded, in its essence, is an interior sentiment. It is the opposite of hatred (שנא) which is the internal homicidal sentiment (cf. v17). The expression בלבבך in v17 makes clear its character of interiority. It expresses itself in acts like vengeance (cf. v16. v18). Since אהב is its contrary, it has the same character of interiority and, like hatred, expresses itself in deeds, but, in this case in opposite deeds, like caring fraternal correction (הוכח תוכיח, v17b) and treating the neighbor like oneself (כמוך, v18β)[9]. As the interior attitude contrary to hatred, it does not seek the death but the life of one's רע. It will not take vengeance, because the life of the רע is as dear to one as one's own life (כמוך). The adversative formulation of v18β, which follows the two prohibitions that proscribe taking of vengeance (v18a) and bearing of grudge (v18α), implies that it is only by identifying oneself with the

---

vengeance on his neighbor punishes himself. Therefore the answer to any injustice one has suffered is not revenge, but love: «and you shall love your neighbor as yourself»», Neudecker, *Ibid.,* 509. Thus, the interconnection between the two verses is clearly brought out by this passage. Similar attempts for interpreting Lev 19,17-18 as one unit from different points of view are also found in post-talmudic commentaries such as that of Nahmanides, Abrabanel, Elijah ben Moses Basyatchi, the supreme Karaitic authority, Gersonides, *Hizzequni* and Rashi. For details see, *Ibid.,* 509-511.

[8] Cf. P. JOÜON, *Grammaire,* 305-306.

[9] Cf. J. MILGROM, *Leviticus, III,* 1653.

other (אהב כמוך), feeling one with him to such a point that his life becomes one's own, that the renunciation of hatred and vengeance is possible. In this identification, one would be able to see that vengeance would only double one's loss instead of compensating it. What is operative here is the principle of familial solidarity, the logic of the sphere of «amity»[10].

How the love involved expresses itself in caring action is shown in v17b, when it commands fraternal correction or confrontation (הוכח תוכיח). It is correction with a positive, caring goal coming from those who are close. Whether it is the behavior of father towards son, or of Yahweh towards his people, of teacher towards his disciple, it is always the behavior of persons linked by the ties of blood or of friendship. (cf. Ps 141,5)[11]. יכח is a form of משפט which does not have the goal of the death of the wrong-doer but his reform and life (cf. v17b). This is particularly evident when the subject of יכח is Yahweh (cf. Prov 3,12; Jb 5,17; 2Sam 7,14). The יכח punishments are not definitive, but open a possibility of change and a new beginning. The goal of יכח judgment is to reestablish the relationships of שלום among the members of the covenant, removing what opposes them (cf. Jb 16,21), of initiating new prospects for a better quality of life (Is 2,3f; cf. Mic 4,3). Thus, יכח stands in contrast to vengeance (v18a) (cf. Ps 6,2; 38,2). It is, in fact, the fruit of love (v18β). Lev 19,17-18 thus demonstrates what this love means by using the concrete case of the treatment of an inimical brother. While hatred leads to vengeance and rancor, love leads to fraternal correction and is an expression of love[12]. The love involved is, thus, love of enemy expressed in caring deeds.

3.2 The Object of Love

The love commandment demands love for the רעך, «your neighbor». It is thus the object of love. The term רע is one of the 4 expressions in vv11-18 for neighbor (רע, בני עמך, עמית, אח) and appears as a constant in varying combinations of these in the three of the four units that make up this passage, and plays a key role in the crescendo that climaxes in the love commandment of v18b which has the effect of rendering the latter the literary and theological climax of the whole passage[13]. But the fact that in vv17-18, the last of the four units, all the four terms oc-

---

[10] Cf. G. BARBIERO, L'asino del nemico, 282-284.

[11] Cf. G. BARBIERO, L'asino del nemico, 271.

[12] Cf. G. BARBIERO, L'asino del nemico, 271-272.

[13] Cf. G.J. WENHAM, Leviticus, 267.

cur stresses inclusiveness in the sense, that these verses «which begins
with the prohibition not to hate and concludes with the command to
love, encompasses every member of the covenant community»[14].

3.2.1 The Term רע vis-à-vis the Plurality of Terms for the Neighbor

רע is only one of the four words available for the neighbor in the
context. But of 4 instances of רע in the Holiness Code, 3 are found in
Ch 19. Here the term means clearly a member of the people. The side
by side use of the expressions for the neighbor points to that[15]. According to M. Noth[16], no appreciable difference exists among these terms
here. But H.P. Mathys points out, that the phrase בני עמך of v18 does
have a specific nuance, in that it contains a national, ethnic meaning.
He further observes, that its presence among these expressions, used
interchangeably, gives this clear reference to the members of the people to the other terms also[17]. Whether the plurality of the words for
neighbor is due to the corresponding number of sources[18] and redactional re-workings, or due to the effort to vary them, the רע in the love
commandment refers to the members of the people[19]. This is clearly
highlighted again by v34, where the resident alien is asked to be included within the range of the love commandment. This explicit demand for his inclusion shows that the commandment of v18 is confined
to the fellow Israelites.

According to E. Gerstenberger, רע springs from vocabulary of kin-
ship and can be translated blood relation, but has acquired an extended
meaning of fellow-human relations based on solidarity. Especially in
ethical and exhortative texts, רע, like אח, occurs very frequently in
Deuteronomy[20]. Mathys, on the other hand, from an examination of the
passages in the Book of the Covenant (Exod 21,14.18.35;
22,6.7.8.9.10.13.25.) concludes that רע is used there as an equivalent
for the «other»[21]. From the expressions theoretically available for the
other- רע, אח, עמית, בן עם- only the «neutral» term רע is used, which
gives an indication that it would not be translated «a member of one's

---

[14] Cf. J. HARTLEY, *Leviticus,* 318.
[15] Cf. H.P. MATHYS, *Liebe deinen Nächsten,* 38.
[16] Cf. M. NOTH, *Leviticus,* 122.
[17] Cf. H.P. MATHYS, *Liebe deinen Nächsten,* 18.
[18] Cf. M. NOTH, *Leviticus,* 122.
[19] Cf. H.P. MATHYS, *Liebe deinen Nächsten,* 39.
[20] Cf. E. GERSTENBERGER, *Das dritte Buch Mose,* 259-260.
[21] Cf. H.P. MATHYS, *Liebe deinen Nächsten,* 31.

own people»[22], or in the context a «fellow countryman»[23]. According to Barbiero, the position is more complex. Israel's experience of the exile, which on the one hand, developed the attitude of exclusion in regard to the גרים, and on the other, the more open-minded attitude of their integration, which is partly also influenced by the vision of the new community after the exile, is reflected in the understanding of the term רע in Leviticus. While it essentially refers to the Israelite, it does not explicitly exclude the גר[24]. Nevertheless, for Lev 19,18 רעך is a synonym of אחיך, עמיתך, and בני עמך, which unequivocally limits the meaning of רע to the members of the people of Israel[25]. The גר does not form part of it, since vv33f sees the need to include him in the love commandment[26].

3.2.2 The Social Context of the Terms for «Neighbor»

In the context of the Holiness Code, and therefore of Ch 19, 11-18, all of these expressions refer to the cultic community of Israel, עדה, the idealistic exilic and post-exilic population united around its God. This community developed in small groups of family and village society where ties of solidarity were strong and important. Uprooted, indigent and devoid of a nation, they conceived of their life in radical terms, like the Israel of the wilderness period. Its designation as עדה is thus the re-

---

[22] Cf. H.P. MATHYS, *Liebe deinen Nächsten*, 32.

[23] Cf. H.P. MATHYS, *Liebe deinen Nächsten*, 38.

[24] Cf. G. BARBIERO, *L'asino del nemico*, 318

[25] Cf. J. MILGROM, *Leviticus III*, 1654. In this connection, H.P. MATHYS, *Liebe deinen Nächsten*, 5, notes that רעך, the object of the verb ואהבת in the commandment to love the neighbor, is rendered not by the usual *nota accusativi*, or by את but by ל. The use of ל in this sense is not rare. Mathys holds that the latter construction is an Aramaism and that there is no significant difference in meaning between the two usages, since in some texts את and ל appear to be used interchangeably (cf. 2Chr 10,6 with 10,9). He thinks that, as an Aramaism, it attests to the relatively late origin of the precept in the exilic period. The connection of רע + אהב occurs again only in Prov 17,17 where it is understood as a «friend», as is the case generally in the Wisdom literature. For details see, *Ibid*. Nevertheless, J. Milgrom, *Ibid*., 1653, while holding that this use of ל is frequently the sign of a direct object as in Aramaic and adding that this is also true of its use with the antonym of «love», namely «hate», (cf. שׂנא לו, Deut 4,42) still observes that, in view of vv33-34, where אהב ל is applied to the resident alien with the meaning of doing him good, or treating him kindly, it could have the sense of for, on behalf of, for the sake of, as the medieval Jewish exegetes have understood it. See also, R. NEUDECKER, «Jewish Interpretation», 503-504, who similarly takes this as a case of *dativus commodi*.

[26] Cf. G. BARBIERO, *L'asino del nemico*, 319-320. Likewise, J. MILGROM, *Leviticus III*, 1654.

sult of a projection of the exilic society to the time of the wilderness period of Israel. Powerless and surrounded by a hostile world, mutual support and brotherly solidarity were essential for its survival. According to Barbiero, this is the social ambiance of the command of non-retaliation and love of enemy of Lev 19,17f. The need to survive forces them to overcome internal oppositions, strengthening the sense of belonging. This situation is reinforced by the voluntary nature of the community as well[27]. It is in line with this, that Lev 19,18 mentions the identification with the other as the motive for non-retaliation and love of enemy: ואהבת לרעך כמוך. Only in a group where human relations are based not on strict reciprocity but amity, renunciation of violence is possible. Such is the cultic community of the exile and post-exile[28].

3.3 The Modality of Love

The type of love that is demanded by the commandment to love the neighbor is phrased כמוך, «*like yourself*». This expresses the modality of the love commanded. The phrase is to be understood as a measure or standard, and not as motivation[29]. In the verse, it is not an autonomous clause whether principal or subordinate, and hence it is incorrect to translate it as «who is like you» or «he is like you»[30]. A comparison with v34, where also כמוך figures («You shall love him [the resident alien] as yourself»), makes clear that such translations are incorrect[31]. On the other hand, from a purely grammatical point of view it is possible to take כמוך as epexegetic apposition of רעך and translate it as «as a man like yourself» or «the like of you»[32]. But against this trans-

---

[27] Cf. G. BARBIERO, *L'asino del nemico*, 321-323.

[28] Cf. G. BARBIERO, *L'asino del nemico*, 328-329.

[29] Cf. H.P. MATHYS, *Liebe deinen Nächsten*, 17. Likwise, J. MILGROM, *Leviticus III*, 1655.

[30] Cf. H.P. MATHYS, *Liebe deinen Nächsten*, 6-7 who also lists the Jewish authors who render it in either of these ways. Similarly, G. BARBIERO, *L'asino del nemico*, 285.

[31] Against R. NEUDECKER, «Jewish Interpretation», 505, who, following certain Rabbinic and later Jewish interpreters, takes it as an adjectival clause «who is like you» or «who as regards his deeds, is like you». As J. MILGROM, *Leviticus III*, 1655, has recently re-emphasized in refuting such readings, its adverbial meaning modifying the verb love, held by most scholars, is demonstrated by its unequivocal use in v34 in this sense. See, also G. BARBIERO, *L'asino del nemico*, 285. According to Milgrom, the verse in the light of what has been said above (cf. n.25), can however mean: «Love (the good) *for* your fellow as you (love the good for) yourself», shortened to «Love for your fellow as yourself.», Milgrom, *Ibid.*

[32] Cf. G. BARBIERO, *L'asino del nemico*, 285; H.P. MATHYS, *Liebe deinen Nächsten*, 9.

lation is an objection in regard to content: it is difficult to explain why after לרעך one should repeat «who is an Israelite like you»[33]. The only possibility left is to take כמוך in the adverbial sense modifying the verb ואהבת[34].

The expression כ + אהב + personal reflexive pronoun is unique in Lev 19,18.34. But אחב כנפש, recurrent in the story of the friendship of David and Jonathan (1Sam 18,1.3; 20,17), is close to it. נפש here has a clearly pronominal value[35]. Though in this sense one would normally have expected the term כנפשך[36], these terms are interchangeable and there is no major difference between them as Mathys has shown[37]. Hence, this also indicates that at this point כמוך is to be taken in the adverbial sense showing the modality of love that is commanded.

---

[33] Cf. H.P. MATHYS, *Liebe deinen Nächsten*, 9, n.111. Also, G. BARBIERO, *L'asino del nemico*, 285. Against R. NEUDECKER, «Jewish Interpretation», 505, who quotes approvingly a number of Jewish interpreters who follow this line.

[34] The opinion of Ben Azzai the disciple/colleague of Rabbi Aqiba who differs from the latter in their search for a basic principle underlying the Torah and the commandments for determining people's behavior towards each other, although both of them had only fellow Jews in mind in the consideration of the commandment, R. NEUDECKER, «Jewish Interpretation», 512, is of interest in the history of Rabbinic interpretation of Lev 19,18b. While R. Aqiba stays with the commandment to love the neighbor (19,18b), Ben Azzai goes beyond it and uses the idea of man as created in the image of God in Gen 5,1 as a more solid basis for a deeper love of neighbor than the former. He considers it further-reaching than the principle of Lev 19,18b which would make love of/for the self the standard for one's treatment of one's neighbor. Ben Azzai argues that, logically, by such a position one would accept to humble the neighbor just as one might humble oneself and relinquish one's own honor, while a consideration of the neighbor as created in the image of God would not justify such a step, *Ibid.*, 513. This image of God theology is considered as going beyond the traditional understanding of Lev 19,18b, since the commandment to love one's neighbor as oneself could mislead one into giving one's neighbor the same treatment as oneself in a predicament and no better, while the understanding that one's neighbor is made in God's image would surpass such an attitude and for this reason would prove to be the superior principle of the Torah, *Ibid.*, 513-514. Ben Azzai's position has merit in so far as it highlights a potentially more fundamental principle for the understanding of one's fellow human being and treatment of him than Lev 19,18b, although it does so by critiquing and surpassing this text in favor of another and developing a theologumenon, H P. MATHYS, *Liebe deinen Nächsten*, 49, out of it.

[35] Cf. G. BARBIERO, *L'asino del nemico*, 287, n.118; P. JOÜON, *Grammaire*, 473f. Cf. H.P. MATHYS, *Liebe deinen Nächsten*, 7.

[36] Cf. J. HARTLEY, *Leviticus*, 305.

[37] Cf. H.P. MATHYS, *Liebe deinen Nächsten*, 7: «כָּמוֹךָ ist...grammatikalisch betrachtet, gleichbedeutend mit כְּנַפְשֶׁךָ.». For the details of the argument see, *Ibid.*, 7-9.

3.3.1 The Classical Example

This modality of love implies that the standard for loving the neighbor is that the person is like one's own self. In the OT, the classic illustration of such love for another is the relationship between David and Jonathan. It is said about their love: «Jonathan loved him like himself» (cf. כנפשו, 1Sam 18,1; cf. 18,3; 19,1; 20,17; 2Sam 1,26). This means that he loved him as his own life or his own self. In other words, Jonathan gave David the strongest imaginable measure of love which one can conceive of[38]. The love involved is voluntary (1Sam 18,1), and in the David-Jonathan story, is translated into a ברית (18,3; cf. 23,18). אהב כנפשו, while involving a strong affective content (cf. 2Sam 1,26), is concretized above all in deeds. Thus, it does away with differences (1Sam 18,4). Following the ברית between them, Jonathan takes off his royal insignia and gives it to the friend. In 23,17 he goes beyond equality and offers to David the precedence. In a self-sacrificing spirit he places himself in the second position in relation to his friend. כמוך thus does not restrict one to equivalence. As we are not on the plane of law but of love or amity, the identification with the loved one could make one give one's life for the other. In this context, the expression means to be so fond of someone and care for him so strongly, that one is ready to do for his life as much as for one's own, indeed to place it above one's own, if needed. It thus emphasizes a measure or standard. But despite the accent on deeds in the understanding of כמוך/אהב כנפשך the stronger weight is on the emotional aspect[39].

3.3.2 The Original *Sitz im Leben*

The original *Sitz im Leben* of the expression כמוך/אהב כנפשך is to be found in the Wisdom Literature. These expressions appear there to characterize the relationship of friendship. The theme of friendship is a classic theme of the Wisdom tradition. Thus, Sir 7,21 comes close to Lev 19,18 when it says: עבד משכיל אהוב כנפש, «an intelligent slave, love him as yourself.». Here כנפש has an adverbial function wholly similar to Lev 19,18. אהב כנפש occurs again in Sir 27,16 (B): רע נאמן תניד חרפה ומסתיר סוד אוהב כנפש: = «A faithful friend drives out dishonor, but one who guards a secret is one who loves as himself». Here

---

[38] Cf. H.P. MATHYS, *Liebe deinen Nächsten*, 14-17.
[39] Cf. H.P. MATHYS, *Liebe deinen Nächsten*, 17.

רע has clearly the typical Wisdom meaning of «friend» (אהב), and כנפש indicates the highest grade of friendship possible[40].

רע occurs in its Sapiential meaning of «friend» in Deut 13,7 (רעך אשר כנפשך) and love for רע is implicit in this expression. The phrase is close to Lev 19,18. In the text of Deut 13,7 רע is connected as in Lev, to אחיך, a term which retains also the original meaning of בן־אמך. This indicates that it is the most intimate sphere of friendship that is meant here[41].

3.3.3 The Preference of כמוך

Barbiero finds a probable key in the comparison between Deut 13,7 (רעך אשר כנפשך) and 10,19 (ואהבתם את־הגר) for understanding how Lev 19,18 (and v34) unites אהב so singularly with כמוך instead of כנפשך. כנפשך puts in relief the emotive and natural aspect of friendship. The substitution of נפש with the corresponding personal pronoun כמוך, according to him, perhaps marks the passage to another type of love, commanded by Yahweh, which is due to the גר where the emotive aspect becomes secondary and the accent falls on deeds[42].

According to Barbiero, this seems to indicate that the original *Sitz im Leben* of the expression כמוך /אהב כנפשך is the relationship of friendship described in the Sapiential tradition. In this context, it expresses, not in contrast but in analogy with blood relationships, the maximum measure of love possible, that is, the solidarity and the identification with the friend to the point of giving one's own life for him[43].

3.4 The Extension of Love (Lev 19,34)

Lev 19,34 extends the commandment to love the neighbor to the גר[44]. The term גר refers to the stranger, the foreigner in the land. Ac-

---

[40] Cf. G. BARBIERO, *L'asino del nemico*, 288.

[41] Cf. G. BARBIERO, *L'asino del nemico*, 291.

[42] Cf. G. BARBIERO, *L'asino del nemico*, 291; H.P. MATHYS, *Liebe deinen Nächsten*, 19-20.

[43] Cf. G. BARBIERO, *L'asino del nemico*, 285-292.

[44] This is a *verbatim* repetition of Deut 10,19 which asks Israel to extend love due to the רע to the גר in the land: ואהבת לו כמוך. Even the motivation mentioned is the same: כי־גרים הייתם בארץ מצרים. Barbiero holds that, though 10,19 is not a very ancient passage in Deut, the constant and univocal direction of relations from Deut to Lev renders improbable a derivation of Deut 10,19 from Lev 19,33f. Thus, we must consider Lev 19,34 as being dependent on Deut 10,19. The reason why Deut 10,19 has the plural ואהבתם while Lev 19,34 uses the singular ואהבת in contrast to the rest

cording to B. Levine, the גר mentioned in the Bible was most often a foreign merchant, craftsmen or a mercenary soldier. The term is not used for the inhabitants of the land who are identified, according to him, by ethnological designations, such as, Canaanites and Amorites, or by other specific terms of reference[45].

In parallel with אהב, Lev 19,33 uses the expression לא תונו, «do not exploit» (v33b). It refers to economic exploitation[46]. The phrase is used in Exod 22,20 in relation to the גר, where the motivation also returns literally: כי־גרים הייתם בארץ מצרים:. It is almost *verbatim* reproduced here. But it is not just protecting the foreigners that is at issue, but affirming the full equality of the foreigners in the land with the Israelites and the obligation of community solidarity (love) towards them[47]. The fair treatment of the גר is enjoined again in Exod 23,9 with the reminder that Israel has known the lot of the stranger in its history, ואתם ידעתם את־נפש הגר, hence with a salvation-historical retrospect as its basis.

In Lev 19,33f, A. Cholewinski has correctly detected the typical tendency of the redactor of the Holiness Code, of taking up the ancient pre-deuteronomic tradition to correct and complete Deut on the basis of the Covenant Code[48]. Thus, from being lumped together with the *personae miserae* in Deuteronomy, the גר, through the Covenant Code, has been given complete equality of treatment with the Israelite in the Holiness Code. If it is a consideration of compassion for the miserable that impels good treatment for him in Deuteronomy, in Leviticus 19,33-34, the גר is considered in this way. He is given full status like that of an Israelite, and the motivation for it is based on Israel's own experience of liberation by God, in their situation as resident aliens in Egypt. They are to remember this and treat others with the same kindness with which God treated them[49].

In the development of this new consciousness towards the גר, the following passages in Ezechiel are of interest. As Barbiero points out, the expressions הגר הגר אתכם / וכי־יגור אתך גר (vv33aα, 34aβ) and

---

of the verse, is because ואהבת לו כמוך is a citation of v18, which is in the singular, G. BARBIERO, *L'asino del nemico*, 292-293.

[45] Cf. B.A. LEVINE, *Leviticus*, 134.

[46] Cf. B.A. LEVINE, *Leviticus*, 134.

[47] Cf. E. GERSTENBERGER, *Das dritte Buch Mose*, 255.

[48] Cf. A. CHOLEWINSKI, *Heiligkeitsgesetz*, 277; G. BARBIERO, *L'asino del nemico*, 293.

[49] For a detailed treatment of the subject see, A. CHOLEWINSKI, *Heiligkeitsgesetz*, 274-277.

כאזרח מכם יהיה לכם (v34aα) find a precise correspondence in Ez 47,22f. The text of Ez, with its great concreteness and detail, seems to be anterior in relation to Lev 19,33f. Ezechiel's text concerns the division of the land in the new idealized community in Chs 40-48. The גר, till now considered a *persona misera*, without a right to own land and dependent on the benevolence of the Israelites, is placed on parity with אזרח, the native Israelite. He is given the right to נחלה, to a portion of the land, in the tribe of his choice (v23).

This parallel with Ez shows the newness of Lev 19,33f in relation to Deut. If the dt law on community (Deut 23,2-9) excludes the foreigners from קהל יהוה, with the exception of the Idumean and the Egyptian, and stipulates, even in their case, that they wait for three generations for their integration, Lev 19,33f stipulates the complete equality of the גר with the Israelite[50].

What כאזרח מכם יהיה לכם (v34aα) actually does, is to underline the parity of economic treatment between Israelites and גרים (cf. לא תונו אתו, v33). It is this aspect, of equality of rights, not the emotional, instinctive aspects of solidarity (since the people involved are not brothers based on religious principle), that is taken up and emphasized in ואהבת לו כמוך of v34a. And since v34a is a citation of v18, its meaning there is also applicable here. This means that you should show the גר the same unconditional love (כמוך), which you are to show to your Israelite neighbor (v18). Thus, the love of oneself applied to the whole covenant community in v18, is now further extended to the גר (vv33f)[51].

As we noted in our discussion of the commandment's preference for כמוך to כנפשך, the former emphasizes deeds rather than emotive aspects. This is also true in v34 which, as a citation of v18, uses the same term כמוך when it prescribes the same love for the גר.

3.5 *The Grounding of the Commandment*

The commandment is concluded with the divine self-introductory formula (אני יהוה in v18; and אני יהוה אלהיכם in v34). It proclaims that the commandment has the authority of God behind it[52]. It also underlines that the love towards the neighbor is a theological love and not a natural one. As in 19,34 and Deut 10,19, so also in the love commandment in Lev 19,18 + v34, the imitation of Yahweh stands as the

---

[50] Cf. G. BARBIERO, *L'asino del nemico*, 294.
[51] Cf. G. BARBIERO, *L'asino del nemico*, 294.
[52] Cf. H.P. MATHYS, *Liebe deinen Nächsten*, 110.

basis of love for the רע. Israel must love the רע and the גר in the way Yahweh has loved it first, through liberation and covenant, when they were a slave people and foreigners in the land of Egypt (Deut 10,18-19). Love of neighbor is the sign of the presence of God among his people, not an expression of natural solidarity[53]. This stress on the unconditional love of Yahweh during Israel's days of גרות in Egypt as the basis of the commandment, also points to the gift character of this love. Before it is a precept, love of neighbor as love of enemy, is a gift[54].

The theological nature of love of רע in Lev 19,18 becomes even sharper when we remember it is one's enemy one is asked to love. We are here called to follow the attitude and conduct of Yahweh, which is different from that of Israel (vv25.29), and which seeks not the death of the wrong-doer but his conversion and life (vv23.32). God's holiness, his separation from us, is powerfully manifested in this attitude of Yahweh in his forgiving and reconciling love. As Barbiero puts it: «La trascendenza, la «santità» di Jahweh è vista nel senso di non trattare l'uomo che pecca come questi meriterebbe, di rompere la ferrea catena «colpa-castigo» con il perdono e la conversione»[55]. The love of neighbor demanded in Lev 19,18 is the imitation of this conduct of God. This also shows that seeking the origin of the precept in familial solidarity, does not take away anything from the theological character of it. The love for רעך which is demanded, is not a «natural» love. To care for the needy brother (vv11-14) and to love one's adversary (vv15-18), is not natural. In fact, the natural tendency towards these categories of רעם, is to dissociate and distance oneself from them. It is for this reason that love is commanded. The love commandment in Lev 19,18 demands precisely for these persons the more radical and unconditional love (אהב כמוך), that very love which is reserved for the dearest friend or closest blood relation[56].

4. The Context of Lev 19,18

4.1 As the Conclusion of Lev 19,11-18

The immediate context of the commandment to love the neighbor is provided by Lev 19,11-18. For determining the significance of this section

[53] Cf. G. BARBIERO, L'asino del nemico, 295.
[54] Cf. G. BARBIERO, L'asino del nemico, 334.
[55] Cf. G. BARBIERO, L'asino del nemico, 295.
[56] Cf. G. BARBIERO, L'asino del nemico, 295.

for the understanding of the commandment, we first point to its unity and division. These will show, on the one hand, the apex position of this commandment (v18), as the crowning demand of God which interprets all others and, on the other, confirm its nature as love of enemy by clarifying its forensic context.

4.1.1 .The Unity of vv11-18 and the apex Position of the Command-ment

Vv11-18 evince a unity based on formal[57] and thematic[58] characteristics, wherein v18 occupies a climactic position. Reinforcing this, is the effect that is produced by means of the term עמית across vv11-18, culminating in v18[59]. Such a crescendo cannot be by chance, but must be the result of a conscious and intended arrangement. The climactic nature of v18 throws it into relief, and makes it the apex of the whole passage (vv11-18). Further, as Barbiero notes, the positive form of the commandment in v18 itself and its conclusive character *vis-à-vis* vv11-18, supports this[60]. The apex nature of v18 illumines the whole passage, and enables us to interpret the entire section and the individual commands as well as prohibitions in it, in terms of it. In other words, these exemplify, both positively and negatively, what in concrete the commandment in v18, «You shall love your neighbor as yourself», means.

---

[57] From the formal point of view, the following data point to its unitary nature: (1) The regular occurrence of the prohibition-form לא + imperfect as a pattern, inter-rupted only occasionally, by generalizing and/or motivating clauses in positive form; (2) The regular occurrence of the divine self-introduction formula in this passage namely, in vv12.14.16.18; (3) The concentric structure of vv11-18. The latter is seen in the following data: vv11f have four clauses introduced by לא; vv13f contain five; vv15f again contain five and v17f have once again four. This patterned distribution gives us an ABB'A' structure, a concentric pattern, G. BARBIERO, *L'asino del nemico*, 244.

[58] These consist in the presence of the plurality of terms for the neighbor found in it. Thus, we have עמית in vv11.15.17; עמם in v16; בני עם in v18; רע in vv13.16.18; אח in v17. The fact that these terms are confined to these verses, and occur here in such profusion, cannot be accidental and must point to their thematic unity, G. BARBIERO, *L'asino del nemico*, 244.

[59] Cf. G.J. WENHAM, *Leviticus* ,267; Also, G. BARBIERO, *L'asino del nemico*, 244, n.200.

[60] Cf. G. BARBIERO, *L'asino del nemico*, 244.

4.1.2 The Division of Lev 19,11-18 and the Forensic Context of vv15-18

Vv11-18, while constituting a unity, also broadly divides into two major units comprising of two pairs of verses each namely, vv11-14 and vv15-18, on the basis of the term אלהיך in the first of these two pairs found only here in vv11-18 (cf. v12b and v14b), and correspondingly, of רעך in the second of the two pairs (vv15-18) (cf. v16b and v18b). These terms are highly significant for Lev 19, as the whole chapter concerns the relation to God and to the neighbor[61], and hence they emphasize that these units are centered on it.

Thematically too, the section divides into vv11-14 and vv15-18. Thus, vv11-14 focuses on the goods of the neighbor and is called «the decalogue on the goods of the neighbor», while vv15-18, which has an original forensic context, is called the «dodecalogue on justice»[62].

The latter, which constitutes a unity, further divides into vv15-16 and vv17-18, which are marked and delimited by the divine self-introduction formula and have a forensic theme and distinct structure[63], which clearly affect the interpretation of the commandment in v18. Thus, thematically, the first subunit, vv15-16, deals with the theme of conduct in court[64]. In fact, לא־תעשו עול במשפט (v15aα) must be considered the title of the paragraph vv15-18, though immediately it introduces the unit 15-16, as is clear from the resuming of the command in v15b. The expression משפט־תשפט in v15aα.b places the unit in a judicial context and the prescriptions here refer to two categories of persons: the judge and the witness. Thus, v15aβγ deals with the activity of judge, and v16 with that of the witness[65].

V16 continues the thought of v15, and deals with the conduct of witness/accuser in a judicial context. But v16a actually goes beyond the context of the court. It forbids going around spreading calumny against עמיך and considers it a grave matter.

Though v16aα, taken in itself, could be understood as not directly judicial, the phrase עמד על in v16b which means to stand up for testifying against someone (Judg 6,31; 1Chr 21,1; Dan 8,25), according to Barbiero, clearly places it in a forensic ambit. Unique in the OT, the expression עמד על־דם in v16b means to make a capital accusation, by

---

61 Cf. G. BARBIERO, *L'asino del nemico*, 246.
62 Cf. G. BARBIERO, *L'asino del nemico*, 246-257; 257-264.
63 For details see, G. BARBIERO, *L'asino del nemico*, 257-258.
64 Cf. E. GERSTENGBERGER, *Das dritte Buch Mose*, 245-246.
65 Cf. G. BARBIERO, *L'asino del nemico*, 259.

which Lev roundly prohibits to bring up such a charge against the neighbor, without in fact distinguishing whether a case is just or unjust. It prohibits a recourse to court procedure itself, involving cases that will lead to a condemnation to death (עלי־דם). Thus, the text commands the renunciation of one's right to go to court, in order to save the life of the «neighbor». Barbiero understands the following strophe, v17f, as intimately connected to this command. Thus, to a capital accusation, the alternative option of fraternal correction is offered (v17), and the whole is motivated with the commandment of love (v18)[66], which gives the latter the character of love of enemy, even though the enemy involved is a fellow-Israelite and the actual expression «you shall love your enemy» does not occur.

4.1.3 The Consequence for Understanding

The most important data that the above consideration of the immediate context of the commandment to love the neighbor (vv11-18) has provided, are: (1) the clarification of the commandment's apex position in this section, as the climactic demand of God which interprets all others; and (2) its character as love of enemy. While the first puts in relief the commandment's preeminent position in the context, the second clearly supports and confirms the interpretation of Lev 19,17-18 as love of enemy. Within the close unity and the internal coherence of the section vv11-18 which concentrates on the welfare of the neighbor and culminates in v18, its second part, vv15-18, as we saw above, manifests a judicial background, though it goes beyond that sphere and integrates the sphere of internalization, involving attitudes and feelings. The original connection with the forensic sphere shows up throughout, and can be seen in vv17-18 as well. It is the personal judicial enemy who should not be hated in the heart but must be reasoned with and confronted, with the goal of his correction in mind (v17). It is again against such forensic personal enemies, that vengeance and rancor is proscribed. The love of neighbor that is commanded includes this sort of בני עמך or רעם. This, as we saw already[67], is clear from the structure of the sentence namely, from the adversative character of the ו which introduces the love commandment (19,18) that clarifies the love demanded as love of enemy. Thus, the consideration of the context supports and confirms the interpretation we have derived from its structural and exegetical analysis. The love commandment crowns in a

---

[66] Cf. G. BARBIERO, *L'asino del nemico*, 262-264.
[67] Cf. 4.

positive generalization the prohibition of capital accusation leading to the death of the judicial enemy, the prohibition against hatred, the injunction of fraternal correction, the prohibition of vengeance and rancor against a personal forensic enemy, and commands love towards him.

4.2 As Center of Lev 19

Lev 19, of which vv11-18 form part, outlines how Israel can imitate God's holiness in all areas of life, a goal 19,2 explicitly enjoins on it. The theme of holiness as the *leitmotiv* of the chapter, is reinforced by the constant repetition of the divine self-introduction formula (in either the shorter אני יהוה, or the longer אני יהוה אלהיכם forms of it) throughout the chapter[68]. The importance of Ch 19 is specially underlined by the change in the schema of mediation through Moses, found in the preceding chapters and repeated in vv1-2. From verse v2, however, God speaks directly to the members of the community throughout the whole chapter, and calls upon the people personally to observe the commandments (v37). This major change reveals the special status of the chapter within the wider context[69].

The theme of holiness, the dominant motif of Ch 19, is developed, under two aspects: (a) that of interpersonal relations of community life; and (b) that of the cult. The two themes are both distinguished and unified, with the result that there is continuity between the profane and sacral spheres. The whole life of the people of God is to be holy, an act of worship, and the relationship with God determines the relationship with the neighbor[70]. This concentration on holiness in Ch 19 reveals that all the legal material in it is a means for Israel for its accomplishment. It also shows that the love commandment (19,18), which comes as a positive crowning conclusion to the prescriptions in vv11-18, has a central position in the holiness Israel is to have[71]. It is in loving the offending brother, one's judicial enemy, that Israel must manifest its holiness above all else, which itself is a reflection of the holiness of God. This point is also made by the role of v18 as the center and climax of the whole of Lev Ch 19[72].

---

[68] Cf. G. BARBIERO, *L'asino del nemico*, 242

[69] Cf. E. GERSTENBERGER, *Das dritte Buch Mose*, 238.

[70] Cf. G. BARBIERO, *L'asino del nemico*, 242.

[71] Cf. J. MILGROM, *Leviticus III*, 1656.

[72] Otto Eckart has shown that, apart from being the crowning conclusion of vv11-18, v18b is actually the center of the whole of Ch 19 of Leviticus. He does this in a

4.3 Within the Holiness Code

A further mediate context for the commandment to love the neighbor is provided by the «Holiness Code», which comprises Lev Chs 17-26, wherein Ch 19 figures. It is called the «Holiness Code» because of its repeated call to Israel to be holy following God's holiness (e.g. 19,2; 20,7-8; cf. 11,43-45). Thus, as in the case of Ch 19, holiness constitutes the determining theological concept of Lev 17-26. The statement, «You shall be holy; for I the Lord your God am holy» (Lev 19,2), gives the basic demand and ground principle of the Holiness Code, while it also expresses the theological rationale of obedience to the law. The holiness Israel is to have is its response to Yahweh's own holiness, manifested in his saving actions. The all-holy God is tabernacled in the midst of his people, and they are called to imitate God's holiness. The legislation of the Holiness Code is offered as a means of realizing this holiness by obedience to it.

We have already seen the dominant place of Ch 19 in the Holiness Code. We also saw the central place the commandment to love the neighbor (19,18) occupies in the chapter, as the crowning positive conclusion of the section vv11-18, and even of the whole Ch 19[73]. Seeing it in the over-all context of the Holiness Code, the commandment to love the neighbor comes across as the climax of the entire Holiness Code[74] which outlines the specific holiness Israel is called to realize, following God's own holiness.

5. The Realizability of the Commandment to Love the Neighbor

The commandment to love the neighbor in its radicalism manifests its programmatic, even utopian, character. As Mathys has observed,

---

comparison of v18b with Lev 19,34, the command to love the resident alien. Eckart considers 19,34 as the social interpretation of the love of enemy. This interpretation and its integration in the structure of the chapter, underscores the function of Lev 19,18b as the center of the chapter. The commandment to love the resident alien (19,34), is not arranged parallelly to the love of enemy (19,18b) as the conclusion of the prohibitive series, but inverted, and hence removed from its parallel position, so that the commandment to love the enemy before the unit Lev 19,19aα can become the center of the chapter. The theological logic underlying this structure, while letting the Decalogue commandments to be the frame and structure of all human action, qualifies the love of enemy as the crowning center of it, defining the holiness to which Israel is called, O. ECKART, *Theologische Ethik*, 248. See also, J. MILGROM, *Leviticus III*, 1656.

[73] Cf. 4.1.1.; 4.1.3; Also, n.72.
[74] Cf. J. MILGROM, *Leviticus III*, 1656.

like the Holiness Code itself, which is the blueprint for the ideal post-exilic community[75], the commandment to love the neighbor is also in the highest measure programmatic[76]. Given its idealistic character, the question of its realizability naturally arises. Is it possible for a community to translate it into reality?

The problem, however, arises only if we take its realization as a purely human achievement. The community which produced it thought of it in totally different terms. It was formulated and redacted by a social group which had no illusions about the ability of human efforts, left to themselves, to bring about its realization. The commandment originated in a community which was taught, by its traumatic experience of the exile, not to put any great faith in human efforts unaided by God. On the contrary, it was firmly convinced, that any new beginning is possible only on the basis of the creative power of God (cf. Jer 31; Ez 36-37). This conviction must be *a fortiori* true of the new world of the commandment. For the Holiness Code and for Israel, thus, the realizability of the commandment to love the neighbor is based on the faith in the creative power of Yahweh. This faith is tellingly expressed in אני יהוה, the divine self-introductory formula, which closes off the commandment[77]. The same faith is expressed by the emphasis on cultic life in the Holiness Code[78]. It is the context for Israel to be taught and energized by Yahweh, present in its midst, worshipped and encountered in the cult. Lev considers the divine cult and a proper relationship with God as central for realizing the program of the Holiness Code, and consequently of the commandment to love the neighbor. Lev 19 shows, how these must penetrate and realize the picture of the new society, envisioned by the Holiness Code. The same faith in the creative power of Yahweh, and the transforming ability of the relationship with God, guarantees the realization of the commandment as program.

---

[75] Cf. H.P. MATHYS, *Liebe deinen Nächsten,* 108.

[76] As H.P. MATHYS, *Liebe deinen Nächsten,* 108, says: «Das Gebot der Nächstenliebe bildet nicht nur Teil des Programmes von Lev 17-26, es ist auch in höchstem Maße programmatisch: Es ist eine der oben aufgeführten idealen, man möchte fast sagen «utopischen» Forderungen, die wesentlich zum programmatischen Charakter des Heiligkeitsgesetzes beitragen. In Lev 19 nur ein Gebot unter andern erhält es einen Teil seiner gesteigerten Bedeutung dadurch, daß es selbst Programm ist.».

[77] Cf. J. MILGROM, *Leviticus, III,* 1653.

[78] Cf. G. BARBIERO, *L'asino del nemico,* 333-335.

3. Conclusion

After an examination of its text form, our study of the command-ment to love the neighbor started with an explanation of the structure of Lev 19,17-18 which forms a unity, offering a contrast structure of 4 prohibitions and two positive general commands. It also showed that Lev 19,18 itself, though in ו-*conversive* form, has an adversative formu-lation which emphasizes, that, instead of taking vengeance against an offending brother and nursing a grudge against him, one must love him as oneself. This was followed by the exegesis of this commandment in which, firstly, the nature and meaning of the love commanded was clarified, which consists of an interior sentiment expressed in caring deeds such as fraternal correction. Clarifying the object of love, רע, we found that it is a fellow-Israelite and covenant brother even if he is an offending person, an enemy. Explaining the modality of love, כמוך, it was found that it has an adverbial meaning namely, as one loves one's own self, the classical biblical example of it being the David-Jonathan relationship, though it emphasizes deeds rather than sentiments. Speaking of the extension of the commandment to love the neighbor in v34 to the גר, we found that it involves the full integration of the resi-dent-alien within the covenant community, with all his legal rights rec-ognized. The divine self-introductory formula, which concludes the commandment, underlines the fact that the commandment rests on the authority of God, while it also emphasizes the theological nature of the love commanded as an imitation of God's own attitude. The discussion of the context of the commandment which followed, first considered the unity and division of 19,11-18, which forms its immediate context. These showed, on the one hand, the apex position of this command-ment (v18) in this section, as the crowning demand of God which in-terprets all others and, on the other, its nature as love of enemy, by revealing its forensic context. The latter thus confirms and supports the understanding of 19,18 as love of the convenant brother, even if he is an enemy, gained from its structural and exegetical analysis. The study of the mediate contexts revealed, that the position of 19,18 as the crowning positive conclusion of vv11-18, puts it into relief as the high point of the holincss proposed to Israel in Ch 19, and in the Holiness Code. This means that it is by loving the offending brother, one's en-emy, that Israel best fulfills its call to imitate God's holiness. The con-cluding reflection on the realizability of the commandment showed, that this depends on Israel's faith in the creative power of Yahweh, present in its midst and encountered in its cult, and on the transforming capacity of its continuing relationship with him.

PART TWO

THE LOVE COMMANDMENT IN MARK

INTRODUCTION

Part II takes up the study of the love commandment in the gospel of Mark (Mk 12,28-34) in two chapters. Thus, Chapter III will investigate this pericope as text in context to bring out its meaning in an integral reading. Chapter IV then considers the fulfillment of the love commandment in the Passion of Jesus which is his teaching on it by example. Together these chapters will demonstrate the Markan interpretation of the love commandment.

The Love Commandment Pericope (Mk 12,28-34):
Text in Context

Chapter III, after briefly introducing the pericope and delineating its structure and form, will study it exegetically, with special emphasis on the text of the love commandments, to bring out its integral meaning. For this purpose special attention will be paid to the commandments' vocabulary in its occurrence within the gospel of Mk.

1. Preliminary Questions

Under this heading we shall first briefly introduce the pericope identifying its place in the gospel. Then we shall also determine its structure and form before starting its detailed exegesis.

1.1 The Place in Mark

The love commandment in Mk (12,29-30) occurs in the context of a *Schulgespräch* about the great commandment (12,28-34). Though a self-contained unit, it forms part of the controversy stories *(Streitgespräche)* in 12,13-37 that are part of the account of Jesus' Jerusalem ministry in Chs 11-12. In this pericope, however, the aspect of controversy is absent and the spirit is that of a discussion between a teacher and a student, the atmosphere throughout being positive and friendly with the result that, at least at the face of it, it may be characterized as a *Schulgespräch*.

In the overall three-day structure of the narrative of the Jerusalem ministry[1] our pericope falls in the activities of the third day (11,20-

---

[1] Cf. K. STOCK, «Gliederung», 483-487. In this treatment the author points out the thematic peculiarities of each of these divisions and their interrelationships among themselves which support this structure. A Synoptic comparison shows that this three-day structure is specifically Markan. Mt 21,1-17 and Lk 19,28-46 place the entry into

12,44). The topographical context of these events is the temple, more precisely the temple forecourt or the court of the Gentiles, except for the special instructions of the disciples (11,12-14; 20-25; 12,41-44) where the first, connected with the fig tree episode (11, 20-25), takes place on the way to the temple and the latter (12,41-44) in the court of the women opposite the treasury[2]. This topographical and chronological commonality gives them a certain formal unity.

1.2 The Structure

Basically, the pericope divides into a question (v28) and answer (vv29-31), followed by its adjuncts: the scribe's approving response (vv32-33), and Jesus' commendation (v34)[3]. Despite this general question-answer structure, however, the particular internal dynamics of the pericope seems to impart to it a chiastic formulation. Thus the posing of the question by the scribe is prompted by his positive and admiring evaluation of Jesus' response to the preceding controversy (cf. v28). This is immediately followed by Jesus' answer, defining and spelling out the two love commandments (vv29-31). A contrary sequence obtains in what follows (vv32-34). Here the scribe's enthusiastic interpretative paraphrase of Jesus' answer on the love commandment (vv32-33) comes first. This leads to Jesus' positive evaluation of the scribe's reply (v34a). If in v28 the scribe's positive evaluation of Jesus' answer in the foregoing discussion leads him to ask a question of his own, in v34 Jesus' positive evaluation of the scribe's response leads him to pay him a compliment as a reaction[4]. Thus the internal dynamics of the pericope's basic question-answer

---

Jerusalem and the driving out of the merchants on the day of Jesus' arrival. The rest of Jesus' activity is not further chronologically divided up by Mt, while in Lk it is enclosed by the summaries of 19,47f and 21,37f in which a longer period of activity is implied, *Ibid.*, n.7. The division is thus purely Markan and, in all probability, redactional.

[2] Cf. H.B. SWETE, *Saint Mark*, l.c. (n.7), 292.

[3] Cf. C.A. EVANS, *Mark II*, 261; R. PESCH, *Markusevangelium II*, 237; R.H. GUNDRY, *Mark*, 709.

[4] For a somewhat similar two-part development of the pericope see, R. PESCH, *Markusevangelium II*, 237; S. LÉGASSE, *L'Évangile de Marc II*, 746, who also observes that "ἰδὼν [......] ὅτι νουνεχῶς ἀπεκρίθη" in v34 with Jesus as subject connects with "ἰδὼν ὅτι καλῶς ἀπεκρίθη" in v28 with the scribe as subject which thus also provides an inclusion to the pericope. For the last point see also, R.H. GUNDRY, *Mark*, 712.

structure gives it also a chiastic development. This can be rendered as follows:

A (v28) The scribe's question motivated by the positive evaluation of Jesus' foregoing answer (cf..... ἀκούσας αὐτῶν συζητούντων, ἰδὼν ὅτι καλῶς ἀπεκρίθη αὐτοῖς ἐπηρώτησεν αὐτόν).

B (vv29-31) Jesus' definition (..ὅτι Πρώτη ἐστίν,'/ δευτέρα αὕτη,....).

B' (vv32-33) The scribe's enthusiastic paraphrase of Jesus' definition (Καλῶς, διδάσκαλε, ἐπ' ἀληθείας εἶπες ὅτι...περισσότερόν ἐστιν πάντων τῶν ὁλοκαυτωμάτων καὶ θυσιῶν).

A' (v34) Jesus' reaction based on his positive evaluation of the scribe's comments.(...ἰδὼν [αὐτὸν] ὅτι νουνεχῶς ἀπεκρίθη...Οὐ μακρὰν εἶ ἀπὸ τῆς βασιλείας τοῦ θεοῦ).

The reaction of the scribe in v32 is taken as an exclamatory comment of agreement (well indeed, teacher!) and not as an expression of evaluation[5] or compliment which introduces his interpretative repetition of Jesus' answer. V34c, καὶ οὐδεὶς οὐκέτι ἐτόλμα αὐτὸν ἐπερωτῆσαι, is taken as a general concluding remark of the whole series of controversies, and not specifically as a conclusion of the present pericope alone, and as such may be considered as being not part of the pericope of the love commandment considered in itself. Thus these phrases do not interfere with this chiastic profile.

1.3 The Form

It is not a *Streitgespräch* or controversy story as it lacks its major characteristic, that is, the questioner being introduced as someone motivated by a hostile intent[6]. Where the latter is present the dynamics lead to conflict and then we have a *Streitgespräch*[7]. On the contrary, our pericope has, from the outset, a friendly atmosphere with mutual recognition and wide agreement between the partners in conversation, and without any sign of ill-will.

1.3.1 It is not a *Schul(Lehr)gespräch*

Most scholars however consider it a *Schul(Lehr)gespräch* since the basic structure of this form, consisting of a question (v28b) and an answer (vv29-31) without a hostile intent on the part of the questioner,

---

[5] Cf. M. ZERWICK-M. GROSVENOR, *A Grammatical Analysis*, 149.

[6] For a differing view see, M. ALBERTZ., *Die synoptischen Streitgespräche*, 25f.; 32f.

[7] Cf. Mk 7,1-7; 7,9-13; 2,23-28.

the latter being rather a sincere seeker of knowledge (v28a), is realized in it[8].

However, it has certain specific traits which actually disqualify it for this form. These, as Klaus Berger has pointed out, include the repetition by the questioner of the answer given (vv32b-33), and the presence of a concluding answer by Jesus, which are very singular among Markan *Gespräche* in its structure[9]. For this reason Berger has elsewhere termed the form of the text as *Chrie/Apoftegma*[10].

Reacting to this M. Mundla has maintained that what really distinguishes *Streitgespräche* from *Schulgespräche* is the presence or absence of the hostile motivation, and that the occurrence of a counter-question is not a necessary trait of it, as in certain instances these are absent and yet they are considered such[11]. Mundla thus holds that the pericope is a *Schulgespräch*, its particular expansions notwithstanding[12]. In similar vein also R. Pesch, who thinks that: «Die besondere Form dieses Schulgesprächs ist durch die wechselseitige Bekräftigung der Übereinstimmung von Frage-steller (vv 32f) und Lehrer V34ab) gegeben; [....]»[13].

K. Kertelge, on the other hand, admits that the normal structure of the *Schulgespräch* is reached with Jesus' definition of the commandments (12,29-31), and observes that the paraphrase repetition by the scribe is not just a statement of agreement but includes an interpreting accentuation of the reply of Jesus, which is a special feature. Despite this admission, however, he prefers to call it a «*zweigipflige Gesprächserzählung*» and includes it under the category of *Schulgespräch*[14]. Thus, Kertelge's position clearly does not do justice to the special feature he has noticed at this point. Actually, a consideration of this feature within the

---

[8] Those who characterize it a *Schul(Lehr)gespräch* or its equivalent include: R. BULTMANN, *Geschichte*, 21; V. TAYLOR, *Mark*, 484; E. LOHMYER, *Markus*, 257; W.GRUNDMANN, *Markus*, 250; R. SCHNACKENBURG, *Markus, II*, 170; J. GNILKA, *Markusevangelium II*, 164; R. PESCH, *Markusevangelium II*, 237; W. HARRINGTON, *Mark*, 190; K. KERTLEGE, *Markusevangelium*, 121; A. SISTI, *Marco*, 346; S. LÉGASSE, *L'Évangile de Marc*, 746.

[9] Cf. K. BERGER, *Gesetzesauslegung I*, 184. He observes: «Das Gespräch der Verse 28b (Frage des Schriftgelehrten) 29-31 (Antwort Jesu), 32b-33 (Wiederholung der Antwort Jesu durch den Schriftgelehrten), 34b (Schlußantwort Jesu)-ist in diesem Aufbau unter den Gesprächen nach Mk völlig singulär».

[10] Cf. K. BERGER, *Formgeschichte des Neuen Testaments*, 80f.

[11] Cf. Mk 7,1-7; 7,9-13; 2,23-28.

[12] Cf. M. MUNDLA, *Jesus und die Führer*, 143.

[13] Cf. R. PESCH, *Markusevangelium II*, 237.

[14] Cf. K. KERTELGE, «Das Doppelgebot», 307.

totality of the pericope, calls for its recognition as *sui generis*, as the following considerations would show.

1.3.2 It is *Dialoggespräch*

The peculiar developments in this pericope, in our opinion, cannot be adequately explained within the structure of the *Schul(Lehr-gespräch)* because they evince unique characteristics. Nor is Bultmann's comment, that the schema of the *Gespräche* originally consisted of a question and an answer and it is indifferent how many conversation exchanges occur further on in the pericope, adequate to explain these away[15]. What matters is the *nature* of those exchanges within the overall development, and when this is taken into account, it becomes apparent that we are dealing with a new form.

Thus, in the so-called repetition of Jesus' answer by the scribe (vv32b-33), there is a creative development. In the rendering of the monotheistic confession the scribe says:...εἷς ἐστιν καὶ οὐκ ἔστιν ἄλλος πλὴν αὐτοῦ·, («...he is one and there is no other but he», v32b). The first part of this has a clear Jewish coloration in the reverential avoidance of the divine name, (cf. εἷς ἐστιν instead of κύριος ὁ θεὸς ἡμῶν); and the second part, οὐκ ἔστιν ἄλλος πλὴν αὐτοῦ·, is a passage closely dependent on the following OT references: Deut 4,35; Ex 8,6 and Is 45,21[16], which accentuates the monotheistic confession. Both add to the Jewishness of the rendering, and in some sense, carries the monotheistic emphasis of the confession forward from Jesus' reply. In the rendition of the love commandment the clear-cut gradation of «the first» and «the second» commandment has been left out, although the order of succession is kept and the two commandments are brought closer together by uniting them with a καί, without mentioning the gradation. But the most important creative contribution is in the addition of the phrase: περισσότερόν ἐστιν πάντων τῶν ὁλοκαυτωμάτων καὶ θυσιῶν (v33b). While this parallels Jesus' comment after the definition of the two love commandments: μείζων τούτων ἄλλη ἐντολὴ οὐκ ἔστιν (v31b), in terms of significance, it develops the meaning of the love

---

[15] Cf. R. BULTMANN, *Geschichte, Ergänzungsheft*, 31

[16] Deut 4,35 runs: ὥστε εἰδῆσαί σε ὅτι κύριος ὁ θεός σου οὗτος θεός ἐστιν καὶ οὐκ ἔστιν ἔτι πλὴν αὐτοῦ, while Ex 8,6 reads: ὁ δὲ εἶπεν εἰς αὔριον εἶπεν οὖν ὡς εἴρηκας ἵνα εἰδῆς ὅτι οὐκ ἔστιν ἄλλος πλὴν κυρίου A. RAHLFS, ed. *Septuaginta*, I and Is 45, 21 has: εἰ ἀναγγελοῦσιν ἐγγισάτωσαν ἵνα γνῶσιν ἅμα τίς ἀκουστὰ ἐποίησεν ταῦτα ἀπ' ἀρχῆς τότε ἀνηγγέλη ὑμῖν ἐγὼ ὁ θεός καὶ οὐκ ἔστιν ἄλλος πλὴν ἐμοῦ....., A. RAHLFS, ed. *Septuaginta*, II.

commandment in a new direction, not explicitly present in Jesus' words. The practice of the love commandment is contrasted with the totality of the sacrificial system, and it is said that the former is - περισσότερόν ἐστιν (more abundant, comprehensive, far-reaching)[17] than it. Because of this progressive development, never present in a *Schul (Lehr)gespräch*, the pericope cannot be adequately assigned to it. Besides, as K. Berger has noted, the concluding comment (v34b) is directed to the scribe personally as dialogue-partner and has nothing to do with his initial question[18], being a reaction to his intelligent answer (v34a). The text emphasizes that he competently tackled the issue (νουνεχῶς ἀπεκρίθη, v34a) and thus made a recognizable contribution to the discussion.

These data, it seems to us, qualify the pericope as a singular one and point to a new form which we may name *Dialoggespräch* or *Dialogal interaction*. The term emphasizes the positive, and mutual-exchange character of the encounter where both partners are involved creatively, and the questioner is not simply at the receiving-end of it. That in this instance Jesus' answer is fundamental to the exchange follows from the nature of things, where he is recognized as a revered teacher which is what prompts the dialogue in the first place (cf. v28a). Despite the defining position of Jesus' answer, there is still a creative exchange which affects both the partners.

We may then outline the structural elements of this form as follows: (a) Well intentioned question; (b) Answer; (c) Appreciation, with paraphrase repetition and in part creatively-developed comment on the answer; (d) Appreciative comment, and recognition of closeness resulting from dialogue.

2. The Exegesis of Mk 12,28-34

According to the unities in the sections seen in the study of structure we shall attempt to demonstrate the contents of this text in detail.

2.1 The Question of the Scribe 12,28

This first introductory verse refers to the intervention of the scribe in a narrative form (12,28a) and to his question in direct speech.

---

[17] Cf. M. ZERWICK-M. GROSVENOR, *A Grammatical Analysis*, 149.
[18] Cf. K. BERGER, *Gesetzesauslegung I*, 184.

2.1.1 His Intervention (12,28a)

The scribe is introduced with an array of three participles (προσελθὼν... ἀκούσας αὐτῶν συζητούντων, ἰδὼν ὅτι καλῶς ἀπεκρίθη αὐτοῖς.,v28a), all of which, on the one hand, point to the pericope's connection with the foregoing and, on the other, reveal his positive, respectful, and knowledge-seeking character. This εἷς τῶν γραμματέων steps forward (προσελθὼν) and asks his question after having heard them disputing (ἀκούσας αὐτῶν συζητούντων), and seeing that he has answered them aptly (ἰδὼν ὅτι καλῶς ἀπεκρίθη αὐτοῖς)[19]. He is thus portrayed as a sincere and open-minded seeker who proceeds to ask the question after being impressed by the way Jesus answered the question of the Sadducees in the foregoing controversy (12,18-27)[20]. It is with admiration for him as a teacher (cf. ἰδὼν ὅτι καλῶς ἀπεκρίθη αὐτοῖς) that he steps forward to put his question. The presentation leaves no doubt about the positive and knowledge-seeking disposition of the man. That this is «one of the scribes» (εἷς τῶν γραμματέων) is at the face of it surprising, given the hostility of the questioners in the immediately preceding controversies (12,13-17; 18-27) and the behavior of the Jewish leadership in the Jerusalem ministry (Chs 11-12).

It is all the more so because the scribes as a group have been presented in the gospel as Jesus' steady and sometimes bitterest ene-

---

[19] H. SWETE, *Saint Mark*, 283, points to the interrelationships among these participles and says that ἀκούσας αὐτῶν here supplies the motive of προσελθὼν and through ἰδὼν of ἐπηρώτησεν also. K. KERTELGE, *Markusevangelium*, 121, stresses the throughout friendly and positive character of the interaction. For details, *Ibid.* Similarly, K. STOCK «Gliederung», 495, who adds that this pericope is governed by the mutual agreement between Jesus and this scribe because of the latter's endorsement of Jesus' reply to the Sadducees which in fact motivates his question (v28) and Jesus' positive evaluation of his position in v32f. This becomes even clearer when one sees it in the context of Jesus' negative characterization of the Sadducees' position at the conclusion of the foregoing episode (cf. πολὺ πλανᾶσθε, 12,27) which builds an inclusion with Οὐ διὰ τοῦτο πλανᾶσθε in 12,24 and thus defines their position as an egregious error. See also, F.D. HAUCK, *Markus*, 148.

[20] Cf. K. STOCK, «Gliederung», 494-495.

mies[21]. The characterization is thus clearly out of character with Mk's usual presentation of the scribes in the gospel[22].

The introductory verse manifests indices which clearly point to its linkage with the foregoing. It opens in v28 with a καί, used here paratactically, a usage of Hebrew origin which is specially conspicuous in Mk[23]. Here it also shows its connectedness to what goes before.

Besides the verse uses personal pronouns to refer to the groups and personalities involved. Thus we have ἀκούσας αὐτῶν συζητούντων which point to the people involved in the discussion. Jesus himself is referred to in this initial verse not by name but with a personal pronoun, αὐτόν (v28b). It is only in v29, to introduce his answer, that he is mentioned by name for the first time[24]. All these are clear pointers to the previous pericope on the question of the resurrection where the Sadducees are involved in a controversy with him on this issue. The use of the series of participles qualifying the scribe who comes to ask the question (προσελθών...ἀκούσας αὐτῶν συζητούντων, ἰδών..., v28a)[25], as

---

[21] In Mark, except for 12,28-34, the scribes are Jesus' consistent enemies either alone or with other groups (Cf. 1,22; 2,6.16; 3,22; 7,1.5; 8,31; 9,14; 10,33; 11,18.27; 12,35.38; 14,1.3.53; 15,1.31). For a systematic treatment of their negative role in Mk see, A. MALINA, *Non come gli scribi*, 7-70. The author shows how their hostile role serves as a foil for highlighting the unique character of Jesus' person and revelation in relation to the appearance of other persons: the disciples, the crowd and the groups of opponents, and in this way fulfills an important narrative function.

[22] There is, however, nothing improbable about this key exception which only means that there have been dissidents among groups antagonistic to Jesus. In this respect this scribe compares well with Joseph of Arimathea, a member of the Sanhedrin which as a body condemned Jesus (cf. 14,53.64), described as one looking forward to the Kingdom of God, thus as one open to Jesus' proclamation, who took courage to ask Pilate for the body of Jesus and, in a threatening situation, did him the honor of a dignified burial (15,43).

[23] Cf. M. ZERWICK., *Biblical Greek*, 153, # 454.

[24] However, unlike Mt and Lk who do not mention Jesus by name in their parallel version of the pericope, Mk does so at two crucial points: first here at the introduction of the answer to the question defining the great commandment (Mk 12,29); second at the beginning of the concluding comment of Jesus to the perceptive answer of the scribe (12,34). The express mention of Jesus' name at these points, seen against the lack of mention of it at the opening verse or anywhere else in the perciope, appears to be intentional. It seems to be meant to add greater solemnity and authority to his pronouncements, first in the definition of the great commandment and then in the positive comment to the scribe.

[25] B. WEISS, *Das Markusevangelium*, 400, n.1, observes that the participles ἀκούσας and ἰδών are not coordinated with each other because the first motivates προσελθών and the second ἐπηρώτησεν for which that is only the pre-supposition. D. RHOADS, and D. MICHIE, *Mark as Story*, 45, on the other hand, point out that the

mentioned, also accentuates the reference to the episode that went before from where the scribe gets the inspiration to pose his own question. Besides, the tenor of v34c which concludes the pericope with its generalizing observation, καὶ οὐδεὶς οὐκέτι ἐτόλμα αὐτὸν ἐπερωτῆσαι, points beyond 12,18-27 to 12, 13-17 as well, or mediately even to the questions and interactions of 11,27-12,28.

The term εἷς in the phrase εἷς τῶν γραμματέων stands for the indefinite article τίς (= γραμματεύς τίς)[26]. The use of εἷς in this sense occurs in Mk 5,22 to refer to Jairus as a certain chief synagogue official (εἷς τῶν...ἀρχισυναγώγων). The combination εἷς τῶν γραμματέων, as partitive genitive, stresses the person to be «one of a group», in this case of the scribes.

The conjunction ὅτι (that) introduces the subordinate noun clause (καλῶς ἀπεκρίθη αὐτοῖς), the object of the participle ἰδών. Καλῶς qualifies ἀπεκρίθη αὐτοῖς and, in this combination, has the meaning «rightly», «well»[27]. The subordinate noun clause underlines the positive perception and evaluation on the part of the scribe of Jesus' reply. The verb occurs in v29 and v34[28]. The occurrence in v34 has a similar positive qualification, νουνεχῶς ἀπεκρίθη, and emphasizes the positive evaluation on the part of Jesus of the scribe's reply. These incidences in the pericope in the opening and ending verses, with a similar positive qualifying adverb in each case, are significant. They create an inclusion which strongly underline the positivity, open-mindedness and agreement that characterize the pericope. The pronominal indirect object αὐτοῖς clearly points back to the preceding controversy (vv18-27) on the resurrection, and refers to the Sadducees involved in it. The instance of the pronominal object αὐτόν of the principal verb ἐπηρώτησεν, as in the case of the foregoing αὐτοῖς also clarifies the direct connection of the pericope and the verse with what precedes. In fact, as mentioned, no substantive has been used so far in this opening v28, except for the indefinite εἷς τῶν γραμματέων. Both the use of the pronouns and the array of participles point clearly to the dependence of the pericope on the foregoing.

---

presence of participles is part of a technique of Markan style to reinforce the rapid movement of action and characters in Mk.

[26] Cf. M. ZERWICK., *Biblical Greek*, 52, # 155.

[27] Cf. *BAGD*, 401.

[28] R. PESCH, *Markusevangelium II*, 237, points to the striking asyndetic line up of participles (ἀκούσας, ἰδών) and verbs ἐπηρώτησεν, ἀπεκρίθη in v28b, on the one hand, and similarly of verbs ἐπηρώτησεν, ἀπεκρίθη in v34a.

2.1.2 His Question (12,28b)

The narrator, after introducing the questioner in the past tense (ἐπηρώτησεν), now moves into direct speech. Thus the question is posed in the present and runs: Ποία ἐστὶν ἐντολὴ πρώτη πάντων; (v28c). The actual question begins with ποία, meaning «of what sort» though here, as often it does, it means «which?»[29] According to R. Pesch, however, it points to the quality of the first commandment which has the first place among all others and which corresponds to the will of God[30]. The question is about ἐντολὴ πρώτη πάντων. According to *BAGD*, πρώτη denotes rank or degree meaning first, foremost, most important, and most prominent of things[31]. Hence the question is about the foremost, most important of all the commandments (v28)[32].

The expression πρώτη πάντων, a partitive genitive, underlines the πρώτη ἐντολή to be foremost, most important within the sum total of all the commandments which stresses comprehensiveness and clarifies its absolutely unique character[33]. As ἐντολή is feminine the expected form of the adjective would be πασῶν. Instead, the masculine form πάντων is used which is difficult to explain. In this connection M. Zerwick points out that πᾶς is sometimes not regularly declined and has even become an indeclinable πᾶσα in modern demotic Greek[34]. This

---

[29] Cf. M. ZERWICK-M. GROSVENOR, *A Grammatical Analysis*, 148.

[30] Cf. R. PESCH, *Markusevangelium II*, 238.

[31] Cf. *BAGD*, 726.; M.J. LAGRANGE, *L'Évangile selon Saint Marc*, 321, following Blass (110), calls it a «kind of superlative».

[32] As R.H. GUNDRY, *Mark*, 710, points out, the anarthrousness of the πρώτη is significant. The omission of the article, where it could be expected, points to the nature or quality of what is signified, M. ZERWICK, *Biblical Greek*, 57-58, # 179. In this sense the anarthrousness emphasizes the quality of firstness. Jesus' reply in v29 also takes it up and has the same emphasis.

[33] J. GNILKA, *Markusevangelium II*, 164, thinks that the formulation aims at the commandment that expresses the quintessence of the will of God. («Dieser fragt nicht nach dem ersten Gebot im Gesetz (wie Mt 22,36) sondern von allem. Er möchte wissen, ob sich die Quintessenz dessen, was den Willen Gottes ausmacht, aussagen läßt».)

[34] Cf. M. ZERWICK, *Biblical Greek*, 5, #12. A. STOCK, *Method and Message*, 311, places the question in the Jewish Rabbinic search for the כלל in catechetical instruction, a kind of total statement which would embrace more detailed particulars, although the questioner speaks of «the first commandment», a numerical ordering which is less exclusively Jewish, but which is also found in this tradition. But since in his reply Jesus speaks of «no greater commandment» (v30), which manifests a qualifying intention, he thinks that, while the questioner uses this phraseology, Jesus extends it. K. KERTELGE, *Markusevangelium*, 121, on the other hand, thinks that the question already involves a hierarchy of commandments. Similarly, R. PESCH, *Markusevangelium II*, 238, who says: «Da in Jesu Antwort ein erstes (πρώτη) und ein zweites (δευτέρα) als die Gebote zitiert werden, im Vergleich mit

irregular situation possibly explains this choice. However V. Taylor, following Alford, takes πρώτη πάντων, as a compound expression with a superlative sense «first of all» (Blass, 108), and explains the πάντων as a stereotyped use of the neuter plural to intensify the superlative. This seems to be a probable explanation[35].

Given the clearly intra-Jewish frame of reference of this discussion, the term ἐντολή here has an unmistakable OT significance[36]. What the

---

denen kein anderes «großer» (μείζων), d. h. vorzüglicher und wichtiger ist, scheint auch in der Formulierung der Frage mit prote panton bereits der Aspekt der exklusiven Erstrangigkeit mitanvisiert zu sein, der im Vergleich V33 fin (περισσότερόν) noch deutlicher hervortritt». C. BURCHARD, «Das Doppelte Liebesgebot», 39, emphasizes the theoretical nature of the question especially compared to Lk. 10,25-28.

[35] Cf. V. TAYLOR, Mark, 485-486. Similarly C.E.B. CRANFIELD, Mark, 377. But E. LOHMYER, Markus, 258, takes πρώτη πάντων as one word, and as such as a kind of superlative. R.H. GUNDRY, Mark, 714, adds that πάντων perhaps occurs stereotypically strengthening πρώτη as superlative, and points to its use in v33 to codify the implied feminine noun θυσιῶν, «sacrifices», as well as the neuter ὁλοκαυτωμάτων, «whole burnt offerings». S. LÉGASSE, L'Évangile de Marc II, 747, on the other hand, suggests that although the question does not mention the Law explicitly, it is not altogether absent from its perspective. It aims at what the Law has as role to communicate, that is, the will of God. It thus asks what is the first «of all» among the commandments from the religious point of view, as God intends it.

[36] This is also its general meaning in the gospel where it occurs 6x inclusive of our context (cf. Mk 7,8.9; 10,5.19; 12,28.31). The first four of these (Mk 7,8.9; 10,5.19) deal with gospel contexts which serve to confirm this understanding. Thus in 7,8.9. Jesus reproaches the Pharisees and scribes (cf. 7,5) for eluding the commandment of God (ἀφέντες τὴν ἐντολὴν τοῦ θεοῦ) and of holding fast to human traditions (κρατεῖτε τὴν παράδοσιν τῶν ἀνθρώπων). In v9 Jesus further states: Καλῶς ἀθετεῖτε τὴν ἐντολὴν τοῦ θεοῦ, ἵνα τὴν παράδοσιν ὑμῶν στήσητε, («You have a fine way of rejecting the commandment of God in order to keep your tradition.») and then goes on to cite the commandment to honor father and mother (Exod 20.12; Deut 5,16) which has been circumvented by the Κορβᾶν practice of the day. The contrast between the commandment of God and the tradition of men clearly confirms the use of the term in its OT sense.

Although in 10,5 the mention of ἐντολή refers to a later Mosaic legislation regarding divorce (10,4), this is rejected by Jesus to reestablish the original will of God intended in the institution of marriage (vv7-8) by means of Gen 1,27 and 2,24. In so far as the former is repudiated, its status as commandment is nullified. Nevertheless, the term is used in the OT sense since it forms part of the book of Deuteronomy despite its not enjoying the sanctity of the will of God.

In Mk 10,19 the term clearly confirms its OT significance in so far as here, to the question of the rich young man about the conditions for inheriting eternal life, Jesus replies: τὰς ἐντολὰς οἶδας· and then lists 6 commandments of the second table, concluding with the commandment to honor father and mother.

scribe is asking for is precisely to know the commandment that is first of all in the entirety of the OT Scriptures[37].

In Mk the scribe, in asking the question, does not address Jesus. The narrator informs us that he posed a question to Jesus (ἐπηρώτησεν-αὐτόν), and then in direct speech gives us his question. In Mt and Lk, however, the questioner addresses Jesus, Διδάσκαλε, (Mt 22,36; Lk 10,25b). In Mt the question is: ποία ἐντολὴ μεγάλη ἐν τῷ νόμῳ; (v36). Mt omits the copula ἐστίν following the Hebrew text. Instead of Mk's ἐντολὴ πρώτη πάντων, Mt has ἐντολὴ μεγάλη ἐν τῷ νόμῳ. The μεγάλη here, though it is only a positive, has a superlative force. The formulation using the positive μεγάλη singles out one from a class (cf. ἐν τῷ νόμῳ)[38]. Mt's mention of ἐν τῷ νόμῳ, instead of the πρώτη πάντων of Mk, points to the discussion as being focused on and confined to the Torah and concerned with the central Jewish religious question. Mk's rendering (πρώτη πάντων) does not have this limitation to the Law and for that reason also sounds more comprehensive.

In Lk the question is not theoretical but is practically-oriented: τί ποιήσας ζωὴν αἰώνιον κληρονομήσω; (Lk 10,25b). It concerns the requirements for inheriting eternal life. The question does not focus on the greatest commandment as in Mt and Mk. However, Jesus' counter-question forces the questioner to look into the Law for the conditions for eternal life. Thus, as a specialist in the Scriptures (νομικός), he is made to spell out those requirements and he cites the same fundamental demands of God enshrined in the Law, that is, the love commandments of Deut 6,5 and Lev 19,18 (cf. Lk 10,27).

2.2 The Answer of Jesus (Mk 12,29-31)

After a short introduction of the Evangelist (12,29a), the reply of Jesus follows. It includes two expressions of ordering (12,29b.31a), the monotheistic confession (12,29c), the commandment of love of God (12,30) and that of love of neighbor (12,31b), and finishes with a conclusive confirmation (12,31c).

---

[37] R. PESCH, Markusevangelium II, 238, observes that the term ἐντολή in the question actually points to an individual or particular commandment in the Law (cf. Mt/Lk par.), the latter being no longer accepted as an indivisible unity (cf. 7,8f; 10,5.19), and that πρώτη πάντων aims clearly at the beginning of the Sh'ma (Deut 6,4), which is not just cited together (v29), and, more importantly, that this question about the «first of all commandments» makes the cult-critical position of the scribe in v33 possible.

[38] Cf. M. ZERWICK, Biblical Greek, 48-49, # 146.

2.2.1 The Introduction of the Evangelist (12,29a)

V29 starts with the principal verb ἀπεκρίθη, («he answered»). The verse is introduced without connective particles or conjunctions linking it with the previous verse and as such it is a case of *asyndeton* and it gives the verse the impression of ease as well as solemnity and weight[39]. These last traits are augmented by the inversion of the subject and predicate (ἀπεκρίθη ὁ Ἰησοῦς). M. Mundla thinks that this inversion might be a Semitic trait[40]. Mt and Lk in their parallels leave out both *asyndeton* and the inversion of the subject-predicate order. Mt has ὁ δὲ ἔφη αὐτῷ (Mt 22,37) and Lk ὁ δὲ ἀποκριθεὶς εἶπεν (Lk 10,27). In both the particle δὲ links the answer of Jesus with the question that precedes. Jesus is not mentioned by name by either of them in the entire pericope. Instead, as mentioned above, the vocative of the substantive διδάσκαλος is employed (cf. Mt 22,34-40; Lk 10,25-28). In Mk, however, Jesus is here referred to by name for the first time in this pericope as the subject. The name of Jesus occurs with the article as is usual practice in the Synoptics though the use of the article is colloquial[41].

The words of Jesus are reported in the direct speech introduced with ὅτι-*recitativum*. It has no significance except marking a direct speech. In Mk it may or may not be used to introduce a direct speech[42]. M. Zerwick points out that there are instances which show that a ὅτι-*recitativum* is preferred when in the direct speech a quotation is found, e.g. (12,32c)[43]. This is the case here, though the quote comes after the designation, Πρώτη ἐστίν. 12,28.29 are also instances where the ὅτι-*recitativum* is introduced by ἀποκρίνομαι, one of the four verbs used for it in Mk[44].

That Jesus answers the scribe's query without a counter-question or an exchange, seems to be significant. Though in the Matthean parallel too the question is answered directly, despite the questioner's malevolent intent, still here in Mk, given the positive tenor of the interaction, it seems to further highlight its friendliness and the dialogal nature of the pericope.

---

[39] Cf. *BDF*, 240-242, # 460- 462.
[40] Cf. M. MUNDLA, *Jesus und die Führer*, 130.
[41] Cf. *BDF*, 240-241, # 260.
[42] Cf. M. ZERWICK, *Markus-Stil*, 41.
[43] Cf. M. ZERWICK, *Markus-Stil*, 48.
[44] Cf. M. ZERWICK, *Markus-Stil*, 39.

2.2.2 The Introduction of Jesus (12,29b)

Jesus' reply starts with Πρώτη ἐστίν which functions as a formula of introduction to the commandment which follows. Πρώτη stands for πρώτη ἐντολή. As an ordinal numeral it denotes rank and position and it takes up the qualification involved in the question in the phrase πρώτη πάντων, and as such corresponds to the question. The omission of the article in the phrase πρώτη ἐστίν points to the nature or quality of what is signified namely, the commandment. Hence the anarthrousness, as we noted already analyzing the question[45], emphasizes the πρώτη as absolutely first underlining the quality of firstness, the first comm andment's (Deut 6,4-5) absolutely first rank[46]. To this corresponds δευτέρα αὔτη in 12,31a which similarly functions as a formula of introduction to the commandment to love the neighbor. Here too the ordinal numeral denoting rank is used without article thus again emphasizing the nature and quality of what is signified by it, that is, the commandment to love the neighbor and its absolutely second rank. It is thus the second most important commandment, second only to the commandment to love God. This methodical ordering, gradation and differentiation of the two commandments thus characterize Jesus' definition in Mk.

2.2.3 The Monotheistic Confession (Mk 12,29c)

The commandment in Mk starts with Deut 6,4, the monotheistic confession[47]. As just alluded to[48], this means that it forms part of Je-

---

[45] Cf. n.32.

[46] Cf. M.. ZERWICK, *Biblical Greek,57-58*, #179.

[47] Among the three Synoptics, the combination of Deut 6,4-5 is cited only in Mk. Mk thus has the commandment to love God along with its inseparable presupposition, Israel's confession of the uniqueness of God (cf. 12,29-30). Deut 6,4-5, originally a confession outlining Israel's fundamental belief and requirement, had by Jesus' time become the daily prayer of Israel, the *Sh'ma*, which each male Jew has to recite twice a day, morning and evening. Jesus' quoting it and qualifying it as the greatest commandment does something exceptionally new to it. On the one hand, it rescues it from domestication by a pious practice, from being rendered harmless by consignment to the realm of daily religious piety. On the other, by defining it as the greatest of all commandments, he invests it with a unique and compelling authority as the most fundamental demand of God, the ἐντολή πρώτη. There is here both restoration and creative development, the former in stressing *Sh'ma* to be far more important as Israel's fundamental confession than as the most important Jewish prayer, the latter in *Sh'ma* being expressly defined as the ἐντολή πρώτη, the first commandment of God (Mk 12,29).

[48] Cf. n.47

sus' definition of the first commandment[49]. In this the Markan formulation is singular, as the formulations of Mt and Lk do not include Deut 6,4 as part of this commandment (cf. Mt 22,37; Lk 10,27). The monotheistic confession is introduced by the address: Ἄκουε, Ἰσραήλ.

a) *Israel Called to Listen (12,29)*

The imperative Ἄκουε, is joined with the vocative of Ἰσραήλ and makes up the formula of address. It directs the following core teaching to Israel considered as a unity involving individuals and community. The term, as we saw in our OT discussion of it, has the meaning of listening with an attitude of obedience[50] which is true in Mk as well. Nevertheless, it would be instructive to see briefly the other instances of these terms, ἀκούω in the imperative and Ἰσραήλ, in the gospel to verify if these contain any special nuances that help us to understand the address form.

The instances of the ἀκούω in the imperative include Mk 4,3.9; 7,14; 9,7 while Ἰσραήλ occurs only once in the gospel in 15,32. An examination of these texts (Mk 4,3.9; 7,14; 9,7) reveals that in the whole of Mk only Jesus directs the command to listen to all the people and demands the acceptance of his teaching. The only exception is 9,7 where God the Father makes the demand to listen but it is addressed to the disciples accompanying Jesus commanding them to listen to Jesus. Following this difference we shall study these texts to see what they offer towards the understanding of the command to listen.

---

[49] Cf. G. BORNKAMM, «Das Doppelgebot der Liebe», 39. With it in fact the monotheistic faith has here become the basic commandment which goes far beyond its role as an introductory formula of the commandment to love God. As the author states: «Bezeichnend ist hierfür bereits die Eingangsformel des Sch'ma Israel (Deut 6,4), die Mk 12,29 in Jesu Antwort auf die Frage nach dem höchsten Gebot begegnet, und ihre Hervorhebung in dem bestätigenden Wort des Schriftgelehrten........Damit wird dem «monotheistischen» Bekenntnis eine eigene, starke Betonung gegeben. Der Glaube an einen Gott im Gegensatz zu aller heidnischen Vielgötterei ist hier das Grundgebot. Von V32f. aus wird deutlich, daß Deut 6,4 in Mk 12,29 also nicht nur als die jedem Juden geläufige Einleitungsformel zum Gebot der Gottesliebe verstanden werden darf.», Bornkamm, *Ibid.*. Similarly, V. P. FURNISH, *The Love Command*, 26. Likewise, C. BURCHARD, «Das Doppelte Liebesgebot», 39, who says: «[.....] aber das erste Gebot ist hier nicht das der Gottesliebe, sondern der Satz vom einen Gott, auch wenn in ihm vorkommt, daß man Gott lieben soll».

[50] Cf. Ch I, 2.; 3.1

(1) Command by Jesus to Listen to him (4,3.9; 7,14).

In Mk 4, 3 the command to listen occurs in its plural form ἀκούετε. It initiates Jesus' parabolic teaching (cf. 4,2) on the Kingdom of God with the parable of the sower (4,3-9). In v9 the command occurs in the indirect imperative form (ἀκουέτω), and closes the same parable with an appeal to the listeners to hear and obey[51]. In both instances it is Jesus who commands to listen and his command is addressed to his vast audience[52]. The two imperatives occur in the beginning and at the end of the parable (cf. 4,3.9) and thus form an inclusion, which gives this command a compelling and insistent character as the one response that is due to Jesus' proclamation.

In 7,14, on the other hand, the command figures in the plural imperative form (cf. Ἀκούσατέ μου πάντες καὶ σύνετε). With this Jesus

---

[51] V. TAYLOR, Mark, 254, thinks that the command in 4,3 emphasizes the importance of the teaching which follows and the need to pay careful attention to it. Similarly, W.L. LANE, Mark, 153; M. D. HOOKER, Mark, 122. Its presence at the end of the parable (4,9) forming an inclusion with 4,3 sets the parable apart as having special significance, W.L. LANE, Mark, 153, and requiring special attention because of its profound meaning and thus prepares for the interpretation which follows, S. LÉGASSE, L'Évangile de Marc I, 257.262. Similarly, R. PESCH, Markusevangelium I, 231. R.H. GUNDRY, Mark, 191, however, affirms that in view of Mk's emphasis on Jesus' didactic authority, his interest lies mainly on these introductory and closing commands to «hear». R.A. GUELICH, Mark, 192, finds the motif to be a thematic running through the parable and its interpretation. Likewise, J. GNILKA, Markusevangelium I, 161; J. MARCUS, Mark, 295, adds that these commands create narrative «gaps» challenging hearers to use all their exegetical skills to understand the narrative, involving them actively in the interpretation. He also finds in them a progression since in the second command it is not everyone who is called to listen, but the one «who has ears to hear», Ibid., 297. While all of these point to the command's significance in one way or the other, Gundry's comment sounds an overstatement.

[52] M. D HOOKER, Mark, 122, thinks that the command to listen echoes the opening word of the Sh'ma. R.A. GUELICH, Mark, 192, on the contrary, says that the thematic use of «hearing» in 4,1-34 makes any connection of 4,3a with it highly dubious and R.H. GUNDRY, Mark, 195, states that the commonness of the command in different kinds of material makes a special allusion to it doubtful. But S. LÉGASSE, L'Évangile de Marc I, 257, n.13, considers it possible. Similarly, R. PESCH, Markusevangeluim I, 231. Against Guelich it must be pointed out that the thematic relation of the motif to listen need not necessarily mean a loss of its role as a command to listen with connections to its further occurrences in the wider narrative. In fact, because of the command's presence apart from 4,3.9 also in 7,14 and 12,29 a certain connection among these is likely from the perspective of narrative unity. And since 12,29 quotes the Sh'ma itself (Deut 6,4) where the command to listen figures prominently in a central passage most important for Israel, a linkage of these commands with it is quite probable.

directs his teaching to his audience on the ethical source of true purity and defilement (7,15-23) rejecting the externalistic Pharisaic-scribal position which makes void the commandment of God to uphold human traditions (7,9-13)[53]. The teaching comes in answer to his opponents' critique of the disciples' non-observance of purity regulations. Addressing the command to all the people, Jesus makes clear that it is to him that they must listen (7,14)[54].

(2) Command by God the Father to Listen to Jesus (9,7)

In 9,7 the command to listen occurs in the context of the theophany in the transfiguration of Jesus (9,2-13) where God the Father testifies about Jesus to his accompanying disciples saying: Οὗτός ἐστιν ὁ υἱός μου ὁ ἀγαπητός[55] and goes on to demand: ἀκούετε αὐτοῦ[56]. The de-

---

[53] Cf. W.L. LANE, *Mark*, 254.

[54] M.D. HOOKER, *Mark*, 178, states that this command to listen (v14) evokes Moses' command to Israel (cf. Deut 6,4), though it also refers to Mk 4,3. Others, while not sharing the former, affirm the latter, W.L. LANE, *Mark*, 254; R.A. GUELICH, *Mark*, 374; J. MARCUS, *Mark*, 453; J. GNILKA, *Markusevangelium I*, 284, adds that Jesus' authoritative call shows that the parable is not easily understood; Likewise S. LÉGASSE, *L'Évangile de Marc I*, 437; R. PESCH, *Markusevangelium I*, 379. But R.H. GUNDRY, *Mark*, 353, while admitting its similarity to 4,3, notes that it carries an object μου unlike the former, underlining Jesus' authority that qualifies him to change even the OT and extending to all (cf. πάντες, v14). In difference to Hooker, W.L. LANE, *Mark*, 254, links the command to the prophetic call to listen as setting for the revelative word of God (cf. Mic 1,2; Wis 6,1), while R. PESCH, *Markusevangelium I*, 379, sees in it an Apocalyptic-Wisdom motif characterizing the wise teacher bringing revelation (cf. Dan 9,23), as it also stresses understanding (Mk 4,12). However, although, if the command is taken in itself, both these are possible, the links to Deut 6,4 would seem to be stronger when it is seen in the wider gospel with other instances of the call, more so because in 12,29 it is actually quoted in an important interaction of Jesus defining the first commandment.

[55] Some consider this a declaration of the messianic sonship of Jesus. Thus V. TAYLOR, *Mark*, 392, thinks that it points back to the confession of Peter (8,29) which is now divinely affirmed. Similarly, R. PESCH, *Markusevangelium II*, 76-77, who takes the term Beloved Son (9,7) as referring to Jesus' messiaship clarified by the demand to listen to him which, he thinks, is a free citation of Deut 18,15. But others believe that it affirms Jesus' filial status like 1,11, M. D. HOOKER, *Mark*, 48; W.L. LANE, *Mark*, 320-321; R.H. GUNDRY, *Mark*, 461. Likewise, J. GNILKA, *Markusevangelium II*, 36, who adds that both texts affirm Jesus' divine sonship without being identical and that here Jesus is enthroned as Messiah for revelation before the chosen disciples. S. LÉGASSE, *L'Évangile de Marc II*, 531, on the contrary, contends that the witness in 1,11 concerns Jesus as the Messiah, while here it goes further in clarifying this Messiah to be the only Son of God. But even those who consider 9,7 in messianic terms presuppose that Jesus is already affirmed as Son of God in 1,11, V. TAYLOR, *Mark*, 162; J. GNILKA, *Markusevangelium II*, 36; R. PESCH, *Markusevangelium I*, 93.

mand has special significance because it comes from God himself and because it also gives» the motivation for the command. Jesus must be listened to because he is God's beloved Son (ὁ υἱός μου ὁ ἀγαπητός)[57]. This demand from God the Father, phrased absolutely, is divine confirmation of all Jesus' commands. It consequently adds divine support and endorsement to his commands to listen.

(3) The Connection of ὁ Χριστὸς ὁ βασιλεὺς Ἰσραήλ (15,32) to the One who Commands to Listen (12,29)

The term Ἰσραήλ occurs in the gospel only in 12,29 and 15,32. In 15,32 it is used along with the term ὁ Χριστός[58] by the high priests with the scribes who employ it in a derisive manner. At the level of the gospel, however, it is a correct designation of Jesus (cf. 8,29)[59]. In 12,29 it is this same ὁ Χριστὸς ὁ βασιλεὺς Ἰσραήλ who takes up the command: Ἄκουε, Ἰσραήλ and presents it as the first commandment. The one who takes up Ἄκουε, Ἰσραήλ in this way and defines it as the first commandment is one who is accustomed to command the people

---

[56] Several scholars take this command as a reference to Deut 18,15: «The Lord your God will raise up for you a prophet like me from among you, from your brethren-him you shall heed», although as Son of God Jesus far surpasses the figure of this end time prophet, V. TAYLOR, *Mark*, 392; M.D. HOOKER, *Mark*, 218; W.L. LANE, *Mark*, 321; J. GNILKA, *Markusevangelium II*, 36; S. LÉGASSE, *L'Évangile de Marc II*, 531; But R.H. GUNDRY, *Mark*, 461, doubts this connection saying that Mk's word order and imperative mood agree with his own in 7,14, but differ from the word order and indicative mood in both the LXX and the MT of Deut 18,15. It is arguable whether this suffices for doubting this connection. On the other hand, even if a linkage exists the quality of divine demand in 9,7 far exceeds Deut 18,15 because it is God's own command while the latter is Moses'.

[57] Thus W.L. LANE, *Mark*, 321, says that the affirmation of Jesus' unique filial relationship to God provides the immutable ground for the solemn admonition in the second clause. Similarly, S. LÉGASSE, *L'Évangile de Marc II*, 531; R.H. GUNDRY, *Mark*, 462.

[58] J. GNILKA, *Markusevangelium II*, 320-321, notes that the title «king of Israel» sums up the two trials of Jesus under the thematic of messiahship and kingship but replaces «king of the Jews» to correspond to the Jewish mode speaking. Similarly, R. PESCH, *Markusevangelium II*, 488. R. H. GUNDRY, *Mark*, 946, points out that the forward position of «the Christ, the king of Israel» emphasizes the rationale behind the challenge that he come down from the cross, which is that a messianic king would not be hanging there.

[59] Thus J. ERNST, *Markus*, 470, points out that this tautological appellation must be read as a conscious antithesis to insult and unbelief in its confessional character by which Mk relativizes the blasphemies without eliminating them and that the phrase has a clearly ironic function. Similarly, D. RHOADS - D. MICHIE, *Mark as Story*, 60, correctly stress the verbal and situational irony involved here by which what is said and intended as insult is in fact true, though the speakers are unaware of it.

thus (4,3.9; 7,14) and is confirmed by God himself in this, in so far as he is ὁ υἱός μου ὁ ἀγαπητός (9,7), ὁ Χριστὸς ὁ βασιλεὺς Ἰσραήλ (15,32).

(4) Its Consequence for Understanding the Commandment to Listen

In so far as in 12,29 Jesus who is ὁ Χριστὸς ὁ βασιλεὺς Ἰσραήλ (15,32) takes up the Mosaic command to Israel, Ἄκουε, Ἰσραήλ (Deut 6,4) and presents it as the first of all commandments, it receives in Mk a specificity. Not only has it thus become part of the first commandment, but it is now the command by ὁ Χριστὸς ὁ βασιλεὺς Ἰσραήλ whose command is confirmed by God himself (cf. ἀκούετε αὐτοῦ), in so far as he is ὁ υἱός μου ὁ ἀγαπητός. By consequence, it has an authority and validity that far exceed its OT status. Besides, listening to him when he defines and presents it as the first commandment is also part of the first commandment. These characteristics pertaining to the person of Jesus enter into the under standing of the command to listen in Mk and give it a specificity *vis-à-vis* its OT understanding.

b) *God as Lord (Κύριος, 12,29): Κύριος used of God/ Κύριος used of Jesus*

After having seen the meaning of the address form Ἄκουε, Ἰσραήλ as part of the first commandment, we shall now see the monotheistic confession as its part analyzing its major elements: κύριος/ὁ θεὸς ἡμῶν/ (κύριος) εἷς ἐστιν. While it is clear that as an OT text it is used in the same sense, we study these elements in their occurrences in the gospel to see if they receive any added nuances from them which enrich its understanding We shall first take up the term, Κύριος.

(1) Κύριος Used of God (11,9; 12,11; 12,36)

Κύριος refers to «master, owner or lord, a person who has control or mastery over someone or something with the power to dispose»[60]. It is in this sense that the term is understood here. It is used in Mk both of God and of Jesus. It is used of God 7x and of Jesus 7x. It occurs in the vocative (Κύριε,) once and otherwise 6x and in parables twice. In Mk the term is used always either of God or of Jesus. This is true of the occurrences in the parables as well, where it figures once each representing God and Jesus. All the 7 instances of the term used of God are

---

[60] Cf. J. A. FITZMYER, «Κύριος», *EDNT*, II, 329.

without article and most of them occur in OT quotations[61]. These are: 11,9; 12,11; 12,29(2); 12,30; 12,36; 13,20. Except for 13,20 all these cases are OT citations and are concentrated in two chapters (Ch 11 and Ch 12). Although 13,20 is not an OT text, the term still has the sense of master, one in control as the context will make clear and thus conveys the same OT meaning. For our study below we shall take up Mk 11,9; 12,11; 12,36; 13,20 which employ the term for God outside of the commandment to love God.

Although all these texts designate God as Lord, a distinction can be made based on their emphases. Thus 12,11 and 13,20 stress the Lord's spectacular deeds manifesting his role as master and one in control, while 11,9 and 12,36 speak of him as Lord in relation to another. We shall investigate them following this difference.

Mk 12,11, a quotation from Ps 118,23, speaks parabolically of the spectacular reversal of the very stone rejected by the builders becoming the cornerstone, and it is applied to the fate of the Beloved Son at the conclusion of the parable of the wicked tenants (12,1-9)[62]. In the context it points to the fate of Jesus who would be rejected by the Jewish leadership, but would be vindicated by his resurrection and exaltation which has the Lord as its source[63]. What is spoken of parabolically by the OT text receives a concrete referent in Mk but it manifests the role of the Lord (Κύριος) as master and one in control in an extraordinary manner[64].

Similarly, 13,20 speaks of the Lord shortening the period of unprecedented eschatological distress in favor of the elect as otherwise

---

[61] Cf. R. MORGENTHALER, *Statistik*.

[62] S. LÉGASSE, *L'Évangile de Marc II*, 718-719, observes that the Lord in the parable (12,9) is a human being (cf. v1) who nevertheless images God. Similarly, R.H. GUNDRY, *Mark*, 663, who notes that «lord-of the vineyard» may have helped lead the Evangelist to the Lord of the building (cf. Jer 1,10; 24,6; 1QS 8,5; 1Cor 3,9; Col 2,7), but also adds that the second figure extends the meaning of the first.

[63] Cf. M. ZERWICK-M. GROSVENOR, *A Grammatical Analysis*, 147. Thus R.H. GUNDRY, *Mark*, 663, says that the marvel of the Lord's making the rejected stone «head of the corner» agrees with Jesus' passion-resurrection predictions (8,31; 9,31; 10,33-34). He notes also that it gets emphasis from the forward position of παρὰ κυρίου,«from the Lord». But he links it to the lordship of Jesus by observing that the giving of the vineyard to others involves Jesus' and the Twelve's judging the twelve tribes of Israel (cf. Mt 19,28 par.; Lk 22,28-30) thus becoming head of a corner referring to rulership following resurrection and not to resurrection itself.

[64] E.P. GOULD, *Mark*, 222, points out that the αὕτη in the phrase παρὰ κυρίου ἐγένετο αὕτη refers to κεφαλὴν γωνίας following the Hebrew original where feminine is used for the neuter referring to the event itself which has God as its author.

no human being would have been saved[65] and thus implies the Lord
(Κύριος) to be in a position to do so as master and one in control[66]. A
competence such as this is spectacular and corresponds to the action of
God in the above instance of extraordinary reversal, although this text
is not an OT quotation. Both these texts, despite their differences, thus
clearly emphasize the spectacular and marvelous aspects of God as
Lord.

11,9 and 12,36, on the other hand, while retaining the core meaning
of the Lord as above, speak of the Lord in terms of another who stands
in a certain relationship to him *vis-à-vis* his will or his lordship. Thus
11,9 speaks of the one who comes in the name of the Lord (ὁ ἐρχόμενος
ἐν ὀνόματι κυρίου) as his representative to accomplish his will, and
calls him blessed. Although originally this OT text connoted the
blessings spoken by the temple priests in the name of the Lord over the
pilgrims arriving in the city for the feast[67], in the gospel context it is
the ecstatic greeting by the people addressed to Jesus in his triumphal
procession and is clearly meant in a messianic sense[68]. Jesus is being

---

[65] V. TAYLOR, *Mark*, 515, points to the Semitic character of v20 seen in the
shortening of a divinely allotted span and the idea of the elect both of which are fundamentally Jewish concepts and also in the anarthrous use of Κύριος characteristic of
OT quotations. The past tenses suggesting a purpose already determined in God's
counsel also supports the same. Likewise, C.S. MANN, *Mark*, 524; In similar vein,
W.L. LANE, *Mark*, 472, thinks that God's saving the elect is an extension of the OT concept of the remnant. All these converge to point to the Κύριος here as a reference to
God.

[66] The text in 13,20 seems to stand in some relation to 13,32 where the Father appears as the only one who knows about the exact day or the hour of the coming of the
Son of Man. Both texts deal with the temporal aspect, the former about the Lord's
shortening the period of the acute and unprecedented distress that would befall the
world in favor of the elect, the latter about the precise time of the coming of the Son of
Man. These extraordinary events are better understood if their agent is God with his
almighty power. Thus this connection also points to the referent of the Κύριος as God.

[67] Cf. V. TAYLOR, Mark, 456-457; W.L. LANE, Mark, 397; R. PESCH, *Markusevangelium II*, 184; J. GNILKA, *Markusevangelium II*, 118-119; S. LÉGASSE, *L'Évangile
de Marc II*, 669; M.D. HOOKER, *Mark*, 259.

[68] Although the text originally contained no messianic overtones, Mk seems to link
the phrase «in the name of the Lord» with the one who comes, whoever, thus converting a
general welcome of the festival pilgrims into a specific proclamation of the arrival of the
one who comes in God's name which could well have messianic significance, M.D.
HOOKER, *Mark*, 259. In this connection it is significant that the acclamation is directed to
Jesus and him alone, J. GNILKA, *Markusevangelium II*, 118-119; R. PESCH, *Markusevangelium II*, 184. Likewise, Hooker, *Ibid.*, thinks that, taken together with the rest of the
acclamation, especially with the reference to the expected coming of the «kingdom of
our father David», it is clearly messianic.

acclaimed by the people as the expected Davidic Messiah who comes ἐν ὀνόματι κυρίου, hence authorized by him as God's representative, to realize the promised liberation[69]. In so far as he comes «in the name of the Lord», the Lord God (Κύριος) is spoken of in relation to him as master and one in control but as one who sends Jesus to accomplish his purpose.

12,36, on the other hand, speaks in the words of Ps 110,1, attributed to David, of the Lord saying to «his Lord»[70] to sit at his right hand «till he puts his enemies under his feet»[71]. The text thus implies that the Lord God (Κύριος) extends his role as Lord to the Messiah Jesus (8,28)[72]. The reason for this extension is his transcendent origin (1,11; 9,7) which is implied in Jesus' rejection of the scribal belief of the Messiah as just son of David to be inadequate involved in his question: καὶ πόθεν αὐτοῦ ἐστιν υἱός; in the context of David's calling the Messiah his Lord (12,37)[73]. Thus, although in the OT the text referred

---

[69] Although in the minds of the people it is mixed with this-worldly Davidic messianic hopes, for Mk it refers to the Davidic Messiah in this sense, C.S. MANN, *Mark*, 437; W.L. LANE, *Mark*, 397; J. GNILKA, *Markus II*, 118-119; R. PESCH, *Markusevangelium II*, 183; E.P. GOULD, *Mark*, 208-209.

[70] In the Hebrew text the initial reference to «the Lord» translates the tetragrammaton Yahweh, while the second τῷ κυρίῳ μου, «to my Lord» renders לאדני found in MT at this point. Since thus in the LXX version which Mk follows both are rendered by Κύριος the problem posed by Jesus clearly exists. Cf. W.L. LANE, *Mark*, 347. Further, R.H. GUNDRY, *Mark*, 720-721, following J.A. Fitzmyer, (*Wandering Aramean*, 90), points out that although the play on the double Κύριος, in v36 and Ps 109,1 LXX does not reflect a similar play in the MT, still by Jesus' time אדני probably substituted for יהוה and a play on two occurrences of the Aramaic מרה is possible.

[71] R. PESCH, *Markusevangelium II*, 253, thinks that the phrase, ἐν τῷ πνεύματι τῷ ἁγίῳ, referring to David's words may indicate not only prophetic inspiration, but special revelation which is spelt out. David hears in the Spirit what the Lord says to this Lord which manifests his immediate closeness to God at his right hand.

[72] R.H. GUNDRY, *Mark*, 718, observes that a heavy emphasis on Christ as Lord is seen in the following data: the repetition of αὐτὸς Δαυίδ, «David himself» (cf. v37a with v36a), the switch from the ordinary aorist εἶπεν (v36a), to the vivid historical present λέγει (v37a), the qualitative thrust of the anarthrous κύριον in the statement as a whole, and the asyndeton which introduces it.

[73] C.S. MANN, *Mark*, 484-485, doubts whether Jesus subscribed to the view that the Messiah would be a physical descendent of David and also whether such a belief was prevalent at the time of Jesus or perhaps the term would have been applied to anyone who effectively established a claim to be the Messiah. He finds it also uncertain whether Jesus is here in any sense claiming to be «son of David» either by physical descent or by messianic claim. R. PESCH, *Markusevangelium II*, 255, however, thinks that, in so far as in early Judaism Ps 110 is not interpreted messianically, the reference to David's words must be seen as Jesus' achievement which the early Church could develop further. Likewise R.H. GUNDRY, *Mark*, 718. S. LÉGASSE, *L'Évangile de Marc II*, 756.758, on the contrary,

to the Davidic messianic king, in the gospel it refers to Jesus who is confessed as the Messiah (8,29) and attested by God himself as his Beloved Son (1,11; 9,7)[74] who, though he is son of David, is for this reason more than that, a fact underlined by David confessing the Messiah to be his Lord (cf. τῷ κυρίῳ μου) implying that he is more than his son[75]. Hence this text, while it fundamentally refers to God as Lord (cf. Εἶπεν κύριος...) in the OT sense, speaks of him extending his quality as Lord to the Messiah Jesus by virtue of his relationship of origin from him.

Thus these four texts which speak of God as Lord in Mk, on the one hand, emphasize in the OT sense his role as master and one in control in a spectacular manner (12,11; 13,20) and, on the other, on the basis of this meaning speak of him as sharing his work and competence as Lord with another either as his representative (11,9) or as one to whom he extends his lordship (12,36) by his sovereign initiative.

(2) Κύριος Used of Jesus (1,3; 12,36)

As mentioned above, the term Κύριος is used in Mk of Jesus also 7 times, one of these being in the parables (13,35). Unlike its use for God, almost fully concentrated in two chapters (Chs 11 and 12) and,

---

considers the particular attribution of this opinion about the Messiah to the scribes in the pericope artificial, because it does not appear to be a doctrine specific to them. While its occurrence in the *Psalms of Solomon*, a work of probable Pharisaic origin, may permit the attribution of certainty about the Davidic descent of the Messiah to the scribes, for the most part followers of the Pharisaic movement, it is certainly a truth rooted in the OT and was substantially shared by contemporary Judaism of Christian origin. However, as W.L. LANE, *Mark*, 436; J. GNILKA, *Markusevangelium II*, 169-170, emphasize the core issue in the text is the relationship of Davidic sonship to the Messiah's transcendent majesty which is presented in the form of a Haggada-question and this is beyond dispute.

[74] Thus J. GNILKA, *Markusevangelium II*, 171-172, notes that for Mk the question of Jesus' sonship is answered only with the affirmation that Jesus is Son of God, a point emphasized by its occurrence at key points in the gospel (1,1; 9,7; 15,39) which also indicates that it is theological reasons that impel the Evangelist to clarify the correct meaning of Jesus' Davidic sonship.

[75] In this connection as R. PESCH, *Markusevangelium II*, 255, stresses that the term Κύριος in v37 is not used as a Messianic title, but means the Lord of David although it is open to a subsequent titular interpretation. Similarly, S. LÉGASSE, *L'Évangile de Marc II*, 760-761, who insists that it is the same title given by the Psalmist to God (v36) and hence is an application to Jesus of a word of scripture where the term Κύριος in the original designates God as in Mk 1,3. Nevertheless, there seems to be a difference between 12,37 and 1,3 in the use of the term in that in the former it is used on the same plane, in so far as the Lord God is extending his Lordship to the Messiah, whereas in the latter it is used in identical sense.

except for 13,20, all figuring in OT citations, its employment for Jesus is scattered through the gospel. They can be grouped into three: passages in which Jesus is directly addressed or called Κύριος (cf. 5,19; 7,28; 11,3); texts which are linked with the Son of Man (cf. 2,28; 13,35); and passages which present citations from OT (cf. 1,3; 12,36). However, not all of these are used in a univocal sense. Some of them, especially when utilized by non-disciples, may not mean more than «Sir» as in the case of the Syro-Phenician woman (7,28) and are open-ended and elastic (5,19; 11,3). Others are employed on the same plane as God without being identical (12,36), while still others are used in an identical sense to the Lord God (1,3). We shall take up the last two types (1,3; 12,36) for our study which come closest to its use for the Lord God.

In Mk 1,3 Κύριος appears in a mixed OT quotation attributed to the prophet Isaiah (40,3) which speaks of one who cries out in the wilderness: «Prepare the way of the Lord, make his paths straight». The Lord (Κύριος) here is Yahweh himself as is clear from MT which has here דרך יהוה, «the way of Yahweh». Mk 1,2f speaks of the appearance of John the Baptist and says that he has come as is written in Isaiah the prophet, that is, as mentioned in this verse[76] thus applying it to John and his role[77]. But in 1,7f John speaks of the coming of the mightier one (ὁ ἰσχυρότερός μου, v7) who would baptize people ἐν πνεύματι ἁγίῳ, with the Holy Spirit, while he himself baptizes with water. He thus sees his work of baptizing as a preparation for the coming and

---

[76] In the citation Mk reproduces the LXX text with significant modifications for the argument. The end undergoes a change: «the paths of our God» becomes «his paths». Thus the antecedent of the possessive is «the Lord» (Κύριος) which indicates Jesus, who, by consequence, takes the place of God in the original. The one who cries out «in the desert» is John whose role the following verse clarifies, S. LÉGASSE, L'Évangile de Marc I, 75-76. Similarly, W. LANE, Mark, 45-46; R. PESCH, Markuse-vangelium I, 78-79; J. GNILKA, Markusevangelium I, 44-45; R.A. GUELICH, Mark, 11. Likewise, R.H. GUNDRY, Mark, 35-36, who observes that the putting of «his» (v3) in place of «for our God» (Is 40,3) reserves the word «God» for later use in reference to the Father of Jesus (cf. v11 with vv14-15) and keeps Mk's audience from misunderstanding Κύριος as God the Father rather than as Jesus.

[77] R. PESCH, Markusevangelium I, 77, thinks that the function of the citation is determined through its syntactic connection to the following narrative and takes the quotation as an anticipatory commentary on it. See also, J. GNILKA, Markusevangelium I, 44-45 and S. LÉGASSE, L'Évangile de Marc I, 72-73. The latter observes that while a scripture passage introduced like this as a rule follows what has to be affirmed by it, here it precedes it which reveals the intimate connection between it and what will be said of John. The quotation (vv2-3) thus provides a scriptural base to the narrative which follows it (vv4-8). For a different view see R.H. GUNDRY, Mark, 30, who links vv2-3 with v1 rather than with v4.

ministry of the mightier one who, as the context unmistakably clarifies, is Jesus, with his immediate introduction and the beginning of his ministry (1,9-15)[78]. Thus the Κύριος of Is 40,3f, originally a reference to Yahweh, is identified here as Jesus who comes after John and whose way he prepares.

The identification itself suggests a relationship between Jesus and Yahweh that is unique and unprecedented which alone can justify the transference of the divine title Κύριος to Jesus[79]. It implies that we see in Jesus the Lord God himself and affirms an identity-in-difference which makes possible the use of this title for Jesus in an identical sense with him.

Likewise Mk 12,36 employs the term Κύριος fundamentally of God but extends it to Jesus as our discussion of this text in relation to its use for God already showed. David's vision expressed in the Psalm 110,1 sees the Lord (Κύριος) speaking to «his Lord» (cf. τῷ κυρίῳ μου) extending God's lordship to him (v36). As becomes clear from this vision David's relation to this other Lord, who as the Messiah is supposed to be his descendent, is that he is his «Lord» (cf. τῷ κυρίῳ μου) like the Lord God. This poses the problem of his descent or origin and makes one reflect on his relation to God, and eventually leads to his divine Sonship as its solution. While the term «Lord» describes his relation to David and following that to human beings, the designation «Son of God» (1,1; 15,19 see also, 1,11; 9,7) denotes his relation to God. But in so far as the term «Lord» is used both of God and of Jesus in relation to humans, it places Jesus alongside God. Nevertheless, the primary reference of the term Κύριος is to God, the lordship of Jesus being a transferred one, accomplished by God himself by his initiative (cf. «Κάθου ἐκ δεξιῶν μου,», 12,36). For this reason, although the title Κύριος is used on the same plane, it is not meant here in an identical sense. The basis of this transferred reality is his unique relation to God as the «Son of God» (cf. 1,1; 15,39) which is attested by God himself (1,11; 9,7). This also throws light on the statement in 1,3 where a text which was used to describe God and his coming with the term Κύριος is transferred to Jesus and his coming. The rationale for it is this same unique relation he has to God.

---

[78] J. GNILKA, *Markusevangelium I*, 40-41, points out that the incidence of the mixed quotation (v2f) and the narrative of the christological proclamation of John (1,7f) designed to stress the role of John as the forerunner, is reinforced by their similar linkage in the Q tradition (cf. Mt 11,10/Lk 7,27 + Mt 3,11/Lk 3,16).

[79] Cf. J. MARCUS, *Mark*, 147.

Thus, because of the gospel's use of the term Κύριος for God in OT terms, it is used in the same sense and primarily refers to him (12,11; 13,20). But in so far as the Lord God is spoken of as having a representative (11,9) and as extending his Lordship to another (12,36) a new dimension enters into its understanding. This becomes clearer and more defined in the use of the term for Jesus on the same plane as the Lord God (12,36) and, in particular, in its use in identical sense as happens in 1,3 because of his relationship of origin from the Lord God as his Son. Because of this wider significance of the use of the term in the gospel, the understanding of the monotheistic confession as part of the commandment becomes enlarged. Moreover, since the confession of the Lord as God is part of the commandment, the acceptance of this wider understanding also forms part of it.

c) God's Relational Character (12,29): ὁ θεὸς ἡμῶν/αββα and 'ο θεός μου.

After having clarified the meaning of the term Κύριος as part of the first commandment in the gospel we shall take up the next element of it, ὁ θεὸς ἡμῶν. The phrase translates the MT אלהינו of the mono theistic confession in the LXX which Mk follows. As our study of the OT revealed, the phrase denotes Yahweh as Israel's God based on election and covenant[80]. It thus emphasizes the relational identity of the Lord God vis-à-vis Israel. Although Mk takes over the LXX usage, we shall investigate the instances of ὁ θεὸς in the gospel in cases where it is employed along with a possessive pronoun as here or in relation to individuals, to see if the phrase has a specific Markan nuance and emphasis.

Outside of the commandment to love God (12,29.30) ὁ θεὸς with a possessive pronoun appears only twice in Mk (cf. 15,34[bis]). Here it is followed by μου. However, apart from these, 12,26 is also relevant in this connection where ὁ θεὸς is spoken of in a possessive relation to the fathers, Abraham, Isaac and Jacob. Like 15,34 this too is an OT quotation. Although it is clear that as part of a citation the phrase ὁ θεὸς ἡμῶν is understood in its OT meaning, we shall study these texts in their contexts to see whether they reveal any nuances which contribute to the understanding of it in the monotheistic confession as part of the commandment.

---

[80] Cf. Ch I, 3.2.; 3.3.1 a)

(1) God as God of the Fathers (12,26).

Here God's self-revelation to Moses (Ex 3,6) is quoted by Jesus in which God speaks of himself as the God of Abraham, Isaac and Jacob, to emphasize his covenant faithfulness and its eternal validity as the solid basis for the assurance of the resurrection of the dead, in the controversy with the Sadducees on this question (12,18-27)[81]. In this revelation God thus identifies himself in relational terms *vis-à-vis* Israel, in so far as he speaks of himself as the God of the fathers. It is significant that it is Jesus who makes this citation, as is also the case in all the other instances of the texts emphasizing the relational character of God (cf. 12,29.30; 15,34). It shows that he not only accepts this aspect of God in its full OT sense, but also emphasizes it. This becomes even clearer from the fact that in 12,26 the citation is made to answer the Sadducees who as a group have grossly failed (cf. 12,24.27) in understanding its import, in so far as they ridicule the belief in the resurrection. In this context it comes as a firm restatement of the relational character of God and its eternal validity.

(2) God as «My God» (15,34) / God as Abba (14,36)

In this OT text (Ps 22,1) cited by the dying Jesus ὁ θεός occurs with the possessive pronoun μου[82] and it thus affirms God as «his» God. Hence it expresses the relational character of God (ὁ θεὸς ἡμῶν) in personal terms in the extreme situation of Jesus' experience of God's ab-

---

[81] W.L. LANE, *Mark*, 430, following F. Dreyfus, thus points to this as the basis of the argument of Jesus. The phrase «God of Abraham...etc.» functions as the symbol of the promise of salvation guaranteed by the covenant which implicitly contains also salvation from death, the ultimate misfortune. Similarly, S. LÉGASSE, *L'Évangile de Marc II*, 741-742.; J. ERNST, *Markus*, 350-351. Likewise, J. GNILKA, *Markusevangelium II*, 159-160. One can therefore say that by this Jesus also manifests God in his relational character as ὁ θεὸς ἡμῶν in a profound way. R.H. GUNDRY, *Mark*, 703, however, contends that Jesus changes the time frame in drawing the conclusion from the quotation, and that, in itself, the text does not imply it. But, as the above authors emphasize, the point of Jesus' argument is that God's covenant faithfulness to the fathers is *eternal* and that therefore it implicitly contains the guarantee of the resurrection. In this the division of the time frame is irrelevant.

[82] It is interesting to note that in the LXX version of this verse the possessive pronoun μου is absent in the first case. The Markan form corresponds to the Hebrew and Aramaic which have it in both. R. PESCH, *Markusevangelium II*, 495, explains the linguistic history of the citation as the Greek transcription of the Aramaic translation of the Hebrew to which a Greek rendering was added by the translator of the pre-Markan passion narrative. See also, S. LÉGASSE, *L'Évangile de Marc II*, 972-973. Be that as it may, its presence in the Markan text seems significant.

sence in his death, as he calls upon God in prayer[83]. But in 14,36 the same Jesus during his agonizing prayer in the garden, faced with his impending Passion and death, addresses God Αββα ὁ πατήρ, confessing his almighty power, asking to avert his harsh destiny, and finally surrendering to his will. This address reveals Jesus' unique relation to God and thus expresses the relational identity of God in singularly personal terms. These texts occurring at the beginning and end of the Passion form an inclusion to it, and together manifest Jesus' experience of God. They do not contradict but complement each other. The Ὁ θεός μου, whose absence Jesus encounters in his death (15,34), is the same Αββα ὁ πατήρ to whom he is uniquely close (14,36).

It is interesting to note that the two texts dealing with the relational character of God in Mk (12,26c and 15,34), have a connection with the human reality of death. In the first, Jesus speaks of this quality of God in the context of his discussion about the resurrection of the dead with people who deny it, in order to emphasize that he is not a God of the dead but of the living, showing how resurrection follows from God's eternal covenant fidelity. In the second, Jesus calls on God Ὁ θεός μου ὁ θεός μου, as he himself confronts death. In both cases, thus, the relational character of God is emphasized in conjunction with death. This means that, in relation to this inevitable human lot, it is specially significant. In these texts thus Jesus seems to emphasize that the relational character of God is especially operative in connection with it. He seems to articulate that God will continue to be «our God» (ὁ θεὸς ἡμῶν), as one confronts this ultimate crisis of human existence.

---

[83] W.L. LANE, Mark, 573, comments on this cry: «Even in the inferno of his abandonment he did not surrender his faith in God but expressed his anguished prayer in a cry of affirmation: «My God, My God». J. ERNST, Markus, 471, finds it significant that precisely here Jesus turns to «his» God. M.A. TOLBERT, Sowing the Gospel, 283.287, finds the *form* of Jesus' words, a prayer *to* God, undercutting their content suggesting that the experience of absence of God may carry within it the possibility of its own resolution. S. LÉGASSE, L'Évangile de Marc II, 973-974, notes that, despite the intensity of the absence of God, the reproach comes from one who would see God's salvation in the future. Likewise, R. PESCH, Markusevangelium II, 494-495. Similarly, J. GNILKA, Markusevangelium II, 231-232; C.A. EVANS, Mark II, 507. Against R.H. GUNDRY, Mark, 966-967; M. D. HOOKER, Mark, 375, who because they miss this wider picture, construe it as a cry of despair. Besides, the repeated address «my God» emphasizes Jesus' relation to God and manifests his trust in him.

(3) Its Consequence for Understanding the Relational Character of God.

Our consideration of ὁ θεὸς ἡμῶν in the monotheistic confession has shown that this God is the God of the fathers whose covenant faithfulness to them is eternal in which is embedded the guarantee of the resurrection (12,26). Jesus' restatement of this fact in the context of the Sadducees' ridiculing the resurrection, which glaringly fails to understand its import, shows his firm emphasis on its permanent validity. On the other hand, this God of Israel is Jesus' own God whose absence he experiences in his death (15,34), but who is at the same time his Αββα ὁ πατήρ, with whom he stands on a unique relationship (14,36). Through both these texts, which are connected with the reality of death, Jesus seems to emphasize that the relational character of God is specially operative in the face of this inevitable human lot. While these texts show Jesus' total acceptance and clear emphasis on God as the God of Israel, they also point to his experience of God and unique relationship with him. As in the case of God as Lord, the study of God's relational character reveals that, while the gospel fully accepts its OT meaning, it manifests unique connections with the person of Jesus. Thus ὁ θεὸς ἡμῶν is also Jesus' Ὁ θεός μου who is at the same time his Αββα ὁ πατήρ. This means that when Jesus proposes the confession of ὁ θεὸς ἡμῶν as part of the first commandment expressing God's relational character, these aspects which emphasize its unique extension to him also enter into its understanding.

d) God's Prerogatives (12,29): The Singularity of God/The Singularity of Jesus

After having seen the meaning of God as Lord, and dealt with his relational character, we shall similarly consider the great prerogative of God of oneness affirmed by the monotheistic confession in the context of the gospel.

(1) The Divine Prerogative of Forgiveness of Sins (2,7)

The great affirmation of 12,29 «..κύριος ὁ θεὸς ἡμῶν κύριος εἷς ἐστιν,»[84], («..the Lord our God the Lord is one») declares oneness as a

---

[84] Here the term κύριος is predicate nominative with ἐστιν to the subject of the sentence ([κύριος] ὁ θεὸς ἡμῶν). As in the subject function the term is used without article. It thus again indicates nature and quality and emphasizes his relationship as Lord vis-à-vis human beings. Thus Κύριος here has the same significance as in its use

unique prerogative of the Lord God, as has been clarified by our OT analysis[85]. However, the gospel offers two other texts (2,7; 10,18) which proclaim two further prerogatives of God with the same vocabulary. While the one (2,7) proclaims the divine prerogative of forgiveness of sins, the other (10,18) affirms the divine prerogative of goodness. We shall consider these texts to see what they contribute to the understanding of the monotheistic confession as part of the commandment.

Mk 2,7 clearly asserts the power to forgive sins as being a unique divine prerogative. The words express the scribes' inner contestation of Jesus' declaration of forgiveness of the sins of the paralytic (2,5), which they consider a usurpation of it[86]. But the belief itself, on which it is based (cf. τίς δύναται ἀφιέναι ἁμαρτίας εἰ μὴ εἷς ὁ θεός;)[87], correctly reflects the biblical teaching[88]. The phrase thus stresses authority to forgive sins as an exclusively divine privilege[89]. Jesus does not deny

---

above except that it is used here predicatively. The term εἷς (one), which translates the Hebrew אחד, completes the predicate with ἐστιν supplied in Greek.

[85] Cf. Ch I, 3.2.

[86] Some, construing ἀφίενταί σου αἱ ἁμαρτίαι as a theological passive, think that Jesus here only declares God's forgiveness, as in 2Sam 12,13. Others see it as his own authoritative act of forgiveness sparking off the controversy, with the scribes considering it as a usurpation of God's unique prerogative. Representing the first, are: W.L. LANE, Mark, 95; R. PESCH, Markusevangelium I, 156; S. LÉGASSE, L'Évangile de Marc I, 142; 145-146; J. MARCUS, Mark, 223-224. Following the second, is M.J. LAGRANGE, L'Évangile selon Saint Marc, 36. Likewise, R.A. GUELICH, Mark I, 85-86, who adds that it corresponds to the ensuing controversy, which peaks in the statement of the Son of man's authority in 2,10. Similarly, C.S. MANN, Mark, 224. According to R.H. GUNDRY, Mark, 112, while ἀφίενταί could imply God's forgiveness yet the implication is unnecessary, since the scribes understand Jesus himself to be the forgiver (v7). The first view takes the verse too much in isolation. Taken as part of the whole pericope, the second seems to prevail as Guelich and Gundry show. Besides, as J. GNILKA, Markusevangelium I, 99, observes, since the forgiveness is mediated through Jesus there is no essential difference between this individual forgiveness and the general statement in v10, given their interrelationship.

[87] That εἷς here means alone is indicated by the Lukan parallel of this verse (Lk 5,21) which has εἰ μὴ μόνος ὁ θεός;, BAGD, 231.

[88] Cf. Ex 34,6f; Ps 103,3; 130,4; Is 43,25; 44,22; 48,11; Dan 9,9. Also, 1QS ii.9; CD iii.18; XX.34; Str.-B I, 421. Likewise, W.L. LANE, Mark, 95, n.14.

[89] Since the term ὁ θεὸς is arthrous it is determined and, in the context, refers to the God of Israel as the only one to whom the authority to forgive sins is reserved. In this connection R.A. GUELICH, Mark, 87, thinks that the phrase εἷς ὁ θεός, v7 probably reflects Deut 6,4 with its emphasis on the singularity of Israel's God, something also appropriate here with the implication that Jesus has blasphemed against God by claiming to do what God alone could do. Similarly, V. TAYLOR, Mark, 196. Likewise, J. MARCUS, Mark I, 219, who adds that it is also standard Markan vocabulary (cf.

this in his reaction to his opponents, but works his healing to underline that the Son of Man has authority on earth to forgive sins (v10). The healing thus comes as a vindication of this authority. The episode then, while asserting forgiveness of sins to be an exclusive divine right, extends it to Jesus. The statement, without denying the scribal belief, clarifies on the basis of it, the mediation of that authority by Jesus. It asserts that he is the mediator of forgiveness through authority transferred to him by God, and by consequence that he stands on an unparalleled relation with God.

(2) The Divine Prerogative of Goodness (10,18)

Mk 10,18 uses the same vocabulary of uniqueness (εἷς ἐστιν) to affirm another divine attribute, goodness. The context is the encounter of the rich man with Jesus. When the enthusiastic rich man reverently asks: «Good Teacher, what must I do to inherit eternal life?» (10,17) Jesus, before answering him, reacts to his address saying: «Why do you call me good? No one is good but God alone» (οὐδεὶς ἀγαθὸς εἰ μὴ εἷς ὁ θεός, v18)[90]. Jesus' statement here neither denies[91] nor affirms ex-

---

10,18; 12,29.32). In similar vein, W. GRUNDMANN, *Markus,* 57; R. PESCH, *Markusevangelium I,* 161; J. GNILKA, *Markusevangelium I,* 100. By contrast, R.H. GUNDRY, *Mark,* 118, while admitting the possibility of an overtone of monotheism, still discounts it because of the anarthrousness of θεός in what he calls «the clearly monotheistic statements» of 1Cor 8,6; Eph 4,6; 1Tim 2,5 and the possibility of a pleonastic use of εἷς. However, he considers the phrase in isolation from the rest of the gospel. Taken together with 10,18 and 12,29.32, the connection to Deut 6,4 would seem natural, more so because it is quoted in 12,29.

[90] V. TAYLOR, *Mark,* 426, following E.F.F. Bishop, suggests the rendering «There is none good save the One», with ὁ θεός as an interpretative Markan addition. While this does not seem to be shared by many, several scholars stress that in the OT and subsequent Judaism only God is characteristically called «good», although it was possible to speak of people as good in a derived sense (cf. Prov 12,2; 14,14; Eccl 9,2; Mt 12,35). The designation of Jesus as «good teacher», however, is virtually without parallel in Jewish sources, W.L. LANE, *Mark,* 364-365; or rare, C.S. MANN, *Mark,* 339; J. GNILKA, *Markusevangelium II,* 85. Similarly, R. PESCH, *Markusevangelium II,* 137-138, who considers it high recognition which seems to extend a divine attribute to Jesus, though firstly it may point to his status as teacher (cf. 12,14). R.H. GUNDRY, *Mark,* 552, adds that it also includes recognition of Jesus' moral virtue. But S. LÉGASSE, *L'Évangile de Marc II,* 610-612, thinks that it expresses Jesus' competence as a teacher, while he, using a kind of play on words, takes the opportunity to refer to God's goodness. This, however, does not seem to explain Jesus' reaction satisfactorily (v18), which presupposes that the address is taken in a univocal sense.

[91] Some seem to suggest that Jesus rejected the address by his question. Thus W.L. LANE, *Mark,* 366-367, speaks of «the apparent repudiation of the epithet». Likewise, D.E. NINEHAM, *Mark,* 270, thinks that he rejects the flattery involved in it.

plicitly that he is good teacher but focuses on the fact that God alone is good[92]. The comment emphasizes goodness as an exclusive prerogative of this God like forgiveness of sins in 2,7[93]. But, as Jesus does not deny that he is «good teacher» but focuses on the goodness of God, his question seems to provide a lead for the rich man's reflection on his person[94]. If he perceives Jesus to be «good teacher», then he should ponder, and discover what his relationship to the God of Israel (ὁ θεός) is, who alone is all good.

This seems to be supported by the development of this pericope, especially by Jesus' response to the rich man. When the latter states that he has been keeping the commandments of God since his youth (v20), Jesus, though he is greatly pleased with him (v21a), tells him that he still lacked one thing ("Ἐν σε ὑστερεῖ, v21b), and goes on to spell out what it is in terms of radical following of him (v21)[95]. Jesus thus de-

---

These, however, miss the implication that Jesus possesses the goodness of God. K. BERGER, *Gesetzesauslegung 1*, 339, similarly, says that because God alone is good, Jesus can do nothing else but point to God's commandments. But, as R.H. GUNDRY, *Mark*, 560, points out, this is to neglect that Jesus does something astonishingly authoritative in telling the rich man that he must follow him radically as an essential condition for inheriting eternal life.

[92] The term ὁ θεός, being arthrous, is determined and in the context points again to the God of Israel.

[93] R.H. GUNDRY, *Mark*, 552-553, remarks insightfully that since in 2,1-12 some scribes asked: «Who is able to forgive sins except one [i.e.] (God)» (cf. εἰ μὴ εἷς ὁ θεός)? and Jesus proceeded to heal a paralytic for proof of his own divine prerogative to forgive sins, here he employs their phraseology to answer the present question for proof of his possession of divine goodness. He also points to Jesus' self-references to divine sonship (13,32; 14,62 with 14,61), as well as others' references to it in Mk (1,1.11; 3,11; 5,7; 9,7; 14,61; 15,39) as support. Because of the narrative interconnection involved this seems possible.

[94] That the Markan version is meant to invite reflection on the identity of Jesus becomes clearer when we compare it with the other Synoptic parallels of this episode. While Lk's version (Lk, 18,18-23) resembles that of Mk, Mt's is markedly different in emphasis. Mt 19,16-22 has small but significant changes from the start. Thus the address is simply Διδάσκαλε, not Διδάσκαλε ἀγαθε, as in Mk and Lk. Jesus' question is: Τί με λέγεις ἀγαθόν; οὐδεὶς ἀγαθὸς εἰ μὴ εἷς ὁ θεός.(v19). The changes are significant, in that the pericope is no longer focused on the person of Jesus. It does not produce a comparison between God, who alone is good (v18), and the «good teacher» (v17). Hence it is not also geared to inviting reflection on Jesus' identity in relation to God, as in Mk.

[95] According to R.H. GUNDRY, *Mark*, 553, Jesus denies that keeping commandments brings eternal life. "Ἐν σε ὑστερεῖ does not mean that the man's past obediences need the addition of one more thing, but that he is lacking in the one and only thing necessary. This, however, contradicts Jesus' referring the man to the commandments, as an answer to his question, S. LÉGASSE, *L'Évangile de Marc II*, 613. Hence the

mands as essential condition for inheriting eternal life, apart from keeping the commandments of God, a radical following of him (v21), thus raising the question as to who he is to make such a demand. As God is the giver of the commandments, it places Jesus on par with God which indirectly implies that, while goodness is an exclusively divine quality, he shares in this like God himself. The overall thrust of the pericope thus provides enough evidence to show that Jesus shares the exclusive divine prerogative of goodness with God. The text, thus, while affirming the unique divine prerogative of goodness, extends it to Jesus like forgiveness of sins in 2,7.

e) *Conclusion*

Concluding our study of the different elements of the monotheistic confession as commandment we may recall that all these, while they primarily apply to God, in each case involves an extension of its meaning to Jesus. Thus, the term Κύριος, as part of an OT quotation, is used in the same sense and primarily refers to God (12,11; 13,20). But, since the Lord God is also spoken of as having a representative (11,9), and as extending his Lordship to another (12,36), a new feature enters into its understanding. This becomes clearer and more specific in the use of the term for Jesus on the same plane as the Lord God (12,36), and, in particular, in its use in identical sense in 1,3 because of his relationship of origin from the Lord God as his Son.

Similarly, the study of ὁ θεὸς ἡμῶν revealed that this God is the God of the fathers whose covenant faithfulness to them is eternal, in which is enshrined the guarantee of the resurrection (12,26). It also showed Jesus' quoting this text as well as making this point to the Sadducees, who as a group grossly fail to understand its import by their ridiculing of the resurrection (12,24.27), to be significant in so far as this manifests his firm emphasis on the relational character of God and its permanent validity. On the other hand, this God of Israel is also the God of Jesus in a unique way. Thus, although Jesus experiences his absence in his death (15,34), yet this God is at the same time his Αββα ὁ πατήρ, with whom he stands on a unique relationship (14,36). Hence, while these show Jesus' total acceptance and emphasis on God's relational character, they also point to a specificity, in so far as this quality of God becomes more personalized for him, in as much as he calls him 'Ο θεός μου and Αββα ὁ πατήρ revealing his unique relationship with him.

---

meaning certainly is that keeping the commandments *alone* cannot bring eternal life, and one must in addition follow Jesus radically.

Thus the study of this character of God demonstrates that, while the gospel fully accepts its OT meaning, it manifests unique connections with the person of Jesus. It is extended to him in a way similar to the conception of God as Lord.

The consideration of the prerogatives of God revealed the same extension. Thus our study of 2,7 showed that, without denying the scribal and OT belief that forgiveness of sins is an exclusive divine prerogative, it clarifies, on the basis of it, the extension of that authority to Jesus. Similarly, 10,18, while it affirms the unique divine prerogative of goodness, extends it to Jesus who enjoys parity with God, in so far as he demands a radical following of him as an essential condition for inheriting eternal life like the commandments of God. Thus, in all these cases, while the OT understanding is faithfully affirmed, it is extended to Jesus by reason of his unique relationship to the Lord God. Because of the wider understanding of these elements of the monotheistic confession as commandment (i.e. God as Lord, the relational character of God and the prerogatives of God) in the gospel, it becomes enlarged. This means that, when Jesus proposes the monotheistic confession as part of the first commandment, it contains this extended understanding and, in view of the command to listen which precedes it, its acceptance also forms part of the commandment.

2.2.4 Love of God (12,30)

Following the monotheistic confession which forms the first part of the first commandment (12,29), comes its second part, the demand to love God with single-minded devotion (v30). Our study of this will consist in the explanation of the content of the love commanded, of the modality of love, and of the object of this love.

a) *The Content of Love (Mk 12,30)*

Our discussion of the content of love will first clarify whether the gospel retains the OT conception of it, and then investigate if it also has a specificity in Mk, and will conclude with a summary and possible consequence.

(1) The Observance of the Decalogue

We saw in our OT analysis of the commandment to love that the content of love consists in the inner holistic orientation of the human person to God based on his/her deliberate decision which is concretized in the observance of God's commandments[96]. The connection of Deut 6,5 with Deut 6,6 made this point abundantly clear[97]. The same meaning seems to prevail in Mk for two reasons. Firstly, Mk does not define love anywhere in the gospel. On the other hand, a consideration of the lone occurrence of the verb love in Mk outside of the commandment and OT quotations (cf. 10,21) yields no specific nuance, which also indicates that the gospel maintains its OT sense. Secondly, the Evangelist repeatedly emphasizes the validity of the OT commandments, especially of the Decalogue (cf. 10,19; 7,8.9.13; 10,9). This too suggests that love is understood in the OT sense, according to which it is concretized in the observance of commandments. The gospel, thus, seems to preserve the OT conception of love. However, we shall examine the texts in Mk where love is spoken of outside of the commandment to love, and those which emphasize the continued validity of OT commandments to verify if these assertions are indeed correct.

The verb for love, ἀγαπάω[98], occurs 5x in Mk[99]. Among these 4 are either in the two love commandments (12,30.31) or in their paraphrase [12,33(2)]. The fifth instance of the term is in Mk 10,21 which is the sole instance of the term in the gospel, outside of OT quotations or their paraphrases.

Here it figures in a free narrative context, where following the rich man's statement that he had kept all the commandments from his youth, Jesus is said to have looked at him and «loved» him (cf. ..ἐμβλέψας αὐτῷ ἠγάπησεν αὐτὸν). The verb expresses Jesus' spontane-

---

[96] Cf. Ch 1, 3.3.1 d)

[97] Cf. Ch 1, 3.3.1 d)

[98] G. SCHNEIDER, «ἀγάπη», EDNT, I, 9, points out that the LXX, which Mk follows, prefers ἀγαπάω for translating אהב, probably because it is more sober, and conveys less affective emphasis than the other terms for love, φιλέω and ἐράω. These classical terms, often used in Hellenistic Greek, are employed much less in the LXX. The NT, in fact, excludes ἐράω completely as a term for love and takes ἀγαπάω to fuller theological development. φιλέω, on the contrary, though used, is given less importance and becomes theologically less relevant. Following this development, the verb form ἀγαπήσεις is used in both the commandments (vv30.31). The author, Ibid., 179, also notes that, apart from Mk, the other two Synoptics also use ἀγαπάω as the most preferred term for love of God and love of human beings.

[99] Cf. G. SCHNEIDER, «ἀγάπη», EDNT, I, 9; V. TAYLOR, Mark, 486-487, observes that this passage and Lk 11,42 are the only ones in the Synoptic gospels which speak of man's love for God. Similarly, there are only five Pauline passages which speak of this theme (Rom 8,28; 1Cor 2,9; 8,3; 16,22; Eph 6,24), a restraint which Taylor, following Moffatt, Love in the NT, 154-163, traces to the reticence of the NT writers in the use of love-language as addressed to God. Likewise, C. S. MANN, Mark, 480.

ous and affective response to the man for his life according to the commandments (10,20)[100]. Although this is an act of integral human love which certainly includes sentiments[101], it is atypical[102]. Besides, it also does not occur in a context of love of God. Hence it has little to contribute to the understanding of the commandment to love God in the gospel. Thus a consideration of the only occurrence of the term in Mk outside of OT quotations indicates no new nuance that adds to the conception of love of God which, in turn, seems to show that the latter is understood in the OT sense.

On the other hand, the text of Mk 7,6, although it does not use ἀγαπάω, «to love» and instead employs τιμάω «to honor» (cf. Οὗτος ὁ λαὸς τοῖς χείλεσίν με τιμᾷ,..., «This people honors me with their lips...»)[103], also seems to have something to contribute to this discussion. This too is an OT citation, though presumably a free one, as the LXX version of it is slightly different (cf. ὁ λαὸς οὗτος τοῖς χείλεσιν αὐτῶν τιμῶσίν με,...., «This people honor me with their lips...») [104]. Like its Markan and LXX versions its MT form also does not employ the term אהב, «to love» but כבד, «to honor» (cf. ובשפתיו כבדוני)[105] as its principal verb. Nevertheless, it seems to offer a parallel to ἀγαπάω in its understanding of human behavior in relation to God.

The term τιμάω occurs in Mk 3x[106]: in 7,6.10; and 10,19. In the first instance (7,6), as can be seen from the quotation above, it certainly

---

[100] Cf. H.B. SWETE, *Saint Mark*, 225; C.S. MANN, *Mark*, 400.

[101] Cf. C. SPICQ, *Agape dans le NT*, 82.

[102] Cf. G. SCHNEIDER, «ἀγάπη», *EDNT*, I, 9-10.

[103] The full text is: Οὗτος ὁ λαὸς τοῖς χείλεσίν με τιμᾷ, ἡ δὲ καρδία αὐτῶν πόρρω ἀπέχει ἀπ᾽ ἐμοῦ· μάτην δὲ σέβονταί με διδάσκοντες διδασκαλίας ἐντάλματα ἀνθρώπων. However, it is noteworthy that a variant reading found in certain MSS (D W a b c) uses ἀγαπᾷ instead of τιμᾷ in this verse. Cf. NESTLE-ALAND, *Novum Testamentum, ad locum*.

[104] Is 29,13 (LXX) reads: καὶ εἶπεν κύριος ἐγγίζει μοι ὁ λαὸς οὗτος τοῖς χείλεσιν αὐτῶν τιμῶσίν με ἡ δὲ καρδία αὐτῶν πόρρω ἀπέχει ἀπ᾽ ἐμοῦ μάτην δὲ σέβονταί με διδάσκοντες ἐντάλματα ἀνθρώπων καὶ διδασκαλίας., A. RAHLFS, ed. *Septuaginta*, II. The last line in the LXX: διδάσκοντες ἐντάλματα ἀνθρώπων καὶ δι᾽ δασκαλίας also varies from Mk's which has: διδάσκοντες διδασκαλίας ἐντάλματα ἀνθρώπων. V. TAYLOR, *Mark*, 337, points out that Mk's version corresponds to that of Paul in Col 2,22 :ἐντάλματα καὶ διδασκαλίας τῶν ἀνθρώπων, which according to him may suggest, rather than direct Pauline influence on the Markan text, that Mk and (perhaps Paul also) was dependent on a form of the Greek text differing from the LXX, perhaps some *florilegium* of OT prophecies current at Rome. While this is a possibility one cannot be certain of it.

[105] The MT version of this verse reads: ויאמר אדני יען כי נגש העם הזה בפיו ובשפתיו כבדוני ולבו רחק ממני ותהי יראתם אתי מצות אנשים מלמדה:

concerns human behavior towards God. Isaiah here critiques the people for «honoring God with their lips» while their «heart», the core of their personality, is far away from him. It is an attack on empty worship which is not accompanied by a life of obedience to God's will embodied in the commandments.

Mk 7,10, on the other hand, is a quotation of the 4th commandment of the Decalogue to honor one's father and one's mother (cf. Ex 20,12; Deut 5,16). It thus also concerns God's will embodied in a commandment and, as such, relates to human behavior towards God, in so far as in fulfilling it one obeys God.

Mk 10,19 also refers to this same 4th commandment in the context of Jesus' answer to the rich man's question concerning the means to inherit eternal life (10,17-20). He cites this commandment, along with others, placing it last, presumably for emphasis[107]. These commandments are a means to inherit eternal life because they embody God's will and fulfilling them involves an expression of human attitude to God. Thus all three instances of the term τιμάω in Mk appear in OT quotations and in texts which deal with human behavior towards God.

This indicates that in Mk both τιμάω and ἀγαπάω are verbs which speak of human behavior in relation to God in an integral, wholistic sense. Their meaning is certainly very similar in the OT citations in which they figure. Like ἀγαπάω, τιμάω also is expressed in the faithful observance of God's commandments. This is perhaps clearest in 7,6-13.

The passage comes as Jesus' response to the Pharisees and certain scribes who had come from Jerusalem, and who question Jesus upon seeing that some of his disciples do not observe the customary rules of Jewish purification (7,1-2). It is meant to expose the externalism of his critics in focusing on these peripheral practices, which are purely human traditions in comparison with the commandments of God which they conveniently evade (7,8)[108], but which in fact ought to have en-

---

[106] Cf. R. MORGENTHALER, *Statistik.*

[107] Cf. W. GRUNDMANN, *Markus,* 211, who observes that the commandments cited all emphasize love of neighbor which caps in this commandment placed last for emphasis.

[108] As M.D. HOOKER, *Mark,* 174, points out the concluding saying opposes the commandment of God to the tradition of men. By giving the latter equal authority with the former, the Pharisees in effect subordinate the Torah to their own interpretation. R.A. GUELICH, *Mark,* 367, observes that this is false teaching and Jesus' opponents are «hypocrites» (v6) because their wrong teaching causes them to neglect Gods' commandment. Similarly, J. GNILKA, *Markusevangelium I,*282. S. LÉGASSE, *L'Évangile de Marc I,* 433, adds that they are hypocrites because they practice a purely exterior

gaged their attention. Concentration on such trivia is «honoring God with one's lips» with one's «heart far away» from him as the passage adds. It is an honoring from which the heart of the matter is missing[109]. The import of Jesus' reply is that true honoring of God is expressed in observing the commandments of God and not in such barren externalism[110].

Here Jesus' conception of «honoring» God is thus very similar to the idea of «love of God» in the OT[111]. This close similarity of meaning, in fact, seems to indicate that «honoring God» (τιμάω) is synonymous[112]

---

religion with their profound indifference to the authentic will of God in their adoption of human precepts in place of the latter.

[109] As R. PESCH, *Markusevangelium I,* 373, observes, in so far as here honoring God occurs only with words, with only one's lips and not with one's heart, there is in fact no honoring of God at all. To focus on human traditions is to pay such lip service to God, while to do so as one makes void the commandment of God is to do the opposite of honoring God. The passage thus also reveals that true honoring of God consists in fulfilling God's commandments from the heart. In this connection Pesch's further comment that Jesus' charge against his opponents' neglect of the commandment of God (7,8), seen in the broader context of Jesus' ministry, refers to the great commandment which demands love of God «with all one's heart» (Deut 6,4-5) seems relevant. They neglect God's commandment because their «heart» is not in their «honor». Similarly, W.L. LANE, *Mark,* 248. In the context of 7,9-13, however, as R.A. GUELICH, *Mark,* 367, observes, the «commandment of God» refers to God's Law as the written law in contrast to «tradition» consisting of «human» commandments, although in either case God's commandment is neglected.

[110] The contrasts between «human tradition» or «your tradition» in 7,8.9.13 and «the commandment of God» or «the word of God» reflects the contrast involved in the Isaian passage of «honoring God with one's lips» and «honoring God with one's heart» (7,6-7) by the observance of his commandments embodying God's will. Also, J. MARCUS, *Mark,* 451; S. LÉGASSE, *L'Évangile de Marc I,* 434, n.51.

[111] Cf. Ch I, 3.3.1f.

[112] In this connection we may recall how our analysis of love of God in Ch I (Cf. Ch I, 3.3.1b) +) revealed that Deuteronomy uses alongside «love», (אהב) other synonymous terms to indicate the same reality which include: «fear», (ליראה את־יהוה אלהיך) «walking with Yahweh», (ללכת בכל־דרכיו), «obedience», (לשמע בקלו) and «service», (..ולעבד את־יהוה אלהיך) (cf. Deut 10,12; 11,13; 30,16.20). These are interchangeable and emphasize both the inner orientation to God and its expression in the observance of the commandments which «love of God» involves. Although «honoring» (כבד) is not one of these terms in Deut, still, as we see in this Isaian text, it expresses the same reality as «loving» God. Besides, it is also pertinent to note that the MT version of this text (Is 29,13) has a clause defining the character of such empty honoring which significantly says: ותהי יראתם אתי מצות אנשים מלמדה:, «so that their fear of me is (only) a human command (that is) memorized.», J.D. WATTS, *Isaiah 1-33,* 384, where thus the term «fear» which in Deut is synonymous «to love» actually figures and which is a revealing pointer to the equation «honoring» = «fearing» = «loving». In view of these data the term «honoring» could legitimately be considered

to «loving God» (ἀγαπάω). This, in turn, is a strong indication of Mk's retention of the OT meaning of love of God as obedience to God's commandments.

Mk' preservation of this OT idea of love of God is also reinforced by the gospel's repeated emphasis on the continued validity of OT commandments in the following texts: 7,8.9.13; 10,9; 10,19. Thus if, as we just saw in 7,8, Jesus critiques the Pharisees' preoccupation with barren externalism even as they evade the commandments of God, vv9-13 go further and describe a concrete example of the way they reject them in favor of their human tradition in the «Corban» practice of the day, which nullifies the Decalogue commandment to care for one's parents through a devious custom by which they license people to circumvent it[113]. Thus Jesus here condemns the Pharisees' infringement of God's commandment either by its substitution by a human tradition or by its annulment[114]. In both cases he defends and reasserts the commandments' permanent validity[115].

However, it is significant that the example Jesus gives in this context of the commandment of God flouted in favor of human traditions, the commandment to honor father and mother (7,10)[116], comes from the Decalogue (cf. Ex 20,12; Deut 5,16). He does not cite any of the other numerous OT prescriptions and ordinances. This surely

---

synonymous to «loving». The variant reading found in a few MSS referred to above, n.103, which in fact has ἀγαπᾶ in place of τιμᾶ in Mk 7,6 perhaps also points in this direction.

[113] The comment of R.H. GUNDRY, *Mark*, 352, that in v9 the sarcasm in v6 turns to irony seems apt in so far as the setting aside the commandment of God for the sake of tradition has sparked the invention of the legal device of Corban, beautiful in its piety, which in accordance with the nature of irony means its opposite, ugly in its impiety. For a different view see, S. LÉGASSE, *L'Évangile de Marc I*, 431, n.32.

[114] Cf. S. LÉGASSE, *L'Évangile de Marc I*, 436-437.

[115] In this connection the argument of R. PESCH, *Markusevangelium I*, 373-375, that Jesus rejects the Corban institution on the basis of his interpretation of the Law based on the undividedness of the love of God and love of neighbor, seems beside the point. While this is admittedly Jesus' fundamental position *vis-à-vis* the Law, the issue in our context is the fulfillment of God's commandment as the true expression of honoring God which is being flouted by Jesus' opponents by its substitution with their human traditions, of which the Corban practice is a telling illustrative example. The latter is rejected because it subverts the commandment of God and supplants it with one of these human precepts, by which they only honor God «by their lips», with their heart far away from him.

[116] R.H. GUNDRY, *Mark*, 350, points out perceptively that the focus on «honoring God» (vv6-8) prepares for this further discussion of «honoring» one's father and mother (vv9-12). The author's point that this interrelationship between the two forms of honoring signals the integrity of the passage is well taken.

is not fortuitous, and seems to indicate that by the commandments of God Jesus means primarily the Decalogue.

This, in turn, also seems to mean that for Jesus love of God as observance of the commandments involves fundamentally the fulfillment of these commandments. In so far as he singles out the Decalogue commandments and emphasizes them, it seems to reveal a specificity *vis-à-vis* the OT understanding which, while it also had a special place for the Decalogue and the demand to love God[117], extended to all the other commandments and ordinances as their specifications. Jesus, by contrast, seems to focus on the former. For him, thus, love of God is expressed primarily in the observance of the Decalogue.

This is, in fact, confirmed by 10,19 where answering the rich man's question as to what he should do to inherit eternal life, Jesus refers him to the OT commandments as the means for it, thus reaffirming OT teaching and restating the commandments' continued validity. But, as in the above case, the commandments cited, except for Μὴ ἀποστερήσῃς[118], are all of them from the Decalogue (cf. Ex 20,13-16;

---

[117] Cf. Ch I, 4.3, the understanding of the שמע as the principal commandment in summary form (elaborated in Deut Chs 5-11) and all the others, the statutes and ordinances, which follow (cf. Deut, Chs 12-28) as individual commandments which are specifications of it, and also its close connection with the Decalogue, especially with its first commandment of which it is considered a commentary and restatement, Ch I, 4.1.

[118] B.M. METZGER, *A Textual Commentary*, 89, observes that Μὴ ἀποστερήσῃς, «Do not defraud» is a reminiscence of Ex 20,17 or Deut 24,14 [LXX MSS AF] or Sir 4,1. The inclusion of this prohibition, according to many, is to be explained by the emphasis in the answer of Jesus on the love of neighbor which characterizes the second table of the Decalogue, from which all the other commandments mentioned come. While the latter emphasize the love given to the neighbor, the former stresses the love that does not withhold what belongs to him. So W. GRUNDMANN, *Markus*, 211; V. TAYLOR, *Mark*, 428, who adds that it may be the negative form of the 9th commandment. Likewise, W.L. LANE, *Mark*, 366, who, however, thinks that it is probably an application of the 8th and the 9th commandments, while R. PESCH, *Markus II*, 139 opines that it replaces the 9th and the 10th. Similarly, S. LÉGASSE, *L'Évangile de Marc II*, 613, who adds that it also indicates that the author is quoting from memory. So also, J. GNILKA, *Markusevangelium II*, 86-87, who, nevertheless, holds that the irregularities in the order of the commandments and the addition betray rather the particular interpretative tradition of the narrator which stresses social morality. In like manner, M.D. HOOKER, *Mark*, 241-242, thinks that it replaces the commandment, «do not covet» and adds that, while no satisfactory explanation has ever been given to this change, it could be because ἀποστερέω which can mean besides «to defraud» or «to deprive», also «to rob», suggested a neat contrast to the demand to give everything to the poor which will be made of the rich man. So too R.H. GUNDRY, *Mark*, 553, who adds that this replacement of the commandment, «do not covet», makes the latter conspicuous by its absence which, as the story progresses, makes it conspicuous in its

Deut 5,17-20)[119], with the commandment to honor father and mother placed at the end[120]. This significantly reveals the gospel's conception of the Decalogue as practically a synonym for the commandments of God[121].

These texts thus, on the one hand, underline the continued validity of the OT commandments and, on the other, identify the latter strongly with the Decalogue in so far as they embody the authentic will of God[122]. They also support the understanding that for Mk love of God concretizes itself in the observance of the commandments of God as in the OT with the specification that these are concentrated primarily in the Decalogue commandments.

(2) The Observance of Jesus' Commands

The gospel not only preserves the OT understanding of love as observance of the commandments of God, primarily understood as the Decalogue, but also extends it to the demands of Jesus. While this extension, as we shall see, occurs in manifold contexts in the gospel, it is seen most fundamentally in 9,7 where God himself effects this

---

applicability to the rich man. It is interesting to note that the one thing common to practically all these opinions is that it paraphrases or replaces one or more of the Decalogue commandments. In this context it is significant that its inclusion along with the Decalogue commandments seems to have been considered inappropriate by both Mt (19,18) and Lk (18,20) who omit it, not to mention many copyists of the Markan text as well, Metzger, *Ibid.*

[119] R. PESCH *Markusevangelium II,* 138, sees the allusion to Deut 6,4, Israel's monotheistic confession, in 10,18b as meant to underline love of God as the basis of the social morality the listing of commandments here (10,19) embodies. The suggestion, though not explicit, seems likely in view of their linkage in the gospel (cf. 12,29-33).

[120] The commandments cited come from the second table and according to M.J. LAGRANGE, *L'Évangile selon Saint Marc,* 266, the order followed is from the more serious sin to the less concluding with a positive commandment.

[121] Cf. J. GNILKA, *Markusevangelium II,* 86; W.L. LANE, *Mark,* 366; R. SCHNACKENBURG, *Markus II,* 90-92.

[122] Though Mk 10,9 is not a «commandment», much less a Decalogue commandment, Jesus here sets aside a piece of Mosaic legislation allowing a man to divorce his wife to reassert the original order of creation established by God the creator (cf. Mk 10,7-8 and Gen 1,27; 2,24). Cf. M.D. HOOKER, *Mark,* 236; C.S. MANN, *Mark,* 391; R. PESCH, *Markusevangelium II,* 124. It is significant, in so far as Jesus in this context reinstates the original will of God for the institution of marriage as indissoluble, superseding a subsequent compromise before human weakness (cf. 10,5). This stress on the genuine will of God is relevant to the conception of love as observance of the Decalogue commandments, since the consistent emphasis on the latter expresses the same stress on the true will of God which they embody.

extension by his word of revelation and command. Thus in this text God the Father, in the context of the transfiguration, reveals Jesus' divine identity to the accompanying disciples in a revelatory declaration: «This is my beloved Son», (Οὗτός ἐστιν ὁ υἱός μου ὁ ἀγαπητός,) and commands that they «listen to him» (...ἀκούετε αὐτοῦ.)[123].

As a divine command expressing the will of God (cf. ...ἀκούετε αὐτοῦ.) it is a commandment of God[124]. It is also a new and definitive commandment of God, because it is the only commandment God himself gives in the gospel. More importantly, this is so because it is based on the new and definitive revelation of God (cf. Οὗτός ἐστιν ὁ υἱός μου ὁ ἀγαπητός,)[125] and embodies the new and definitive revelation of his will (cf. ...ἀκούετε αὐτοῦ.)[126]. As such it has a fundamental position in the gospel.

As the most fundamental commandment of God it integrates itself into the commandments which the gospel considers important, namely the Decalogue and the love commandment (12,29-31). Because of its fundamental stature it also imparts to all the demands of Jesus the firm basis of divine authority. All his other demands are qualified by it, based on it, and follow from it. At the same time, by imparting divine authority to them, it also integrates these demands of Jesus into the commandments of God. Because of it to obey Jesus is to obey God himself.

Although «listening to Jesus» is not called «love of God» in the gospel, this integration of Jesus' demands into the commandments of God, considered in the context of the OT understanding of love of God as observance of God's commandments which Mk retains and reinforces, it involves precisely this. Thus in Mk «to listen to Jesus», to

---

[123] The command involves, as in the OT, listening with an attitude of obedience, Ch I, 2. 3.1. In this connection M.D. HOOKER, *Mark*, 218, observes that «the words remind us also of the repeated commands in the OT to listen to -and to obey- God himself.» See also S. LÉGASSE, *L'Évangile de Marc II*, 450, n.49. R.H. GUNDRY, *Mark*, 462, adds that the *asyndeton* puts further emphasis on the command to hear Jesus.

[124] Cf. G. SCHRENK, «ἐντολή», *TDNT*, II, 545-556; M. LIMBECK, «ἐντολή» *EDNT*, I, 459-460; R. F. COLLINS, «Commandment», *ABD*, I, 1097-1099.

[125] Cf. M. D. HOOKER, *Mark*, 48; W. LANE, *Mark*, 320-321; R.H. GUNDRY, *Mark*, 461; J. GNILKA, *Markusevangelium II*, 36; S. LÉGASSE, *L'Évangile de Marc II*, 531.

[126] Cf. V. TAYLOR, *Mark*, 392; M. D. HOOKER, *Mark*, 218; W.L. LANE, *Mark*, 321; J. GNILKA, *Markusevangelium II*, 36; S. LÉGASSE, *L'Évangile de Marc II*, 531. Taylor, *Ibid.*, 391-392, adds that Mk's interest in this episode centers in the message, Οὗτός ἐστιν ὁ υἱός μου ὁ ἀγαπητός, ἀκούετε αὐτοῦ.

obey his commands, is to love God, just as much as to observe the Decalogue commandments is to love God.

In this connection it is significant that the term ἀγαπάω occurs in Mk, prescinding from 10,21, only in the two love commandments and their paraphrase (12,30-33). As the former is atypical and unconnected with the context of love of God, this means that the term actually figures in the gospel in relation to love of God only in the comm andments of God.

Significantly too, the semantically related term ἀγαπητός, used by the Father to characterize the Son, appears only in the following passages: 1,11; 9,7 and 12,6. Of these, the first two are the words of the Father about Jesus in the revelatory contexts of Jesus' baptism[127] and transfiguration[128] respectively, while the last (12,6) comes from the narrator referring to the owner of the vineyard who images the Father

---

[127] In 1,11 the appellation is addressed to Jesus himself (cf. Σὺ εἶ ὁ υἱός μου ὁ ἀγαπητός,..) while at the transfiguration it is directed to his three accompanying disciples (cf. Οὗτός ἐστιν ὁ υἱός μου ὁ ἀγαπητός,.. 9,7). The term is used with two articles which, with their focus on the individual, M. ZERWICK, *Biblical Greek*, 57, #177, point to the accurate determination of the Son in question. Several scholars trace the language of this statement to Ps 2,7 and Is 42,1, V. TAYLOR, *Mark*, 162; W.L. LANE, *Mark*, 57; J. GNILKA, *Markusevangelium I*, 52-53; S. LÉGASSE, *L'Évangile de Marc I*, 91-92; J. MARCUS, *Mark I*, 162; R.H. GUNDRY, *Mark*, 49-50. Similarly, M.D. HOOKER, *Mark*, 47, who, however, considers the connection with the latter text dubious. Regarding these possible connections it is noteworthy that the term υἱός does not occur in Is 42,1, and that in Ps 2,7 it figures in the words of the newly enthroned king communicating the formula of his investiture, whereas here it is directly spoken by God himself to Jesus which is a significant difference. In regard to the meaning of ἀγά πητός, Hooker, *Ibid.*, 47-48, thinks that, given its use in the LXX for an *only* child, its position after υἱός both in 1,11 and 9,7 indicates that these words are to be taken together to mean «my only son». Gundry, *Ibid.*, however, qualifies this by saying that, although ἀγαπητός has come to mean «only», since an only son is naturally beloved, the primary meaning «beloved» remains, and is clarified by the next phrase: «in you I am well pleased». The term denotes Jesus' unique status and is the declaration of his identity, while the following clause suggests his obedient response to the divine will which causes God to delight in him, Hooker, *Ibid.*, 47-48. Similarly, Taylor, *Ibid.*, who, however, adds that the words are best understood as an assurance, or confirmation of Jesus' filial relationship to God rather than a revelation. Likewise, R. PESCH, *Markusevangelium I*, 93; Légasse, *Ibid.*, 92. So also, Lane, *Ibid.*, 58, who observes that the second clause is based on the first which makes this verse a direct parallel to 9,7. Similarly, Pesch, *Ibid.*, 93; Légasse, *Ibid.*, 91-92. Likewise, Gundry, *Ibid.*, 49, who notes that Mk puts Σύ in the first position to accent the identification of Jesus as God's Son.

[128] Cf. n.55; Also n.127.

in the deeply christological parable of 12,1-12[129] to speak about his son. Hence the term ἀγαπητός figures in Mk only in the words of the Father, or of the narrator referring to the Father, to characterize Jesus' divine origin and his uniquely profound communion with him.

This parallelism of the usage of ἀγαπάω, apart from the atypical instance of 10,21, only in the love commandments to observe which is to love God, and that of the term ἀγαπητός exclusively in characterizing Jesus' divine status as Son and his singularly profound union with God, also serves to underline the equivalence of obedience to Jesus' commands to observance of the commandments of God. The former is to love God just as much as the latter, all the more so, because in the former one obeys the Beloved Son who is uniquely close in a most profound union to God who demands absolute obedience of his Son's

---

[129] In Mk 12,6 the term υἱός ἀγαπητός is spoken of by the narrator who, after describing the slaves dispatched by the owner earlier who were rejected (12,2.4.5), mentions him as the only one left for him to send. It is significant that the terms used, δοῦλος and υἱὸς ἀγαπητός, occur without article, thus stressing their nature and quality as opposed to their individuality, M. ZERWICK, *Biblical Greek*, 53.55, #165.171. Similarly, S. LÉGASSE, *L'Évangile de Marc II*, 714, n.34, who adds that the term ἕνα in v6 stands in opposition to πολλούς in v5 and υἱὸν ἀγαπητόν is an apposition to it. Likewise, V. TAYLOR, *Mark*, 475; C.S. MANN, *Mark*, 465; M.D. HOOKER, *Mark*, 276. So too R. PESCH, *Markusevangelium II*, 217-218, who, however, considers υἱὸν ἀγά πητόν not just an addition but as interpreting ἕνα, «the only one» in line with 1,11 and 9,7. The latter's difference is also indicated by the owner's calling him «my son» (v6b), and expecting a different treatment for him than given to the slaves (12,6); and also by the fact that he severely punishes his murder (12,9). All this show that, while both have the same mission (cf. ἀπέστειλεν, 12,2.4.5.6) and are treated similarly, they differ in their quality of relation to the owner. While the first are slaves, the second is a beloved son who is also an only son (cf. n.127), Taylor, *Ibid.*; Mann, *Ibid.*; Hooker, *Ibid.*. Similarly J. GNILKA, *Markusevangelium II*, 146, who adds that, as the last sent, the son is also the possessor of eschatological authority. Likewise, Pesch, *Ibid.* So also, R.H. GUNDRY, *Mark*, 660-661, who notes that the *asyndeton* in v6a and v6b heightens the contrast between the two. These data thus serve to reveal the meaning of the term «beloved son» in the parable. While the term «son» underlines the state in which a person stands in relation to another person (father), the adjective «beloved» seems to put in relief the personal and cordial character of this relation.

On the other hand, 12,10f which speak expressly of the action of God clarify that the owner of the vineyard is God, W.L. LANE, *Mark*, 420; Taylor, *Ibid.*, 477; Mann, *Ibid.*, 467; Gnilka, *Ibid.*, 145.148; Pesch, *Ibid.*, 220-221; Hooker, *Ibid.*, 277; Gundry, *Ibid.*, 662-663, and according to 12,12, Jesus' opponents recognize that he said this parable against them, and they see themselves in the role of the wicked tenants. The parable thus clearly demonstrates that the term «beloved son» signifies Jesus' unique relation to God in contrast to all others who preceded him in sacred history and expresses his singular closeness to God, Lane, *Ibid.*; Hooker, *Ibid.*. Similarly,. Gnilka, *Ibid.*, 149. Likewise, Pesch, *Ibid.*, 223. So also, Gundry, *Ibid.*, 663-664.

commands and gives them unique divine authority (9,7). It also underscores that to listen to Jesus, to obey him, is to obey God and hence to love God.

Moreover, it is significant that this demand of God to listen to Jesus is made to the disciples in the presence of Moses and Elijah (9,4). These epic OT figures symbolize the Law and the Prophets, and as such the totality of the OT. Their presence has relevance in the context of God's fundamental command to listen to Jesus, and means that the OT continues to have validity and relevance, in so far as Jesus integrates it into his teaching. As the new and definitive revelation of God (cf. ..ὁ υἱός μου ὁ ἀγαπητός,) and of his will (cf. ...ἀκούετε αὐτοῦ.) Jesus and his teaching is the measure of both. The OT and its revelation are valid and relevant, in so far as they are taken up and confirmed by him[130].

As we saw above, this is to be found substantially in the Decalogue and in the love commandments. Obviously, it also follows from this that, what Jesus rejects and annuls of the OT, ceases to have any validity and relevance as commandments embodying God's will (cf. 10,2-12). They are superseded and overcome and no longer qualify as such.

All this results in reinforcing 9,7 as the most fundamental commandment of God in Mk which, as mentioned, invests all the demands of Jesus with divine authority. We shall now turn to these demands of Jesus in the gospel which thus have parity with God's commandments. They are found in the following places in the gospel: 1,17; 2,14; 8,34; 8,17.21; 8,35; 8,38; 10,21.

The first three of these (1,17; 2,14; 8,34) along with 10,21, concern the demand to «follow». Thus in 1,17 Jesus makes this demand of Simon and Andrew (1,16) and they respond to him immediately and follow him leaving everything (1,18). The demand is phrased in absolute terms (cf. Δεῦτε ὀπίσω μου, 1,17) which underlines its unqualified and unconditional character[131]. The response is also

---

[130] In this connection M. D. HOOKER, *Mark*, 218, rightly observes that because of his unique authority, these figures give way to Jesus and vanish from the scene, so that the disciples' attention may be focused on him alone. Similarly, R. PESCH, *Markusevangelium II*, 77; R.H. GUNDRY, *Mark*, 461-462. Likewise, W.L. LANE, *Mark*, 321, who aptly observes that at this point the disciples are confronted with the truth that «His (Jesus') word and deed transcend all past revelation.»

[131] The absolute character of the demand is underlined also by the fact that it is unexpected and invasive. It is particularly seen in its authoritative and overwhelming nature, R.A. GUELICH, *Mark I*, 51; R.H. GUNDRY, *Mark*, 67. J. GNILKA, *Markusevangelium I*, 73, sees the latter stressed by the fact that only in regard to the response the ones called appear in the subject function. J. MARCUS, *Mark I*, 185, hears the compel-

absolute and unconditional[132]. In 2,14 Jesus similarly calls Levi the tax-collector, as he sat at his tax-office, with the same absolute demand, Ἀκολούθει μοι, who also responds instantly by following him, thus manifesting absolute obedience to Jesus' call[133].In these cases the demand to follow is made to particular individuals.

In 8,34 however the same demand is addressed to all, to the multitude along with the disciples, laying down the unequivocal conditions for such following. Three such conditions are mentioned, two being decisive and a third implying a continuous relationship. The first is to «deny oneself» (ἀπαρνησάσθω ἑαυτόν) which carries the nuance to utterly deny or disown oneself by placing discipleship before one's own wishes and plans; the second is to «to take up one's cross» (καὶ ἀράτω τὸν σταυρὸν αὐτοῦ), which involves accepting the last consequences of obedience expressed here metaphorically, cross being understood as an instrument of death (cf. 15,21.30.32). The third requirement is sustained loyalty in discipleship (καὶ ἀκολουθείτω μοι.). The call also lays emphasis upon willing, (cf. Εἴ τις θέλει). The demands are relevant only in the case of the one who accepts discipleship freely and consciously[134]. But it is noteworthy that,

---

ling voice of God in Jesus' call, while Gnilka, *Ibid.*, 74, stresses that Jesus calls out of his own authority. Likewise, R. PESCH, *Markusevangelium I*, 111. Similarly, S. LÉGASSE, *L'Évangile de Marc I*, 116.118.180; W. LANE, *Mark*, 68-69, links the suddenness of the call and the nature of the response to the eschatological urgency of Jesus' mission.

[132] The response is immediate (cf. εὐθύς, 1,18) and without qualification and as such it underlines absolute obedience. It corresponds to the call, R.A. GUELICH, *Mark I*, 51; W.L. LANE, *Mark*, 69. Similarly, V. TAYLOR, *Mark*, 169, who sees the decisiveness of the response in those called leaving their nets (1,19). So also, C.S. MANN, *Mark*, 209. Likewise, M.D. HOOKER, *Mark*, 60; R.H. GUNDRY, *Mark*, 67, who observes that the act of leaving the father by the Zebedee brothers intensifies the impact of Jesus' call; So too, S. LÉGASSE, *L'Évangile de Marc I*, 119, who points out that the mention of the father twice in the account enables the author to enrich the object of renunciation to the maximum; R. PESCH, *Markusevangelium I*, 111. According to, Taylor, *Ibid.*, 203, the immediateness of the response in 2,14 is expressed by the aorist, ἠκολούθησεν.

[133] The absoluteness of the response in the case of Levi is also expressed in the irrevocable nature of the renunciation of his profession as tax-collector. Unlike the fishermen he never returns to it even on occasion, V. TAYLOR, *Mark*, 203; C.S. MANN, *Mark*, 229.

[134] Cf. V. TAYLOR, *Mark*, 381; C.S. MANN, *Mark*, 349; M.D. HOOKER, *Mark*, 208. Similarly, J. GNILKA, *Markus II*, 24, who, however, thinks the third condition to be a summarizing restatement of the other two; R. PESCH, *Markusevangelium II*, 59-60, who adds that the denial stands as contrast to the confession of God and his Messiah (cf. Lk 12,8f par.) and that the cross-bearing in the context of 8,31.35 expresses

although willing following is stressed, the conditions themselves are phrased stringently and in absolute language, which admits of no compromise. This is clear from the fact that no qualifiers are added to them. Anyone who wants to follow Jesus must necessarily accept these conditions uncompromisingly.

In 10,21 we have the last instance of the command to follow. The context is the episode of the rich man who comes to Jesus with the query about the means to inherit eternal life. He is told that for this, besides observing the OT commandments, he must also renounce everything and follow Jesus radically. The observance of the Deca logue commandments, important as it is, alone does not suffice for it (cf. Ἕν σε ὑστερεῖ·, 10,21)[135]. He must, in addition[136], give up everything and follow Jesus[137]. Although the gospel does not term the demand of Jesus a «commandment», it has this status, as we saw above, because of the fundamental revelation and command of God in 9,7. These integrate the demands of Jesus into the commandments of God and give them parity with them based on his equality and profound communion with him. By reason of them it embodies God's will like God's commandments.

In fact it is important and essential as part of the new and definitive revelation of God's will. This seems to be the reason why here following Jesus is demanded as a *necessary* step to inherit eternal life, like the observance of Decalogue commandments. Without it the man

---

the determined readiness for martyrdom, and finally ongoing Christian asceticism. Likewise, S. LÉGASSE, *L'Évangile de Marc II*, 510-511, who observes that the term «deny» (ἀρνέομαι) is employed elsewhere for what is equivalent to apostasy (cf. Mk 14,68.70 par.; Mt 10,33; Lk 12,9) and is used here reflexively, implying thereby pre-scinding from one's person; W.L. LANE, *Mark*, 306-307, who, however, holds that this call to follow points to the common commitment to Jesus which differs from «discipleship» in the technical sense. So also, R.H. GUNDRY, *Mark*, 434-435 who adds that the positive formulation of the call makes it a command.

[135] Against C.A. EVANS, *Mark II*, 98, who asserts that Jesus here accepts that keeping the commandments *by itself* secures eternal life.

[136] Against R.H. GUNDRY, *Mark*, 554, who claims that Jesus here denies obser-vance of commandments as having even a contributory role in bringing eternal life.

[137] In this respect the Markan position is clearly different from that of Matthew. The latter states: «If you would enter life, keep the commandments (19,17)», thus in-dicating that the observance of the commandments suffices for it. The radical following of Jesus is demanded in Mt only in relation to perfection: «If you would be perfect, go, sell what you possess and give to the poor, and you will have treasure in heaven; and come, follow me.» (19,21).

cannot attain it as he would be lacking in the «one thing» crucial for it[138].

Although 8,17.21 do not appear like the rest of the demands of Jesus, as they do not have the form of a direct demand nor employ an external phraseology of absoluteness (cf. οὔπω νοεῖτε οὐδὲ συνίετε; [v17]; Οὔπω συνίετε; [v21]), yet they unquestionably contain a clear-cut expectation of Jesus on the disciples: that they «understand». It is also not left as something indifferent or immaterial whether they did so or not. The energy and the effort that Jesus expends in the context on making sure that they do understand (cf. 8,14-21) suggest that it is in fact essential and indispensable to their role as disciples and their relationship with him. Without it they remain obdurate (8,17c), blind, and deaf (8,18) and thus fail to measure up to their role. Besides, the fact that Jesus' efforts eventually yield results and they reach the desired understanding (8, 29), also points in the direction of its crucial character[139]. All this seems to converge to qualify the will of Jesus expressed here as involving an absolute demand on the disciples.

The text occurs in the context of Jesus' warning them of «the leaven of the Pharisees and the Herodians», referring to their evil influence[140] while the disciples misunderstand this reference to the leaven and dispute about the fact that they have no bread (8,16), as they had forgotten to take some with them (8,14). Jesus' reproach, «Do you not

---

[138] Against J. GNILKA, *Markusevangelium II*, 87, who, while admitting that this radical demand goes beyond the first, still thinks that it is not meant as either its substitute or complement but is an opening to the will of God for this man. Though it is not its surrogate, it surely has a crucial and irreplaceable character in so far as it is a *necessary* step along with the first. Also, against S. LÉGASSE, *L'Évangile de Marc II*, 614, who asserts that the new condition is mentioned not because it is necessary for inheriting eternal life, but for revealing the superior conditions for it beyond the simple observance of the commandments. The text, with the forward position of Ἕν in the phrase Ἕν σε ὑστερεῖ· (10,21) which emphasizes it, clearly affirms that without this step the man simply does not measure up to inherit eternal life.

[139] Reinforcing this is the role of 8,29 as the center of the gospel, marking the high point in the revelation of Jesus' identity in the first part and dividing the gospel narrative into two halves. Cf. I. dE lA POTTERIE, «De Compositione», 135-141.

[140] While «leaven» is a Jewish metaphor for such negative influence, the leaven of the Pharisees and the Herodians consists in their unbelief, leading to hard-heartedness. The disciples are being warned against falling into the same danger because of their failure to understand the import of the multiplication miracles, J. GNILKA, *Markusevangelium I*, 310-311; V. TAYLOR, *Mark*, 365; W.L. LANE, *Mark*, 280-281; R.H. GUNDRY, *Mark*, 408; R. PESCH, *Markusevangelium I*, 414. Similarly, R.A. GUELICH, *Mark I*, 427; M.D. HOOKER, *Mark*, 195; J. MARCUS, *Mark I*, 510; S. LÉGASSE, *L'Évangile de Marc I*, 481-482.

yet perceive or understand?», comes as an exasperated response to it[141]. It does not specify the object of understanding, which, in the case of these transitive verbs (cf. νοεῖτε, συνίετε;), is exceptional and intriguing, and this suggests that it is to be understood from the context[142].

A consideration of the preceding context in fact clarifies that the object has to do with the identity of Jesus. The disciples, despite their having witnessed and participated in the great multiplication miracles (6,30-44; 8,1-10), have failed to understand their true import, in so far as they fret about the fact that they have no bread with them, though the same Jesus is with them. Had they understood its significance, they would have realized that Jesus, who took care of such a large number of people, is capable of dealing with their situation of want as well. It thus points to their lack of understanding of his identity, and the stinging reproach on their not understanding (8,17), is an indirect demand to understand the significance of these miracles, and to make a break-through in the comprehension of his person as the one who is able to take care of them, that is, as the Messiah[143].

The following statements seek to conduct the disciples to this strongly desired understanding by recalling to their memory, through question and answer, the important details of the two multiplication miracles and conclude with the further aggravated and tenacious question: «Do you not yet understand?» (Οὔπω συνίετε;, 8,21). The unrelenting character of this expectation that they understand which this context clearly evinces, thus seems to characterize it as an absolute demand. It is the strongly expressed will of Jesus that they decidedly

---

[141] Cf. R.A. GUELICH, *Mark I*, 424; W.L. LANE, *Mark*, 281; M.D. HOOKER, *Mark*, 195.

[142] Cf. R.A. GUELICH, *Mark I*, 424; W.L. LANE, *Mark*, 282-283.

[143] This christological significance of the demand «to understand» in this context is supported by the following scholars: W.L. LANE, *Mark*, 282-283, who observes that what the disciples should understand from the miracles of the loaves is the secret that Jesus is none other than the Messiah and Lord; M.D. HOOKER, *Mark*, 196; J. GNILKA, *Markusevangelium I*, 311-312. R.A. GUELICH, *Mark I*, 427, who adds that it refers to the disciples' comprehension of the uniqueness of Jesus and his ministry. V. TAYLOR, *Mark*, 366-367, specifies that it refers to the power of Jesus to supply their need. Similarly, R.H. GUNDRY, *Mark*, 410; S. LÉGASSE, *L'Évangile de Marc I*, 484. R. PESCH, *Markusevangelium I*, 414, however, interprets it symbolically and says that it points to Jesus' significance as the one bread that suffices for Jews and Gentiles.

cut through their obduracy and opaqueness and reach the goal of understanding[144].

In 8,35 as part of his instruction after his call to follow[145] addressed to the disciples and to the crowd and hence to all, Jesus makes the demand «to lose one's life» (...ἀπολέσει τὴν ψυχὴν αὐτοῦ)[146] for his sake and for the gospel's (ἕνεκεν ἐμοῦ καὶ τοῦ εὐαγγελίου.) to save it (...σώσει αὐτήν). The demand is made in the form of a paradoxical statement which has the nature of a conditional clause introduced by a relative pronoun[147]. It contrasts two scenarios: (1) of whoever attem

---

[144] This seems to be particularly implied in the rhetorical question in 8,21. Despite its note of distressed irritation, it contains the belief and the promise that the disciples will eventually understand. This is also highlighted by this pericope's placement between the healing of a deaf-mute (7,31-37) and a blind man (8,22-26) «which bespeaks Jesus' healing power for the "deaf" and "blind" disciples», R.A. GUELICH, *Mark I*, 426. Also, J. MARCUS, *Mark I*, 515. Similarly, J. GNILKA, *Markusevangelium I*, 311, who adds that the reproachful question is meant to stimulate them to comprehension. Likewise, W.L. LANE, *Mark*, 282-283, who rightly observes that it points forward to the miracle of understanding in 8,27-30. In similar vein, R. PESCH, *Markusevangelium I*, 415.

[145] As R. PESCH, *Markusevangelium II*, 61, points out, the logion comes as a rationale for the call to follow which the initial γάρ clarifies. It thus implies that denying of oneself and carrying of the cross (v34) have to do with saving and losing of life. In this connection R.H. GUNDRY, *Mark*, 434, shows how the entire section 8,34-9,1 is bound together by catchwords, similarities of grammatical structure, and connections of thought pointing to its literary and thematic unity. For details see, *Ibid.* S. LÉGASSE, *L'Évangile de Marc II*, 511-512, n.9, speaking of the particle γάρ, however, thinks that it establishes not a properly causal relationship but one of explanation or complementarity.

[146] Several scholars point out that the term ψυχή, «life» is used here in a double sense: existence on, the one hand, and one's real, perduring self or personality, on the other. To cling to the first, is to lose one's real self in the eschatological recompense, V. TAYLOR, *Mark*, 382; M. D. HOOKER, *Mark*, 209; W. GRUNDMANN, *Markus*, 176. Similarly, W.L. LANE, *Mark*, 308, who sees in the saying a call to radical loyalty in martyrdom, rejecting the temptation to save one's earthly life through disloyalty to Jesus and the gospel; J. GNILKA, *Markusevangelium II*, 24, however, sees the saying not so much contrasting earthly life with eternal life, but rather speaking of genuine, perduring life arising out of the sacrifice of passing life. In like manner, R. PESCH, *Markusevangelium II*, 61, sees its double sense in considering concrete life in its totality before God, in view of God's judgment. Likewise, S. LÉGASSE, *L'Évangile de Marc II*, 513; So too, R.H. GUNDRY, *Mark*, 437, who adds that it carries alternating connotations of present life and eternal life.

[147] V35 uses ὃς γὰρ ἐὰν + subjunctive. Regarding this R.H. GUNDRY, *Mark*, 437, comments that it contrasts the θέλει + indicative mood in v34 which made for a strong condition, «if anyone really does want to follow behind me.». The formulation with subjunctive here results in a weak condition, «for whoever would want to save his life.». The subjunctive is chosen because, unlike the former, this is not to be encour-

pting to save his life by clinging to it ending up losing it, and (2) whoever losing it for Jesus and for the gospel saving it[148]. Both cases are formulated absolutely. This will be true in every case without exception. By means of this absolutely phrased contrastive paradox, Jesus thus makes the demand to his would-be followers to make their radical choice of losing their lives for him to really find it in full measure.

It is significant that this absolute demand is «for my sake and for the sake of the gospel» (ἕνεκεν ἐμοῦ καὶ τοῦ εὐαγγελίου., 8,35)[149]. It underlines that it is not any sort of losing one's life that would save it, but losing it for these. The phrase, «..and for the gospel» (...καὶ τοῦ εὐαγγελίου..), is used as an equivalent of the person of Jesus (ἕνεκεν ἐμοῦ), in so far as the gospel is all about him or more precisely himself, or identified with him[150]. The full phrase thus underlines the crucial

---

aged, as it would lead to its opposite, that is, to losing one's life. On the other hand, it is significant that the indicative mood reappears on the positive side of this verse: «but whoever will lose (..ἀπολέσει, «will in fact lose», not just «would want» or «or be willing to lose») his life...will save it», thus underlining that it is something to be encouraged, as it leads to a most positive result. The verse also manifests a chiastic structure: (a) wanting to save your life; (b) losing it; (b') losing your life; and (a') saving it, emphasizing this paradoxical maxim.

[148] R. PESCH, *Markusevangelium II*, 61-62, interprets the paradoxical saying thus: Faced with the decision for God which is radically addressed to man anew in Jesus' call to conversion (1,15), one who clings to life loses it, because he trusts only himself and takes death as the only eschatologcal reality and does not accept life as a gift of the creator who can preserve it in death. Similarly, the one who gives it away keeps it because he trusts in God as the Lord over life and death, as the Lord of the living. Following this perspective, Pesch sees resurrection faith (12,17-27) as the basis of the saying which is reflective of Jesus' own faith in God's unlimited power as creator that overcomes death, his hope in the resurrection and his offering of his existence in love and trust in God, who reveals himself as love which defines his «courage of life», and adds that it is relevant for the discussion on Jesus' understanding of his death and the emergence of the resurrection faith. Similarly, W. GRUNDMANN, *Markus*, 176.

[149] M. D. HOOKER, *Mark*, 209, sees the phrase «for my sake», (ἕνεκεν ἐμοῦ) indicating a claim to absolute authority.

[150] The phrase ἕνεκεν ἐμοῦ καὶ τοῦ εὐαγγελίου. is a specifically Markan formula and it is not found in Mt and Lk. For Mk Jesus and the gospel about him proclaimed by the Church belong firmly together, and provide the motivation for this radical disregard of the disciple's own interests, M.D. HOOKER, *Mark*, 209; V. TAYLOR, *Mark*, 381-382, who considers it as an explanatory comment. Similarly, W.L. LANE, *Mark*, 308; R.H. GUNDRY, *Mark*, 454. Likewise, J. GNILKA, *Markusevangelium II*, 24, who adds that the saving of life now depends on the connection with Jesus. In like manner R. PESCH, *Markusevangelium II*, 62, who sees it as reflecting a call to readiness for martyrdom for Jesus' sake on the part of the witnesses, which Mk explains with the mention of «the gospel», for which it is demanded. Lane, *Ibid.*, 308-309, clarifies the phrase further and says

role of the person of Jesus in this paradoxical process of saving one's life by losing it[151].

We see here the same emphasis on the person of Jesus found in 10,21, which calls for the following of him and not just of some absolutized abstract cause for inheriting eternal life. In both cases, the demand is closely related to the person of Jesus. This gives the demand and its absoluteness a specificity. Ultimately, this relation to Jesus is rooted in the fundamental command of the Father to «listen to him» (cf. ...ἀκούετε αὐτοῦ.), which imparts to all the demands of Jesus unique divine authority[152].

In 8,38, concluding his instruction in the wake of his call to follow addressed to all, Jesus makes yet another demand, the requirement «not to be ashamed» of him[153]. The radical formulation of the verse stresses the absolute nature of the demand[154]. Nothing should be allowed to

---

that the identity between Jesus and the message is underlined by the reference to suffering for the gospel, and points out that in the second half of Mk «the gospel» always denotes the message announced by the Church, of which Jesus is the content (cf. 8,35; 10,29; 13,10; 14,9), precisely as in 1,1. For a different view see S. LÉGASSE, *L'Évangile de Marc II*, 513.

[151] The next verses (vv36-37) support v35 by carrying the thought of the supreme value of the life farther. There is no greater gain (v36) and no price can be put upon it (v37), V. TAYLOR, *Mark*, 382; W. GRUNDMANN, *Markus*, 176; S. LÉGASSE, *L'Évangile de Marc II*, 513-515. Similarly, W.L. LANE, *Mark*, 309, who adds that if the loss even of ordinary human life is in no way compensated by winning the world, it is all the more true of eternal life, and when a man has forfeited the latter, he experiences absolute loss. By thus highlighting the supreme value of life, these rhetorical questions heighten the pressing character of the choice to find one's true self by losing one's passing and perishable earthly one for Jesus' sake and the gospel's. Likewise, J. GNILKA, *Markusevangelium II*, 25, who, however, thinks that these verses, following OT religiosity (cf. Ps 49), highlight the danger of false confidence in riches, just as v35 warns of a falsely presumed security of life which ultimately leads to death. Accordingly, the conceptual presupposition of these verses is not that human being is as valuable as the entire creation but that he should consider the endangering of his life, which is more than the earthly, and act correspondingly. Similarly, R. PESCH, *Markusevangelium II*, 63, who adds that the resurrection faith holds together vv35-37, which warn against self-security and encourage sacrifice.

[152] Cf. 2.2.4 a) (2)

[153] J. GNILKA, *Markusevangelium II*, 25, clarifies that the term ἐπαισχυνθήσεται concerns public apostasy. Similarly, W.L. LANE, *Mark*, 309-310; S. LÉGASSE, *L'Évangile de Marc II*, 515. In contrast, R.H. GUNDRY, *Mark*, 438, sees here the situation of a non-disciple having to choose to become a disciple, who shies away from it for fear of abuse and contempt from his fellows.

[154] Loyalty or disloyalty to Jesus now as the criterion for a person's acceptance or rejection before the Son of Man, W.L. LANE, *Mark*, 310-311, emphasizes the demand's absolute character, while its formulation as eschatological *ius talionis*, R.

compromise one's allegiance to Jesus, not even the loss of one's life. It is thus a call to unrelenting loyalty in situations where one is tempted to compromise it before the powers-that-be to save one's life[155], and to let go of it in the service of ultimate faithfulness[156]. It is based on the certainty that the one to whom one is showing such radical fidelity is the Son of Man who will return in triumph, «in the glory of his Father with the holy angels»[157], and judge these powers at the eschatological judgment. It also holds out the threat of final rejection by the same Son of Man of those who, through apostasy, attempt to save their life[158] which also seems to augment the absolute character of the demand.

(3) The Content of Love in Mk

The gospel, on the one hand, preserves the OT idea of love of God as observance of the commandments, with the specification that these are primarily to be found in the Decalogue and the love commandments. On the other, it extends it to the demands of Jesus. Principally, this is done by God himself in his fundamental command to listen to Jesus in 9,7, embodying the new and definitive will of God

---

PESCH, *Markusevangelium II*, 64; S. LÉGASSE, *L'Évangile de Marc II*, 516-517, seems to accentuate it.

[155] The world before which the denial is done is defined qualitatively as «an adulterous and sinful generation» which is an expression colored by the strictures of the prophets against idolatry (cf. Is 1,4.21; Ezek 16,32; Hos, 2,4), W.L. LANE, *Mark*, 309-310, who also adds that denial confirms this world in its idolatrous character and approves the unfaithfulness to God expressed in its rejection of Jesus and of those who display uncompromising loyalty to him. So also, R.H. GUNDRY, *Mark*, 438; V. TAYLOR, *Mark*, 383; J. GNILKA, *Markusevangelium II*, 26; C.S. MANN, *Mark*, 350. Similarly, R. PESCH, *Markusevangelium II*, 64, who, nevertheless, thinks that it now refers to Israel which rejects Jesus by its rejection of his apostles. Likewise S. LÉGASSE, *L'Évangile de Marc II*, 516, who adds that in the Markan context it also includes the Gentiles before whom the Christians confess or deny their Lord.

[156] In this connection, R. PESCH, *Markusevangelium II*, 65, points out that the passage is an exhortation to readiness for martyrdom.

[157] J. GNILKA, *Markusevangelium II*, 26, observes that here not only does the Son of Man and Son of God Christology become interlinked (cf. 8,31 + 9,7) but the very heavenly form of the Son of Man is recognized unambiguously as that of Jesus, the Son of God. The passage thus interprets the Son of Man in terms of Son of God. Similarly, V. TAYLOR, *Mark*, 383; R. PESCH, *Markusevangelium II*, 64; S. LÉGASSE, *L'Évangile de Marc II*, 516-517.

[158] As W.L. LANE, *Mark*, 309-310, points out v38, like each of the successive statements to v35a, reinforces the latter's irony that the man who gains his life through denial of Jesus and the gospel suffers infinite loss. The character of the loss is defined with reference to the final judgment where the Son of Man is judge. Thus v38 is parallel in structure to v35 and carries it to its final consequences.

based on his new and definitive revelation about Jesus as his Beloved Son and his closest communion with him. This command of God integrates into the commandments of God which the gospel considers important namely, the Decalogue and the love commandment and, as the most fundamental commandment in the gospel, also gives divine authority to all the demands of Jesus converting them into God's commandments on par with the former.

Moreover, as the new and definitive commandment of God, it is even more fundamental than OT commandments, since the latter have continued validity and relevance, only in so far as Jesus takes them up and confirms them. This central command of God thus affects both Jesus' demands and OT commandments at the same time. It also harmonizes them perfectly. Because of it, they are simultaneously both commandments of God and Jesus' demands.

On the other hand, since, in the gospel, to obey God's commandments is to love, and since both the OT commandments confirmed by Jesus and the demands of Jesus are commandments of God, to obey these is to love God. Consequently, the content of love of God in Mk is to obey Jesus' commands and the OT commandments confirmed by him, such as the Decalogue and the love commandment.

Further, since both proceed from the one new and definitive divine revelation about Jesus and God's will, this love is also wholly integrated. Because of their divine identity and profound unity as the Father and the Beloved Son, to obey Jesus' words (both his demands and the OT commandments confirmed by him) is, at the same time, to love God and to love Jesus.

b) *The Modality of Love (Mk 12,30)*

After having seen the content of love of God, we shall now turn to the study of the modality of this love in the gospel. It will first examine whether Mk retains the OT conception of it, and then consider if it also has a specificity in the gospel, and will close with a concluding summary.

(1) The Integral Character of Love (Mk 12,30.33)

Our OT discussion on the formulary of the commandment to love God revealed, that this three-fold formula is meant to emphasize the wholeness of love commanded, with the three phrases expressing totality in a climactic fashion. It thus underlines the integral character of the response emphatically[159]. This seems true also in Mk who basically reproduces the OT formulary. However, in so far as the Markan text has a four-fold formula instead of the three-member one of the OT with the addition of the phrase καὶ ἐξ ὅλης τῆς διανοίας σου[160], it could be said that it slightly accentuates this note of totality even further. Thus Mk not only preserves the OT meaning[161] but also emphasizes it.

Besides, a consideration of this formulary in the gospel reveals that as a four-fold formulary of totality it is confined to the commandment to love God (12,30). A three-member form of it occurs in the paraphrase of this commandment (12,33) and, although this drops two of the terms of the four-fold formulary (ψυχή and διάνοια) and introduces a third one (σύνεσις), it still functions clearly as a formula of totality. The formula does not figure in either of these forms or in the form of its individual constituents anywhere else. This also indicates that it is understood here in its OT sense.

---

[159] Cf. Ch I, 3.3.2

[160] The Markan text also has καὶ ἐξ ὅλης τῆς ἰσχύος σου in place of καὶ ἐξ ὅλης τῆς δυνάμεώς σου of the LXX. Cf. Ch I, 1.2. In this connection, M. MUNDLA, *Jesus und die Führer*, 131-132, observes that διάνοια, and ἰσχύς which replace δύναμις of the LXX, come from the rational and psychological fields respectively, and occur only in this pericope in Mk (vv30.33). He also suggests that the four-fold formula arose from a double translation of the Hebrew לב, first with διάνοια, and then with καρδία. Similarly, M.J. LAGRANGE, *L'Évangile selon Saint Marc*, 321-22; C.E.B CRANFIELD, *Mark*, 377; D.E. NINEHAM, *Mark*, 327; K. BERGER, *Gesetzesauslegung I*, 177. K. KERTELGE, «Das Doppelgebot», 316, on the other hand, thinks that these Markan specialties *vis-à-vis* LXX are a sign not only of a different textual transmission, but also of a hellenistically-inspired intensifying of the commandment. J. GNILKA, *Markusevangelium II*, 164-165 shares the latter point. Likewise, Berger, *Ibid.*, 178-179. R.H. GUNDRY, *Mark*, 710-711.715, on the contrary, downplays the Hellenistic influence and suggests that these changes which underline the intellectual dimension are meant to link the love of God to the scribe's activity of studying the scriptures and to stress that it should not stop at analyzing God but must progress to loving God accordingly. While all three views are hypothetical, the changes do stress the role of intelligence in the love of God.

[161] There is overwhelming consensus on this among scholars. Thus those who hold the formulary's emphasis on the total character of the love demanded consequent upon the reality of Israel's God include: W. GRUNDMANN, *Markus*, 251-252; J. GNILKA, *Markusevangelium II*, 164-165; R. PESCH, *Markusevangelium II*, 240; W.L. LANE, *Mark*, 432-433; C. S. MANN, *Mark*, 479; R.H. GUNDRY, *Mark*, 710-711; S. LÉGASSE, *L'Évangile de Marc, II*, 748-749.

(2) The Absolute Character of Jesus' Demands

Although the four-fold formula of totality as the modality of love is understood in Mk in the OT sense, and is limited to the commandment to love God, with a modified three-member form of it figuring in its paraphrase, still it seems to receive a translation and extension, and thus an equivalency, in the modality of response demanded by Jesus' commands. This also seems to follow most fundamentally from the new and definitive revelation of God and his will in 9,7[162], in so far as the fundamental commandment of God here is phrased in absolute terms (cf. ...ἀκούετε αὐτοῦ, 9,7)[163] which entails that the response to it has to be absolute as well. Phrased absolutely, it is also comprehensive and applies to all the demands of Jesus. Besides, its fundamental character as the only new and definitive commandment of God in the gospel, imparts its absoluteness to all the demands of Jesus also.

Following this, the demands of Jesus in the gospel themselves manifest, directly or indirectly, a character of absoluteness[164]. Thus all the instances of the demand «to follow» in the gospel are constructed absolutely. Andrew and Simon, the first ones to be called, are told: Δεῦτε ὀπίσω μου, (1,17). The formulation is absolute. Similarly, Levi the Son of Alphaeus, the tax-collector, is commanded: Ἀκολούθει μοι (2,14), again in absolute terms. Although the general call to follow addressed to all is phrased conditionally (cf. Εἴ τις θέλει ὀπίσω μου ἀκολουθεῖν,...) to underline that no one is forced to follow Jesus against his will and that the choice has to be *free*, the demands of following themselves are phrased absolutely and are valid in every case without exception (cf......ἀπαρνησάσθω ἑαυτὸν καὶ ἀράτω τὸν σταυρὸν αὐτοῦ καὶ ἀκολουθείτω μοι, 8,34). As in all cases of the call to follow addressed to particular individuals we have seen so far, the demand of Jesus to the rich man to follow him, in addition to the observance of the OT commandments, is couched in absolute language (cf. ...καὶ δεῦρο ἀκολούθει μοι, 10,21). As an absolute statement, with no qualification, it expresses totality and admits of no exceptions. Interestingly, this absoluteness is also true about the steps that go before the demand to follow (cf. ὕπαγε, ὅσα ἔχεις πώλησον καὶ δὸς [τοῖς] πτωχοῖς,..), all of which are thus also phrased absolutely. The same note of absoluteness is encountered in the demand to sell *everything* (cf. ὅσα ἔχεις) and give

---

[162] Cf. 2.2.4 a) (2).

[163] Cf. J. GNILKA, *Markusevangelium II*, 36; R.H. GUNDRY, *Mark*, 461; C.A. EVANS, *Mark II*, 39.

[164] Cf. The discussion in 2.2.4 a) (2).

[them] to the poor. Hence, a complete renunciation is demanded admitting of no compromises. Thus in the entirety of the demand, the absolute character of the modality of the response is strongly underlined by the manner in which it is expressed.

The insistent nature of the expectation that the disciples «understand» in 8,17-21 we noted above, also qualifies it as an absolute demand even though it is not expressly couched in the absolute mode. By it, the disciples are made to realize, that they ought to work through their obduracy and reach comprehension as something essential and indispensable to their role as disciples and their relationship with Jesus. This seems to be also indicated by the fact that they eventually reach the understanding insisted upon (cf. 8,29). Thus the demand «to understand» is also an absolute demand which the disciples are called upon to reach, despite their serious problems along the way.

The formulation of the demand «to lose one's life» for the sake of Jesus and for the gospel's (8,35) is also formulated absolutely. Its construction in the form of a conditional clause introduced by ὃς γὰρ ἐὰν θέλῃ τὴν ψυχὴν αὐτοῦ σῶσαι.../....ὃς δ' ἂν ἀπολέσει τὴν ψυχὴν αὐτοῦ...[165] universalizes and absolutizes the statement[166]. It is thus true in all instances and as such has an absolute character which is also augmented by its radical content[167].

The uncompromising nature of the demand «not to be ashamed» (cf. 8,38) similarly seems to stress the absoluteness of the demand. Nothing should be allowed to undermine one's loyalty to Jesus, not even the loss of one's dear life. It is thus a call to absolute loyalty in situations

---

[165] Cf. n.147.

[166] Thus, as V. TAYLOR, Mark, 382, observes, v35 has the nuance that even if death ensues one who does so has preserved or gained his true self, which thus indicates that absolutely nothing, not even death, can cause a different outcome. W.L. LANE, Mark, 308, further sees the «the phrase for my sake and for the sake of the gospel» unequivocally expressing the absoluteness of Jesus' claim upon people's allegiance to his own person, although as R.H. GUNDRY, Mark, 454, points out this is not the first time it appears in the gospel as Lane claims. Similarly, J. GNILKA, Markusevangelium II, 24, who underlines the importance of the connection with him for the saving of life. Likewise, R. PESCH, Markusevangelium II, 62. Besides, as Gundry, Ibid., 437, notes, the chiastic arrangement of v35 heightens its absolute character.

[167] Additionally, it is stressed by the rhetorical questions which follow (vv36-37) that support the saying (v35), in so far as they can only be answered in the negative which thus rules out a different possibility. There is simply no greater gain than one's authentic life (v36), and no exchange can be found for it (v37), V. TAYLOR, Mark, 382; W.L. LANE, Mark, 309; J. GNILKA, Markusevangelium II, 25; R. PESCH, Markus II, 63-64; S. LÉGASSE, Marc II, 513; W. GRUNDMANN, Markus, 176-177; R.H. GUNDRY, Mark, 437.

where one is tempted to compromise it before the powers-that-be to save one's life, and to sacrifice it in the service of loyalty unto death. The absoluteness of the demand seems to be augmented by the threat of ultimate rejection by the same Son of Man which the verse contains of those who, through disloyalty to him, attempt to save their life. The stakes for that loyalty are extreme, and so are those for compromising it. Both emphasize the absoluteness of the demand, and consequently of the response to it.

In so far as both the fundamental command of God in 9,7 and all the demands of Jesus in the gospel are thus either phrased absolutely or imply absoluteness, they may be said to translate the integral character of the four-fold formulary of the modality of love into the modality of the response to Jesus in the gospel. In this sense, these can be characterized as parallel to the formulary of the modality of love. They form its functional equivalents, and in them it is translated in the gospel *vis-à-vis* these demands. For the same reason, they are its extension to them. Thus, in so far as the latter have a total and absolute character, they translate and extend the formula of modality of love in the gospel to Jesus' demands, and lend the latter equivalency.

(3) The Modality of Love in Mk

The above considerations reveal, on the one hand, that in Mk the OT sense of the modality of love prevails. As in the OT it emphasizes the integral character of the love commanded, with the phrases involved expressing totality in a climactic fashion, although the gospel seems to accentuate this note of totality even further, because of its use of the four-fold formulary instead of the three-fold one of the OT. The fact that this formula is confined to the commandment to love God (12,30) and in a somewhat modified form to its paraphrase (12,33), also indicates that it is understood in the gospel in the OT sense.

Nevertheless, this conception of the modality of love seems to receive a translation and extension, and thus an equivalence, in the modality of response demanded for Jesus' demands in the gospel. This follows most basically from the fundamental commandment of God in 9,7 which is phrased in absolute terms (cf. ...ἀκούετε αὐτοῦ), indicating that the response demanded is absolute. As an absolute demand it is also comprehensive and applies to all the demands of Jesus and, as the only new and definitive commandment of God with a fundamental character, it lends its absoluteness to all of them. Following this, the demands of Jesus in the gospel themselves manifest an absolute quality which is clear from the manner in which they are either phrased or accentuated which, in spite of their differences, all imply absoluteness either directly or indirectly. They thus define an integral response which admits of no exception and compromise.

As this coincides with the OT meaning of the formulary of the modality of love, they can be understood as its functional equivalents in the gospel *vis-à-vis* the response to Jesus' demands. They thus constitute the translation and extension to the demands of Jesus of the formula of modality of love *vis-à-vis* his demands.

c) *The Object of Love (Mk 12,30)*

After having considered the modality of love of God in Mk, we shall now examine the object of this love. The study will first ascertain whether the gospel maintains its OT conception, and then explore whether it also has a specificity in it, and will conclude with a summary and possible consequence.

(1) The Lord God as Object of Integral Love

Our OT analysis of the commandment to love in Ch 1 showed that it is intimately connected with the monotheistic confession that precedes it, in the sense, that the latter is understood as a consequence of what is asserted in the former[168]. Thus, the commandment to love is a response to the reality of God as the unique Lord God. It is because the Lord God is what he is that he should be loved with an integral love. This dependence of the commandment on the assertion about the reality of God, made in the monotheistic confession, is expressed in the ו-*conversive* formulation (cf. ואהבת)[169] with which the commandment begins and which the LXX translates with the phrase καὶ ἀγαπήσεις., a rendering which Mk reproduces[170]. This unveils the Lord God as the object of the commandment to love single-mindedly[171]. As an OT quotation it is obviously understood in its original OT sense.

---

[168] Cf. Ch 1, 3.3

[169] Cf. Ch 1, 3.3

[170] In this connection, M. REISER, *Syntax und Stil,* 125, points out that as in the OT, going beyond a paratactic function, the καὶ.. here implies a connection of consequence between the preceding sentence and the following one. Thus the meaning is: «Hear O Israel! The Lord our God is one and therefore *(as a consequence)* you shall love the Lord your God with all your heart...,etc..»

[171] Those who emphasize this connection of the monotheistic confession with the commandment that follows include: B. WEISS, *Markusevangelium,* 401; J. KNABENBAUER, *Markus,* 327; E. LOHMEYER, *Markus,* 258; G. WOHLENBERG, *Markus,*

(2) Jesus as Object of Absolute Obedience (9,7)

While Mk clearly retains the OT sense of Lord God as the object of love, the gospel also speaks of Jesus as the object of absolute obedience. The most fundamental statement in the gospel to this effect again comes from God himself[172] in his new and definitive revelation (cf. Οὗτός ἐστιν ὁ υἱός μου ὁ ἀγαπητός)[173] followed by the new and definitive revelation of his will (cf. ἀκούετε αὐτοῦ, 9,7). The designation ὁ υἱός μου ὁ ἀγαπητός, «my Beloved Son» reveals Jesus' divine identity as well as his most intimate union with God[174]. The command that follows is a consequence of this unique divine revelation. The disciples must listen to him because of Jesus' divine identity and unique closeness to the Father as the Beloved Son[175].

Thus the text of 9,7 has the same fundamental structure as 12,29-31. Just as in the latter, the uniqueness of Yahweh is first revealed and is followed by the demand for integral love as a consequence of it[176], in the former, God the Father first reveals Jesus as his unique Son, and this is followed by the command to «listen to him» as a consequence of it. The only difference between these is that, while in 12,29f Jesus, the royal Messiah (15,32), makes his own the words of Moses (Deut 6,4-5) and proposes to Israel the OT revelation of the uniqueness of Yahweh her God[177], and demands undivided love as the only adequate response to him, in 9,7 God the Father pronounces the words of revelation about Jesus as his Beloved Son to his disciples, and demands absolute obedience to him as the only commensurate response to him. But in both cases, it is divine revelation followed by divine command, with the second rooted in the first.

319; E.P. GOULD, *Mark*, 232; V. TAYLOR, *Mark*, 486; C.E.B. CRANFIELD, *Mark*, 377; R. SCHNACKENBURG, *Markus II*, 172; W.L. LANE, *Mark*, 432; A. STOCK, *Method and Message*, 313; J. RADERMAKERS, *Marc*, 322; W. GRUNDMANN, *Markus*, 251; J. HUBY, *Marc*, 285; A. SISTI, *Marco*, 347; R. PESCH, *Markusevangelium*, II, 239-40; J. GNILKA, *Markusevangelium II*, 164-165; M.D. HOOKER, *Mark*, 287; K. KERTELGE, «Das Doppelgebot», 316-317; C.A. EVANS, *Mark II*, 263.

[172] Cf. 2.2.4 a) (2).

[173] For a critical discussion of scholarly opinion on the christological significance of this designation and its relation to 1,11 see, n.55.

[174] Cf. 2.2.4 a) (2).

[175] Cf. M. D. HOOKER, *Mark*, 218; W.L. LANE, *Mark*, 321; J. GNILKA, *Markusevangelium II*, 36; R. PESCH, *Markus II*, 77; S. LÉGASSE, *L'Évangile de Marc II*, 531; R.H. GUNDRY, *Mark*, 462; C.A. EVANS, *Mark II*, 38-39. For a critical discussion of opinions on the import of this demand see, n.56.

[176] Cf. 2.2.4 c) (1)

[177] Cf. 2.2.3 a)

This identity of structure between 9,7 and 12,29-31, and the fact that both the revelation and the command in the former come from God himself, most unequivocally reveal Jesus as the object of absolute obedience in the gospel.

Based on this, the demands of Jesus in the gospel also present him as the object of such absolute obedience. This becomes clear from the way they are expressed. Not only are they either phrased absolutely or imply it, indicating that the response to them has to be absolute obedience, but they focus on the person of Jesus as the unique object of this response.

Thus, in the first vocations, the persons involved are commanded to follow *him*. Peter and Andrew are told: Δεῦτε ὀπίσω μου, «Follow *me*» (1,17) and leaving their nets they follow *him*[178] (cf. καὶ.....ἠκολούθησαν αὐτῷ, 1,18) and when Jesus calls the Zebedee brothers we are told that they too followed *him* (ἀπῆλθον ὀπίσω αὐτοῦ., 1,20b)[179]. In like manner, the call of Levi illustrates the same emphasis on the person of Jesus. He is called to follow *Jesus* (cf. Ἀκολούθει μοι) and he does so (cf. καὶ ἀναστὰς ἠκολούθησεν αὐτῷ.) in 2,14[180]. The general call to discipleship is likewise a demand to follow the *person* of Jesus and not just a cause (cf. Εἴ τις θέλει ὀπίσω μου ἀκολουθεῖν,...καὶ ἀκολουθείτω μοι., 8,34b)[181]. Similarly, in 10,21, the last instance of the demand to follow, the rich man is asked, in addition to observing OT commandments, to renounce everything, to give them to the poor and to follow *him* (cf...καὶ δεῦρο ἀκολούθει μοι...)[182] in order to inherit eternal life. The call to follow in all instances, thus, involves absolute obedience to the person of Jesus[183]. He is its proper object[184].

---

[178] Cf. J. MARCUS, *Mark*, 185; R.A. GUELICH, *Mark I*, 51.52; J. GNILKA, *Markusevangelium I*, 74.

[179] Cf. W.L. LANE, *Mark*, 69; C.S. MANN, *Mark*, 209; R.A. GUELICH, *Mark I*, 51.

[180] Cf. C.S. MANN, *Mark*, 229; R.A. GUELICH, *Mark I*, 101. Besides, the unqualified response in all the three cases of the call points to its unconditionality before the absolute call of Jesus. Cf. R. PESCH, *Markusevangelium I*, 109, n.3.

[181] Thus, V. TAYLOR, *Mark*, 380, following Goguel, 385, points out that Jesus here «asks for attachment to his person, and not only for the acceptance of his message.». He further requires sustained loyalty in discipleship. *Ibid.*, 381. Also, M.D. HOOKER, *Mark*, 209; R.H. GUNDRY, *Mark*, 435; C.S. MANN, *Mark*, 349; J. GNILKA, *Markusevangelium II*, 23; C.A. EVANS, *Mark II*, 30.

[182] Cf. V. TAYLOR, *Mark*, 429; C.S. MANN, *Mark*, 401; W.L. LANE, *Mark*, 368; D. LÜHRMANN, *Markus*, 74-75; A. STOCK, *Method and Message*, 273; R. SCHNA - CKENBURG, *Markus II*, 90-92. See also 2.2.4 a) (2).

[183] In this connection S. LÉGASSE, *L'Évangile de Marc*, 115, correctly observes that the person of Jesus and his dignity give to the call to follow a specificity all its own for which there is no model in surrounding cultures. It is an enterprise for and

This is also true about the other demands of Jesus. Thus the insistent demand «to understand» concerns Jesus' person, in so far as its object is his true christological identity (8,17.21)[185].

Thus the absolute demand to lose one's life (8,35) in the instruction following the call to follow, is clearly focused on the person of Jesus, as it is «for *him* and for the gospel» (ἕνεκεν ἐμοῦ καὶ τοῦ εὐαγγελίου), that one is asked to do so, the last phrase, «and for the gospel», being closely linked with the person of Jesus[186].

Similarly, the demand «not to be ashamed» (8,38) relates to uncompromising allegiance to Jesus' person even in the face of threat to one's life. The formulation of the verse in the form of an eschatological *ius talionis*[187], wherein the one who is disloyal is threatened with ultimate rejection by the end-time judge, also clearly underlines the person of Jesus as the object of the absolute obedience demanded[188]. Though the verse mentions being «ashamed of *me* and *my words*» (ὃς γὰρ ἐὰν ἐπαισχυνθῇ με καὶ τοὺς ἐμοὺς λόγους), the «words» are in question because they are *his* words (cf. τοὺς ἐμοὺς λόγους)[189] which again lays stress on the person of Jesus as the object of the radical response. Thus all these demands converge on emphasizing Jesus as the object of absolute obedience which all of them categorically require.

Now, as noted above[190], this conception of the gospel of Jesus-as-object-of-absolute obedience resembles its motif of God-as-object-of-

---

with him which includes the way of the cross «behind» him (8,34). Similarly, R. PESCH, *Markusevangelium I*, 113. Likewise, R.A. GUELICH, *Mark I*, 52, 53.

[184] Cf. J. GNILKA, *Markusevangelium I*, 74.

[185] Cf. W.L. LANE, *Mark*, 282-283; R. PESCH, *Markusevangelium I*, 414; J. GNILKA, *Markusevangelium I*, 311-312; M.D. HOOKER, *Mark*, 196; R.A. GUELICH, *Mark I*, 427; R.H. GUNDRY, *Mark*, 410 who, however, finds it as pointing to the superadequate power of Jesus.

[186] Cf. n.150.

[187] Cf. R. PESCH, *Markus II*, 64; S. LÉGASSE, *L'Évangile de Marc II*, 516-517; C.A. EVANS, *Mark II*, 27.

[188] Cf. W.L. LANE, *Mark*, 305-306; 310-311; J. GNILKA, *Markusevangelium II*, 25; M.D. HOOKER, *Mark*, 210; C.A. EVANS, *Mark II*, 27; R. PESCH, *Markusevangelium II*, 65, who stresses the readiness for martyrdom for Jesus' sake involved in this demand. Also, R.H. GUNDRY, *Mark*, 439. To the point is the contrast in the verse between the two situations of denial and eschatological rejection which lays stress on Jesus as the object of shame and denial, on the one hand, and him as subject of eschatological rejection, on the other. In both cases the person of Jesus is at the center.

[189] The placement of the possessive adjective before the substantive marks emphasis, *BDF*, 149, #285,1.

[190] Cf. 2.2.4 c) (2)

integral love. Just as the latter is a direct consequence of the reality of the Lord God, the former is the result of the reality of Jesus *vis-à-vis* God, as his «Beloved Son» (9,7). This is the true basis of the consistent emphasis on the person of Jesus as the object of absolute obedience which we see in the demands of Jesus. This, in turn, seems to imply a relationship between Lord God-as-object-of-integral love and Jesus-as-object-of-absolute obedience.

This relationship becomes clear from the gospel's evaluation of Jesus' demands. Because the latter are based on the fundamental commandment of God in the gospel (9,7), they are on par with God's commandments in the OT[191]. Indeed, in so far as God the Father himself gives this most fundamental commandment to «listen to him», Jesus' demands are God's commandments[192]. Even OT commandments are now actually dependent on Jesus, since they continue to be God's commandments only in so far as they are taken up and confirmed by him[193]. The gospel thus asserts, on the one hand, that all the commandments of God continue to be God's commandments in so far as Jesus takes them up and confirms them, and on the other, that all the demands of Jesus are simultaneously God's commandments, because of the absolute demand of the Father in 9,7.

On the other hand, the Gospel retains the OT conception of God as object of integral love[194]. In the context of this subordination of OT commandments to Jesus, the fundamental commandment of God to listen to Jesus (9,7) involves the integration of God-as-object-of integral love with Jesus-as-object of absolute obedience. Indeed, in this perspective God-as-object-of integral love is the same as Jesus-as-object-of absolute obedience. The demands of Jesus are God's demands and the OT commandments of God confirmed by Jesus are Jesus' commandments. There is complete parity between the two. Thus, in the conception of the gospel, God-as-object-of integral love and Jesus-as-object-of absolute obedience merge into an integral reality. Hence, as in all the above cases, (the God as Lord, the relational character of God, the prerogatives of God, the content of the love of God, the modality of this love), the object of love of God also opens in the gospel to integrate the reality of Jesus.

---

[191] Cf. 2.2.4 a) (2)
[192] Cf. 2.2.4 a) (2)
[193] Cf. 2.2.4 a) (2)
[194] Cf. 2.2.4 c) (1)

On the other hand, as we saw above[195], the gospel extends the modality of the love of God to the response to the demands of Jesus, in so far as it translates the latter in the language or quality of absoluteness which characterizes the modality of the response to Jesus' demands and articulates it as an integral response which the formula of the modality of love expresses. The clarification of the merger in the gospel of God-as-object-of-integral love with Jesus-as-object-of-absolute obedience, unveils the authentic basis of this translation and extension.

(3) The Object of Love in Mk

The above investigation shows that the gospel preserves the OT conception of the reality of the Lord God as the object of love of God. It is because the Lord God is the unique Lord that he should be loved with an integral love. However, parallely, it also speaks of Jesus as the object of absolute obedience. Most fundamentally, the latter is established by the new and definitive revelation of God and his will in 9,7 by God himself. Its similarity of structure to 12,29-31 shows that it is because of the divine identity of Jesus as the Beloved Son that he should be listened to absolutely. This structural similarity between the two texts and the fact that the fundamental revelation and command in 9,7 come from God himself, unveil Jesus as the object of absolute obedience in the gospel.

Following this, all the demands of Jesus are also made in absolute terms either directly or indirectly and focus on the person of Jesus. These too thus show that he should be obeyed absolutely because of his identity as the Beloved Son.

On the other hand, the fundamental absolute command of God to listen to Jesus has a unifying and integrating function *vis-à-vis* the twin conceptions of the gospel of God-as-object of integral love and Jesus-as-object of absolute obedience. The Father's revelation and command reveal Jesus as the measure of both. OT commandments retain their validity and relevance, in so far as they are taken up and confirmed by Jesus and Jesus' commands are at the same time God's comm andments. The Father's command thus merges God-as-object-of-integral love with Jesus-as-object-of-absolute obedience in the gospel. There is complete parity and integration between the two. Hence God-as-object of integral love and Jesus-as-object of absolute obedience are the same in the gospel. This also perfectly corresponds to the revelation

---

[195] Cf. 2.2.4 b) (2)

of God about the divine identity of Jesus and his most profound union with him as the Beloved Son in 9,7.

Besides, this also unveils the ultimate rationale of the translation and extension in Mk of the modality of love of God to the response to the demands of Jesus, which is this same fact that the reality of Jesus-as-object-of-absolute obedience includes God-as-object-of integral love and they form one reality.

2.2.5 Love of Neighbor (Mk 12,31)

After having seen the exegesis of the first commandment (12,29-30) in Mk, which includes the call to listen, the monotheistic confession and the demand to love God integrally, we shall now turn to the study of the second commandment (12,31), that of love of neighbor. It will consist of the consideration of the status of this commandment, its object, and the modality of the love commanded.

a) *The Status of the Commandment (12,31)*

Jesus gives the commandment to love the neighbor by defining it as the second commandment. As this is a denotation of status we shall first clarify its significance.

(1) The Second Most Important Commandment

Jesus mentions the commandment to love the neighbor with a formula which also introduces it namely, δευτέρα αὕτη, (cf. 12,31). Δευτέρα means «second» of a series[196] and thus marks gradation in itself. The anarthrousness of δευτέρα with its implied noun ἐντολή emphasizes its nature or quality of being the second commandment[197] in relation to the first. It thus serves to mark the gradation very strongly[198]. Besides, δευτέρα also exhibits *asyndeton* in its formulation, and taken together with its anarthrousness, it clearly stresses its nature of being the second most important commandment[199]. One may also point to the intensive character of the term αὕτη, which sets the δευτέρα (ἐντολή) off from the πρώτη (v29) and all else, emphasizing and contrasting[200], thus again stressing its status as the second most important commandment.

---

[196] Cf. *BAGD*, 177.
[197] Cf. M. ZERWICK, *Biblical Greek*, 57-58, # 179.
[198] Cf. R.H. GUNDRY, *Mark*, 710.
[199] Cf. R.H. GUNDRY, *Mark*, 711.
[200] Cf. *BAGD*, 122.

As our OT analysis showed, the commandment to love the neighbor did have an important position in the book of Leviticus where it figures (cf. Lev 19,18). It marked the high point of a series of injunctions centered on the neighbor in its immediate context (cf. Lev 19,11-18). It thus had an apex position in this section as the crowning demand of God which interprets all others, and in so far as it has a character of love of enemy[201]. It retained this dominant status also in the wider context of Lev Ch 19 which demands imitation of the holiness of God (Lev 19,2), in so far as it is in loving an offending brother, an enemy, that Israel should manifest this[202]. Besides, given the important position of Ch 19 in the Holiness Code, it also remained the climax of the latter[203]. Nevertheless, the commandment to love the neighbor in Leviticus was *one* of the demands of God and it was never *defined* as having a status greater than any other commandment. This is also inherent in the OT and Jewish conception of Law where all the commandments have the same importance and validity and none is greater than others[204]. By

---

[201] For details see, Ch II, 4.1f; 4.1.3

[202] Cf. Ch II, 4.2

[203] Cf. Ch II, 4.3

[204] Cf. K. BERGER, *Die Gesetzesauslegung I*, 175-176, who contends that the conception of the great commandment as an individual commandment and as something like the sum of the Law understood as the expression of the will of God has no support in the OT and is independent of it. Similarly, C. BURCHARD, «Das Doppelte Liebesgebot», 54, who adds that the grading of the commandments into «first» and «second» (12,29.31), do not correspond to the Palestinian view of the Law since there, despite attempts to summarize the Law and to break the commandments down into small and great, each commandment always retained absolute validity. Likewise, R.H. GUNDRY, *Mark*, 713, who observes that «[.....] Rabbinic literature never combines the two love-commandments and make them the most important». Against Berger's, *Ibid.*, and Buchard's, *Ibid.*, contention of Jewish Hellenistic influence, however, Gundry, *Ibid.*, while admitting that Greek and Hellenistic Jewish writings associate εὐσέβεια and δικαιοσύνη, points out that the language of those writings tends strongly toward that of moral philosophy, especially toward Stoic language of that sort, and that, not even Hellenistic Jewish literature, ever quotes Deut 6,4-5 and Lev 19,18 *in tandem*. In similar vein, R. PESCH, *Markusevangelium II*, 243-247; J. GNILKA, *Markusevangelium II*, 167; K. KERTELGE, «Das Doppelgebot», 315-317. So also, J. PIPER, *Love your Enemies*, 91-95, who, while granting that the substance of the love commandments is found reflected in *The Testaments of the Twelve Patriarchs*, Test. Iss. 5,2. and Test. Dan 5,3, still points out that here the commandments are not called «first» or «second» nor do they provide a sum of all the other commandments. Besides, Gundry's, *Ibid.*, observation in this connection, that we also have to reckon with the possibility of Christian influence on, if not Christian composition of, *The Testaments of the Twelve Patriarchs*, is also to be considered. In this context, the statement of A. NISSEN, *Gott und der Nächste*, 416, after his extensive analysis of the substance of the love commandments in Judaism, is pertinent: «Doppelgebote als Summe der Tora sind mithin un-

contrast, Jesus here *defines* the commandment to love the neighbor as the second most important commandment. His act of definition thus does something new to it, in so far as it invests it with a new status which goes beyond its commanding position in the Holiness Code. It is now the second most important commandment, second only to the first commandment (Mk 12,29-30). This is a striking innovation *vis-à-vis* its OT status. Its new position is also clearly expressed in its literary formulation (cf. δευτέρα αὕτη,). It is, moreover, a Markan specificity as the formulations of Mt and Lk do not bring this out as clearly as that of Mk[205]. In Mk, by contrast, it emerges with a clearly denoted status as the second most important commandment because of Jesus' definition.

---

möglich, ein Doppelgebot der Liebe ist, wäre es mehr als eine Koppelung zweier großer Gebote, nicht jüdisch.».

Nevertheless, the commandment to love the neighbor has been interpreted by more than one Rabbi as one of the great general principles of the Law. Thus, R. Aqiba has said: «Du sollst deinen Nächsten lieben, wie dich selbst, Lev 19,18; das ist ein größer allgemeiner Grundsatz in der Torah זה כְּלָל נדול בתורה s.S.357f» Cf. Str.-B., I, 907. Similarly, regarding the same commandment Hillel has observed: «Was dir unliebsam ist, das tu auch du deinem Nächsten nicht. Das ist die ganze Torah, das andere ist ihre Auslegung», *Ibid.*. This is the «Golden Rule» in its negative formulation which comes close to Jesus' understanding of this commandment.

However, even these are not a true reduction of the entire Law into this commandment. Ultimately, in fact, Rabbinic Judaism considers all 613 individual laws of the Torah to have the same value. Even when the Rabbis divide these into «easier» and «more difficult» ones, *Ibid.*, 901, it is never understood that any of them could be neglected or left out. The same is true about attempts on the part of certain of them to speak of general principles (in this connection, cf. Ch II, n.34). These are essentially catechetical and interpretative efforts which may not be taken as attempts at reducing individual laws into one or two principles which alone suffice. The Rabbinic position on the value of individual laws is well summarized in the following statement of R. Abba ben Kahana: «Die Schrift macht das leichteste unter den leichten Geboten שבקלות קלה מצוה dem Schwersten unter den schweren Geboten דמורה מן הדמורות gleich», *Ibid.*, 902. This clearly differs from Jesus' position which summarizes the entire Law into the love commandments.

[205] Thus Mt adds after the naming of the first commandment: αὕτη ἐστὶν ἡ μεγάλη καὶ πρώτη ἐντολή. (Mt 22,38) which makes the primacy of the love of God clear enough. But he introduces the second with the phrase: δευτέρα δὲ ὁμοία αὐτῇ, (v39a), which links the second commandment closely with the first without underlining the gradation among them. In the Lukan version the commandments do not have any introductory formulas at all. (cf. Lk 10,25). The two commandments are also not named «first» and «second» (Lk 10,27). Besides it links them with a simple καί. Both these peculiarities do not help create a clear affirmation of gradation of the commandments.

(2) Unity in Difference with the First Commandment (12,31b)

While Jesus' definition grades the first and the second commandments within a hierarchical whole, with their distinction and gradation clearly underlined, they are not separate from each other. Despite their distinctiveness they form a unity as the ἐντολὴ πρώτη πάντων (v28b), without one collapsing into the other. Their unity and relatedness are also underlined by the comment of Jesus: μείζων τούτων ἄλλη ἐντολὴ οὐκ ἔστιν., «There is no other commandment greater than these» (v31b), in so far as they are referred to together, emphasizing their unique importance and contrasting them with all others[206]. As a unity of the two supreme commandments, they also seem to have a summary character in relation to all other commandments. This seems indicated by Jesus' statement that greater than these there is no other commandment.

However, this qualification (v31b) emphasizes also their distinction and difference within this unity. They keep their individuality and hierarchical gradation within it. Thus the commandment to love God has absolute primacy and is not reducible to the second. Similarly, the commandment to love the neighbor ranks after the first and has thus a distinct status with its own individuality and is not reducible to the first. Mk thus affirms a clear hierarchy among the love commandments[207]. This means that while they constitute a unity, they cannot be merged into each other. Their distinction is further underlined by Jesus' reference to the two commandments as «these» (cf. μείζων τούτων...., v31b) rather than «this» (v31)[208]. But, as already mentioned, though they keep their individuality they cannot be separated from each other, but are intrinsically related as parts of a hierarchically-ordained whole[209]. The commandment to love the neighbor thus constitutes a unity-in-difference with the first commandment within a hierarchically-founded totality[210].

---

[206] As G. WOHLENBERG, *Markus*, 318-319, comments: «Der Herr unterscheidet eine ἐντολὴ πρώτη und δευτέρα, faßt dieselben aber doch wieder zu einer Einheit zusammen, 31b: [........].»

[207] Cf. M. MUNDLA, *Jesus und die Führer*, 195; R. PESCH, *Markusevangelium II*, 240.

[208] Cf. R.H. GUNDRY, *Mark*, 716; R. PESCH, *Markusevangelium II*, 241.

[209] Cf. M.D. HOOKER, *Mark*, 288; W. HARRINGTON, *Mark*, 191; W.L. LANE, *Mark*, 433; K. KERTELGE, *Markusevanglium*, 121-122; ID., «Das Doppelgebot», 318-319.

[210] In this context it seems highly significant that, although no reference has been made to a second commandment in the question, Jesus adds it, H. B. SWETE, *Saint*

Both these characteristics come from Jesus' definition. In the OT, Deut 6,4-5 and Lev 19,18 were not related or brought together anywhere. They were texts far apart from each other in the Torah, and were never coupled or quoted *in tandem*. Needless to say, they were also not defined as first and second commandments within a hierarchically-conceived unity as happens here. All these characteristics which these texts now possess in Mk, therefore, must be affirmed as resulting from Jesus' definition.

(3) The Status of Love in Mk

Although the commandment to love the neighbor did have a pre-eminent position in the context of Lev 19,11-18, as also in Lev Ch 19, and even in the Holiness Code as a whole, it still remained an individual commandment. Within the framework of Jesus' definition, however, it receives a new and defined status as the second most important commandment, second only to the first most important commandment. This is expressed also in its literary formulation as δευτέρα αὕτη, which manifests anarthrousness and *asyndeton*, both of which underline its character as the second most important commandment. While its formulation, paralleling that of the first commandment, underlines the distinction and gradation of the two great commandments, the gospel also maintains their relatedness. In their distinction and gradation they also constitute a certain unity. The commandment to love the neighbor thus receives a new status in Mk resulting from Jesus' definition as the second most important commandment, constituting a unity-in-difference with the first commandment within a hierarchically-ordained totality. A comparison with its OT situation reveals that all these features of this commandment in Mk are new, and result from Jesus' act of definition.

b) *The Object of Love (12,31a)*

After clarifying the status of the commandment to love the neighbor and its relationship of unity-in-difference with the first commandment, we shall now study its object. It will first briefly restate its OT

Mark, 285; M.J. LAGRANGE, *L'Évangile selon Saint Marc,* 322; V. TAYLOR, *Mark,* 487; M.D. HOOKER, *Mark,* 287-288; J. GNILKA, *Markusevangelium II,* 164-165;

R. PESCH, *Markusevangelium II,* 240; S. LÉGASSE, *L'Évangile de Marc II,* 749, with this definition and as forming part of the one great commandment. It sharply emphasizes this unity-in-difference nature of the Love commandments. Similarly, J. WELLHAUSEN, *Das evangelium Marci,* 103, who adds that this combination is important to the meaning of the whole.

conception, and with this background, investigate the commandment's specificity in the gospel, and close with a concluding summary.

(1) Covenant Brother, Resident Alien, even as Enemy

The object of the second commandment to love is πλησίον[211]. It is the LXX rendering of the Hebrew term רע found in Lev 19,18 which meant a compatriot or a fellow-Israelite.

Our OT analysis of this text in Ch II showed that the neighbor, as the object of the commandment to love (רע / πλησίον), is a covenant brother[212]. The רעים thus are one's own people as members of the covenant community, although Lev 19,34 extends the commandment to love to the resident alien as well[213]. But we also saw that the רע or covenant brother involved in the context is a personal and judicial enemy. It is such a רע against whom retaliation and rancor is forbidden and who, instead, must be loved by the concrete step of caring fraternal correction[214]. This also follows from the structure of the sentence namely, from the adversative character of the ו which initiates the commandment (cf. 19,18). It has, thus, the meaning: «You shall not take vengeance or bear a grudge against the sons of your own people (בני עמך = fellow-Israelites) but you shall love your neighbor as yourself» which, with its contrast structure, clarifies the love commanded as love of enemy[215]. The commandment thus enjoins love for רעם, the members of the covenant community, even when they are enemies.

(2) All Human Beings, even as Enemies (Mk 9,35; 10,44; 14,24)

It can be said that in Mk the same OT meaning obtains, as there is nothing within the pericope to suggest a difference in meaning. The Evangelist also does not define πλησίον anywhere, indicating a changed nuance. The two instances of the term πλησίον in the gospel figure either in the commandment to love the neighbor (12,31) or in its

---

[211] This neuter form of the adjective πλησίον used as masculine noun has, besides the meaning «neighbor», the nuances of «one who is near» / «close by», or «fellow-human being», *BAGD*, 672.

[212] Cf. Ch II, 3.2.1

[213] Cf. Ch II, 3.4

[214] Cf. Ch II, 2.2

[215] Cf. Ch II, 2; 2.1; 2.2; 3.1

paraphrase (12,33). The fact that it occurs nowhere else, except in these places, indicates that, at least at the face of it, the term is used in its OT meaning[216].

This situation not withstanding, the conception of the term in the gospel seems to go beyond the OT sense in view of the following texts: Mk 9,35; 10,44; 14,24, where Jesus either teaches the disciples on the path to true greatness, or interprets the meaning of his life and death in relation to others. Thus in 9,35 taking up the question of rivalry for greatness among the Twelve Jesus tells them that «he who wants to be first of all must be last of all and servant of all». What Jesus enunciates by this is an absolute rule as the terms «first» (πρῶτος), «last» (ἔσχατος), «servant» (διάκονος) and «all» (πάντων) are all used absolutely[217]. The meaning thus is that the path to absolute greatness, to being absolutely first, is to be absolutely last and absolutely servant of all without exception[218]. The will to greatness is not condemned and is thus taken to be a valid pursuit for which the correct way is shown[219]. In doing so Jesus reveals the attitude that has the highest premium in the gospel, as the path to absolute greatness. It is to be last of all and servant of all. The «last» (ἔσχατος) here emphasizes the role one must adopt in relation to others[220] while the term «servant» (διάκονος) expresses the obligation that goes with it[221]. He must be absolutely servant of all

---

[216] Although this seems to be the case in Mk at first sight, a glance at Lk 10,29-34, which addresses this issue, shows that in the gospel tradition πλησίον does receive a clear universal application in the teaching of Jesus. The example-story of the good Samaritan clearly overcomes the limitation of Lev 19,18 to the fellow-Israelite + resident alien and opens up to every needy human being, even if he/she is a national enemy, H. SCHÜRMANN, *Das Lukasevangelium II*, 147; J. A. FITZMYER, *Luke II*, 884. As the latter, *Ibid.*, puts it: «The point of the story is summed up in the lawyer's reaction, that a "neighbor" is anyone in need with whom one comes into contact and to whom one can show pity and kindness, even beyond the bounds of one's own ethnic or religious group.».

[217] Cf. K. STOCK, *Boten*, 118-120.

[218] Cf. K. STOCK, *Boten*, 120; J. GNILKA, *Markusevangelium II*, 56-57; R. PESCH, *Markusevangelium II*, 104, who adds that the terms «first» and «last» denote rank. Similarly, R.H. GUNDRY, *Mark*, 509, who points out that the forward position of πρῶτος emphasizes firstness and the chiastic positions of ἔσχατος and διάκονος strengthen the contrast between firstness and lastness, or servanthood, while πάντων, used twice, universalizes the contrast. Its placement before ἔσχατος and again before διάκονος intensifies that universalism. Likewise, S. LÉGASSE, *L'Évangile de Marc II*, 568.

[219] Cf. A. STOCK, *Method and Message*, 256; K. STOCK, *Boten*, 118.

[220] Cf. K. STOCK, *Boten*, 119.

[221] Cf. K. STOCK, *Boten*, 119. Thus to be last in relation to others means to serve them. *Ibid.*, n.350; J. GNILKA, *Markusevangelium II*, 56-57.

without exception (πάντων)[222]. The term «διακονεῖν», «to serve» as opposed to δουλεύειν, «to slave» emphasizes person-oriented service in distinction to the service of a slave, characterized by the subjection of the one who serves[223].

Although Jesus gives this teaching in relation to the way to true greatness, it reveals the value that has the highest premium *vis-à-vis* others in his teaching. It, consequently, contains an interpretation of the commandment to love of neighbor which defines the attitude commanded by God in relation to others[224]. Since it demands service in absolute terms extending to all (cf. «last of all»; «servant of all»), it reveals the object of love of neighbor as *all* human beings without exception, hence inclusive of even enemies, which clearly goes beyond the limitation to one's own people.

In 10,44 the same teaching is repeated and deepened in the context of the ambitious request of the Zebedee brothers and the Ten's indignation at it (10,35-41). In his instruction Jesus says in response that in direct contrast to the attitudes that prevail among the great ones of the world (v42)[225]: «....whoever would be great among you (μέγας)[226] must be your servant (διάκονος), and whoever would be first among you must be slave of all» (v44)[227]. Here too the conception of the role and service, despite its being addressed to them (cf. «among you», ἐν ὑμῖν), is not confined to the Twelve but covers all, since the greatness in-

---

[222] So not limited to a group or circle but in the widest possible, unlimited sense. Cf. K. STOCK, *Boten*, 120. See also. n.120.

[223] Cf. K. STOCK, *Boten*, 119-120.

[224] Cf. W.L. LANE, *Mark*, 339, who observes pointedly that: «This surprising reversal of all human ideas of greatness and rank is a practical application of the great commandment of love of one's neighbor (Ch 12,31; Lev 19,18) [......]».

[225] V. TAYLOR, *Mark*, 444; J. GNILKA, *Markusevangelium II*, 100; R. PESCH, *Markusevangelium II*, 154, think that this verse characterizing the behavior of the worldly rulers is formulated in a synonymous parallelism, while K. STOCK, *Boten*, 138, considers it uncertain, as it may be talking of two types of rulers.

[226] V. TAYLOR, *Mark*, 444, following M. Black, points out that μέγας represents a Semitic usage of the positive being employed as superlative. (cf. also *Ibid.*, 405, n.11). R.H. GUNDRY, *Mark*, 580, however, thinks that it is the counterpartness of πρῶτος in 9,35 with it and the parallel with πρῶτος in 10,44 which escalate its meaning from «great» to «greatest».

[227] Vv 43 and 44 exhibit synonymous parallelism in its formulation, V. TAYLOR, *Mark*, 444; W.L. LANE, *Mark*, 382; C.S. MANN, *Mark*, 414; J. GNILKA, *Markusevangelium II*, 100; R. PESCH, *Markusevangelium II*, 154; S. LÉGASSE, *L'Évangile de Marc II*, 639. For a different view see, M.F. VAN IERSEL, *Mark*, 336, who finds the two verses forming a concentric structure.

volved is not limited to their circle[228]. It is both open to all and the one who takes up the service of all in this manner will be first of all without exception, first of all absolutely[229]. The change from διάκονος to δοῦλος in this formulation highlights an emphasis. While the first underlines the nature of the service demanded as person-oriented service[230], the second accentuates the obligatory character of this service[231]. For the disciples of Jesus such service is not a matter of choice but of obligation. This is clarified by 10,45 which gives the validating reason why it is so. They must serve all without exception necessarily «because the Son of Man also came not to be served but to serve[232] and to give his life as a ransom for many» (cf. καὶ γὰρ..., v45)[233]. It follows as an obligation for them from their participation in the way of Jesus (cf. ἀναβαίνομεν, 10,33)[234].

Here too the absolute use of the object of service (cf. πάντων δοῦλος) indicates its universal and unlimited range. As the preeminent

---

[228] Cf. K. STOCK, *Boten*, 140. Against R.H. GUNDRY, *Mark*, 586, who denies an extension from a reference to the Twelve in «of you» to a reference to all people in «of all» and thinks that the repetition of «among you» shows that «slave of all» means «slave of you all» in parallel with «servants of you» for fear that «otherwise we have a disjunction of being a slave of all society but being first only among the Twelve».

[229] Cf. K. STOCK, *Boten*, 120.

[230] Cf. K. STOCK, *Boten*, 119.140; C.E.B. CRANFIELD, *Mark*, 341.

[231] Cf. K. STOCK, *Boten*, 140.

[232] The term διακονῆσαι again underlines the person-oriented character of the Son of Man's service which, in fact, culminates in his giving his life as ransom for the many who are all (λύτρον ἀντὶ πολλῶν). Just as the Son of Man's service knows no limits but goes to the extent of laying down his life for all, so also the service of the Twelve should not be limited, K. STOCK, *Boten*, 142-143. The personal character of the Son of Man's service seems to be heightened by the use of the preposition ἀντί which has the nuance that in the act of deliverance the «many» not only benefit but receive what they cannot effect, V. TAYLOR, *Mark*, 444. Similarly, W.L. LANE, *Mark*, 384, stresses the substitutionary nature of Jesus' death implied by the preposition. Likewise, J. GNILKA, *Markusevangelium II*, 104; R. PESCH, *Markusevangelium II*, 164; R.H. GUNDRY, *Mark*, 590; S. LÉGASSE, *L'Évangile de Marc II*, 642. For a different view see, C.S. MANN, *Mark*, 419, who following M.D. Hooker, takes the phrase as meaning Jesus' giving his life for the community as a servant deliverer.

[233] K. STOCK, *Boten*, 141, stresses the validating nature of this phrase. It places the reason and what is validated on the same plane of comparison and thus underlines their similarity. According to the connection that it establishes the example of Jesus becomes the standard for the behavior demanded of the Twelve, while it also grounds this demand. Also, A. STOCK, *Method and Message*, 283. Similarly, R. PESCH, *Markusevangelium II*, 162. Likewise, M.D. HOOKER, *Mark*, 247-248, who adds that they must follow the Son of Man's example not simply because he is their model, but because his death is for their benefit, and provides the force for them to follow it.

[234] Cf. K. STOCK, *Boten*, 143-144.

attitude in relation to others, it expresses the commandment to love and its unrestricted extension and thus clarifies its object as *all* human beings without exception, inclusive of enemies. The same extension is underlined by the grounding statement about the Son of Man whose example obligates the service of the disciples. It too has an unlimited extension (cf. λύτρον ἀντὶ πολλῶν, v45), since the «many» (πολλοί) is a Semitic expression which is not opposed to «all» but may denote «all, who are many»[235].

This same unlimited extension recurs in 14,24 as well where Jesus speaks of the cup of his blood as the blood of the covenant which is poured out for «many» (ὑπὲρ πολλῶν), thus interpreting the meaning of his self-offering by using the same terminology of inclusion[236].

Hence, in view of these texts which either define the preeminent attitude to others of absolutely humble service of all as the path to true greatness, or interpret the salvific meaning of Jesus' life in relation to all others which, consequently, involve an expression of the commandment to love the neighbor, the object of love in the gospel is *all* human beings without exception, inclusive of enemies. It thus indicates a major break-through in meaning compared to its understanding in the OT.

It is also noteworthy that both these decisive texts on the relation to the neighbor in Mk have a special position in the gospel. 9,35 occurs at the beginning of the central instruction of the Twelve (9,35-50) in the «way section» (8,27-10,52)[237]. Similarly, 10,43-45 figures as the

---

[235] Cf. M. ZERWICK-M. GROSVENOR, *A Grammatical Analysis,* 143. V. TAYLOR, *Mark,* 546, further clarifies that its meaning is not «some, but not all» but «all in contrast with one». Similarly, J. GNILKA, *Markusevangelium II,* 104, stresses its universal reference and points to 1Tim 2,6 (ὑπὲρ πάντων) in support. For a different view see, C.S. MANN, *Mark,* 419, who thinks that it stands for the covenant community.

[236] Cf. V. TAYLOR, *Mark,* 546; A. STOCK, *Method and Message,* 361; M.D. HOOKER, *Mark,* 343; R.H. GUNDRY, *Mark,* 589-590; J. GNILKA, *Markusevangelium II,* 246, who adds that, although in Qumran writings the term connotes the community, against the background of the Servant songs (cf. Is 53,11f), it cannot be limited to Israel (against R. PESCH, *Abendmahl,* 177f; ID., *Markusevangelium, II,* 360; C.A. EVANS, *Mark II,* 394) but has a universal application. Similarly, S. LÉGASSE, *L'Évangile de Marc II,* 871, who also notes that it is on this basis that the gospel proclamation to all the peoples (13,10) is demanded.

[237] The way section is the first section of the second part of the gospel which is centered on the theological theme of Jesus' way to Jerusalem that will eventually culminate in his Passion and death, a way that the disciples must also follow. It divides into three units on the basis of similarity of construction. They start with the Passion and resurrection predictions (8,31; 9,30-31; 10,32-34) which dominate these units, and are followed by a reference to the misunderstanding by the disciples (8,32-33; 9,32-34;

unique theme of their last instruction (10,38-45). As these instructions have the greatest importance in the Twelve's following of Jesus by virtue of their participation in his way (cf. ἀναβαίνομεν, 10,33) based on their radical call to follow (8,34f), their significant placement underlines their crucial importance. Interestingly, the pre-eminent position of these texts containing the gospel's expanded understanding of the commandment to love parallels its pivotal position in the book of Leviticus[238], a point which also seems to enhance their importance.

(3) Object of Love in Mk

On the one hand, the gospel seems to retain the OT conception of the object of love of neighbor which denoted a member of the covenant community and resident alien even as enemy, since there is nothing in the pericope to suggest a change in meaning and since the gospel also does not define πλησίον anywhere indicating a different nuance, its occurrence being limited to the commandment (12,31) or its paraphrase.

On the other hand, it seems to extend the meaning of neighbor to absolutely all human beings without exception even as enemies, in view of 9,35; 10,44; 14,24, thus overcoming the limitation to one's own people inherent in the OT conception.

In the first two of these texts (9,35; 10,44) this follows from Jesus' teaching on true greatness which affirms that, to be greatest of all, one must absolutely be servant of all without exception. As a definition of the gospel's preeminent attitude in relation to others, it expresses the commandment to love the neighbor, and in so far as it insists on the service of all human beings without exception, it points to the extension of the object of love to all, inclusive of enemies. This is deepened further christologically in 10,45 by grounding it in the example of the Son of Man whose life is defined by service to the point of giving it as a ransom for all. This text, which interprets the meaning of Jesus' life and death in terms of its impact on others in inclusive terms, involves the commandment to love and, as such, also indicates the same extension of the object of love to all without exception. Mk 14,24 reinforces this by interpreting in similar terms the meaning of Jesus' redeeming death using the same inclusive language. Thus both these texts also witness to the extension of the object of love of neighbor in the gospel.

10,35-37), and conclude with an instruction on discipleship by Jesus (8,34-38; 9,35-50; 10,38-45), I. dE lA POTTERIE, «De Compositione», 139-140. See also, S. KUTHIRAKKATTEL, *The Beginning,* 52-53; M. D. HOOKER, *Mark,* 245.
    [238] Cf. 2.2.5 a) (1); Ch II, 4.1f; 4.1.3; 4.2; 4.3;

Hence, in difference to its OT meaning, it is *all* human beings without exception, inclusive of enemies, which, thus, indicates a major break-through in meaning compared to the former.

c) *The Modality of Love (Mk 12,31a)*

After having clarified the object of love of neighbor in Mk, we shall now see the modality of this love. It will first restate its OT meaning, then explore its specific Markan understanding, and conclude with a short summary of the discussion.

(1) As Oneself (ὡς σεαυτόν, Lev 19,18)

The modality of love of neighbor is termed ὡς σεαυτόν which is the LXX rendering followed by Mk of the Masoretic כמוך, «as yourself». In Lev 19,18 (+v34) כמוך meant a measure or standard and not a motivation. The כמוך there is equivalent to כנפשך, «as your own self». It has the adverbial sense which points to the modality of love that is commanded[239]. This emphasizes that the standard for loving the neighbor is that the latter is like one's own self[240]. Our study of the OT meaning of the modality of love revealed that the choice of כמוך over כנפשך in Lev 19,18 (+v34) highlighted the type of love involved in the commandment. While כנפשך puts in relief the emotive and natural aspect of friendship, כמוך underlines the transition to a different type of love towards the רע (v18) and the גר (v34) commanded by Yahweh, where the emotive aspect becomes secondary and the accent falls on deeds[241]. Thus, one is to care for the neighbor and behave towards him in a manner corresponding to his rights, as in one's own case[242]. It thus respects equality of rights. The love involved has to be concretized in deeds, considering the neighbor like oneself and treating him/her as one would oneself even when he/she is a an enemy.

The stress on deeds becomes clear also in the commandment's context in Leviticus. In 19,18 the offending covenant brother, a personal or judicial enemy, is to be loved by renouncing vengeance and rancor against him and by means of the concrete step of caring fraternal correction[243], while in 19,32 the resident alien is to be loved by recognizing his full equality of rights with the members of the covenant

---

239 Cf. Ch II, 3.3
240 Cf. Ch II, 3.3.1
241 Cf. Ch II, 3.3.3
242 Cf. R. PESCH, *Markusevangelium II*, 241.
243 Cf. Ch II, 2.2

community[244]. «As yourself» as the modality of love thus respects the equality of rights that is due to the covenant brother and resident alien even when he is an enemy, although the emotional aspect of identification with them is not lacking in it.

(2) As Servant of All and Slave of All

The modality of love implied by כמוך (ὡς σεαυτόν, «as yourself») in the commandment in the OT seems to continue to have the same meaning and emphasis in Mk at first sight, as no change of nuance is indicated in the pericope[245]. Despite this, however, as in the case of the extension of the object of love of neighbor, the gospel seems to widen the idea of the modality of love. This is suggested by the texts, 9,35 and 10,44-45, where as we saw above, Jesus, on the one hand, teaches the disciples on the way to true greatness and, on the other, speaks of his life as defined by service to the point of giving it as a ransom for all (10,45). Just as our analysis of these texts revealed the extension of the object of love of neighbor to all human beings, inclusive of enemies, they also seem to unravel the modality of the love that is due to them in the attitude *vis-à-vis* these that they embody.

Based on our study of 9,35[246], then, it can be affirmed that the disposition of being «last of all» and «servant of all», as an expression of the gospel's fundamental attitude towards others which, as such, expresses the commandment to love the neighbor, also articulates the modality of the love in question. Thus it consists in being last of all and servant of all without exception, by necessarily rendering person-oriented service to them[247].

The teaching in 10,45 reinforces and grounds this modality christologically in the example of the Son of Man who has come not to be served but to serve and to give his life as a ransom for many and also underlines that it follows as an obligation for the disciples of Jesus from their association with him and their participation in his way (cf.

---

[244] Cf. Ch II, 3.4

[245] Mk also does not define (ἀγαπᾶν) ὡς σεαυτόν anywhere indicating a change of nuance. The two instances of its use with ἀγαπᾶν in the gospel appear either in the commandment itself (12,31) or in its paraphrase (12,33), with the second actually being (ἀγαπᾶν)... ὡς ἑαυτὸν as required by the indirect discourse. The fact that it occurs nowhere else also indicates that the term is used in its OT meaning.

[246] Cf. 2.2.5 b) (2).

[247] Cf. W.L. LANE, *Mark*, 339-340.

ἀναβαίνομεν, 10,33)[248]. Both these texts thus embody the modality of
love of neighbor in the gospel, the second deepening it further[249].

While these texts reveal the gospel's conception of this modality,
Mk also provides both positive and negative illustrative models of it.

The positive model is offered in 9,36-37 in a concrete depiction[250].
Jesus here stands a child in the midst of the 12 and, embracing
(ἐναγκαλισάμενος) it, tells them: «Whoever receives one such child in
my name receives me.». Both the gesture of Jesus and his words appear
to illustrate his teaching on greatness through being absolutely last of
all and servant of all. It is an example of what it means «to be servant
of all» because the children[251] too belong to the «all»[252] and one serves
them in so far as one receives them. Δέχεται, with its meaning of receiving warmly[253], has a relation to διακονεῖν which has the basic
meaning of «serving at table» (cf. Lk 10,38.40). It thus stands for all the
care and trouble which go with reception[254]. To receive is a total service which cannot, for instance, be compared to almsgiving. Jesus' action of embracing the child also has a similar meaning. It declares that
one surrounds it with all one's love and care and that it is wanted and

---

[248] Cf. 2.2.5 b) (2). With «ransom for many» is indicated an area which is reserved
to Jesus alone since his deed is once-for-all and since the disciples cannot follow him in
it. However, they are obligated to follow him, in so far as it is person-oriented service.
In this it is not excluded that their service and giving of life have an analogically similar
effect as the deed of Jesus, K. STOCK, *Boten*, 143, n.426.

[249] Cf. W.L. LANE, *Mark*, 374; J. GNILKA, *Markusevangelium II*, 103; R. PESCH,
Markusevangelium II, 162.

[250] Cf. H.B. SWETE, *Saint Mark*, 206; W. LANE, *Mark*, 341; R. PESCH, *Markusevangelium II*, 107.

[251] Some consider the child, though representative of its class, as a symbol of the
disciples, H.B. SWETE, *Saint Mark*, 206; W.L. LANE, *Mark*, 340. However, there
seems to be no basis in the Markan text for this assumption. It is not also a picture of
humility that must characterize the disciple, as the context is not concerned with this
but with receiving those who are humble and unimportant, M.D. HOOKER, *Mark*, 228.
Lane's attempt, *Ibid.*, 340-341, to justify the former with a reference to 6,11f, therefore, seems far-fetched. R.H. GUNDRY, *Mark*, 518-519, hits the nail on its head when
he says: «All interpretations of v36 that point to a childlike virtue worthy of imitation-
innocence, trustfulness etc.- fail to consider that v37 goes on to make a child the object
of reception, not of imitation.». Likewise, S. LÉGASSE, *L'Évangile de Marc II*, 569.

[252] Besides, as A. STOCK, *Method and Message*, 256; J. GNILKA, *Markusevangelium II*, 57, remind us, they were also considered as persons of no importance in the
Jewish culture of the time.

[253] Cf. V. TAYLOR, *Mark*, 405; R.H. GUNDRY, *Mark*, 519.

[254] Cf. R.H. GUNDRY, *Mark*, 519.

cherished[255]. By this he underlines that it is not concern over one's rank and strife around it but care for a child, the service to the little ones, that makes one great. Thus Jesus here offers an example of what it means to be «servant of all»[256] and, as such, illustrates the modality of love in the gospel.

Although in 9,36-37 the nuance of obligation to serve is not present which v35b, taken in itself, has, still what happens in such an act of reception is clarified, and this obligates the reception of such a child. This happening is that one who receives such a child thus receives God. Hence 9,37 has the same dynamic as 9,35b: what is considered inferior and unimportant reveals itself as the greatest; the absolutely last is the absolutely first. Reception of a child means reception of God. Here we see another dimension of the connection between 9,35b and 9,37. 9,37 not only concretizes what it means to be «servant of all», but also reveals why it is the source of genuine greatness. The servant of all, the servant of the little ones, serves God. Thus, what was characterized in 9,35b in terms of connection is clarified in 9,37 on the basis of its reason[257]. The disclosure of this reason for service in the context of this illustration thus enriches also the understanding of the modality of love in the gospel, as it clarifies its deep motivation.

This is further deepened by the phrase ἐπὶ τῷ ὀνόματί μου (v37) which gives the basis for the reception[258] of the child. The child is welcomed «for Jesus' sake», from the relationship with him[259]. Its reception is a reception of Jesus and of the one who sent him. This shows that in the exercise of the modality of love in the gospel Jesus has a central role[260]. Thus 9,37 reveals the full perspective of the modality of

---

[255] Cf. J. GNILKA, *Markusevangelium II*, 57; R. PESCH, *Markusevangelium II*, 106; R.H. GUNDRY, *Mark*, 510; C.A. EVANS, *Mark II*, 62.

[256] Cf. K. STOCK, *Boten*, 121-122; A. STOCK, *Method and Message*, 256; R.H. GUNDRY, *Mark*, 519; S. LÉGASSE, *L'Évangile de Marc II*, 569; C.A. EVANS, *Mark II*, 61. For a different view see M.F. VAN IERSEL, *Mark*, 307, who finds here the contrary relations first/last, master/servant, evoking a whole paradigm of binary oppositions centered on the basic antithesis superior/inferior, of which two are expressed: adult/child, ruler/messenger, with the first made visible in a metaphorical action. However, although it is possible to perceive such a relation here, the elaboration seems to ignore the dominant theme in the context of greatness through necessary service of absolutely all.

[257] Cf. K. STOCK, *Boten*, 121-122; J. GNILKA, *Markusevangelium II*, 58; R. PESCH, *Markusevangelium II*, 106-107.

[258] Cf. V. TAYLOR, *Mark*, 405; R.H. GUNDRY, *Mark*, 510.

[259] Cf. M.D. HOOKER, *Mark*, 228.

[260] Cf. A. STOCK, *Method and Message*, 256-257; M.D. HOOKER, *Mark*, 228; R. PESCH, *Markusevangelium II*, 106; R.H. GUNDRY, *Mark*, 510.

love demanded in 9,35b. Being servant of all makes one great because the service involved is done for Jesus' sake, and because it is done to him[261]. Jesus is the connecting link between the visible deed of the disciple and God. Similarly, it is also implied that the relationship of the disciple to Jesus is realized in the service to the little ones[262]. In the little ones Jesus encounters him/her and through service to him he/she is related to Jesus. This connection to Jesus involved in «being servant of all» further enriches the modality of love of neighbor in the gospel[263]. In «being servant of all» one encounters Jesus and the service itself is ultimately done to him. Thus, compared to its OT conception, this indicates a major deepening and extension of the modality of this love.

The negative model, on the other hand, is found in 10,42. Here Jesus responds to the ambitious request of the Zebedee brothers for assured places to his right and left in his glory and the Ten's indignation at it (10,35-41) by first referring to the grossly negative attitudes that prevail among the rulers and great ones of the world in their exercise of power, to which the disposition of humble service of all, that must characterize the community of his disciples, stands in direct contrast (v42). Since the former concern people's behavior towards others, they touch the

---

[261] Cf. J. GNILKA, *Markusevangelium II*, 57.

[262] Cf. K. STOCK, *Boten*, 121-122; J. GNILKA, *Markusevangelium II*, 57; S. LÉGASSE, *L'Évangile de Marc II*, 572-573.

[263] As K. STOCK, *Boten*, 124-129, demonstrates Mk 9,38-50 appears to add to this. Thus seeing 9,38-41 in the light of Jesus' teaching in 9,35b this episode means that it does not behoove those who should be «servant of all» to judge those outside harshly and rigorously. They should serve also in seeing everything positively and in recognizing the value of what they do. Similarly, 9,42-49 implies that one who is servant of all will avoid every offense. It also seems to point to the 12 as being in danger of failing the little ones in their faith, perhaps specially through their rivalry around rank and the attitude that produces it. Likewise, 9,50, the final parabolic exhortation which seems focused on the maintenance of character and its loss, appears to refer to the fundamental theme of being «servant of all». The exhortation, «have salt and keep peace» with its reference back to the beginning, seems to suggest that this is to be concretized through the commandment of 9,35b. Thus, «being servant of all» appears to be the essential attitude that the 12 must always preserve. All three passages thus seem to emphasize specific aspects of the modality of love in its application. Supporting the literary and/or thematic unity of 9,33-50 is W.L. LANE, *Mark*, 339; R.H. GUNDRY, *Mark*, 507-508.516; C.A. EVANS, *Mark II*, 66.74-75. Likewise, J. GNILKA, *Markusevangelium II*, 63, who thus sees v40 providing a summarizing inclusion with v33f. For a different view see, S. LÉGASSE, *L'Évangile de Marc II*, 563-564; 587-588, who, while finding a reference back to vv33-35 in v50, fails to see the uninterrupted thematic commonality in the intervening section. Likewise, V. TAYLOR, *Mark*, 414. See also, R. PESCH, *Markusevangelium II*, 103.

commandment to love and, in so far as Jesus enjoins the Twelve to reject them categorically, it would seem that he is thereby giving them an illustrative model of the modality of love in negative terms.

Jesus begins his response by referring to the common knowledge which the disciples have about the behavior of the rulers and great ones of the Gentiles (cf. Οἴδατε ὅτι...,v42)[264]. Two categories are mentioned: «those who are supposed to rule over the Gentiles» (οἱ δοκοῦντες ἄρχειν τῶν ἐθνῶν)[265] and, «the great men who exercise authority over them» (οἱ μεγάλοι αὐτῶν). The first «lord it over» or «rule over» them[266] (cf. κατακυριεύουσιν αὐτῶν). The second «exercise authority over», (cf. κατεξουσιάζουσιν αὐτῶν), or more precisely, «tyrannize over» them[267].

It is significant that both the verbs in the two clauses are compound verbs starting with κατά which has a distinct negative nuance of «against», thus connoting a misuse of power and authority against the people involved to one's own advantage[268]. This pejorative nuance is

---

[264] As R. PESCH, *Markusevangelium II*, 161, points out, this signals a point of agreement between the speaker and the hearer.

[265] V. TAYLOR, *Mark*, 443, thinks that the phrase οἱ δοκοῦντες ἄρχειν which qualifies the rulers carries with it a note of irony with the meaning «the so-called rulers» or «those who are supposed to rule». Similarly, W.L. LANE *Mark*, 382; C.S. MANN, *Mark*, 414. Likewise, J. GNILKA, *Markusevangelium II*, 103, who adds that it implies God to be the real ruler of this earth; M.D. HOOKER, *Mark*, 247, considers it ambiguous, but as probably intended to indicate their rule to be only apparent and unreal in the eyes of God. For a different view see, S. LÉGASSE, *L'Évangile de Marc II*, 638, who thinks that instead of the latter it reflects a common opinion from the perspective of the people, understandable in a Jewish-Christian author preoccupied with keeping a distance from pagan power. Similarly, R.H. GUNDRY, *Mark*, 579, who thinks that it reflects recognition based on fact namely, these as actual rulers among the Gentiles. At any rate, as R. PESCH, *Markusevangelium II*, 161, also observes, the characterization does seem to involve an attitude of distance.

[266] Cf. M. ZERWICK-M. GROSVENOR, *A Grammatical Analysis*, 143. S. LÉGASSE, *L'Évangile de Marc II*, 638, points out that it has the sense of exercising a dominating power and, *Ibid.*, n.48, occurs in this sense in 1Pt 5,3; in Act 19,16 and in LXX, Gen 1,28; 9,1; Ps 9,26.31.

[267] Cf. M. ZERWICK-M. GROSVENOR, *A Grammatical Analysis*, 143.

[268] Cf. K. STOCK, *Boten*, n.410. Similarly, S. LÉGASSE, *L'Évangile de Marc II*, 638, n.48, following Lagrange, thinks that these two verbs formed with κατά on the same theme convey a pejorative sense. Likewise, C.S. MANN, *Mark*, 414; J. GNILKA, *Markusevangelium II*, 103; H.B. SWETE, *Saint Mark*, 239, adds that, while both connote arbitrary rule over their subjects, the first points to misrule as Lords paramount (κατακυριεύουσιν αὐτῶν), the second as subordinates (κατεξουσιάζουσιν αὐτῶν). So also, R. PESCH, *Markusevangelium II*, 161. In any case, they involve a decidedly negative nuance. As R. Pesch, *Ibid.*, quoting K.G. REPLOH, *Markus*, 165, observes: «Jedenfalls klingt in beiden Verben "das Gewalttätige Mißbräuchliche, auf reinen Eigennutz

further augmented if these clauses are in synonymous parallelism which is a possibility[269]. But even if they are not, and instead speak of two different types of rulers (great and small) which is also a possibility[270], this stress on the misuse of power clearly stands.

This negative characterization of the Gentile rulers may be because generally worldly power is misused to lord it over and exploit subject peoples[271]. But it may be also aimed at destroying every parallelism between worldly rulers and the Twelve to emphasize the stark contrast between them, in order to eliminate all temptations on the latter's part to model themselves on them[272]. In any case, the formulation makes a factual statement about the way worldly rule is exercised. It is characterized by misuse expressed in tyranny and exploitation of others.

After this stark portrayal of worldly power, Jesus makes a normative statement: «But it shall not be so among you.....», (οὐχ οὕτως δέ ἐστιν ἐν ὑμῖν,). Although there exists a variant of this clause with ἔσται in place of ἐστιν which corresponds to the translation, its authenticity is firm[273] and it has to be understood more as a categorical statement than as a statement of fact[274]. This becomes clear from the vv43b + 44

Bedachte der Herrscher an, denen nicht das Wohl ihrer Völker das erste Anliegen ist, sondern eigener Machtgewinn auf Kosten dieser Völker." ».

[269] Cf. n.227. Also, S. LÉGASSE, L'Évangile de Marc II, 638-639; C.S. MANN, Mark, 414.

[270] Cf. n.227.Also, S. LÉGASSE, L'Évangile de Marc II, 639, who, somewhat differently, makes a distinction between rulers (emperors and kings) and «great ones». Similarly, R. PESCH, Markusevangelium II, 161; R.H. GUNDRY, Mark, 579.

[271] In this sense, it may also, perhaps, reflect the contemporary situation in Israel under Roman and Herodian rule, W.L. LANE, Mark, 382. Or, as J. GNILKA, Markusevangelium II, 103, suggests, it may express the experience of the addressees of the despotism of Nero.

[272] Cf. K. STOCK, Boten, 140. Similarly, S. LÉGASSE, L'Évangile de Marc II, 639, who thinks that the reason for the harsh characterization is because it is needed to draw the lesson which follows.

[273] According to B. M. METZGER, A Textual Commentary, 91, the future tense, which is supported by A C³ K X Π and most minuscules (followed by the Textus Receptus) appears to be a scribal amelioration designed to soften the peremptory tone of the present ἐστιν. He also considers it possible that the future may have arisen from assimilation to ἔσται in the next line.

[274] Thus V. TAYLOR, Mark, 443-444, following Swete, 239, states that this authoritative statement «suggests a principle which is operative in the new Israel». Similarly, S. LÉGASSE, L'Évangile de Marc II, 639. Likewise, C.S. MANN, Mark, 414, who adds that its present tense is emphatic and dramatic. In similar vein, R. PESCH, Markusevangelium II, 161, who further observes that against the negative model, the contrast is established, first with this formal statement that it ought not to be so in the community of disciples, and then by the following community norm in vv43-44.

which furnish normative statements with ἔσται (*bis*), and which consequently are not declarations of reality already achieved but norms and
values that have validity in the community[275].

Hence in v43a, making a comparison with the pattern among normal
worldly rulers, Jesus states that this pattern of behavior has absolutely
no normative validity for the Twelve, and then in vv43b-44 puts forward in categorical terms the norms that should actually characterize
their behavior[276]. It thus contrasts sharply an actuality with a normative
reality which they must strive after. But, in so far as v43a forbids in
negative categorical terms (cf. οὐχ οὕτως δέ ἐστιν ἐν ὑμῖν,) the mode
of behavior of worldly rulers, it defines in negative terms the attitude
that should absolutely never figure *vis-à-vis* the disciples' disposition to
others[277] and, as such, concerns the commandment to love the neighbor. It thus defines negatively what is involved in its practice. In other
words, Jesus here gives us a negative model of the modality of love of
neighbor in the gospel.

Thus, Mk 9,36-37 and 10,42, as positive and negative illustrations of
the modality of love enunciated in 9,35 and 10,43b-45, give it a powerful and imaginative concretization.

(3) The Modality of Love in Mk

Following its OT sense, the modality of love seems to mean the
same in Mk, since at the level of the pericope there are no indications
for a change of nuance. However, although as an OT quotation the modality of love appears to retain this meaning in the pericope, the gospel

---

[275] Cf. K. STOCK, *Boten*, 138; R. PESCH, *Markusevangelium II*, 161.

[276] In this connection, the interrelations among the two pairs of clauses (v42 and
vv43-44) are significant. Thus, as K. STOCK, *Boten*, 138, points out, they are linked to
each other chiastically and this is manifested in the following data: the μέγας of v43b is
related to the μεγάλοι of v42 and corresponds to it. While μεγάλοι of v42 occurs in
the second clause of the first pair, the μέγας of v43 occurs in the first clause of the second pair.

There are also the following relations of contrast between different elements of
these pairs of clauses: κατεξουσιάζουσιν of the second clause of the first pair stands in
contrast to the ἔσται ὑμῶν διάκονος of the first clause of the second pair; οἱ δοκοῦντες
ἄρχειν of the first clause of the first pair stands in contrast to the πρῶτος of the second
clause of the second pair, and κατακυριεύουσιν of the first clause of the first pair contrasts the ἔσται πάντων δοῦλος of the second clause of the second pair. These last cor-
respondences show that these pairs of clauses contrast each other not only globally but
also in details.

[277] The forward position of οὐχ οὕτως, with which the clause starts, emphasizes
this nuance.

also extends and deepens this meaning in 9,35; 10,43b-44. While these articulate being absolutely servant of all human beings without exception as the gospel's pre-eminent value in relation to others and, as such, touch the commandment to love the neighbor and firstly points to the object of this commandment in the gospel, they also embody the modality of this love. The latter consists in being absolutely servant of all human beings without exception, rendering person-oriented service as a servant (cf. πάντων διάκονος). This teaching is deepened in 10,44-45 which stresses that for the disciples of Jesus this manner of service is a matter of obligation based on their participation in the way of Jesus (cf. ἀναβαίνομεν, 10,33) whose pattern of life was defined by it to the point of giving his life for the liberation of all. This shows that compared to its OT conception, the gospel's teaching on the modality of love of neighbor manifests a major deepening and extension.

Mk also follows up this teaching with positive and negative illustrative models, the first in 9,36-37 and the second in 10,42f. While the first illustrates how to be «servant of all» in concrete, the second exemplifies how it most certainly ought not to be. Together they provide mutually complementary and unforgettable models in the concrete realization of the modality of love in the gospel.

2.2.6 The Concluding Confirmation (Mk 12,31b)

Following the definition of the second commandment, Jesus concludes his answer with a closing statement which brings out their joint importance *vis-à-vis* all others. Our study of it will consist in indicating the special status of these commandments in the OT, and their new status following Jesus' definition, and close with a brief summary of these.

(1) The Special OT Status of these Commandments

Our OT analysis of these commandments demonstrated that already in their original contexts both of them had an important, even pivotal position. Thus the text of the first commandment, the שמע, had a central position in the book of Deuteronomy. On the one hand, as our examination of the context of שמע showed, it is connected with the Decalogue which precedes it in Ch 5 (cf. Deut 5,6-22). The Decalogue is given with the statement in 5,6: «I am the Lord your God, who brought you out of the land of Egypt, out of the house of bondage (Deut 5,6) which is succeeded by the first commandment: «You shall have no other gods before me» (Deut 5,7) and then by the other commandments

(5,8-22). The שמע and the rest of Ch 6 which come after this, is considered as a commentary and restatement of the first commandment of the Declaogue[278] which points to its importance in this context.

On the other hand, its prominence is even more clearly highlighted by the section which follows the Decalogue in Ch 5. This centers on the exclusive loyalty to Yahweh consisting in the whole-hearted observance of his commandments and thus deals with the המצוה, «the commandment» as opposed to החקים והמשפטים, «the laws and judgments». This המצוה opens with the שמע in this part, and is elaborated in the paranaetic sermons in the succeeding chapters till Ch 11. The chapters which follow (Chs 12-28), by contrast, deal with החקים והמשפטים, the specifications of the main commandment. The first part (Chs 5-11) thus concerns the principal commandment and the second (Chs 12-28) the individual commandments. Within this division Deut 6,4-5 itself constitutes the המצוה or the principal commandment in summary form in so far as it deals with Israel's fundamental confession of faith and its greatest religious obligation[279]. which demonstrates that, as such, it has clearly a pivotal status in Deuteronomy.

Similarly, the text of the second commandment had an important position in the book of Leviticus. There it marked the crowning of a series of injunctions centered on the neighbor in its immediate context (cf. Lev 19,11-18). It thus had an apex place in this section as the climactic demand of God which elucidates all others and by reason of its character as love of enemy[280]. It retained this dominant status also in the wider context of Lev Ch 19 which demands imitation of the holiness of God (Lev 19,2), in so far as it is by loving an offending brother, an enemy, that Israel is to demonstrate this[281]. Besides, given the importance of Ch 19 in the Holiness Code, it also stood as the climax of the latter[282]. The texts of both commandments thus had an important position in the respective books of which they are part.

(2) Their New Status (Mk 12,31b)

Despite these texts' significant position in their OT contexts Jesus' definition gives them a new status in a number of respects. Firstly, their

---

[278] Cf. Ch I, 4.1
[279] Cf. Ch I, 4.3
[280] Cf. Ch II, 4.1f, especially 4.1.3
[281] Cf. Ch II, 4.2
[282] Cf. Ch II, 4.3

prominence not withstanding, Deut 6,4-5 and Lev 19,18 were not related or brought together anywhere in the OT. They were texts distant from each other in the Torah and were never coupled or quoted *in tandem*. While in the later Jewish tradition there are signs of a possible linkage of these texts[283] they nowhere reach the development that is seen in the Markan text[284]. This is something which results from Jesus' act of definition[285].

Secondly, despite their distinguished position in their OT contexts, they were never *defined* in their pivotal status. Needless to say, they were also not characterized as the first and second commandments. In Mk, by contrast, Jesus specifically *defines* them as such. Jesus' act of definition marks them off as the most important commandments, the first and the second most important, within a hierarchically-conceived totality. Their new status, as already noted briefly[286], is also expressed in their formulation. Thus the first commandment is introduced by the formula of gradation: πρώτη ἐστίν, with πρώτη standing for πρώτη

[283] Cf. Test. Dan. 5,2. Test. Iss. 5,2; 7,6. But, as has been noted already, although these texts contain the substance of the ideas of the two love commandments, the latter are not termed «first» or «second» by them nor characterized as the sum of all the other commandments. For a fuller discussion on this and related issues see, n.204.

[284] K. BERGER, *Die Gesetzesauslegung I*, 134-176, as noted in passing in n.204, (cf. also «General Introduction», 2. Status Quaestionis and the Focus of Our Study) attempts to show that the reduction of Law into the two principles of love of God and love of neighbor has been prepared for in Hellenistic Judaism and completed in Hellenistic Jewish Christianity under the influence of the great principles of Hellenistic piety, εὐσέβεια and φιλανθρωπία. However, this remains a hypothesis. For a succinct critique of this theory and a detailed discussion on related opinions on the question see, n.204.

[285] In this connection, W. DIEZINGER, «Zum Liebesgebot», 81-83, has suggested that Jesus reached the combination of Deut 6,4-5 and Lev 19,18 into the love commandment through a well-known technique of biblical exegesis in contemporary Rabbinic Jewish tradition which consists of associating texts, even those far apart, with the same key terms and seeing in their combination a deeper understanding of the will of God. The hook-word involved in this instance is «אהבת», thus not the usual imperative but a second person masculine perfect used as jussive, figuring only in four places in the Pentateuch: twice in Deut with God as its object (6,5 ;11,1), and twice in Lev with neighbor as its object (19,18; 19,34). The commandment «you shall love», «אהבת», thus, has only two objects in the Torah: God and neighbor. The association reveals that these belong together as one inseparable commandment because they are linked by the same term, while it also emphasizes that no object other than these is worthy to claim love in this sense. Although this may be a possibility, one is far from certain that Jesus employed this technique. Besides, even if this were true, Jesus, as we see, does far more than couple these texts and see a new significance in their combination. He *defines* them into the first and second most important commandments within a hierarchically-ordained totality with a character of unity-in-difference and gives them a summary character *vis-à-vis* the Law.

[286] Cf. 2.2.2.

ἐντολή, and with its character as an ordinal numeral denoting rank and position. Besides, its anarthrousness points to the nature or quality of what is signified (the commandment), emphasizing the first as absolutely first and thus highlighting the first commandment's absolutely first rank[287].

Likewise, the second commandment is introduced by the formula of gradation: δευτέρα αὕτη (12,31a), with the ordinal similarly denoting rank and its anarthrousness articulating the nature and quality of what is signified, the second commandment of love of neighbor, underlining its absolutely second rank. It is thus the second most important comm andment, second only to the commandment to love God.

Besides, both πρώτη and δευτέρα here also exhibit *asyndeton* in their formulation and taken together with their anarthrousness they clearly emphasize their nature of being the first and the second most important commandments[288]. Jesus' definition in Mk is thus characterized by this systematic ordering and gradation of the two commandments.

However, Jesus' concluding confirmation: «There is no other commandment greater than these» (v31b) following the commandments' definition underscores that in their individuality and gradation they form a unity. The statement accentuates their unique importance, on the one hand, by referring them together and, on the other, by contrasting them with all others. Both ways their unity within a hierarchically-ordained totality is affirmed. It means to say: these commandments in combination are the greatest; no other commandment is as great as them; what other commandments there may be, are secondary, inferior to these two and reducible to them[289].

As a unity of the two supreme commandments they also appear to have a summary character in relation to all other commandments. This also seems indicated by Jesus' statement that greater than these there is no other commandment[290]. Such a conception of them, as we already noted, is also a new feature compared to the OT and Jewish conceptions of Law which holds that all 613 laws which comprise it have the

---

[287] Cf. n. 46. R. PESCH, *Markusevangelium II*, 239, observes that the introduction of the answer, corresponding exactly to the question, is, in this respect, singular in Mk. The first commandment, the most important, is first defined and then the second, the one next in importance. Further, it is expressly stated that there is no commandment greater than these two. Such systematic differentiation and concluding general evaluation clearly implies a hierarchical difference of commandments in the Law which is expressly affirmed in v33.

[288] Cf. R.H. GUNDRY, *Mark*, 711.

[289] Cf. 2.2.5 a) (2).

[290] Against H. SARIOLA, *Markus und das Gesetz*, 202, who, because he misses this aspect of unity of the two love commandments, fails to see their summary character *vis-à-vis* the Law.

same rank and validity[291]. None was more important than the other. Much less could any of them alone, or in combination with another, summarize the Law. In contrast to this, Jesus' definition here seems to invest these commandments with a summary character *vis-à-vis* the Law[292].

But this statement emphasizes also their distinction and difference within this unity. They keep their individuality and hierarchical gradation within it. In fact, the formulation πρώτη/δευτέρα, which accordingly means «the first most important», and «the second most important», involves a parallelism between them which emphasizes precisely their distinction and gradation[293]. Thus, the commandment to love God has absolute primacy. It is not reducible to the second. But there is a second commandment, the commandment to love the neighbor, which ranks after the first. It also has its individuality and distinctiveness and is not reducible to the former. Mk, thus, affirms a clear hierarchy among the two love commandments. This means that, while they constitute a unity, they cannot be reduced into each other. Their distinction is further underlined by Jesus' reference to the two commandments as «these» (cf. μείζων τούτων.., v31b) rather than «this» (v31)[294]. All these aspects, which make up the new status of Deut 6,4-5 and Lev 19,18 in Mk, proceed from Jesus' definition.

(3) These Commandments in Mk

Our consideration of the concluding confirmation of Jesus (12,31b) indicated first that the texts of both commandments enjoyed a pivotal importance in their original OT contexts. Nevertheless, Jesus' definition of the two commandments adds a number of features to them that are new. On the one hand, as distinct from the OT, it brings them together *in tandem*. While in the OT, despite these texts' pre-eminent

---

[291] Cf. A. SUHL, *Die Funktion*, 87; For a detailed discussion on this and related questions see, n.204

[292] C.A. EVANS, *Mark II*, 265, following Allison, affirms that these two commandments summarize the Decalogue, the first summarizing its first table and the second its second table, and as such has a summary character in Jewish piety. While this may be true from an interpretative or catechetical point of view, it is highly unlikely as a true reductive summary in the sense that by observing these two commandments one observes the whole Decalogue (cf. n.204). But even if this were true, the difference is that here Jesus' concluding confirmative statement: «there are no commandments greater than these» involves a *formal definition* of their joint-status *vis-à-vis* all others which as such did not exist before him.

[293] Cf. B. WEISS, *Das Markusevangelium*, 401.

[294] Cf. R.H. GUNDRY, *Mark*, 716.

position, they were not *defined* in their pivotal positions, Jesus defines them the first and second most important commandments within a hierarchically-conceived totality. Their gradation and distinctiveness are also expressed in their literary formulation as πρώτη and δευτέρα, in their anarthrousness and in their asyndeton. However, though hierarchically-ordered and distinct, they constitute a unity, underlined by Jesus' declaration that greater than these there is no other commandment, which at once sees them as distinct and one. They also seem to have a summary character *vis-à-vis* the Law which is also articulated by the same statement. All these characteristics found in the Markan formulation of the commandments thus proceed from Jesus' definition.

2.3 The Answer of the Scribe

The definition of Jesus and his concluding confirmation is followed by the response of the scribe, characterized by his complimenting comments and his interpretative paraphrase of Jesus' words. Our following study of this will first dwell on his approving comments, and then take up his rendition of Jesus' words, and clarify its emphases. It will conclude with a reflection on the function of this response in the interaction.

2.3.1 His Complimenting Words (Mk 12,32)

The scribe reacts to Jesus' definition with a complimenting statement: «Your are right, Teacher; you have truly said that he is one...» (Καλῶς, διδάσκαλε, ἐπ' ἀληθείας εἶπες ὅτι εἷς ἐστιν...)[295]. His statement seems to be complimentary in two senses: (1) of Jesus as teacher, (2) of the teaching he has just given. His compliment to Jesus as teacher is expressed in the words, Καλῶς, διδάσκαλε,[296]. Καλῶς, an adverb used as exclamation, meaning «quite right», «that is true», «well said»[297], expresses enthusiastic agreement, admiration in itself. But, because of the direct address to Jesus which immediately follows it (cf. διδάσκαλε,), it refers the compliment primarily to Jesus as teacher as

---

[295] As an interpretative version of Jesus' answer, this response of the scribe is unique in the gospels, S. LÉGASSE, *L'Évangile de Marc II,* 750; W. HARRINGTON, *Mark,* 191. The former, following R. PESCH, *Markusevangelium II,* 242, adds that the succession of terms in its introduction (v32a) is also without parallel in Mk.

[296] R.H. GUNDRY, *Mark,* 711 thus thinks that it points to Jesus' having proved his didactic superiority.

[297] Cf. *BAGD,* 401.

evidenced by the interactions that he witnessed[298]. The address probably also emphasizes Jesus' by now recognized role as teacher in Israel.
Perhaps, it also further expresses the respectful remembrance of the
special quality of Jesus as teacher, as one who taught with his own
authority, as distinct from the people of his own class, the scribes (cf.
Mk 1,22 par.; Mt 7,28f; cf. Lk 4,32).

On the other hand, scribes as a group have consistently opposed Jesus as teacher[299] taking offense at his teaching (3,6), accusing him of
blasphemy (2,7), maneuvering to trap him in word (12,13), and attempting to do away with him (12,12; 14,1). In this general context of
opposition, conflict, and enmity it is extremely significant that one of
them should react to him enthusiastically as teacher, and compliment
him for his didactic quality. That the matter in question concerns the
core demands of God, the greatest commandment in the Law, (cf.
12,28b) augments its significance even further as this is a most important matter. That on this momentous question one of them compliments
Jesus as teacher shows that there is no substantial issue that divides
them at all, and that the opposition of his colleagues towards him is
motivated and *mala fide*[300].

The scribe's compliment to Jesus as teacher is intensified further by
the following phrase, ἐπ᾽ ἀληθείας. The term ἀλήθεια points to «truth»
or «reality» as opposed to mere appearance (πρόφασις). The phrase ἐπ᾽
ἀληθείας, «in accordance with the truth»[301] thus underlines his integrity
as teacher. This too is something which has been widely recognized in
Israel, since even his enemies, in their attempt to trap him, are forced to
confess this quality of his. Thus, in 12,14b the Pharisees and the Herodians, deputed by his mortal enemies to trap him in word (12,13), and
who for this purpose bring up the thorny issue of the legitimacy of
paying taxes to Caesar, approach Jesus with a statement that they know
him to be ἀληθής, «true» (a person of integrity) and go on to state that
he «truly teaches the way of God», (ἐπ᾽ ἀληθείας τὴν ὁδὸν τοῦ θεοῦ

---

[298] Cf. S. LÉGASSE, *L'Évangile de Marc II*, 750, who observes that the scribe rec-
ognizes him as a teacher whose teaching objectively conforms to the will on God.
Following his inner approval of Jesus' response to the Sadducees (v28), he now expresses his agreement in a declaration. Similarly, R.H. GUNDRY, *Mark*, 711, who adds
that the address διδάσκαλε, is respectful and the exclamation Καλῶς which precedes it
augments it as it expresses Jesus' already demonstrated didactic superiority by the way
he dealt with the tricky Pharisees, the blundering Sadducees and now the inquiring
scribe himself. Likewise, C.A. EVANS, *Mark II*, 265.

[299] In this connection see, n.21.

[300] Cf. R. PESCH, *Markusevangelium II*, 248.

[301] Cf. *BAGD*, 36

διδάσκεις), meaning that he also teaches with integrity and without human respect. Even though this is a hypocritical reference and a motivated attempt to suborn him, it is nevertheless significant that they say so. It testifies to Jesus' acknowledged reputation as an upright teacher. In direct contrast to this deceptive use of his reputation[302] the scribe here sincerely and spontaneously affirms Jesus' quality as a teacher of integrity[303].

Secondly, the statement of the scribe is also a complimentary comment on the quality of Jesus' *teaching*[304]. This is made probable by the fact that the phrase Καλῶς,......ἐπ' ἀληθείας could be taken together, meaning «well indeed!», or with εἷς and ἄλλος referring to ὁ θεός (cf. v29)[305]. The scribe is enthusiastically in agreement with Jesus' teaching about the greatest commandment in the Law which brings together two central passages, qualifying them «the first» and «the second» most important commandments within a hierarchically-ordained whole, giving them a summary quality in it[306]. He might also be struck by the newness in this definition, and his complimentary reference might have to do with this as well. This seems to be part of the reason why he repeats the teaching in an interpretative paraphrase. It is not only an act of agreement. It also contains his reflection on Jesus' teaching, in an attempt to integrate its novelty into his Jewish frame of reference. This seems to explain the new elements in the scribe's answer, as we shall see shortly. At any rate, he is thereby quickened to go deeper in the dialogal interaction, and this is manifested in the interpretative additions of his paraphrase. Thus, one may safely conclude that the complimenting words of the scribe have both these functions. On the one

---

[302] The contrast between these two situations is striking. In the former, the compliment is paid by Jesus' enemies who employ it pompously and insincerely for bending him through flattery to trap him. In the latter, it is made by his dialogue-partner spontaneously and sincerely for recognizing his quality as a teacher of integrity to honor him. They thus create a sharp contrast between πρόφασις (pretense) and ἀλήθεια (truth).

[303] Coming from the dialogue-partner in response to the teacher's definition, this reaction of the scribe also seems to have a formal role in the interaction, in highlighting the latter as a *Dialoggespräch*. In this connection, see the proposed structure of this new form in 1.3.2

[304] Cf. C.A. EVANS, *Mark II*, 265.

[305] Cf. M. ZERWICK-M. GROSVENOR, *A Grammatical Analysis*, 149.

[306] Cf. C.A. EVANS, *Mark II*, 265. In this connection R.H. GUNDRY, *Mark*, 711, pertinently observes that the exclamation Καλῶς, διδάσκαλε, makes the following sentence start with *asyndeton*: ἐπ' ἀληθείας... and that the *asyndeton* and the forward position of ἐπ' ἀληθείας highlight the truthfulness of Jesus' speech.

hand, it is directed to Jesus as teacher, and concerns his role as a teacher of integrity. On the other hand, it concerns the quality of Jesus' teaching on the greatest commandment. He is compelled to reflect on it and react to it, which is shown in his interpretative comments.

2.3.2 His Interpretative Paraphrase (12,32-33)

Following his complimentary comments about Jesus and his teaching, the scribe adds an interpretative paraphrase of Jesus' answer which manifests a substantial dependence on the words of Jesus, as well as a creative and constructive commentary on them. We shall first briefly indicate its dependence on Jesus' definition, and then dwell on its newer elements.

The words of the scribe (vv32-33) till the phrase ὡς ἑαυτόν in v33 contain the scribe's paraphrase of Jesus' reply (vv29-31b), the rest of v33 being an interpretative addition[307]. The following points show its dependence on the definition. Firstly, there is the phrase εἷς ἐστιν. It is a clear reference to the foregoing citation of the monotheistic confession in v29, without the mention of the phrase Κύριος ὁ θεὸς ἡμῶν. Another element of dependence is the substitution of the two instances of ἀγαπήσεις, the future indicatives used in an imperative sense[308] found in them, by two substantivized and determinate infinitives with a neuter article marking their substantivization and giving them an anaphoric significance (cf. τὸ ἀγαπᾶν(2), v33)[309]. Because of the latter, they refer to the well-known texts which demand integral love of God (Deut 6,5), on the one hand, and love of neighbor as oneself (Lev 19,18), on the other[310].

In paraphrasing the modality of love required for the neighbor, the phrase ὡς σεαυτόν is rendered ὡς ἑαυτόν, which is an expected adaptation for the reported-speech employed with no modification of mean-

---

[307] Some scholars insist that the paraphrase is an expression of agreement, S. LÉGASSE, *L'Évangile de Marc II*, 751; K. KERTELGE, *Markusevangelium*, 112. ID., «Das Doppelgebot», 313, thus states that the agreeing intention of the text becomes evident when the scribe's introductory complimenting words in v32: «You are right teacher you have truly said..» (Καλῶς, διδάσκαλε,..) are seen in combination with Jesus' affirmation that «he has answered wisely» (νουνεχῶς... , v34). A.M. AMBROSIC, *The Hidden Kingdom*, 180, adds that the repetition is «typically Semitic», and also that the latter, along with the remark «he answered wisely», serves the purpose of stressing the importance of the commandment.».

[308] Cf. M. ZERWICK, *Biblical Greek*, 94, #280.

[309] Cf. *BDF*, 205, #398.

[310] Cf. *BDF*, 205-206, #399.

ing. The use of αὐτόν, the personal pronoun in v33, again refers to the κύριον τὸν θεόν of v30.

However, in the elements marking the totality of love demanded for God, only 3 terms (καρδία, σύνεσις, ἰσχύς) figure in the scribe's paraphrase, among which only καρδία and ἰσχύς are repetitions from the reply of Jesus. The two commandments are linked to each other with a coordinating καὶ in the scribe's version. Although from a formal point of view, this seems to contrast with Jesus' definition of the two commandments in a clear hierarchical gradation as «the first» and «the second», it still seems to preserve the primacy of the commandment to love God[311].

The scribe's paraphrase thus contains all the three major steps of Jesus' definition namely, the monotheistic confession, the commandment to love God single-mindedly, and the commandment to love the neighbor in their original order and sequence. It also maintains the unity of these commandments. In fact, the linking of the three elements with καὶ seems to emphasize it[312].

The paraphrase commentary of the scribe, while it is dependent on the words of Jesus, also involves a number of new emphases and nuances. As alluded to above, these include the stress on monotheism, on the reasonableness of the love of God, and the superordination of love over cult.

(1) The Monotheistic Emphasis (12,32)

The paraphrase of the monotheistic confession of the commandment to love God in v29, is rendered by the scribe thus: εἷς ἐστιν καὶ οὐκ ἔστιν ἄλλος πλὴν αὐτοῦ· (v32). As seen above, the first part εἷς ἐστιν is the equivalent of Deut 6,4 quoted in Mk 12,29a: κύριος ὁ θεὸς ἡμῶν κύριος εἷς ἐστιν. However, in the affirmation of εἷς ἐστιν, the oneness of God is underlined emphatically[313]. The copula ἐστιν, supplied in Greek, brings out the subject of whom the oneness is predicated, the κύριος ὁ θεὸς ἡμῶν of v29. The only difference here is that the scribe's words avoid the divine name, with the subject of the clause in the pronominal form contained in the verb. There are two possible reasons for

---

[311] In this connection, the observation of H. B. SWETE, *St. Mark*, 286, that the repetition of the substantivized infinitive (cf. καὶ τὸ ἀγαπᾶν... καὶ τὸ ἀγαπᾶν..., v32) is due to a desire to keep the two commandments separate is pertinent, in so far as they are mentioned in the same order.

[312] Cf. R.H. GUNDRY, *Mark*, 711-712.

[313] Cf. R. PESCH, *Markusevangelium II*, 248; J. GNILKA, *Markusevangelium II*, 165-166.

this: (1) the fact that it is a reference to the just concluded definition of Jesus, and (2) the Jewish practice of the reverential avoidance of the divine name. Of these, perhaps, the second is a weightier motive, considering that it comes from the scribe, a Jewish theologian or specialist in the Law[314].

The oneness of God is further emphasized by a contrastive negation, ruling out the existence of any other beside κύριος ὁ θεὸς ἡμῶν namely: καὶ οὐκ ἔστιν ἄλλος πλὴν αὐτοῦ· (v32). The αὐτοῦ here again avoids the divine name but clearly refers to κύριος ὁ θεὸς ἡμῶν. V32 seems to be also structured as an antithetic parallelism, wherein the first member affirms in positive terms the oneness of κύριος ὁ θεὸς ἡμῶν (Yahweh), while the second negates the existence of any other that could challenge his absolute oneness. The use of this literary pattern thus accentuates, through affirmation and negation, the stress on the absolute oneness of God remarkably.

The second part of the confession: καὶ οὐκ ἔστιν ἄλλος πλὴν αὐτοῦ· is closely dependent on three OT passages: Deut 4,35; Exod 8,6 and Is 45,21[315]. All these are contexts which underscore the uniqueness of Yahweh, unequivocally. If Deut 6,4 could be understood in a henotheistic way or as affirming Yahweh as Israel's' unique God, without necessarily denying that other gods exist[316], in these passages the possibility of such an interpretation is obviated by this negative definition, which rules out all other competitors. It is characteristic of these passages in the OT to unambiguously proclaim the monotheistic confession, and they are reflective of post-exilic theology[317]. This monotheistic emphasis which, subsequently, became characteristic of orthodox Judaism is being represented in this formulation. It thus adds a new

---

[314] Cf. M.J. LAGRANGE, *L'Évangile selon Saint Marc*, 324; V. TAYLOR, *Mark*, 488-489; C.S. MANN, *Mark*, 481. W.L. LANE, *Mark*, 433, adds that it is grounded in the third commandment (Ex 20,7). For a dissenting view see, S. LÉGASSE, *L'Évangile de Marc II*, 751, who considers the repetition of the divine name superfluous after what precedes, of which it is a paraphrase. Similarly, R.H. GUNDRY, *Mark*, 716, who adds that in reciting the *Sh'ma* twice daily the scribe would have pronounced those names any way. However, taken together with other typically Jewish elements in the words of the scribe, the former view seems to prevail.

[315] Cf. 1.3.2, in particular, n.16. In this connection, M. F. VAN IERSEL, *Mark*, 379-380 observes that by putting his approval in the form of an implicit quotation of several passages from the Scriptures, which repeat the same commandment in other words, the scribe displays his professional competence. It thus goes to reveal his quality as a Jewish theologian.

[316] Cf. Ch I, 3.2, where N. Lohfink takes this view, while M. Weinfeld rejects it.

[317] Ch I, 1.3.2, where N. Lohfink takes this position, and M. Weinfeld nuances it.

nuance which interprets the statement of the citation in v29 in Jesus' words more emphatically[318].

Besides, if Καλῶς,......ἐπ' ἀληθείας (truly) (v32) is to be taken with εἷς and ἄλλος which is a possibility[319] referring to God and his oneness, then this qualification further accentuates the uniqueness of God as an enthusiastic endorsement of it. Even if the phrase Καλῶς,......ἐπ' ἀληθείας is taken together with the meaning «well indeed!», it can also be seen as an enthusiastic exclamation at Jesus' statement in v29[320]. The term εἷς, though it means «one» in contrast to more than one, has also the sense of «single», «only one»[321]. The εἷς in v33 falls in this category with an emphasis on the character of one, thus meaning *«only one»*. The formulation thus emphasizes uniqueness in unequivocal terms. The ensemble of these nuances thus contrive to give the formulation a distinctive monotheistic emphasis, which is characteristically Jewish[322].

(2) The Reasonableness (12,33)

A second nuance that ensues in the interpretative paraphrase, is the reasonableness of the love of God. This is hinted at by the changes in the formula of the modality of love in the words of the scribe. Thus, in listing the faculties emphasizing integral love, the scribe reduces the number of terms from 4 to 3, dropping two of the original expressions in the Markan form of the commandment namely, διάνοια and ψυχή and bringing in a new word, σύνεσις. This last term is fairly close to διάνοια in that both have a connection with understanding[323]. Σύνεσις,

---

[318] Those who agree on a monotheistic emphasis here include M.J. LAGRANGE, *L'Évangile selon Saint Marc*, 325; K. KERTELGE, *Markusevangelium*, 122; G. BORNKAMM, «Das Doppelgebot der Liebe», 39; V. P. FURNISH, *The Love Command*, 28; J. GNILKA, *Markusevangelium II*, 165-166; R. PESCH, *Markusevangelium II*, 242; S. LÉGASSE, *L'Évangile de Marc II*, 751.

[319] Cf. n.305.

[320] Cf. M. ZERWICK-M. GROSVENOR, *A Grammatical Analysis*, 149. However, in this connection see also 2.3.1, in particular, n.298.

[321] *BAGD*, 231, points to Gal 3,20 (...ὁ δὲ θεὸς εἷς ἐστιν.) as an example of this.

[322] Besides, as R.H. GUNDRY, *Mark*, 711-712, observes, the omission and addition involved in the scribe's words here together bring out more clearly the connection between monotheism and undivided love.

[323] M. MUNDLA, *Jesus und die Führer*, 171-173, however, observes that while διάνοια and σύνεσις belong more to the narrower field of the discursive intelligence, the latter emphasizes the aspect of more fruitful and sharper intelligence. Similarly, G. BORNKAMM, «Das Doppelgebot der Liebe», 40-41; V. TAYLOR, *Mark*, 488-489. J. GNILKA, *Markusevangelium II*, 165-67, adds that its preference thus emphasizes the rea-

however, has further nuances of its own. While the word means in general, understanding, intelligence, faculty of comprehension, acuteness, shrewdness[324], more specifically, it means insight or understanding in the religio-ethical realm which God gives to his people (cf. LXX; Test.; Rueb.6,4; Lev 18,17)[325]. In this sense, as the references indicate, it occurs both in the LXX and in the Jewish tradition.

Here it would be instructive to recall the context of Solomon's request to God for «an understanding mind» (1Kgs, 3,9)[326] at Gibeon when God appeared to him in a dream and invited him to ask for what he wished. This is meant to serve him to «discern between good and evil», (ἐν δικαιοσύνῃ τοῦ συνίειν ἀνὰ μέσον ἀγαθοῦ καὶ κακοῦ, v9). Here it becomes clear that σύνεσις has to do with discerning understanding. God was pleased with Solomon's preference for this gift to other mundane blessings, such as long life, riches, or victory over enemies (v11). In God's response to Solomon «the understanding mind» (v9) he asked for is identified with σύνεσις (cf. σύνεσιν τοῦ εἰσακούειν κρίμα, v11). This clarifies that it is the faculty of discerning intelligence, an ability for moral discernment and judgment which is a God-given talent in the religio-ethical realm that enables one to see and choose the best moral option[327].

It is thus intelligence like διάνοια (though sharper than it), but also with a special emphasis on its religio-ethical character. The formulation of the first commandment in the words of the scribe, as in the definition of Jesus, states that the totality of one's faculties and powers must be brought to the love of God, but here he singles out discerning intelligence (σύνεσις) as an important factor in this totality which,

---

sonableness of the love of God. Likewise, R. PESCH, *Markusevangelium II*, 242-243, who, similarly thinks that it possibly stresses the rational handling of the will of God. K. BERGER, *Gesetzesauslegung I*, 180-181, on the other hand, holds that σύνεσις shortens and summarizes ψυχή and διάνοια of the definition. In a different perspective, R.H. GUNDRY, *Mark*, 710-711; 711-712 thinks that both διάνοια and σύνεσις here have the purpose of relating the distinctively scribal activity of thinking about the meaning of the OT Law to the love commandments. S. LÉGASSE, *L'Évangile de Marc II*, 751, however, holds that σύνεσις does not substantially modify the stress on intelligence, already found in διάνοια. Despite the differences, practically all these authors thus grant the sharpening of the aspect reasonableness which σύνεσις conveys.

[324] Cf. *BAGD*, 788.

[325] Cf. *BAGD*, 788.

[326] Cf. A. RAHLFS, ed. *Septuaginta*, I.

[327] Both this context, and its frequent occurrence in the Wisdom literature emphasize the character of σύνεσις as a *divine* gift and hence not as a natural capacity as among the Greeks. In this connection see, M. MUNDLA, *Jesus und die Führer*, 171-173.

given its nuances, seems to accentuate the reasonableness of the love of God.

σύνεσις occurs only twice in all the gospels, once each in Mk (12,33) and Lk (2,47). The sole occurrence in Mk, is in these words of the scribe paraphrasing the commandment to love God. In Lk it occurs in the Infancy Narratives (2,47), hence in a place which has nothing to do with the love commandment. The verse forms part of the pericope that narrates the incident of the boy Jesus being lost and found in the temple (Lk 2,41-52). Remaining back in the temple as his parents left, Jesus joined the people listening to and participating in the discussion of the Rabbis on religious questions, most likely matters relating to scriptural interpretation. Those who heard him were struck by the quality of his understanding and answers[328]. The term σύνεσις is used in this context to refer to Jesus' understanding. It has here the meaning we have seen above namely, religio-ethical insight, discerning understanding, though the aspect of perception of moral option is not to the fore. However, it covers most of the range of meanings we have seen. The other NT incidences of σύνεσις are: 1Cor 1,19; Eph 3,4; Col 1,9; 2,2; 2Tim 2,7. None of these are connected with either of the two love commandments. This means that in the NT σύνεσις occurs only once in relation to the love commandment, and this is in Mk 12,33.

In the context of the above data, the choice of the term in Mk seems to accentuate a nuance, that is, the emphasis on the intellectual faculty with a stress on religio-moral insight and discernment which adds to the understanding of the commandment to love God. It thus underlines the reasonableness of the love of God. Since the shade of meaning involved is a contribution to the conception of the commandment to love God, it also shows the scribe's dialogal interaction to be constructive and to a certain degree creative[329].

(3) The Superordination (12,33)

A third nuance that characterizes the scribe's interpretative response, is the superordination of love over cult. It is, in fact the most constructive addition to the words of Jesus found in it. The motif is

---

[328] Lk 2,47 states: «And all who heard him were amazed at his understanding and his answers», (ἐξίσταντο δὲ πάντες οἱ ἀκούοντες αὐτοῦ ἐπὶ τῇ συνέσει καὶ ταῖς ἀποκρίσεσιν αὐτοῦ.).

[329] Incidentally, this, in some measure, corroborates our identification of the new form *Dialoggespräch*, where this aspect of creative development in the interaction is an integral part. Cf. 1.3.2.

contained in his statement that the praxis of the two combined love commandments is «...much more than all whole burnt offerings and sacrifices», (...περισσότερόν ἐστιν πάντων τῶν ὁλοκαυτωμάτων καὶ θυσιῶν., v33). Although περισσότερον means «more abundant», «more», in the context it must be understood as «more comprehensive» or «far-reaching»[330]. With the following phrase in genitive of comparison (cf. πάντων τῶν ὁλοκαυτωμάτων καὶ θυσιῶν), it means «much more (more far reaching) than all whole burnt offerings and sacrifices» (v33)[331]. In this clause, the assertion is made that the double commandment of love of God and love of neighbor counts much more (περισσότερον ἐστιν) than all holocausts and sacrifices[332]. The formulation provides a comprehensive (cf. πάντων τῶν..) contrast between the properly graded unity of the two love commandments and the whole system of holocausts and sacrifices. This is a significant statement and has allusions to several passages in the OT: such as 1Sam 15,22; Hos 6,6; Amos 4,4; 5,4. 21f; Is 1,11f; Mich 6,6-8; Jer 6,20; 7,1f; 7, 21-28; Ps 40,6-8; Ps 51,15-16; 18-19; Prov 21,3.

An idea that unifies all these texts, is that God demands the fulfillment of his will manifested in the covenant, which consists in inner obedience to him and covenant justice toward the neighbor, and this cannot be substituted by purely external sacrifices unaccompanied by them. Thus, Hosea says that God looks for steadfast love (ἔλεος = חסד, which in the book of Hosea is equivalent to obedience to covenant demands), rather than sacrifices and an experiential knowledge of him (ἐπίγνωσις = דעת אלהים), rather than burnt-offerings (Hos 6,6)[333]. Similarly, 1Sam 15,2 emphasizes that sacrifices and holocausts cannot replace obedience to God, while Amos 4,4-6; 5,4-6; 5,21; Is 1,11f, af-

---

[330] Cf. M. ZERWICK-M. GROSVENOR, *A Grammatical Analysis*, 149.

[331] As R.H. GUNDRY, *Mark*, 712, observes, the scribe's paraphrase which turns the foregoing Ἀγαπήσεις, (12,29.30), into an articular infinitive (καὶ τὸ ἀγαπᾶν, v33), on the one hand, makes undivided love the subject of the statement and, on the other, the phrase «is much more than all whole burnt offerings and sacrifices» its added predicate.

[332] R.H. GUNDRY, *Mark*, 716-717, rejects the charge that the scribe weakens Jesus' statement by shifting from μείζων, «greater», to περισσότερον, «much more», and from «all» to «all burnt offerings and sacrifices», M. MUNDLA, *Jesus und die Führer*, 203-204.213; K. BERGER, *Gesetzesauslegung I*, 256-57, and says that it does the scribe an injustice since both adjectives are comparative and neither one overmatches the other in meaning. Besides, «all burnt offerings and sacrifices» limits the earlier «all» no more than Jesus' «another commandment» did (cf. vv28.31) but it selects an example of what a lesser light than Jesus might have falsely identified as the most important commandment.

[333] Cf. F.I. ANDERSEN, and D.N. FREEDMAN, *Hosea*, 430.

firm that sacrifices without justice and obedience to God are an abomination to him.

Thus, Amos rejects the national cultic celebrations, on the ground that they obscure the basic issue of justice and covenant faithfulness in which Israel has failed[334]. He avers, that a sacrificial system devoid of justice and righteousness, is false and worthless, and is in fact only an occasion for greater sin. The true seeking of God begins in the heart, and in the practice of justice and righteousness, in the pursuit of good and rejection of evil. Those who seek God in this way will encounter him anywhere[335]. In the same way, Isaiah maintains that God's demand from his people is inner conversion, expressed in shunning evil, doing good, seeking justice, correcting oppression, defending the fatherless, and pleading for the widow[336]. So long as these are missing, the people's system of sacrifices, with their variety and pomp, are plain abomination to him.

Jeremiah goes even further, and declares that such inauthentic sacrifices actually invite divine displeasure and judgment (Jer 6,20; 7,1). Mere external compliance, expressed in bringing costly materials for sacrifices (v20), will not save them, as these remain empty. People would face judgment and down-fall, in consequence of their refusal to heed the call to conversion (vv16-17)[337]. In 7,21-28, on the other hand, Jeremiah underlines the rejection of sacrifices because of their lack of religious significance, in so far as they are devoid of obedience to God, the principal command given to the people after the Exodus. He reminds them that, despite its known primacy, they have repeatedly preferred external cults to it which only brought them disaster[338].

Continuing this perspective, Micha 6,6-8, in a celebrated text of the OT that echoes the great message of the eighth-century prophets like Amos (5,24) and Hosea (6,6), states that it is none of the external gifts or sacrifices, be it the most impressive and difficult, that God seeks from his worshipper, but a humble attitude which loves to serve God and practices justice toward his fellow-human beings[339]. Similarly, Ps 40 emphasizes the primacy of obedience and interiority, while it relegates sacrifices clearly to a subordinate position in relation to it (Ps

---

[334] Cf. F.I. ANDERSEN, and D.N. FREEDMAN, *Amos*, 481.
[335] Cf. F.I. ANDERSEN, and D.N. FREEDMAN, *Amos*, 481-482.
[336] Cf. J. WATTS, *Isaiah*, 20.
[337] Cf. P.C. CRAIGIE; P.H. KELLEY, J.F. DRINKARD, JR, *Jeremiah* 1-25, 106-107.
[338] Cf. P.C. CRAIGIE; P.H. KELLEY, J.F. DRINKARD, JR, *Jeremiah* 1-25, 124.
[339] Cf. R.L. SMITH, *Micah-Malachi*, 50.

40,6-8)[340]. Likewise, the subordination of sacrifices to the interiority of «a broken and contrite spirit» expressing genuine repentance for forgiveness of grave sins is unequivocally articulated by Ps 51,15-16[341].

However, none of these texts assert that sacrifices are useless in themselves. This is particularly evident in Ps 51, which after affirming inner repentance as the real sacrifice acceptable to God for forgiveness vv15-16, still goes on to indicate a role for external sacrifices offered with the right disposition in a renewed Jerusalem in vv18-19.[342].

The prophetic position on sacrifices is shared by Proverbs as well, although it stands in the Wisdom tradition. Like the prophetic literature, it too teaches that obedience to God and justice toward fellow human beings have primacy over them. However, interestingly, it does not deal with the question of sacrifices accompanied by righteousness, perhaps because they are clearly proper[343].

Thus, in one way or the other, all these texts combine in affirming the primacy of obedience to God (love of God) and covenant justice (love of neighbor) over external sacrifices. However, they do not reject the sacrifices *per se*. Nevertheless, to be authentic and acceptable they have to be firmly based in life, and must be the expression of obedience to God and covenant justice toward the neighbor, failing which they become worthless. These texts thus converge to superordinate love of God and love of neighbor to cult.

The observation of the scribe (v33b), has to be understood in this perspective. He says that the double commandments of love of God and love of neighbor is much more than all whole burnt-offerings and sacrifices (12,32-33)[344]. Thus, the properly graded double-comm andment of love is compared to the entire sacrificial system, and the observation is made that the former counts «much more»[345]. In other

---

[340] Cf. P.C. CRAIGIE, *Psalms 1-50*, 315.

[341] Cf. M. E. TATE, *Psalms 51-100*, 28

[342] Cf. M. E. TATE, *Psalms 51-100*, 29-30.

[343] Cf. T.H. CRAWFORD, *Proverbs*, 30.

[344] R. PESCH, *Markusevangelium II*, 243, opines that especially Hos 6,6 could be the background for the cult-critical words of the scribe, as here, besides this general theme of superordination of love over cult, the term ἐπίγνωσις is also found, the latter being related to σύνεσις, figuring in the scribe's response. Although the suggestion looks ingenious, it is more likely that, as a Jewish theologian, well-versed in the scriptures, he has this rich larger background behind his comment. See, in this connection, C.A. EVANS, *Mark II*, 265-266.

[345] In this perspective, the statement of R.H. GUNDRY, *Mark*, 711, following M.J LAGRANGE, *L'Évangile selon Saint Marc*, 324, that «from the primacy of love the scribe

words, an interiorized morality, embodying the very sum and substance of Law (cf. v31b), is compared to the system of external rites, and the first is declared to be the core of the matter.

The thinking is along the same lines as in the OT passages seen above, which assert the primacy of obedience to God and practice of covenant justice toward the neighbor over sacrifices and holocausts. Similarly, the primacy of God's will manifested in the commandments is affirmed, and is opposed to the practice of purely external rites. As in the passages above, here too it is not said that the burnt-offerings and sacrifices are of no account, if accompanied by the praxis of God's will, manifested in the two love commandments. Hence, the statement of the scribe is not in itself a denial of the value of cult, but asserts the primacy of the combination of love of God and love of neighbor over it. It is when the external cult is devoid of the latter that they become valueless[346]. This clarification of the significance of the scribe's comment in v33b shows that it adds a new nuance to the discussion on the great commandment, not explicitly present in the definition of Jesus[347] and as such could be characterized as a creative contribution to the discussion[348].

---

has correctly deduced the inferiority of sacrifices in the temple» seems correct. Cf. Also, J. WELLHAUSEN, *Das Evangelium Marci*, 103;. F. D. HAUCK, *Markus*, 148.

[346] As R.H. GUNDRY, *Mark*, 716, aptly observes: «To say that loving God and your neighbor is "much more than" offering sacrifices is not to displace the sacrifices with love, but to superordinate love to them.». Similarly, J. GNILKA, *Markusevangelium II*, 166. Against C.A. EVANS, *Mark II*, 262, who takes the scribe's words as suggesting «that Jesus' teaching potentially renders the temple activities of the priests redundant» and as representing «one more criticism of the temple establishment».

[347] In this connection, the observation of S. LÉGASSE, *L'Évangile de Marc II*, 752, that the πάντων, in the phrase περισσότερόν ἐστιν πάντων τῶν ὁλοκαυτωμάτων καὶ θυσιῶν in the scribe's comment, reinforces the import of these OT texts *vis-à-vis* cult seems valid. The scribe's comment thus adds a new shade, though it is only by way of emphasis.

[348] Some point to the special sharpness these cult-critical words, especially coming from a Jewish theologian, acquire in the macro-text of the gospel, not only because these are spoken in the temple precincts, but also after Jesus' action on the temple (11,15-19), J. GNILKA, *Markusevangelium II*, 166-167; J. ERNST, *Markus*, 356, and also almost immediately before his prophecy of its destruction in 13,1f, M.D. HOOKER, *Mark*, 290. For the latter, it shows that Mk considered the scribe's words as an endorsement of Jesus' condemnation of the temple worship as inadequate.

Others see this text with its superordination of love over cult as redefining true worship of God which consists not in offering sacrifices prescribed by the Law but in the doing of the will of God expressed in love of God and love of neighbor, K. KERTELGE, *Markusevangelium*, 122. The ethicizing of the worship and the de-emphasis on sacrifices involved here corresponds to a Law-critical tendency found

Thus, the scribe's interpretative paraphrase (12,32-33) has made a number of points on Jesus' definition of the two love commandments. It reflects an enthusiastic and essential acceptance of it, and a partly creative commentary on it. As we saw above, the comments of the scribe contribute something to the whole development, and adds a new emphasis to Jesus' definition. It has thus positively contributed to the interaction, and for this reason could be justifiably termed a dialogal contribution. Concretely, it has stressed the oneness of God (v32); the reasonableness of the love of God, expressed by the addition of σύνεσις, a term, meaning the faculty of discerning intelligence in the religio-ethical realm, to the formulary of the modality of love and by the retention in it of καρδία which is considered the seat of intelligence (v33); and the superordination of love to cult (v33b).

These, however, do not alter Jesus' definition substantially. Thus, the scribe's response contains all three major steps of the definition of Jesus namely, the monotheistic confession, the commandment to love God integrally, and the commandment to love the neighbor as oneself in their original order and sequence. The stress on the monotheistic confession only puts in relief what is present in Deut 6,4. His comments do not negate Jesus' qualification of the love commandments as «the first» and «the second». The unity of the two love commandments is also maintained. In formal terms the linking of the three elements with the coordinating καί serves to emphasize their unity (v33). Besides, the scribe's enthusiastic acceptance of Jesus' answer (v32), and the general atmosphere of agreement and dialogal empathy that pervade the whole interaction, show that, despite the absence in his comments of certain details of Jesus' definition, the scribe concurs with his explicitly stated positions in it.

---

elsewhere in Mk too (2,18-22; 2,23-28; 3,1-6; 7,1-23; 11,15-19; 14,58). In these texts it involves not so much the rejection of the sacrificial system *per se* but points to the origin and core of all worship namely, the thankfulness due to the creator by creation which is none other and no better than the recognition and doing of the will of God interpreted by Jesus. The observation in 12, 34 clarifies this Law-critical interpretation of the two love commandments as corresponding to Jesus' intention, ID., «Das Doppelgebot», 320. For R. PESCH, *Markusevangelium II*, 243, on the other hand, the superordination of two love commandments over cult is a reflection of Hellenistic Judaism. While the first two points seem valid, Pesch's statement about the scribe's observation as reflecting Hellenistic Judaism seems doubtful and unnecessary because of their deep roots in the OT tradition.

2.3.3 Its Function

After having examined the answer of the scribe, which included his complimenting words as well as his interpretative paraphrase with its three-fold emphases, we shall now determine its function.

In the context of the above investigation, the comments of the scribe (12,32-33) must be said to express the endorsement and acceptance of Jesus' definition (12,29-31) in the frame-of-reference and cultural emphases of a Jewish theologian. This is particularly true about the first two nuances namely, the stress on the oneness of God (v32) and the reasonableness of the love of God (v33). The third, the superordination of love to cult (v33), though perhaps does not reflect the commonly prevailing Jewish thinking, belongs firmly to the OT heritage, especially to the prophetic tradition, as the above discussion demonstrates, and hence can also be considered as forming part of his frame-of-reference, besides being emphatically part of Jesus' teaching and praxis (cf. Mt 23,23 par.; Lk 11,4)[349]. Hence, these perspectives of the scribe's reaction must be characterized as expressing his enthusiastic agreement with Jesus in his Jewish idiom, with its typical emphases.

This also seems to be the way Jesus perceives them, considering the positive reaction that follows the scribe's comments (cf. ἰδὼν [αὐτὸν] ὅτι νουνεχῶς ἀπεκρίθη...., v34). It indicates Jesus' recognition of the perceptive nature of the scribe's comments, with their distinctive emphases. It also shows that none of these are unacceptable to him and, on the contrary, that he is in accord with them.

The standpoints in the scribe's comments thus can be characterized as an enthusiastic Jewish validation of Jesus' definition of the two love commandments[350]. They underline that fair-minded and right-thinking

---

[349] Mt saw this well and, consequently, inserted quotations of Hos 6,6 in 9,12; 12,7, R. H. GUNDRY, *Mark*, 714. Also relevant in this connection, is Jesus' cleansing of the temple (Mk 11,15-19) and his critique of the scribes (in Mk 12,38-40), both of which manifest it unambiguously.

[350] Scholarly opinion on its function include nuances that are both similar and different. Thus, J. KIILUNEN, *Das Doppelgebot*, 64, analogously, speaks of 12,32-33 as an instance of Christianity being legitimated out of Judaism. A. STOCK, *Method and Message*, 314, sees it as expressing a basic agreement between the two. Others find in it a missionary intent of wooing Judaism by means of scriptural argument, J. GNILKA, *Markusevangelium II*, 163-164, and by demonstrating that the proclamation of Jesus and the Church can be expressed in OT terms, S. LÉGASSE, *L'Évangile de Marc II*, 754. For still others, this witness by one from among Jesus' consistent enemies in Mk on his concurrence with the fundamental truths of biblical-Jewish faith, has the function of stressing his orthodoxy and, as conclusion to the Jerusalem-controversies, of exposing the ill-will of the Jewish authorities and establishing him as the fulfillment of Israelite-Jewish

Judaism is in accord with Jesus' position on the core demands of God (12,28) as being constituted by these commandments (12,29-31)[351].

Further, it seems to us, that from a narrative point of view, these have also the function to give expression to the aspect of creative contribution on the part of the scribe in the interaction, and thus to invest the pericope with an individuality as a *Dialoggespräch* since this, as we have seen, is not part of either a *Schul(Lehr)gespräch* or a *Streitgespräch*[352].

2.4 Jesus' Reaction (Mk 12,34)

Following the scribe's comments on his definition of the two love commandments, comes Jesus' reaction to him. This is characterized, on the one hand, by a positive evaluation of his words and, on the other, with an intriguing observation that he is not «far from the Kingdom of God» (12,34b). In our following consideration, we shall first dwell on the complimentary nature of Jesus' comments, and then take up its character as an invitation to a fuller understanding, and conclude with a reflection on the import of this statement.

2.4.1 Jesus' Positive Evaluation of the Scribe (Mk 12,34)

(1) His Answer as Ingenuous and Acceptable (12,34a)

The editorial comment about Jesus' reaction to the scribe's words, affirms that Jesus made his statement in v34b «seeing that he answered wisely» (cf. ἰδὼν [αὐτὸν] ὅτι νουνεχῶς ἀπεκρίθη..., v34a)[353]. It implies a positive and complimentary appraisal of the scribe's comments on the part of Jesus. The term used for «wisely» in this context is νουνεχῶς, an

---

tradition, R. PESCH, *Markusevangelium II*, 248-249; Légasse, *Ibid.*, 753-754. While these are possible, they need not be conceived as *motivated*. They could very well be based on the character of Jesus' teaching as perceived by an open-minded Jewish theologian and as the working out of its consequences.

[351] Needless to say, this validation does not include the scribe's perception and acceptance of the wider meanings of the two love commandments in the gospel as we have seen in our investigation, since these go beyond the parameters of a Jewish frame-of-reference. This, however, does not exclude the possibility that they might have a relevance in the progression of the dialogue.

[352] Cf. 1.3.

[353] C.S. MANN, *Mark*, 481, points out that the use of the accusative [αὐτὸν] as anticipating the subject of the dependent clause, is found also in 7,2; 11,32 and in one version of Lk 9,31 as well as in Lk 24,7.

adverb from νουνεχής and means «with understanding», «intelligen-tly»[354], or even «thoughtfully»[355]. A *hapaxlegomenon* in the NT which thus stresses intelligence, it underlines that the scribe has understood Jesus' teaching correctly and reacted thoughtfully to it (cf. ἀπεκρίθη....). Hence, the narrator's comment clearly implies Jesus' as-sessment of the scribe's comments as being intelligent and ingenu-ous[356] and as such acceptable, at least as far as they go. The evaluation is both complimentary to the scribe and expresses agreement between them on the question about the great commandment and its interpreta-tion to a considerable extent[357].

(2) The Qualification οὐ μακρὰν εἶ (12,34b)

After this positive estimate of the scribe's comments, Jesus tells him: «You are not far from the kingdom of God» (Οὐ μακρὰν εἶ ἀπὸ τῆς βασιλείας τοῦ θεοῦ., v34b). The phrase οὐ μακρὰν εἶ is intriguing. Οὐ μακρὰν, «not far (away)»[358], is used here metaphorically[359] in rela-tion to the Kingdom of God (cf. ἀπὸ τῆς βασιλείας τοῦ θεοῦ). The statement of Jesus evaluates the scribe and his position in relation to the fundamental thematic of Jesus' proclamation, the Kingdom of God (cf. 1,15)[360]. It contains a double emphasis, in so far as it expresses a simultaneous closeness and distance *vis-à-vis* the Kingdom[361]. In the context, it points, on the one hand, to the prevailing extent of agree-ment between the scribe and Jesus on the interpretation of the love commandment. On the other, it also hints that the agreement is not to-tal, that further steps might be necessary for full agreement, and for adequately belonging to the Kingdom. It is thus complimentary and

---

[354] Cf. M. ZERWICK-M. GROSVENOR, *A Grammatical Analysis*, 149.

[355] Cf. *BAGD*, 544.

[356] Cf. J. ERNST, *Markus*, 356. II.B. SWETE, *St. Mark*, 287, adds that the scribe displays intelligence not only in accepting Jesus' judgment about the two primary com-mandments, but in detecting and admitting the principle on which it rested namely, the su-periority of moral over ritual obligations.

[357] Cf. F. D. HAUCK, *Markus*, 148.

[358] Cf. *BAGD*, 487.

[359] Cf. *BAGD*, 487.

[360] The phrase «the Kingdom of God» (ἡ βασιλεία τοῦ θεοῦ) occurs 14 times in Mk (cf. 1,15; 4,11.26.30; 9,1.47; 10,14.15.23.24.25; 12,34; 14,25; 15,43) and appears for the first time in the programmatic summary (1,14-15) at the outset of the narrative of Jesus' Galilean ministry.

[361] As M. F. VAN IERSEL, *Mark*, 380, observes this is the only time in the gospel that someone is told that he is not far from the Kingdom of God.

thought-provoking at the same time. The verse thus provides an open and dynamic conclusion[362].

(3) Its Positive Role

The positive role of this observation, refers back to the creative comments of the scribe on Jesus' definition, with their three-fold emphases: of the oneness of God, the reasonableness of the two love commandments, and their superordination to cult. These gave the scribe's understanding of Jesus' definition a specific Jewish color, while they essentially agreed with his interpretation. Jesus' comment underlines their positive and acceptable character. His perspectives have not distorted Jesus' interpretation but has only intelligently (cf. νουνεχῶς ἀπεκρίθη...) adapted it to his Jewish frame-of-reference. Jesus' positive reaction, contained in the comment οὐ μακρὰν, shows that he appreciates them as an ingenious achievement, with which he empathizes and essentially agrees. More importantly, it implies that his interpretative version of Jesus' answer brings him close to «the Kingdom of God», the fundamental thematic of Jesus' proclamation (cf. ἀπὸ τῆς βασιλείας τοῦ θεου). Jesus' observation thus affirms the scribe's closeness to the Kingdom of God, because of his position in relation to it, manifested in his understanding of Jesus' teaching about the two love commandments.

2.4.2 Jesus' Invitation to a Fuller Understanding (Mk 12,34b)

After having seen the complementary and affirmative part of Jesus' reaction, we shall now discuss the wider import of his comment.

(1) The Hint of Insufficiency

Despite the scribe's earlier agreement with Jesus' reply to the Sadducees on the resurrection (cf. 12,28) in the previous pericope (12,18-27), and despite the considerable agreement between Jesus and him at this point, and the consequent closeness of the scribe to the Kingdom of God, Jesus' observation οὐ μακρὰν εἶ simultaneously contains also a hint that the accord is not total and that, although the scribe is close to the Kingdom, he does not actually belong to it. The comment thus seems to imply that while the concurrence is substantial, further steps are necessary to reach full agreement and to actually belong to the

---

[362] Cf. K. STOCK, «Gliederung», 495.

Kingdom[363]. The phrase thus has a certain dynamism built into it, which seems to take the problematic of complete agreement and full belongingness further[364]. In this sense, it contains an invitation[365] to go further to achieve both these by taking the steps that are necessary for them[366].

---

[363] As regards the significance of the mention of the Kingdom of God here K. KERTELGE, «Das Doppelgebot», 321-322, following J. Becker, observes that the open conclusion of the pericope makes clear that the two love commandments are «directed to» the comprehensive relationship to Jesus' Kingdom-proclamation for unlocking their precise meaning, as the distinctive teaching of Jesus, the Messiah. This seems to us to be fully valid, underlining a correct perspective.

[364] Most scholars agree on the dynamic nature of this statement, and a majority on its christological import, though they articulate these differently. Some stress the dominical authority which it evinces, E. LOHMEYER, *Markus*, 260; V. TAYLOR, *Mark*, 490. Similarly, J. GNILKA, *Markusevangelium II*, 166. Others see it as an invitation to see the person of Jesus as the embodiment of the Kingdom, C.E.B. CRANFIELD, *Mark*, 380; J. SCHNIEWIND, *Markus*, 162; E. SCHWEIZER, *Markus*, 253; J. ERNST, *Markus*, 356; M. MUNDLA, *Jesus und die Führer*, 212-213; A. STOCK, *The Method and Message*, 314. Still others take it in terms of the scribe's subjective condition *vis-à-vis* discipleship for entering the Kingdom, J. HUBY, *Marc*, 289; A. AMBROZIC, *The Hidden Kingdom*, 181; G. WOHLENBERG, *Markus*, 321, while others rule this out in favor of steps at the theoretical level, K. BERGER, *Die Gesetzesauslegung*, 201. Similarly, K. STOCK, «Gliederung», 496. Among the minority who reject its possible christological import are G. BORNKAMM, «Das Doppelgebot der Liebe», 42; C.BURCHARD, «Das Doppelgebot», 58 and V. P. FURNISH, *The Love Command*, n.12, who take it a case of «*litotes*» indicating that the scribe is on the right way to the Kingdom, with no suggestion of any lack still to be filled. S. LÉGASSE, *L'Évangile de Marc II*, 753, adds that as a judgment of Jesus it is sure and guaranteed by his authority.

The authority of the statement is undoubtedly striking, but its christological import seems to be the core of the matter. But this has to do with steps at the theoretical level as the whole pericope, indeed the whole section 12,13-37, is centered on teaching (cf. 12,14). Agreement on this level is already considerable (cf. 12,28.32-33.34b), but remains to be completed. Those who deny this and take it as *litotes* ignore the larger context, as mentioned, as well as the literary and thematic connections between 12,28-34 and 12,35-37 which necessarily carry the problematic of the former into the latter. These include the hook-word γραμματεύς and the term κύριος in v29 which provide a basis for the thematic connection between the discussion on the descent of the Messiah from the Lord God and the Lord God of the monotheistic confession. They indicate that the comment of Jesus (cf. v 34b) does involve an invitation to reflection, and to further steps on the part of the scribe to fully belong to the Kingdom.

[365] Cf. W. HARRINGTON, *Mark*, 191. Similarly, K. KERTELGE, *Markuevangelium*, 122.

[366] This, incidentally, seems to fit into the positive and dynamic character of the interaction as a *Dialoggespräch* as well.

(2) The Solution to Insufficiency

The nature of that insufficiency and how it is to be overcome seems to be revealed, with high probability, in the immediately following pericope where the descent of the Messiah is discussed (Mk 12,35-37). In this connection, it is also significant that the question is raised by Jesus himself, which seems to suggest that its content has relevance for the solution of this problem indicated by his observation[367].

By his statement Jesus seems to be calling attention to an important point which the scribe should have realized, but has not yet succeeded in, despite his intelligent reaction to his definition. Jesus' authoritative interpretation of the two love commandments with their clear gradation, their linkage and their summary character *vis-à-vis* all other commandments (and his suggestion that their interpretation hinges on his proclamation of the Kingdom[368]) involve a certain implicit claim that he is the true interpreter of God's will which should have raised questions about his identity, especially in this well-disposed and perceptive dialogue-partner[369]. As this has not happened, Jesus' pointed comment (v34b) followed by the discussion about the identity of the Messiah, a question which he himself raises (Mk 12,35-37), seems to be a delicate invitation to the scribe to reflect on, understand and accept his true identity by which his insufficiency in the way of full agreement and adequate belongingness will be remedied[370]. Thus the solution to the scribe's insufficiency seems to be offered in this discussion which follows[371].

---

[367] Significantly, this is the first time in the Jerusalem ministry (Mk Chs 11-12) that Jesus himself raises a question for discussion (in all other cases, the questions are posed by his opponents or sympathetic hearers) which may also indicate that it has to do with the problem of insufficiency he has just hinted at.

[368] Cf. K. KERTELGE, «Das Doppelgebot», 321-322. Also, n.363.

[369] Cf. J. GNILKA, *Markusevangelium II*, 167.

[370] Cf. K. KERTELGE, «Das Doppelgebot», 320-321, underlines that the reference to the Kingdom here points to the person of Jesus in whom and in whose words and deeds it has come close to people and insists that this has to be the case especially after Mk 4,11 which closely links the former with the latter.

[371] As K. STOCK, «Gliederung», 498, argues, this assumption that the pericope on the descent of the Messiah (Mk 12,35-37) contains the answer to the question as to what the scribe lacks, follows from the logic of the situation as well. Because of the pericope's close connection with the foregoing, where the scribe's position has been characterized as not fully adequate (v34b), one would expect that the missing completion would be revealed in the answer to the question which Jesus himself raises immediately after it. When this happens to be the only question raised by him and his last public interaction in the Jerusalem ministry, it becomes virtually certain that in its answer this missing completion would be found. This is further corroborated by the fact that the question is raised before all the people, with no limitation on the audience, al-

(3) The Import of Jesus' Invitation

The import of Jesus' invitation thus seems to be contained in the interrelationships that exist between the two pericopes. In this connection, the following data are important. First, the fact that the context of Mk 12, 28-34 is not only one of commandments proper (Deut 6,5; Lev 19,18) but also of Israel's monotheistic confession (Deut 6,4) forming part of the first commandment (Mk 12,29). Second, the circumstance that the definition of the commandments occurs in an animated dialogue (Mk 12,32-34) which ends in the open-ended and inviting comment: «You are not far from the Kingdom of God, v34b». Because of these the love commandment pericope with this comment of Jesus seems to connect perfectly with the following one, with its question of the descent of the Messiah (12,35-37). The answer to that question would thus seem to be the basis for the solution of the scribe's insufficiency.

In this context, as hinted at above, the fact that in the Markan version the monotheistic confession: «Hear O Israel, the Lord your God is one Lord» (Deut 6,4) has become part of the first commandment (cf. Mk 12,29), is significant. The confessional formula is about the uniqueness of the Lord God. It concentrates on the person of the Lord God and his significance. Similarly, what is discussed in the following pericope (12,35-37) has also to do with the person of the Lord God, in so far as the descent of the Messiah is discussed in relation to him. Besides, it is about the person of the Messiah and its significance namely, his real origin and descent. This concentration on the person of the Messiah and its import, parallels the concentration in the confessional formula on the person of the Lord God and its significance. The origin and descent of the Messiah, is essentially linked with the Lord God. His connection with David, is considered to be only one aspect, and that

---

though soon after this in 12,41-44 there is a change from the general public to the small group of disciples. These underline the importance of this question and the teaching it contains for the expected completion. Apart from here nowhere else in the gospel is this question of what the scribe lacks clarified. All this makes it practically certain that the answer to it is contained in the content of this pericope, as it cannot be that it is left unanswered. The point of the narrative is that, while Jesus and the scribe agree on the acceptance of the Lord God and on the basic meaning of the two love commandments, the scribe must correct his conception of the Messiah to correspond to the Kingdom of God. *Ibid.* Also, H. SARIOLA, *Markus und das Gesetz*, 202, n.56, who characterizes this as «eine berechtigte Deutung».

too a secondary one[372]. In fact, the conclusion implied in the pericope, is that the Messiah, whom David calls Lord, actually belongs to the realm of the Lord God (v37)[373]. That is his real source of origin and descent, not David. Though he is David's descendant, he is his Lord.

In so far as the pericope clarifies the true identity of the Messiah as belonging to the realm of the Lord God sharing his lordship, or rather as the one to whom the Lord God has transferred his lordship (v36), it unravels a reality that concerns the Lord God[374]. The Messiah is his Son, his descendant, though he is also linked with David[375]. Since the clarification of the true descent of the Messiah concerns an important dimension of the person of the Lord God, in so far as it affirms a relationship between the Messiah and him which also affects his lordship, it is a dimension of the monotheistic confession which proclaims the unique personal significance of the Lord God. It means that, to understand the full meaning of the lordship of the Lord God, it is important to recognize and accept the lordship of the Messiah and his essential

---

[372] In this connection, R. PESCH, *Markusevangelium II*, 252, usefully points out that in 12,35b the indeterminate υἱὸς Δαυίδ, expected in its function as predicate noun, compared to the determinate ὁ Χριστός does not emphasize the non-titular versus titular but the direction of the question which aims at the nature and quality of the sonship of the Messiah.

[373] As R. PESCH, *Markusevangelium II*, 254 underlines: «Unausgesprochen bleibt: der Messias muß, da David ihn Herrn nennt, mehr als Davids Sohn sein (vgl. Mt 12,41f), ein anderer Sohn: der Menschensohn = Gottes Sohn.». Similarly, W.L. LANE, *Mark*, 438.

[374] As S. LÉGASSE, *L'Évangile de Marc II*, 760-761, points out the terms «son of David» and «Lord» cannot go together. The second is the title which the Psalmist gives to God and, consequently, represents in our gospel an application to Jesus of a word of scripture where the term κύριος designates God (Mk 1,3). This being the case, Mk here echoes the rest of the NT where the title «Lord» addressed to Jesus is a recognition of his association with the Divinity. In relation to this transcendent status, the Davidic sonship appears as secondary.

[375] In this connection, J. GNILKA, *Markusevangelium II*, 171-172, correctly points out that although with this discussion Mk wants to clarify the Davidic sonship of Jesus in the context of the Jerusalem ministry, it is in fact relativized. This suggests that for the evangelist the question about the sonship of Christ is only answered, with the discovery that Jesus is the Son of God. Although this is not indicated in the immediate context, the emphasis on this title in the beginning, at the end, and in the middle of the gospel, establishes it sufficiently. According to him, this also shows that it is not political considerations but theological ones that moved the author to bring the Davidic sonship into the appropriate relationship. Similarly, W. HARRINGTON, *Mark*, 193, who adds that for Mk «this title (of Son of David) can be understood only when one acknowledges who Jesus is: the Son of God already on earth (1,11) destined to be exalted to the right hand of God (14,62)».

relationship of descent from him. If one limits oneself to the confession of the uniqueness of the Lord God, as the scribe does, he is only «not far» (οὐ μακράν) from the Kingdom (v34). To belong to the Kingdom, it is necessary to understand and accept this further reality. It is to this step, that the scribe is invited by this pointed and expectancy-creating comment[376].

Thus, in this pericope (12,35-37) the commandment which proclaims the uniqueness of the Lord God (12,29) is offered a wider interpretation and application[377]. This consists in the recognition of the true identity of Jesus and his singular relationship to God, whose unique Lordship is professed in the confessional formula. Recognizing and accepting Jesus' true identity as the Son of the Lord God, one realizes adequately one's relation to the Lord God and his lordship of which the commandment speaks (12,29). It is to this wider interpretation and application of the first love commandment that the scribe must progress, before he could fully belong to the Kingdom. With only the confession of faith in God as one Lord in its OT form, the scribe would only be «not far» (οὐ μακράν) from the Kingdom, and not really belong to it. Although the OT recognition of the unique God remains fundamental (12,29f; v32), this must be completed by the recognition of Jesus as the Son of this unique God (12,35-37), in whom he has manifested and realized his Lordship or Kingdom.

---

[376] That Jesus' comment here leads to the question of his identity which is discussed in the following pericope (12,35-37) is supported among others by B. WEISS, *Das Markusevangelium*, 402.404; J. SCHNIEWIND, *Markus*, 162.164; G. MINETTE DE TILLESSE, *Le Secret Messianique*, 151-52; K. STOCK, «Gliederung», 498; J. GNILKA, *Markus II*, 167; K. KERTELGE, «Das Doppelgebot», 320-321; H. SARIOLA, *Markus und das Gesetz*, 202.251; W. WEISS, *«Eine neue Lehre»*, 254. The latter also insightfully points to the significance of the occurrence of the terms σύνεσις in 12,33 and νουνεχῶς in 12,34a in leading to the motif of the recognition of the Son. He sees this already contained in v32 where the «way of God» spoken of in 12,14 is verified in the two love commandments, a point stressed by the hook-word ἐπ᾽ ἀληθείας found in both verses, though it reaches its high point when Mk links the comment of v34a with that of v34b that the scribe is not far from the Kingdom. In v32f it is made out, on the one hand, into an understanding (νουνεχῶς) of the τὴν ὁδὸν τοῦ θεοῦ in the double commandment of love, with the impossibility of belonging to the Kingdom through the cult and, on the other, into the right understanding (σύνεσις) of love of God in the confession of Jesus, the unique teacher, as the Son. *Ibid.*, 254.

[377] We may recall at this point our exegesis of the monotheistic confession as part of the first commandment, where it was found that in the context of the wider gospel the OT confession of the Lord God opens to include the lordship of Jesus as well, 2.2.3. b). The interpretation of Jesus' words in 12,34b thus confirms its truth.

2.5 General Conclusion

We have reached the end of our investigation of the love commandment pericope as text in context. It remains for us to complete our study with a general conclusion. As we have offered a summary of our inquiry at every step, we shall here synthesize the main points in their interrelationships.

(1) In our investigation of the pericope, we have, after a short introduction, depiction of its structure and form, examined it exegetically, with special stress on the text of the two commandments, to bring out its meaning in context. For this, we paid particular attention to the commandments' vocabulary in its occurrence within the gospel. The study revealed that, while the commandments retain their basic OT meaning, they also acquire distinctive Markan enrichments, resulting in a two-level meaning.

Thus, on the one hand, the gospel confirms the OT understanding of the two love commandments. On the other, an integral reading of the pericope also unravels another dimension of meaning which widens its horizon. Thus, for instance, our study of the monotheistic confession as part of the first commandment in the Markan formulation of the latter emphasizes, like Deut 6,4, Israel's call to listen, God as Lord, and the relational character of God. However, an integral reading also reveals that the gospel extends all these affirmations to Jesus, and adds further prerogatives to God and to him, such as forgiveness of sins and goodness. This produces a wholistic conception of the monotheistic confession as commandment, wherein the reality of Jesus coheres integrally in the reality of the Lord God whose acceptance also forms part of this commandment, in view of the command «to listen» at the beginning (12,29)[378]. Thus, as a part of the integral narrative, the commandment has this wholistic meaning wherein both these dimensions are coherently integrated. As we shall see, this is true of the commandment to love God which follows, as well as the commandment to love the neighbor.

However, Markan specificities are found also at the level of the pericope vis-à-vis the OT texts. These include their definition as commandments, their clear hierarchical gradation into the first and the second commandments, their unity-in-difference character within this gradation, and the commandments' summary role in relation to all others (12,29.31). These characteristics clearly go beyond the OT concep-

---

[378] Cf. 2.2.3, in particular 2.2.3 e).

tion of them, as neither Deut 6,4-5 nor Lev 19,18 had any of these peculiarities.

On the other hand, the two levels of meaning, as mentioned, are not restricted to the interpretation of the monotheistic confession, but extends to the entirety of the love commandments. Thus, in the commandment to love God integrally (12,30), this extension is seen in the content of love, the modality of love and the object of love.

On the one hand, the content of the commandment to love is understood in the OT sense, as one's inner wholistic orientation to God based on one's deliberate decision which is concretized in the observance of God's commandments, which the gospel identifies with the observance of the Decalogue (10,19). On the other, it extends this to obedience to Jesus' commands (cf. 1,17; 2,14; 8,34; 10,21; 8,17.21; 8,35; 8,38). Most fundamentally, this is accomplished by God himself in 9,7 where following God's new definitive revelation of Jesus as the Beloved Son, the disciples are commanded to «listen to him». This new fundamental commandment of God embodying God's definitive will, not only integrates into the commandments of God which the gospel values as important, such as the Decalogue and the two love commandments, but gives all the demands of Jesus divine authority, making them at once commandments of God like the former. Besides, given the fundamental character of this command, even the latter continue to be God's commandments, only in so far as Jesus takes them up and confirms them as such[379].

Although the gospel does not explicitly call the demands of Jesus «commandments», and obedience to them is not named «love», they are in fact both, because of this pivotal divine command. Besides converting them into God's commandments, in as much as to obey God's commandments is to love God, it also entails that to obey these is to love God. Thus, in the gospel to obey Jesus' commands is to love, just as much as observing the Decalogue commandments is to love[380], thus expanding the content of love. Besides, as both of these proceed from the one definitive revelation of God and his will, they are also perfectly integrated. Consequently, because of their divine identity and profound communion as the Father and the Beloved Son, to obey Jesus' words (both his demands and the OT commandments confirmed by him) is, simultaneously, to love God and to love Jesus.

---

[379] Cf. 2.2.4 a) (2)
[380] Cf. 2.2.4 a) (2)

A similar extension-integration is also seen in the modality of love. While the gospel understands it in the same OT sense of integral love (cf. the formulae of the modality in 12,30), it also translates and extends this to the modality of obedience to Jesus' commands. This too follows, most basically, from the fundamental command of God to listen to Jesus in 9,7 which is phrased absolutely (cf. ...ἀκούετε αὐτοῦ.) and which, as such, indicates that the response demanded is absolute and which, as the most fundamental commandment, also invests all the commands of Jesus with the same absoluteness. Its phrasing in absolute terms involves also that it is comprehensive and applicable to all the demands of Jesus[381]. This means that the modality of response to Jesus' commands, necessarily has the same quality as the modality of response to the commandments of God. Additionally, this also follows from the fact that obedience to Jesus' commands has an absolute character in the gospel, manifested in the manner in which they are themselves either phrased or depicted which, despite their differences, all imply absoluteness either directly or indirectly, and which thus expresses the same reality as an integral response. The gospel thus translates and extends the modality of love of God to obedience to Jesus' commands in this language or expression of absoluteness[382].

The same extension and integration is found also in the object of love. While the gospel faithfully restates the OT conception of the Lord God as the object of undivided love, it also integrates the reality of Jesus into it, in so far as he is the object of absolute obedience, which is clarified again by the fundamental absolute command of God to listen to him in 9,7, following the new and definitive revelation of God about Jesus as his Beloved Son. Given its structural similarity to 12,29-31, with the revelation of God followed by the consequent commandment of God, this unique divine command unravels Jesus as the object of absolute obedience. The disciples must listen to him because of Jesus' divine identity and unique closeness to the Father as the Beloved Son[383]. In addition, it follows from the fact that resultant from this, the absolute demands of Jesus in the gospel also focus on the person of Jesus[384].

This means, that in Mk Jesus-as-object-of-absolute obedience is most profoundly united with God-as-object-of-integral love. Indeed, because of the divine identity of Jesus and his most profound union

---

[381] Cf. 2.2.4 b) (2)
[382] Cf. 2.2.4 b) (2)
[383] Cf. 2.2.4 c) (2).
[384] Cf. 2.2.4 c) (2).

with God, decisively clarified in 9,7, Jesus-as-object-of-absolute obedience is identical to God-as-object-of-integral love. In the gospel they
merge into one reality[385], with the concomitant result that to obey Jesus
is to love God, and to obey God's commandments is to love Jesus. This
also clarifies the true basis of the translation and extension of the modality of love in the gospel to the modality of obedience to Jesus'
commands, which is this same union and identification.

(2) Similarly, the two-level meaning is seen also in the case of the
commandment to love the neighbor. While the gospel concurs with its
OT meaning at the face of it, in so far as its wording remains the same,
an integral reading reveals that the latter enriches it in regard to its
status, object and modality. Its rich OT meaning is accepted and further
deepened.
     Thus, in regard to its status, its central position in the book of Le-
viticus as expressive of the demand to imitate the holiness of God,
above all by loving the offending covenant brother, a judicial enemy,
and resident alien in caring deeds, here becomes the second most important commandment, second only to the commandment to love God
and, together with the latter, evince a character of unity-in-difference
within a hierarchically conceived totality, while they summarize all
other commandments (12,31)[386].
     As regards its object, likewise, although the gospel does not exclude
the OT understanding of it as covenant brothers and resident aliens,
inclusive of enemies among them, it extends it to all human beings
without exception, hence even as enemies (cf. 9,35; 10,44; 14,24).
These texts in so far as they insist, as the path to true greatness, the
necessary person-oriented service of all without exception, express the
preeminent attitude of the gospel vis-à-vis others and, as such, manifest
the commandment to love the neighbor and, in so doing, points to the
extension of its object to absolutely all human beings, inclusive of
enemies, thus overcoming its limitation to one's own people[387].
     Its modality, similarly, consists not only in loving «as yourself» re-
specting the equality of rights of the covenant brother and resident alien
even when inimical, but in «being last of all» and «servant of all» (9,35;
10,34), thus necessarily rendering person-oriented service to absolutely
all human beings without exception, hence even to enemies. While this

---

385 Cf. 2.2.4 c) (2)
386 Cf. 2.2.5 a)
387 Cf. 2.2.5 b)

teaching, as mentioned, reveals the gospel's pre-eminent attitude in relation to others and, as such, expresses the commandment to love the
neighbor, the disposition it embodies articulates the modality of this
love[388]. The latter is further enriched by the positive and negative illustrative models of this service, the first by Jesus' receiving the child
(9,36-37) which shows what it means to be «servant of all», thus concretely demonstrating the modality of love in the gospel. The reality of
Jesus also enters into this enrichment, not only because he is the source
of this teaching but because it is based on his life characterized by such
person-oriented service to the point of laying it down as ransom for all,
which has a paradigmatic nature *vis-à-vis* the disciples because of their
association with him as his followers (10,45)[389]. It is further ennobled
by the fact that in such rendering of humble person-oriented service of
all, especially of the lowly, it is Jesus himself and God who sent him
who are served.

The second, the negative illustrative example, on the other hand, is
offered by the comparison with the tyrannical and exploitative manner
in which worldly power is exercised by the Gentile rulers and the great
ones of the world over their subjects, which Jesus categorically forbids
as a model for the community of his disciples (cf. οὐχ οὕτως δέ ἐστιν
ἐν ὑμῖν), thus delineating the modality of love further by exemplifying
what it most certainly is not[390]. The prohibition defines in negative
terms the attitude that should absolutely never figure *vis-à-vis* the disciples' disposition to others, and hence, touches the commandment to
love the neighbor. It thus defines in negative terms what is involved in
its practice, and illustrates the negative model of the modality of love
of neighbor in the gospel.

As the concluding confirmation of Jesus clarifies, the two levels of
meanings are found integrated in the gospel, in so far as the commanding positions of Deut 6,4-5 and Lev 19,18 in their original contexts
come to be enhanced in the definition of these into the first and second
commandment within a hierarchically-constructed totality with a character of unity-in-difference. It is also seen in their summary role in relation to all other commandments[391]. These characteristics of the
commandments reach their fullness of meaning when they are seen
against the background of their integral richness in the gospel, wherein
at every point the reality of Jesus is integrated.

---

[388] Cf. 2.2.5 c)
[389] Cf. 2.2.5 c)
[390] Cf. 2.2.5 c)
[391] Cf. 2.2.6

(3) If the two love commandments in their integral reading reveal the above wealth of meaning, a study of the dialogal interaction of the scribe (12,32-34) shows that it enthusiastically affirms Jesus' definition of these commandments in their first level of meaning. Thus his words affirm and compliment both the quality of Jesus as a teacher of integrity and the quality of his teaching. The comments of the scribe contribute something to the whole development and add a new emphasis to Jesus' definition. It has thus contributed positively to the interaction and hence with good reason could also be called a dialogal contribution. The three emphases perceived in the scribe's comments: monotheistic emphasis, reasonableness and superordination of love over cult, manifest the distinctive features of a Jewish frame-of-reference which thereby affirm and integrate Jesus' definition in the latter[392]. As its function is to provide a Jewish validation of the two love commandments as far as it can go, their integral meaning does not form part of it, since the latter lies outside its ambit.

(4) Jesus' reaction to the scribe's comments, defined by dialogal empathy, friendliness and positive valuation (v34a), underlines his agreement with the scribe's understanding of his definition to a large extent[393]. However, his concluding comment «You are not far from the kingdom of God» (v34b) shows that, while the agreement is considerable, it is not total. Though it commends the scribe's sharpness and resourcefulness, it also contains a hint of insufficiency in this rider, which delicately invites him to go beyond his perception to discover its fullness of meaning, so that he could be not just «not far» but actually belong to the Kingdom.

In this connection, Jesus' raising the question of the identity of the Messiah (12,35-37) becomes significant, as the import of Jesus' invitation seems to be contained in the interrelationships that exist between it and the love commandment pericope. As we just saw, this question which critiques the inadequacy of the scribal interpretation of the issue and reveals the Messiah's transcendent origin, supplies the key to the solution of the scribe's insufficiency, as it is this recognition that he must reach as a precondition to belong to the Kingdom[394]. This identification indicates how the unique Lordship of the Lord God confessed in the first commandment (12,29b), integrates the reality of Jesus the

---

[392] Cf. 2.3
[393] Cf. 2.4.1
[394] Cf. 2.4.2

Messiah by virtue of his relationship of descent from him (12,35-37). The underlying rationale why this recognition secures for the scribe belongingness to the Kingdom, seems to be the fact that this integral conception of the Lordship of the Lord God is fundamental to the Kingdom of God-understanding of the two love commandments[395] which the gospel embodies.

(5) For this reason, this key revelation, beyond meeting the scribe's lack in belonging to the Kingdom, appears to entail further consequences. Firstly, it seems to underline the correctness of the integral meaning of the two love commandments we have seen. Not only does it corroborate our finding, that in the wholistic reading of the monotheistic confession the Lordship of the Lord God integrates the Lordship of Jesus, but it also legitimizes the other aspects of its integral meaning. This is because the latter depends on and flow from the former. Thus, from the revelation that Jesus belongs to and integrates into the reality of the Lord God and his Lordship, it follows that he shares also in these other aspects, such as his relational character and his prerogatives of oneness, goodness and forgiveness of sins. The same is also true about the rest of the two love commandments' integral meaning, in so far as these too are dependent on the reality of Jesus who integrates into the Lord God.

Secondly, the recognition that the reality of the Lord God integrates the reality of Jesus as fundamental for belonging to the Kingdom, implies that these other aspects of the integral meaning of the two love commandments have also a relationship to the Kingdom of God. Although a recognition and acceptance of these aspects is not demanded of the scribe as a precondition for belonging to the Kingdom, yet the fundamental character of the former [the recognition that the reality of the Lord God integrates the reality of Jesus being essential for belonging to the Kingdom] involves that the latter [the other aspects of the integral meaning of the two love commandments] go along with it and, as such, are also associated with the Kingdom, like it. But with the clarification of Jesus as integrating into the reality of the Lord God and his Lordship, *the key* to the recognition of these as part of the commandments' integral meaning and of their connection to the Kingdom is provided. Though not a precondition, the one who accepts this key demand thereby enters a world of which these are part, and is set on the road to recognize and accept them as part of that world. Thus, this key

---

[395] Cf. K. KERTELGE, «Das Doppelgebot», 321-322. Also, n.363.

revelation implicitly points to the other aspects of the integral meaning of these love commandments as forming part of their Kingdom of God-understanding[396].

In this context it seems also correct to say that the invitation to recognize Jesus as integrating into the reality of the Lord God and his Lordship as a precondition to belong to the Kingdom, indirectly implies an openness to the recognition and acceptance also of the other aspects of the integral meaning of these love commandments as forming part of their Kingdom of God-understanding, even though this is not explicitly demanded, nor presented as a condition of belongingness. However, further considerations on this comment actually belong to the scope of the next chapter which will investigate the «Fulfillment of the Love Commandment in the Passion of Jesus» and represents Jesus' instruction by example following his instruction by word.

---

[396] Cf. K. KERTELGE, «Das Doppelgebot», 321-322. Also, n.362.

CHAPTER IV

The Fulfillment of the Love Commandment
in the Passion of Jesus

The teaching of Jesus in 12,28-34 on the love commandment which we have seen in the previous chapter, raises the question as to how Jesus himself has lived, observed it. We shall now turn to consider this issue. Although the question can be raised and studied *vis-à-vis* the whole gospel[1], we shall confine ourselves to the Passion of Jesus[2] where it reaches its culmination[3].

---

[1] A conception that facilitates this is the approach that takes 10,45 as a programmatic summary of the whole career of Jesus defined by service in obedience to God culminating in the Passion and, as F. NEIRYNCK, *Duality*, 32-72, thinks, as a case of Markan duality. As the latter, the verse is an instance of parallel clauses constituting a two-step progression, although the parallelism is antithetical, with a first negative step (v45a), followed by a second and more precise step in the affirmative, (v45b), as D. RHOADS - D. MICHIE, *Mark as Story*, 47-48, point out. As part of a duality, the second step of the parallelism adds precision and clarification to the first. Although the negative first step clarifies the purpose of the Son of Man's coming by stating what it is not, yet the emphasis falls on the second, which not only defines the purpose of his coming positively, but also shows to what extreme extent it goes and interprets its significance in terms of its ransoming effect on all.

In this vision, the duality of 10,45 also provides the gospel the same structure at the macro-level. Thus its first half (1,1-8,27) concerns Jesus' ministry in active service of teaching, healing and exorcism and activities or episodes linked to these. The second, (8,31-16,8), on the other hand, focuses on his Passion destiny where he gives his life as a ransom for all, as the final act of such service. Although these are intimately linked, in so far as both are service, yet there is a clear progression from the first to the second. The latter represents not only the climax of the former, but it also interprets the significance of the service involved. For a similar understanding see, Rhoads - Michie, *Ibid.*, 48-49. Such an approach also underlines the Passion as the climax of the whole gospel, and justifies our concentration on it.

[2] The love commandment (12,28-34) occurs in the central section (11,1-13,37) of the second part of the gospel of Mark (8,27-16,8), I. DE LA POTTERIE, «De Composi-

1. Jesus' Passion as Love of God

In the gospel, following its OT sense, to love God means to do the will of God. This follows from the equation of love of God with the observance of the commandments, since the latter are the embodiments of the will of God. In the following treatment, we shall investigate how Jesus does the will of God in the Passion, and thus fulfills the commandment to love God[4]. It will consist in: Jesus' revelation of the

---

tione», 139-141; S. KUTHIRAKKATTEL, *The Beginning*, 52-60, and is on the one hand, preceded by the way section (8,27-10,52) which sets in motion the journey of Jesus to the cross and prepares for the events of the Passion and, on the other, is followed by the narrative of the actual events of his Passion, death and resurrection, the fulfillment of the Mystery of the suffering Son of Man (14,1-16,8).

This structural location of the commandment within the sweep of the narrative events which precede and follow it, seems to link it inevitably with them and also point to them as its christological realization. See also, M. MUNDLA, *Jesus und die Führer*, 231-233. In this connection, it is significant that it is uttered by the Messiah who is consciously moving to the Passion as the will of God for him (cf. 8,31; 9,31; 10,32-34), and as the concretion of this commandment defining his life (10,45), who will soon concur with it definitively in the prayer in Gethsemane (14,36), and speak of the cup of his blood at the Last Supper as the blood of the new covenant and as the sacrificial outpouring for all (14,24). This circumstance particularly links the love commandment and the Passion and underlines the latter as the christological fulfillment of the former.

[3] A further narrative connection between the love commandment and the Passion seems to be created by the incidence in 12,34b of the phrase «ἡ βασιλεία τοῦ θεοῦ», «the Kingdom of God». While, in the first place, this renders the important teachings in the section 12,13-34 essentially related to the Kingdom of God, the principal thematic of Jesus' Galilean proclamation (1,14-15), K. STOCK, «Gliederung», 508, the phrase also seems to link the love commandment specially to this proclamation. Indeed, the privileged occurrence of this phrase in the love commandment pericope in this section, reveals the latter to be uniquely connected to the Kingdom of God. On the other hand, this connection which the reference to the Kingdom of God in 12,34b establishes between the two, entails that the love commandment is intimately connected with the entire ministry of Jesus which centers on this theme, a point underlined by the inclusion provided by this phrase to the macro-text of the gospel (cf. 1,14-15 + 15,43). Within this general inclusion, however, the phrase further rings the Passion narrative (cf. 14,25 + 15,43) which suggests that, while Jesus' entire ministry is related to the Kingdom of God, the Passion is specially connected to it, as its most intense and climactic phase. Given the close connection of the love commandment and the Kingdom of God, this involves that, while Jesus' entire ministry is defined by this commandment, his Passion is determined by it *par excellence*.

[4] A lack of the OT understanding of the equation between love and obedience leads R. B. HAYS, *The Moral Vision*, 84-85, to assert that: «Unlike Paul and John, Mark nowhere explicitly interprets Jesus' death as an act of "love"» and that: «The way of the cross is simply the way of obedience to the will of God [...] ». But, as our detailed treatment of the love commandment in its OT context has clearly demonstrated, love of God consists in the inner holistic orientation of the human person to God based on his/ her deliberate decision

Passion as the will of God with implicit acceptance; his explicit acceptance of it as the will of God, and his living it out as the will of God.

1.1 Jesus Reveals the Passion as the Will of God with implicit Acceptance

Under this heading we shall study the texts in the gospel, in which Jesus reveals the Passion as a divine necessity for the Messiah in God's plan, and hence as the will of God for him. While this is primarily found in the concept of δεῖ (8,31), there are also several other texts which express the same reality in one way or the other, which we shall also cover briefly in this connection.

Jesus reveals the Passion as the will of God for him in a number of texts in the gospel. With their language and phraseology, all these texts characterize it as a divine necessity for him. These include: δεῖ (8,31); the Passion predictions (8,31; 9,31; 10,33f); the theological passives (9,31; 10,33; 14,41); and the other texts that depict the Passion as the will of God such as, the γέγραπται phrases: πῶς γέγραπται (9,12); καθὼς γέγραπται (9,13; 14,21); ὅτι γέγραπται, (14,27); and the contrast between divine will and human will (8,33)[5]. All these are found in the second part of the gospel[6].

---

which is concretized in the observance of the commandments, that is, in the obedience to the will of God contained in them, Ch I, 3.3.1 d). In this OT conception which Mk follows, Ch III, 2.2.4 a), obedience is the concretion of love. Consequently, Jesus' obedience to his God-willed Passion destiny is surely the expression of his love of God. Given this intrinsic connection between the two, a lack of explicit use of the term love in Mk in interpreting the Passion cannot be taken to mean that the Evangelist does not understand it as an expression of the love of God. When the gospel characterizes the Passion as obedience to the will of God, it means precisely that it is the concretion of love.

In this connection, it is also pertinent to recall that the book of Deut employs a number of synonymous expressions to denote the reality of love of God. These include «fear of Yahweh», «walking in his ways», «obedience», and «service», (Deut 10,12; cf. 11,13; 30,16.20; Ch 1, 3.3.1 b-d). All these terms involve both one's inner free holistic orientation to God and its expression in the observance of the commandments, Ibid, resulting in an equation among them.

Moreover, the intimate nexus between obedience and love is corroborated by the gospel of Jn. For this gospel obedience to the commandments is the real touch-stone of love without which there is no genuine love (cf. Jn 14,15.21.23-24; 15,9-10.14). It also explicitly speaks of Jesus' obedience to his divinely-willed Passion destiny as the expression of his love of God. (cf. 14,31). Jn's emphasis on their intrinsic connection also demonstrates that this conception cuts across the two Testaments. See also, M. MUNDLA, Jesus und die Führer, 233.

[5] Cf. S. KUTHIRAKKATTEL, The Beginning, 39-40.

[6] Cf. I. DE LA POTTERIE, «De Compositione», 138-141.

(1) δεῖ

Among the texts that reveal the Passion as a divine imperative δεῖ (8,31) is the first and the clearest[7]. This term initiates the first Passion prophecy (8,31) and hence also the whole series of such announcements in the gospel. Mk 8,31, where it figures, says: «And he began to teach them that the Son of Man must (δεῖ) suffer many things, and be rejected by the elders and the chief priests and the scribes, and be killed, and after three days rise again».

The prophecy is introduced as Jesus' teaching to the disciples. As the gospel depicts Jesus' teaching as authoritative (cf. 1,22), this teaching about his destiny has the same character. 8,31 is one of the few texts in the gospel (4,2; 8,30; 9,31; 11,17; 12,35) which indicate the content of the teaching of Jesus. It is also one of the two such texts whose teaching is reserved to the disciples, with an identical content that concerns the destiny of the Son of Man (cf. 8,31; 9,31).

The prediction has as its subject, ὁ υἱὸς τοῦ ἀνθρώπου, (the Son of Man), a literal Greek rendering of the Aramaic בר נשא or בר אנשא, which Jesus uses as a self-designation[8]. The destiny itself is described in four verbs: (1) «suffer» (παθεῖν) reinforced by the object «many things» (πολλά), which refers to the sufferings of Jesus in the Passion[9]; (2) «be rejected», (ἀποδοκιμασθῆναι) meaning to be morally disapproved and rejected after examination which refers to the role of the

---

[7] Cf. W. GRUNDMANN, «δεῖ», *TDNT*, II, 21-25.

[8] It occurs in the NT only in the gospels apart from Acts 7,56; and (without the double article) in Hb 2,6; Rev 1,13; 14,14. Though it appears in their narrative section, it is found only in the words of Jesus who by this term refers to his person. However, in Jn 12,34 [*bis*] the people repeat a word of Jesus and refers to it. The term serves only as a subject of which something is said, and it never occurs in a predicative function. In Mk, Jesus uses it in three different contexts: speaking of his authority (2,10.28); his destiny (8,31; 9,9.12.31; 10,33.45; 14,21[*bis*].41) and his parousia (8,38; 13,26; 14,62). All three Passion-resurrection predictions (8,31; 9,31; 10,33f) are referred to the Son of Man and are realized in the narrative of the Passion, death and resurrection of Jesus (Chs 14-16). For details Cf. COLPE, «ὁ υἱὸς τοῦ ἀνθρώπου», *TDNT*, VIII, 403-489. The shift from «the Christ» (v29) to «the Son of man» (cf. especially, 9,9.12.31; 10,33) is probably because of Jesus' preferring the latter phrase for oblique reference to himself, perhaps, also because of the strangeness of suffering to the prevailing notions of messiahship, R.H. GUNDRY, *Mark*, 428. For the last point see, also C.A. EVANS, *Mark II*, 16, who, following J.D. Kingsbury, adds that it thus involves a correction of Peter's confession.

[9] S. LÉGASSE, *L'Évangile de Marc*, II, 502-503, points out that it is a global reference to the details of the Passion which are then mentioned. R. PESCH, *Markusevangelium II*, 49, adds that it recalls a fundamental motif in the traditions of the suffering righteous man.

three groups of Jewish authorities, the elders, the scribes and the high priests, who constitute the Synedrion[10]; (3) «be killed» (ἀποκτανθῆναι) which points to the result of the condemnation leading to Jesus' violent death; and (4) «[after three days] rise again», (ἀναστῆναι) which expresses the overcoming of the inflicted death in the act of the resurrection[11]. These verbs in their order and totality define what is covered by the δεῖ.

The term δεῖ is an impersonal verb meaning «it is necessary» and has the sense of «divine destiny or unavoidable fate»[12]. In our text, it stresses the fact that Jesus' Passion destiny, as spelt out in the prediction, is the will of God, and hence that it is unalterable[13].

Although the term occurs 6x in Mk (cf. 8,31; 9,11; 13,7.10.14; 14,31), only 4 of these connote divine necessity (cf. 8,31; 9,11; 13,7.10)[14]. Among these 4 only 8,31 actually expresses the divine ne-

---

[10] Cf. S. LÉGASSE, L'Évangile de Marc II, 503. R. PESCH, Markusevangelium II, 49, adds that the term ἀποδοκιμασθῆναι recalls Ps 118,22, used here to refer to the rejection and condemnation of Jesus. Similarly M. D. HOOKER, Mark, 206. Likewise, C.A. EVANS, Mark II, 17.

[11] As S. LÉGASSE, L'Évangile de Marc II, 503, stresses, the resurrection appears at the end, as in the other two announcements (9,31;10,33-34), as the indispensable prolongation and counterpart to the drama just evoked. It underlines that this death is not definitive. C.A. EVANS, Mark II, 17, adds that it, in all probability, involves a reference to Hos 6,2.

[12] Cf. BAGD, 172. Several scholars emphasize the emphatic character of the term and its nuance of inevitability based on the will of God. Thus, M. D. HOOKER, Mark, 206; W.L. LANE, Mark, 300; R. PESCH, Markusevangelium II, 49; R.H. GUNDRY, Mark, 428; S. LÉGASSE, L'Évangile de Marc II, 502.

[13] W.L. LANE, Mark, 295, n.72, thinks that δεῖ in 8,31 refers to a compulsion, behind which is the expressed will of God, and corresponds to γέγραπται in 9,12; 14,21.49. Similarly, S. LÉGASSE, L'Évangile de Marc II, 502, n.30, who adds that, as an expression of the scripturally-based divine necessity, the former is synonymous to the latter. Likewise, J. GNILKA, Markusevangelium II, 16; R. PESCH, Markusevangelium II, 49; C.A. EVANS, Mark II, 16.

Regarding its content V. TAYLOR, Mark, 378, remarks that the teaching concerning Messianic suffering and death is bound up in the mind of Jesus with his sense of vocation, and thinks that it is based on a unique combination of the idea of the suffering servant of Is 53 with that of the Son of Man.

[14] The other two instances (13,14; 14,31) have different connotations. Thus in 13,14 the phrase has the meaning of «ought not to be» and occurs in reference to the desolating sacrilege in the context in the phrase: «When one sees it standing where it ought not to be....». Used with the negative particle οὐ, it thus has the nuance of «what is not proper», BAGD, 172. In 14,31, on the other hand, it conveys the idea of an inner necessity growing out of a given situation, Ibid., and occurs in Peter's boastful claim that he would not deny Jesus, even if it means dying with him. Neither of these thus implies divine necessity.

cessity of the Passion, while the other 3 imply divine necessity in other contexts and *vis-à-vis* other realities[15].

The occurrence of δεῖ in the first announcement of the Passion itself serves to highlight at the very outset of Jesus' references to the Passion their character as the unalterable will of God. It also gives perspective and clarity to the rest of the Passion predictions and the remaining texts dealing with the necessity of the Passion, although the term is not repeated in them. It qualifies all these and the whole destiny of Jesus with its different stages and details as determined by the will of God. While people do act, what they do is integrated into the salvific plan of God. For this reason, this first prediction defined by δεῖ is the most important, expressing its character as divine revelation of the Passion as God's determined will which Jesus announces and shares with his disciples. On the other hand, this sharing announcement of his God-willed Passion destiny also points to Jesus' implicit acceptance of it. Both its characterization as his teaching (cf. Καὶ ἤρξατο διδάσκειν αὐτοὺς ὅτι.., v31) and the narrator's further comment that he spoke plainly about the matter (cf. καὶ παρρησίᾳ τὸν λόγον ἐλάλει.,v32) also indicate this implicit acceptance.

(2) The Passion Predictions

Apart from the prediction in 8,31 articulated by δεῖ, there are two other Passion announcements in the gospel which occur in 9,31 and 10,33-34 respectively. It is noteworthy that the first prediction (8,31) immediately follows the Messianic confession of Peter in the middle of the gospel at Caesarea Philippi (8,29b), which indicates that it is meant to reveal the true nature of Jesus' messiahship as the suffering Son of

---

[15] Thus in 9,11 it occurs in the disciples' question to Jesus regarding the scribal teaching that Elijah must come first, a belief with which Jesus concurs, while maintaining that he has already come in the person of John the Baptist. Here, δεῖ has the meaning of divine necessity and connotes that it is according to the pre-determined plan of God, J. GNILKA, *Markusevangelium II*, 41. Similarly, in 13,7 it occurs in the apocalyptic discourse, in reference to the beginning of woes, where Jesus says: «And when you hear of wars and rumors of wars, do not be alarmed; this must take place..». Here too it clearly expresses divine necessity, as these are thought of as divinely-ordained, and hence must take place. In 13,10 likewise, it also figures in the apocalyptic discourse in the context of Jesus' prediction about the persecutions the community would undergo (13,9-13), where he adds that «..The gospel must first be preached to all nations». It thus also involves divine necessity, in so far as it suggests that it is the pre-determined will of God that this should happen first.

Man[16]. It is further clarified and reinforced by the second (9,31) and the third (10,33f) predictions. These occur at further points in the «way section»[17] (8,31-10,52) where Jesus is on a journey that will eventually take him to Jerusalem[18]. Thus the second (9,31) is made as Jesus passes through Galilee on his journey, and the third (10,33-34) as the destination of this journey is clearly specified as Jerusalem for the first time (cf. 10,32.33). These announcements, made as Jesus and the disciples are «on the way» (cf. ἐν τῇ ὁδῷ), also serve to emphasize the way involved as a journey to the Passion[19].

All three predictions are occasions where Jesus formally announces his Passion destiny as the will of God. Their revelatory character is indicated by the language used, which expresses divine necessity. While the first prediction presented this by means of δεῖ, the other two employ theological passives to articulate the same (cf. παραδίδοται in 9,31 and παραδοθήσεται in 10,33).

The three-fold schema of these announcements, formally made by Jesus himself, also underlines their importance as divine revelation concerning his Passion[20]. Additionally, its repetitiveness serves as a

---

[16] This becomes clear from the fact that the time, place and persons involved in 8,31f remain the same as in the former episode (8,27-30), with only the thematic of the identity of Jesus as the Messiah followed by the clarification of the nature of the messiahship involved. In this connection, see also W.L. LANE, *Mark*, 292-293; C.A. EVANS, *Mark II*, 16.

[17] Cf. I. dE lA POTTERIE, «De Compositione», 139-140; See also, Ch III, n.237.

[18] Thus in 8,27 Jesus goes on with his disciples to the villages of Caesarea Philippi; in 9,30 he passes through Galilee; in 9,33 he comes to Capernaum; in 10,1 he goes to the region of Judea and beyond the Jordan; in 10,32f they are on the road going up to Jerusalem, and in 10,46 they come to Jericho. Although only in 10,32.33 Jerusalem is explicitly mentioned as the destination for the first time, it is implicit from the beginning as the journey begins at Caesarea Philippi, Israel's northernmost and farthest point, and winds its way to the Jewish capital. This is suggested by the mention of «the elders and the chief priests and the scribes» in 8,31, since the holy city is their seat of power.

[19] The phrase ἐν τῇ ὁδῷ in the way section (cf. 8,27; 9,33.34; 10,17.32.46.52), embodies the theological motif of Jesus' way to Jerusalem, climaxing in his Passion and death, a way the disciples should also follow. Its occurrence in 8,27 and 10,52, the beginning and end of this section, functions as an inclusion and constitutes the intervening section as a unity defined by this theme, I. dE lA POTTERIE, «De Compositione», 139-140; S. KUTHIRAKKATTEL, *The Beginning*, 53. See also, D. RHODES - D. MICHIE, *Mark as Story*, 70, who point to the «funneling effect» the journey produces for the whole gospel story causing the settings of the story channel the characters, the conflicts, and the actions toward a dramatic conclusion in Jerusalem, thereby intensifying the latter's climactic character.

[20] Cf. W.L. LANE, *Mark*, 293.

concrete means of instruction of the disciples, enabling them to pro-
gressively accept the Passion destiny of the Messiah which diametri-
cally contradicts their expectations about him[21].

Among the three Passion predictions, the second is the shortest, and
says: «The Son of man will be delivered into the hands of men, and
they will kill him; and when he is killed after three days he will rise.».
It is thus not detailed, and indicates only the essential facts and stages
of the fate of the Son of Man, and is crafted in a formulation that fits
the lot of every righteous sufferer[22]. Its first verb παραδίδοται, («will
be delivered»), though in the present form, has a future value[23], and as
passive, globally denotes the fate which will befall Jesus.

The phrase «to be delivered into the hands [of men]» (παραδίδοται
εἰς χεῖρας [ἀνθρώπων]), in 9,31 is a Semitic idiom found both in the
OT and in the NT in both active and passive voices[24]. The hand is a
symbol of power[25] and hence the picturesque phrase indicates the
handing over of the Son of Man into the power of men with all that it
implies[26]. Thus it underlines Jesus' being exposed to the hatred, cru-
elty, arbitrariness and malice of people and becoming the fatal victim
of these vicious forces to the point of being dubbed a blasphemer and a
messianic pretender and unjustly condemned to death and crucified.

However, the use of the passive could also involve the affirmation
that the handing over in question does not lie outside God's providence,
but is in fact integrated into God's salfivic plan. It is thus a theological

---

[21] Cf. W.L. LANE, Mark, 293.

[22] Cf. R. PESCH, Markusevangelium II, 99.

[23] Cf. R.H. GUNDRY, Mark, 504; R. PESCH, Markusevangelium II, 99; Also, S.
LÉGASSE, L'Évangile de Marc II, 559, n.7.

[24] Thus, in the OT (LXX) the phrase is found in the active in Deut 1,27; Jer 33,24;
Jdth 6,10; 1Macc 4,30; 1 Esdr 1,50; and in the passive in Jer 39,4.36.43; Sir 11,6; Da
11,11. In the NT it occurs in the active in Act 21,11; and in the passive in Mt 17,22;
26,45; Mk 9,31; 14,41; Lk 9,44; 24,7; Act 28,17. BAGD, 614. R.H. GUNDRY, Mark,
503, adds that the phrase «into the hands of men» indicates oppressive and violent treatment. Similarly, J. GNILKA, Markusevangelium II, 54.

[25] Cf. M. ZERWICK-M. GROSVENOR, A Grammatical Analysis, 137.

[26] As J. GNILKA, Markusevangelium II, 54, puts it: «Das einprägsame Wortspiel
artikuliert das Skandalon der Passion, das darin besteht, daß Gott seinen Erwählten der
brutalen Gewalt der Menschen preisgeben wird.». R. PESCH, Markusevangelium II, 99,
adds, that it corresponds to the Jewish theology of the just sufferer, and perhaps that
of the suffering Servant. Likewise, S. LÉGASSE, L'Évangile de Marc II, 561. Also,
C.A. EVANS, Mark II, 57, who, however, thinks that the reference is to Dan 7,13-14.

passive[27]. As such it stresses the fact that the action and deed are an expression of the will of God and is intended by God. In and through the chain of human actions God's purpose is realized, so that it becomes at the same time a divinely-intended event, with the human agency cohering into the divine plan[28]. The prediction further speaks of the people's negative action of killing Jesus (ἀποκτενοῦσιν) being reversed in time by the resurrection (ἀναστήσεται)[29]. Thus, the second Passion prediction expresses the divine necessity of the Passion by means of the use of theological passive.

The third Passion prediction, clearly placed «on the way» of Jesus and the disciples to Jerusalem (10,32.33), characterizes its content in a summarizing expression in the introductory verse as τὰ μέλλοντα αὐτῷ συμβαίνειν, («what was to happen to him», v32) which thus plainly indicates this as the future destiny of Jesus and also clarifies «the Son of Man» in the prediction as himself (v33). The prediction, addressed to the Twelve, states: «Behold, we are going up to Jerusalem; and the Son of man will be delivered to the chief priests and the scribes, and they will condemn him to death, and deliver him to the Gentiles; and they will mock him, and spit upon him, and scourge him, and kill him; and after three days he will rise.».

The phrase:«Behold, we are going up to Jerusalem..» (Ἰδοὺ ἀναβα ίνομεν εἰς Ἱεροσόλυμα,...) with which Jesus begins this prediction reveals in itself that he has implicitly accepted his Passion, since Jerusalem is the place of this divinely willed destiny and the announcement of his journey to it indicates his determination to face it.

Coming to the prediction itself, among the future verbs which speak of the Son of Man there, the first and the last are in the third person singular, while the intervening ones are in the third person plural. The first, παραδοθήσεται, («will be delivered»), is a theological passive and hence refers, not only to the action of Judas (cf. 3,19; 14,10) but also to the plan of God (cf. 9,31; 14,41). Thus, as above, there is here the inter-

---

[27] Those who emphasize this interpretation include: V. TAYLOR, *Mark*, 403; M. D. HOOKER, *Mark*, 226; J. GNILKA, *Markusevangelium II*, 54. See also, C.A. EVANS, *Mark II*, 57.

[28] Cf. K. STOCK, *Boten*, 157-158; W.L. LANE, *Mark*, 337; M. D. HOOKER, *Mark*, 350; R. PESCH, *Markusevangelium II*, 99; S. LÉGASSE, *L'Évangile de Marc II*, 560.

[29] R. PESCH, *Markus II*, 99, speaks of the prediction thus dominated by the contrast-schema «killing - rising» found in 8,31. Similarly, S. LÉGASSE, *L'Évangile de Marc II*, 561.

twining of the divine and the human agencies[30], the latter cohering within and serving the over-arching plan of God who has intended the event in all its concreteness[31].

The last, ἀναστήσεται, speaks of the conclusive action of the Son of Man who will rise. Such inclusion also shows that the intermediate human actions do not have a definitive significance. Thus, the prediction has the same structure as 9,31[32]. Hence, the third Passion prediction, like the second, expresses the divine necessity of the Passion by means of another theological passive, and thus interprets it as the certain will of God for Jesus.

(3) Other Theological Passives

Apart from the second and third Passion predictions, 14,41 also employs a theological passive to express the divine necessity of the Passion. This last instance occurs at the end of Jesus' agonizing prayer in Gethsemane. Although he had asked his three disciples, Peter, James and John, the inner circle of the Twelve whom he had taken along with him to witness this critical event in his life to remain and watch while he went ahead and prayed, when he came to them in between his prayer at three different times, he found them asleep. At the third encounter after his prayer, being now ready and resolute to face the ordeal, as he

---

[30] Among these the authorities named are the high priests and the scribes. Among the human actions, their juridical actions are mentioned at first: condemnation to death (cf. 14,64) and handing over to Pilate (cf. 15,11), and then in a crescendo, come three forms of maltreatments: mocking (cf. 15,20.31), spitting upon (cf. 14,65; 15,19), scourging (cf.15,15), and finally killing. All these verbs have their object in the singular referring to the Son of Man, except the term ἀποκτενοῦσιν. See also, S. LÉGASSE, L'Évangile de Marc II, 629.

[31] Cf. J. GNILKA, Markusevangelium II, 97; R. PESCH, Markusevangelium II, 149; A. STOCK, Method and Message, 279; S. LÉGASSE, L'Évangile de Marc II, 628-629. Failure to recognize the interlocking of human and divine agencies with the former's integration into the latter leads R.H. GUNDRY, Mark, 507, to deny a theological passive in the passion predictions and to claim that following up the passive with an active, referring to human action in 10,33; 14,41-42, undermines it.

[32] Cf. R. PESCH, Markusevangelium II, 149. In this connection, the view that this Passion prediction is a vaticinium ex eventu with the vocabulary of the Passion Narrative, as V. TAYLOR, Mark, 438; A. STOCK, Method and Message, 277, et al. claim, is to be rejected, as the sequence in the prediction does not reflect that in the PN. Thus, W.L. LANE, Mark, 375, notes that «the more precise details in verse 34 are actually enumerated in the inverse order in which they occur in Ch 15,15-20; moreover, there has been no attempt to conform the vocabulary of the prophecy to the fulfillment (see Ch 15,15).». For more details see, Lane, Ibid. See also, R.H. GUNDRY, Mark, 574-575; S. LÉGASSE, L'Évangile de Marc II, 626, n.2; C.A. EVANS, Mark II, 106.109.

found them still asleep, Jesus tells them in friendly irony: «It is enough» and adds: «the hour has come; the Son of Man is handed over (παραδίδοται) into the hands of sinners...» (v41).

The term παραδίδοται is a theological passive. In this case, the implied divine agency seems to be stressed more emphatically. This becomes clear from the second part of the clause where it is said that the Son of Man is handed over «into the hands of sinners», a reference to the people who are involved in Jesus' arrest and process. This act of being handed over to the sinners, who are in opposition to God, is the act of God. The emphasis on the divine agency is also clear from the clause that precedes which speaks of «the hour» that has come. The hour is the divinely appointed hour, for the Son of Man to be handed over[33]. The action of the human agencies, «the sinners», is at a different plane which fits into the divine plan. Thus, the whole Passion destiny is thought of as divinely-willed and brought about by God in all its historical actuality, although the text in this case highlights the divine agency as pre-eminent in the interplay of the two[34]. The statement again reveals the Passion as God's unalterable will for Jesus which he shares with his disciples.

Thus, our survey of the instances of theological passives relating to Jesus' Passion, both in the Passion predictions (9,31; 10,33f) and in 14,41, has shown that the latter is divinely-willed, with God as its principal agent. There is, however, the causality of a chain of human agents who act to bring this about historically. But these integrate into the over-arching divine plan. These theological passives in Jesus' Passion-announcements to the disciples thus reveal it as the firm will of God for him.

(4) The γέγραπται Phrases

While the above texts express divine necessity by means of δεῖ and theological passives, the γέγραπται phrases express the same by means of the idea of scriptural necessity. They do so by stating that something is scripturally necessary by means of such phrases as: πῶς γέγραπται (9,12), καθὼς γέγραπται (9,13; 14,21), ὅτι γέγραπται (14,27).

These phrases involving scriptural necessity express divine necessity because the Scriptures are the embodiment of God's will, and hence what they state must necessarily happen. The above 3 types of phrases denoting scriptural necessity employ the term γέγραπται preceded by

---

[33] Cf. V. TAYLOR, *Mark*, 557; R. PESCH, *Markusevangelium II*, 394.
[34] Cf. J. GNILKA, *Markusevangelium II*, 263.

terms like πῶς (9,12), καθὼς (9,13; 14,21) or ὅτι (14,27)[35] . These are
the only instances of such γέγραπται phrases in Mk expressing scriptural necessity. We shall now proceed to study these.

πῶς γέγραπται (9,12)

This phrase, a combination of the interrogative particle πῶς[36] with
γέγραπται, a perfect passive, meaning «in what sense is it written?» occurs in 9,12. The use of the perfect tense underlines the continuance of
the effect of the action of being written to the present as a perduring,
lasting reality[37] . Underlining this nuance we may translate the phrase:
«How (in what sense) does it stand written?» The will of God expressed in the Scriptures perdures, and as the will of God it must certainly happen. It also demands obedience. The phrase thus expresses
divine necessity because of the inevitability and finality of the expressed will of God involved.

In 9,12 Jesus asks this question partly in answer to the disciples who
queried him about the scribal belief that Elijah must (δεῖ) come first
(v11)[38] . Agreeing with this belief, he says that Elijah does come first to
restore all things but goes on to pose a question regarding the Son of
Man's Passion destiny of which the Scriptures testify: «And how is it
written of the Son of Man that he should suffer many things and be
treated with contempt?» (9,12b). The question seems to imply that
these are at variance and have to be reconciled. Elijah would, indeed,
return and the Son of Man would suffer many things and be treated
with contempt. Both are right and according to God's will (cf.
γέγραπται, vv12b,13)[39] .

Jesus then goes on to identify in the appearance, ministry, and fate
of John the Baptist the return of Elijah and the fate he met with. He
also seems to imply by the question about the Passion destiny of the
Son of Man, that in the fate of Elijah returned, identified as John, there

---

[35] The term γέγραπται actually occurs 7 times in Mk but of these two, (1,2, καθὼς
γέγραπται; and 7,6, ὡς γέγραπται), do not express scriptural necessity but introduce
the biblical passages cited. These have thus a purely reporting function. A third instance, 11,17, though it emphatically expresses the divine will for the temple as a
house of prayer for all the peoples, does not express a destiny willed by God, and
hence does not belong to the group of γέγραπται texts expressing scriptural necessity.

[36] Cf. *BAGD*, 732.

[37] Cf. M. ZERWICK, *Biblical Greek*, 96, #285.

[38] R.H. GUNDRY, *Mark*, 446, rightly points out that this allusion, along with the explicit appeals to Scripture in Mk 9,12; 14,21, and the use of δεῖ at 9,11 in a paraphrastic
quotation of Mal 3,23 (4,5), show that δεῖ refers to scriptural necessity (cf. Lk 24,26 with
24,27; Jn 20,9; Act 3,21).

[39] Cf. W.L. LANE, *Mark*, 325, n.34.

is the foreshadowing of the destiny of the Son of Man whom John was to precede and usher in. The use of γέγραπται thus concerns the Passion destiny both of the precursor and the Messiah, and emphasizes that both are a scriptural necessity, and hence that they are both a divine necessity[40]. It thus contains a revelation on the part of Jesus of his Passion as the will of God.

καθὼς γέγραπται (9,13)

Another instance of γέγραπται implying divine necessity occurs in 9,13 preceded by καθὼς, thus constituting the formula, καθὼς γέγραπται. Its context is the same. After posing the question about the scriptural necessity of the Son of Man's suffering destiny, Jesus asserts solemnly that Elijah has come and they did to him whatever they pleased, adding, «as it is written of him», (καθὼς γέγραπται ἐπ' αὐτόν, 9,13). As we have just noted, Jesus here identifies Elijah returned in the person, ministry, and fate of John the Baptist, and implies that the passion destiny of John, Elijah returned, is according to the Scriptures[41] and therefore involves divine necessity. Jesus also affirms in this identification that John was treated as Elijah had been (1Kg 19,2.10). John paid for his mission with his life as Elijah was persecuted and threatened with death because of his mission (cf. 1Kg 18,20-40).

Although this text does not directly deal with Jesus' Passion, yet in so far as the passion of John is spoken of in relation to the Passion of the Son of Man (cf. 9,12), it does indirectly imply the latter also and as such involves a revelation of the Passion destiny of Jesus.

καθὼς γέγραπται (14,21)

In 14,21 there is yet another γέγραπται statement introduced by καθὼς appearing in the context of the Last Supper. As the meal got underway, Jesus foretells his betrayal by one of the Twelve. As the disci-

---

[40] Cf. M. D. HOOKER, *Mark*, 220; R.H. GUNDRY, *Mark*, 465; J. GNILKA, *Markusevangelium II*, 42; S. LÉGASSE, *L'Évangile de Marc II*, 538-539. See also, C.A. EVANS, *Mark II*, 44.

[41] As W.L. LANE, *Mark*, 326, n.35, notes, it is necessary to assume that the phrase «even as it is written of him» refers to prophet Elijah in the framework of his historical ministry, since no passage of Scripture associates suffering with Elijah's eschatological ministry, and there is no evidence that pre-Christian Jewish apocalyptic circles expected Elijah to face suffering upon his return. See also, S. LÉGASSE, *L'Évangile de Marc II*, 539-540. In fact, the concept of Elijah's sufferings is alien to the Jewish expectations of his role as the Restorer. In this sense, Lane, *Ibid.*, n.36, the suffering of the Elijah returned and, even more, his identification with the captive, murdered prophet John, a *dead* Elijah, is just as offensive as the statement that crucified Jesus is the Messiah. Mk has thus radicalized and transformed the Elijah expectation even while the old framework is preserved.

ples were sad at his announcement and began asking him one by one whether it was he, Jesus replies that it was one of the Twelve who was dipping bread into the dish with him and then adds: «For indeed the Son of Man goes as it is written of him but woe to that man by whom the Son of Man is betrayed. It would have been better for that man if he had not been born», (14,21).

The formulation clarifies that the Son of Man goes as marked out for him in the Scriptures which expresses the will of God. What stands written (γέγραπται) in them is the Passion destiny of the Son of Man. While he freely and faithfully accepts that destiny, the one who betrays him would not be without guilt because of this[42]. In fact, the guilt of betrayal would be so great and reprehensible that it would have been better if the betrayer had never been born[43]. Thus the statement involves a clear revelation of the divine necessity of the Passion and hence its nature as the will of God[44]. It also shows implicitly that Jesus fully accepts God's will.

Moreover, the phrase, «the Son of Man goes..» (ὑπάγει) in this statement, taken in itself, is also significant. It is a euphemistic reference to dying that is actively accepted by Jesus and corresponding to the will of God manifested in the Scriptures. A comprehensive reference to the Passion and death of Jesus found in Mk only here, this

---

[42] For M. D. HOOKER, *Mark*, 337, this conception «demonstrates the way in which Mk holds together divine predestination and human freedom: Judas is the one by whom Jesus is betrayed, an act of treachery so vile that it would have been better for the man if he had never been born; but he is also the one through whom God achieves this purpose to hand Jesus over to his executioners.». Similarly, W.L. LANE, *Mark*, 503. Likewise, J. GNILKA, *Markusevangelium II*, 238. Also, S. LÉGASSE, *L'Évangile de Marc II*, 864.

[43] These words are construed differently by different scholars. Thus V. TAYLOR, *Mark*, 542, thinks that the «woe»' pronounced over him is not a curse, but a cry of sorrow and of anguish: «Alas! for that man» and takes the saying «it were better.., etc.» not as a threat, but as a sad recognition of facts. Similarly, J. GNILKA, *Markusevangelium II*, 238, thinks that, although the statement refers to the eschatological judgment, it does not necessarily imply damnation. W.L. LANE, *Mark*, 503, on the other hand, holds that the purpose of Jesus' poignant warning is not primarily to affirm the fate of Judas but to emphasize his own assurance of vindication, although the betrayer is morally responsible for his action and for the horrible character of its consequences, both for Jesus and for himself. For a somewhat harsher view see, S. LÉGASSE, *L'Évangile de Marc II*, 865. Also, C.A. EVANS, *Mark II*, 378.

[44] However, the γέγραπται here is a global reference and not a specific one to an individual text, though it probably refers to the Servant Songs of Isaiah (cf. Is 42,1-4; 49,1-6; 50,4-11; 52,13-53,12). Cf. J. GNILKA, *Markusevangelium II*, 238. However, R. PESCH, *Markusevangelium II*, 351, thinks that Ps 41 (also 55,13f) might be in view.

phrase also thus manifests Jesus' implicit acceptance of his God-willed Passion destiny[45].

ὅτι γέγραπται (14,27)

The context of this text is Jesus' prediction as he walks to the Mount of Olives with his disciples after the Last Supper (14,26) about the falling away and scattering of the disciples following the crisis of his Passion. He says: «You will all stumble» and to substantiate this he quotes the Scriptures (Zech 13,7) with the introductory formula ὅτι γέγραπται, «for it is written»: «I will strike the shepherd, and the sheep will be scattered,» (v27), and adds: «But after I am raised up, I will go before you to Galilee» (v28).

The latter quotation from Zech 13,7, constitutes a messianic oracle which is closely linked with Zech Chs 9-11[46]. The sword that strikes is Yahweh's sword of judgment which usually strikes Israel's enemies but also those within Israel who disobey his word. But in exilic or post-exilic sources, it also reflects the destruction of Yahweh's own people as a group including its leaders[47]. In this context the shepherd image must refer to Israel's ruler as in the usage of Jeremiah and Ezechiel, both of whom have strongly influenced Zechariah[48].

Yet, given its eschatological setting, it has also an eschatological meaning. In the latter sense the theme of the oracle is understood as the theme of God's shepherd being smitten for the sheep. The striking of the shepherd is part of God's design. Though it destroys temporarily, yet this deed of judgment has a saving intent[49]. After the death of the shepherd, a remnant of his flock will be purified and saved. However, its immediate result is the falling away, the scattering, of the sheep. But

---

[45] Cf. J. GNILKA, *Markusevangelium II*, 238. Similarly, R. PESCH, *Markusevangelium II*, 351.

[46] V. TAYLOR, *Mark*, 548, points out that in the quotation in v27 from Zech 13,7 both the Hebrew and the LXX have the imperative «Smite», and that the use of the future in Mk may be due to either early *Testimonia* (cf. Swete, 337), or to original in the Hebrew, or to Jesus himself (cf. Lagrange, 383). M. D. HOOKER, *Mark*, 344, thinks that the change underlines the point that even human weakness and hardheartedness are part of the divine purpose. What happens is both foretold in scripture and accepted in obedience by Jesus.

[47] Cf. C.L. MEYERS - E.M. MEYERS, *Zechariah 9-14*, 384.

[48] Cf. C.L. MEYERS - E.M. MEYERS, *Zechariah 9-14*, 385. The passage thus refers to Israel's tragic history of its king and princes being captured and put to death at the end of the monarchic period, with the monarchy in this way effectively finished and its people either slain or scattered. It thus points to the catastrophic events of the end of monarchic rule. *Ibid.*, 387.

[49] Cf. J. GNILKA, *Markusevangelium II*, 252-253; C.A. EVANS, *Mark II*, 401.

eventually, this smiting of the shepherd would bring about healing and salvation for the remnant.

This pattern is verified in the gospel in relation to Jesus and his disciples[50]. Following the prediction of the striking of the shepherd[51] and the falling away of the sheep[52] Jesus foretells that he would go before the disciples to Galilee. After his redeeming death (10,45) he would be vindicated by God and then he would go before them to Galilee, like the shepherd before the flock (14,28), leading them into a new future[53]. The text thus reveals Jesus' Passion destiny and its scattering impact on the disciples which, despite this, will ultimately end both in his vindication and in the restoration of the community of his disciples as being a scriptural necessity, and thus as the will of God.

(5) Contrast between Divine Will and Human Will (8,33)

The gospel underlines the same idea of divine necessity of the Passion by contrasting the Divine will and the human will[54] which the polarity between «the things of God» (τὰ τοῦ θεοῦ) and the «things of humans» (τὰ τῶν ἀνθρώπων) in 8,33 expresses. Its context is Peter's reaction to the first Passion prediction (8,31) where Jesus strongly reacts to his attempt to dissuade him from his way, so firmly clarified by him (cf. καὶ παρρησίᾳ τὸν λόγον ἐλάλει, v32)[55] as a matter of divine

---

[50] Cf. R. PESCH, *Markusevangelium II*, 380; R. GUNDRY, *Mark*, 845; S. LÉGASSE, *L'Évangile de Marc II*, 877.

[51] R. PESCH, *Markusevangelium II*, 380, thinks that the nearness of 14,25 to this text implies the shepherd's giving of his life for the sheep as in Jn (cf. 10,11.14-15).

[52] It is significant that in vv 27.29 «being scandalized» (cf. σκανδαλισθήσεσθε, v27; σκανδαλισθήσονται, v29) is spoken of in absolute mode, without the addition of a qualifier, as in Mt. (cf. ἐν ἐμοι, and ἐν σοί in Mt 26,31.33). It would seem that Mk, by not choosing to add such precisions, wants to emphasize that the Passion of the master is the scandal *par excellence* for the disciples, resulting in deep disturbance, loss of trust in Jesus, and disruption in their following of him. See also J. GNILKA, *Markusevangelium II*, 252. Likewise, S. LÉGASSE, *L'Évangile de Marc II*, 877, who adds that this is literally verified in 14,50 at the arrest of Jesus.

[53] Cf. J. GNILKA, *Markusevangelium II*, 253; C.A. EVANS, *Mark II*, 401, who adds: «[...] implicit in the promise to "go before you" is anticipation of regathering the sheep that had been scattered when the shepherd was struck down (in v27, quoting Zech 13:7.». Likewise, S. LÉGASSE, *L'Évangile de Marc II*, 878, who further observes that the prophecy also contains comfort and pardon for the disciples.

[54] Cf. S. KUTHIRAKKATTEL, *The Beginning*, 40.

[55] R.H. GUNDRY, *Mark*, 431, points out that: «The addition of παρρησίᾳ, its placement in first position after the conjunction, and the advance of τὸν λόγον to second position, ahead of the verb, put great weight on the point that Jesus really did teach the disciples beforehand about his passion and resurrection.». C.A. EVANS, *Mark*

necessity for him (cf. 8,31). Jesus uncompromisingly rejects Peter's suggestion with the words: «Get behind me, Satan! For you do not think the things of God, but of men.» (Ὕπαγε ὀπίσω μου, σατανᾶ, ὅτι οὐ φρονεῖς τὰ τοῦ θεοῦ ἀλλὰ τὰ τῶν ἀνθρώπων, v33).

The first part of this reaction : «Get behind me, Satan», (Ὕπαγε ὀπίσω μου, σατανᾶ,)[56] is a command of Jesus to Peter to return to his place behind the master as disciple to follow his lead. By his present misadventure Peter has relinquished his position as disciple and is playing the role of Satan, the adversary of God and, in so far as he is attempting to divert Jesus from his divinely-willed destiny, he is even personifying Satan[57]. Hence he is commanded to get back in line[58] where he belongs as a disciple[59].

II, 18, adds that with the phrase Mk is emphasizing that Jesus spoke of these events not metaphorically but quite literally.

[56] Cf. M. ZERWICK-M. GROSVENOR, *A Grammatical Analysis*, 133, V. TAYLOR, *Mark*, 380, understand this to mean: «Get out of my sight, Satan». In this sense these words recall Mt 4,10, Ὕπαγε, Σατανᾶ· and suggest that Peter's interposition implies the same kind of temptation Jesus faced in the wilderness, that of accepting the popularly expected messianic role. Likewise, M. D. HOOKER, *Mark*, 206. However, since Mk must be interpreted primarily in terms of Mk, the correctness of this view must be decided on the basis of the precise role of Satan in the gospel.

[57] In this connection, the similarity between the action of Satan described in 4,15 in the explanation to the parable of the sower and the action of Peter in 8,32 is striking. In the former, Satan comes and immediately carries away the word of Jesus (αἴρει τὸν λόγον) from people. In the latter, Peter reacts immediately against the word of Jesus (cf. τὸν λόγον ἐλάλει, v32) without even a modicum of willingness to receive it. Peter is thus acting like Satan in opposing Jesus' divinely-revealed Passion destiny. In this connection, C.A. EVANS, *Mark II*, 19, correctly observes that Jesus' use of this epithet is adjectival referring to Peter's current role and not an identification.

[58] Cf. M. D. HOOKER, *Mark*, 206-207; R.H. GUNDRY, *Mark*, 433; J. GNILKA, *Markusevangelium II*, 17; R. PESCH, *Markusevangelium II*, 54; C.A. EVANS, *Mark II*, 19.

[59] This understanding of the command of Jesus is supported by the parallelism between Δεῦτε ὀπίσω μου, (1,17) and Ὕπαγε ὀπίσω μου, (8,33). Both have a similar formulation: an imperative connoting motion followed by an indication of the place one must occupy. The first command is the call of Peter and Andrew as disciples; the second, the command here. Following this parallelism, the latter must be construed as the command that recalls Peter's call to discipleship and puts him back on its track. This is particularly so because the phrase ὀπίσω μου is a characteristic term for discipleship in the gospel (6 times in Mk and except for 13,16, nearly always in the combination ὀπίσω μου [in 1,20 the form is ὀπίσω αὐτοῦ.], that is, in relation to the person of Jesus, save in 1,7 where it refers to John the Baptist (cf. 1,17; 8,33.34). The appellation «Satan» does not make this understanding strange, as M. D. HOOKER, *Mark*, 206-207, remarks, as this is explained by Peter's current role in deflecting Jesus from the path of God where he personifies Satan. (cf. n.57). Cf. Also, R.H. GUNDRY, *Mark*,

The second part of the reaction gives the reason for Jesus' stern disapproval: «For you do not think the things of God, but of men.», (ὅτι οὐ φρονεῖς τὰ τοῦ θεοῦ ἀλλὰ τὰ τῶν ἀνθρώπων). The phrase τὰ τοῦ θεοῦ in this statement means the things that pertain to God, the concerns of God[60]. In the context, it is the divinely-willed Passion destiny of Jesus[61]. This is contrasted to the τὰ τῶν ἀνθρώπων, the things of men, the concerns of humans. The latter, what humans consider important and strive after, stand in direct contrast to God's will[62]. In so far as Peter opposes the divinely-willed Passion destiny of Jesus, he is intent on (φρονεῖς) these. He lets himself be determined by τὰ τῶν ἀνθρώπων, in opposition to τὰ τοῦ θεοῦ. This sharp contrast wherein Peter is shown to be opposed to the Passion destiny announced by Jesus, the τὰ τοῦ θεοῦ in the context, underlines implicitly that this destiny is determined by God (cf. δεῖ in 8,31)[63]. By this uncompromising position *vis-à-vis* the will of God regarding his future, Jesus thus once again reveals it as the will of God for him.

Concluding Summary

The foregoing study has shown that the gospel presents Jesus as revealing the Passion as the unalterable will of God for him in a variety of texts. While this is most fundamentally seen in the δεῖ in 8,31 which speaks of it in terms of divine necessity, the same revelation is also made in the other Passion predictions (9,31; 10,33f) where Jesus formally and openly announces his divinely-willed future to his disciples. It is clarified in particular by the theological passives found in these predictions (9,31; 10,33) and outside them (14,41) in the gospel which, while they underline the intertwining of the divine and the human agencies, integrate the latter in the overarching character of the former. Further, the same idea of divine necessity of the Passion is expressed by the γέγραπται texts (9,12; 9,13; 14,21; 14,27) that speak of its

---

433; J. GNILKA, *Markusevangelium II,* 17; R. PESCH, *Markusevangelium II,* 54; S. LÉGASSE, *L'Évangile de Marc II,* 507; C.A. EVANS, *Mark II,* 19.

[60] Cf. M. ZERWICK-M. GROSVENOR, *A Grammatical Analysis,* 134.

[61] Cf. R.H. GUNDRY, *Mark,* 433; R. PESCH, *Markusevangelium II,* 55, who adds that it refers clearly to the δεῖ of 8,31. Similarly, C.A. EVANS, *Mark II,* 19. Likewise, J. GNILKA, *Markusevangelium II,* 17, despite the suggestion that the contrast weakens the enormity of the danger for discipleship of rejecting the crucified and fits better in 7,8.

[62] This contrast seems to reflect contexts in the gospel where humans appear in a certain contrast to God (cf. 7,7f; 10,27; 11,30.32; 12,14).

[63] Cf. R. PESCH, *Markusevangelium II,* 55; C.A. EVANS, *Mark II,* 19.

scriptural necessity, in so far as the latter is an expression of the will of God embodied in them. Finally, the gospel expresses the divine necessity of the Passion in the contrast between the τὰ τοῦ θεοῦ and the τὰ τῶν ἀνθρώπων in 8,33 where Jesus rebukes Peter's attempt to divert him from his Passion as the revealed will of God, in so far as in the context the contrast clarifies his just announced Passion destiny (8,31) to be the τὰ τοῦ θεοῦ which must always prevail. Through this rich variety of texts the gospel thus portrays Jesus as unambiguously revealing the Passion as the determined will of God for him and as implicitly accepting it.

1.2   Jesus explicitly Accepts his Passion as the Will of God (14,36; 14,41; 14,49)

After having seen in the foregoing section how Jesus reveals the Passion as the will of God for him, we shall now see how he explicitly accepts it in obedience to God, which constitutes the second step in his fulfillment of the commandment to love God. While this is basically seen in 14,36 in Jesus' clear-cut and formal acceptance of the will of God in the prayer in Gethsemane, it is further revealed as a frame of mind in 14,41 at the end of his prayer, and in its character of resoluteness in 14,49 in the context of his arrest. Together, these texts and contexts clarify the second step in Jesus' fulfillment of the commandment to love God, as in these he categorically goes beyond revealing the Passion as the will of God to its explicit and unambiguous personal appropriation.

1.2.1   Jesus' Formal Acceptance of the Passion (14,36)

We shall first see how Jesus explicitly and formally accepts the Passion as the will of God for him during his prayer in Gethsemane in 14,36.

While the texts we saw in the previous section unequivocally reveal the Passion as the determined will of God for Jesus, they do, as we have noticed, more than just communicate this bare information and actually intimate Jesus' implicit concurrence with this divine will as part of his destiny. This is particularly clear in 8,33 where Jesus violently rejects Peter's attempt to deflect him from this fate as the will of God for him, identified as the τὰ τοῦ θεοῦ, and assigns that attempt to the τὰ τῶν ἀνθρώπων which stands in diametric opposition to it. Nevertheless, these texts we shall now investigate focus on the aspect of

Jesus' explicit and formal acceptance of the divine will and as such reveal it explicitly and formally.

Thus, the gospel's account of Jesus' prayer in Gethsemane presents his struggle with the bitter prospect of the Passion and his reverent and trustful request to his Father to remove it if it is possible, with the readiness to accept it if that is his will, the latter pointing to his explicit acceptance of it.

On reaching Gethsemane Jesus, after instructing the rest of the disciples to sit there while he prayed (14,32), takes Peter, James and John, the inner circle of the Twelve, with him and shares with them that he was profoundly sad and troubled and asks them to remain there and watch (14,34)[64].

Jesus thus manifests extreme anxiety and sadness at the beginning of this prayer (14,33f)[65]. In this context, the falling on the ground mentioned in v35 and expressed with the imperfect (cf. ἔπιπτεν), may indicate this state of mind more than an act of reverence[66]. Jesus' prayer was a long and intense one and both these qualities of it are also indicated by the imperfect προσηύχετο (v35). However, although he thrice (v41) interrupts his prayer to reach out to the threesome whom he had asked to remain and watch but who in fact failed to do so, still there is no change in the content of the prayer (v39) which remains the same to the end. The content itself is presented both in indirect (v35)[67] and in direct speech (v36)[68].

The prayer form in direct speech has four elements: address, affirmation, request and resignation. All the elements in this prayer form

---

[64] M. D. HOOKER, *Mark*, 348, points out that the command to the three disciples to keep watch picks up the theme of the final parable in Mk 13 (cf. 13,32-37).

[65] J. GNILKA, *Markusevangelium II*, 259, thinks that v33b characterizes Jesus as the righteous sufferer in the words of lamentation Psalms (cf. Ps 42,6.12; 43,5). Similarly, R. PESCH, *Markusevangelium II*, 389, who adds that they also express his reaction before the danger of death, while R.H. GUNDRY, *Mark*, 867, holds that, besides the fear of death, the treachery, the disloyalty and the denial by his disciples as well as the knowledge that he would be handed over into the hands of sinners also contributes to it.

[66] Cf. R.H. GUNDRY, *Mark*, 854-85; C.A. EVANS, *Mark II*, 410.

[67] R. PESCH, *Markusevangelium II*, 390, stresses that the conditional clause in the version of the prayer in the indirect discourse, εἰ δυνατόν ἐστιν, does not contradict the almighty power of God (v36b) but expresses Jesus' surrender to the will of God. Similarly, J. GNILKA, *Markusevangelium II*, 261.

[68] V. TAYLOR, *Mark*, 553, thinks that this procedure of reporting in both assures the reader's attention and adds that the mention of the «hour» in v35 has eschatological significance (cf. Dan. 9,40.45), here connoting the fulfillment of Jesus' Messianic destiny. M. D. HOOKER, *Mark*, 348, observes that it picks up from 13,11 and v32, the crucial hour of testing. Similarly, J. GNILKA, *Markusevangelium II*, 261.

are formulated in the second person singular with a direct personal address to God his Father. In 14,36 the address has the form Αββα ὁ πατήρ,, «*Abba*, Father», which is a combination of the Aramaic and the Greek terms, found only twice again in the NT (cf. Rom 8,15; Gal 4,6)[69].

The term ὁ πατήρ, substitutes the vocative[70] and hence is a direct address. Αββα is the Greek transliteration of the Aramaic term אבא, and is an irregular emphatic used vocatively (its expected regular form being אבא) of the substantive אב, «father»[71]. All the three NT uses of אבא (Mk 14,36; Gal 4,6; Rom 8,15) seem to confirm it as this form, since they accompany it with the Greek equivalent ὁ πατήρ. The term אבא was for long considered as originally belonging to the language of small children[72] embodying the familiar relationship between a child and its father[73] and Jesus was claimed as having such a relationship with God his Father expressed in his address of God with this term, considered distinctive of him[74].

Recent research has, however, altered this understanding[75]. As is being pointed out, there is now an example of the author of the Dead Sea Scroll prayer-psalm addressing God in Hebrew as «my Father» (4Q372: אבי), and in the Greek OT there are several instances of Jews speaking to God as «Father» in prayer[76]. The Gospels portray Jesus

---

[69] J. A. FITZMYER, «*Abba* and Jesus' Relation», 31, points out that, while this formula may reflect a customary usage in Hellenistic communities, the retention of the Aramaic אבא along with the Greek ὁ πατήρ, its Greek rendering, when the vocative πατήρ was being used to address God in some Greek-speaking communities (cf. Lk 22,42; Jn 17,1.5.11.25), actually supports the contention that אבא was indeed *ipsissima vox Jesu*. It was preserved in Jesus' own mother-tongue even in these communities, precisely as the sign of his use of it. Similarly, M. D. HOOKER, *Mark*, 348.

[70] Cf. *BDF*, 81, # 147, 2.; J. A. FITZMYER, «*Abba* and Jesus' Relation», 19.

[71] Cf. J. A. FITZMYER, «*Abba* and Jesus' Relation», 17-24.

[72] Cf. G. KITTEL, «Αββα», *TDNT*, I, 6; J. JEREMIAS, *Abba*, 59-60.

[73] Cf. G. KITTEL, «Αββα», *TDNT*, I, 6; J. JEREMIAS, *Abba*, 59-60.

[74] Cf. G. KITTEL, «Αββα», *TDNT*, I, 6; J. JEREMIAS, *Abba*, 59-60.

[75] A synthetic presentation of the state of research on this question is found in, G. SCHELBERT, «Abba, Vater!», 257-281. However, a more recent critical summary of the important issues involved in this discussion is offered by R.E. BROWN, *Death of the Messsiah I*, 172-175.

[76] Cf. 3 Macc 6,3; Wis 14,3; Sir 23,1, E.M. SCHULLER, «The Psalm», 67-69, especially 77. It must, however, be noted that most biblical usage, whether in Hebrew or Greek, of «Father» for God is in relation to corporate Israel (Deut 32,6; Isa 63,16) and that usage by an individual appears very seldom and then too only in the last period before Jesus: Sir 23,1,4, a text found only in Greek and in canticles like Sir 51,10 (in Hebrew) and 1QH 9,35 where the individual may be speaking collectively, J. A.

using various expressions to address God such as «My Father» and «Father» (πατήρ μου, πάτεπ, πατήρ) and it cannot be assumed that all represent Aramaic אבא[77]. In fact, Mk 14,36 is the only instance of the term in the gospels which is in Greek transliterated form. On the other hand, research has revealed that in attested Aramaic for the period 200 BC-200 AD אבי is normal for a child's address «My father».The term אבא, where it occurs during this period, is found in contexts where it is clearly used by adults to address or refer to their father[78]. This shows that the understanding of אבא in Jesus' usage as representing the language of small children («Daddy») is no longer tenable[79].

A further important datum is that only in literature to be dated after 200 AD does אבא replace אבי in addressing an earthly parent. Besides, even here it is not used of God in the Mishna, and only once in the Onkelos and Jonathan Targums (Mal 2,10 being a statement and not an address). When all this is taken into consideration, it becomes clear from the available evidence that Jesus' use of אבא to address God is highly unusual[80]. For this reason, it does point to Jesus' consciousness of his relationship with God[81], although it is not the only datum in the gospel tradition that expresses it [82].

FITZMYER, «*Abba* and Jesus' Relation », 25-26.; R.E. BROWN, *Death of the Messsiah I*,173.

[77] Cf. R.E. BROWN, *Death of the Messsiah I*, 172-173.

[78] Cf. J. A. FITZMYER, «*Abba* and Jesus' Relation», 22; .J. BARR, «'Abbā», 38, who adds that this datum also corresponds to the NT usage, since wherever Αββα is used there, it is translated with ὁ πατήρ, or πατήρ, that is, with a term used by adults and not with a diminutive, despite ancient Greek possessing a diminutive like «ὁ πάπας» apt for the purpose.

[79] Cf. J. BARR, «'Abbā», 28-47, who convincingly elaborates this point.

[80] Cf. R.E. BROWN, *Death of the Messsiah I*,173. As J. A. FITZMYER, «*Abba* and Jesus' Relation», 28, after surveying relevant linguistic and historical data about this term observes: «There is no evidence in the literature of pre-Christian or first-century Palestinian Judaism that *'abbā'* was used in any sense as a personal address for God by an individual — and for Jesus to address God as *'abbā'* or "Father" is therefore something new.».

[81] As J.P. MEIER, «Jesus» *NJBC* (78),1323, observes: «[....]one is justified in claiming that Jesus' striking use of *Abba* did express his intimate experience of God as his own father and that this usage did make a lasting impression on his disciples.».

[82] In this connection, see J. A. FITZMYER, «*Abba* and Jesus' Relation», 36, where the author broadbases the source of Jesus' unique relationship to God, in addition, also on Lk 10,21-22 and Mt 11,25-27 which refer to the knowledge that the Son has about the Father and the knowledge that only he can transmit to his followers.

The fact that it is the only instance of Αββα in the Synoptic gospels is significant[83]. The gospel transmits to us this term in Jesus' original language precisely in his prayer of Gethsemane, the occasion of his greatest test of obedience towards his Father. In doing so it underlines that «[....]as characteristic of Jesus it expresses a new relationship to God: the Sonship of Jesus manifested in his unconditional obedience in 14,36.»[84]..

After this filial address, Jesus confesses the almighty power of God and says: «All things are possible to thee», (πάντα δυνατά σοι, v36)[85]. Thus, even at this critical point he is absolutely certain of God's ability to accomplish all things. With this trustful certainty he directs his request to the Father to be freed from the bitter destiny[86] that is near, qualifying this request with an ἀλλά clause: ἀλλ' οὐ τί ἐγὼ θέλω ἀλλὰ τί σύ, «Not what I will but what thou willst», (v36).

Although Jesus' address to God with the term Αββα ὁ πατήρ, at this point of crisis underlines in itself his attitude of obedience, his trust in God is manifested also in this request to be freed of the bitter destiny with the full awareness of his Father's almighty power which he explicitly affirms (v36)[87]. But it is in the concluding qualifier: ἀλλ' οὐ τί ἐγὼ θέλω ἀλλὰ τί σύ[88], «not what I will but what thou willst» (v36)[89]

---

[83] As R. PESCH, *Markusevangelium II*, 391, comments: «Jesu Gebet in v36 überliefert mit der Anrede das Herzstück seines Gottesglaubens.»

[84] R. PESCH, *Markusevangelium II*, 391.

[85] R.H. GUNDRY, *Mark*, 855, points out that the ellipsis (ἐστιν) between πάντα and δυνατά σοι emphasizes the almighty power of God and (indirectly) all the more that Jesus' crucifixion will be God's will. See also, C.A. EVANS, *Mark II*, 418.

[86] The «hour» (v35) and «the cup» (v36) of which Jesus speaks are symbols of the fate which looms large as his Passion destiny. According to V. TAYLOR, *Mark*, 554, the cup Jesus asks to be taken away is not just of personal suffering and death, but also of redemptive suffering, involving the bearing of sin, which seems to be indicated by the bewilderment and anguish of ἐκθαμβεῖσθαι καὶ ἀδημονεῖν M. D. HOOKER, *Mark*, 349, adds that the cup image has already been used for Jesus' sufferings and death in 10,38. Similarly, S. LÉGASSE, *L'Évangile de Marc II*, 889; Likewise R. PESCH, *Markusevangelium II*, 390.

[87] Thus M. D. HOOKER, *Mark*, 349, points out that the prayer is set, on the one hand, in the context of an affirmation of God's power and, on the other, of the acknowledgment that God's will must be done, which thus manifests Jesus' obedience to God. Similarly, S. LÉGASSE, *L'Évangile de Marc II*, 890.

[88] R. PESCH, *Markusevangelium II*, 391, points out that the prayer closes with an address to God (cf. σύ), as it began (cf. Αββα ὁ πατήρ,). This inclusion underlines Jesus' prayer as utterly centered on God, his Father.

[89] As W.L. LANE, *Mark*, 518, states: «Jesus' desire was conditioned upon the will of God, and he resolutely refused to set his will in opposition to the will of the Father». Similarly, S. LÉGASSE, *L'Évangile de Marc II*, 890, who adds that the word of Jesus

that Jesus reaches the culmination of his prayer, in so far as it fully and unambiguously expresses his obedient surrender to God's will[90].

In this process of acceptance of the will of God, the reference in 14,39 of Jesus' return to his prayer after reaching out and exhorting the three sleeping disciples to watch and pray (v38) saying the very same words (cf. καὶ πάλιν ἀπελθὼν προσηύξατο τὸν αὐτὸν λόγον εἰπών.), underlines his single-minded application to surrender to the divine will. As such, it symbolically manifests Jesus' loving God with all his heart, with all his soul, with all his mind, and with all his strength (12,30).

1.2.2 Jesus' Acceptance as a Frame of Mind (14,41)

While 14,36 demonstrates Jesus' clear and formal acceptance of the will of God, 14,41 reveals this acceptance as an established frame of mind which we shall now see.

Jesus' acceptance of the will of God is further seen in his words of reaction to his failed disciples at the end of his prayer: «It is enough; the hour has come; the Son of man is handed over into the hands of sinners» (vv41b-42). While several interpretations are proposed for the term «it is enough» (ἀπέχει)[91] in this , the most appropriate in the context seems to apply to Jesus himself and may point to the end of his prayer and his reaching full accord with the divine will[92]. More pre-

---

gives in advance a full and unconditional acceptance of the will of God. Likewise, R. PESCH, *Markusevangelium II*, 391. R.H. GUNDRY, *Mark*, 854-85, observes that «both the strength of the adversative ἀλλά, its repetition and the further ellipsis in «but [I request] not what I want, but [I request] what you [want]» underscore the admirableness of Jesus' subordinating his will to that of his Father.»

[90] Cf. M. D. HOOKER, *Mark*, 349; G. SCHRENK, «θέλω», *TDNT*, III, 49, expresses the mystery of this obedience of Jesus, the Beloved Son (1,11; 9,7), to his Father thus: «This synthesis in His life of omnipotent and effective will on the one side and patient obedience in lowliness on the other is most clearly and radically expressed in the balanced ἀλλ᾽ (πλὴν) οὐ τί (οὐχ ὡς) ἐγὼ θέλω ἀλλ᾽ ὡς σύ of His prayer in Gethsemane [....]. Here the position of the Son is as follows. Humanly he has the possibility of an independent will, but this will exists only to be negated in face of the divine will. Its perfect agreement with the divine will finds agreement in the declaration of this negation.»

[91] As M. ZERWICK, *Biblical Greek*, 45, #132, notes, the term ἀπέχει means receiving what is due to one, perhaps payment of a debt. Based on this the following explanations are suggested: it may apply to Judas and may mean that he has received the sum agreed upon; or it may refer to the disciples and may mean that they have slept enough. Similarly, R.H. GUNDRY, *Mark*, 856. For a different view see, C.A. EVANS, *Mark II*, 416-417, who takes it as a question meaning «is it [i.e. the end] far off?», implying it is not.

[92] Cf. J. GNILKA, *Markusevangelium II*, 263.

cisely, it might mean that now his free activity is over and the decisive turn is taking place with the pre-determined will of God manifesting itself. This last, in fact, is supported by the correspondence between 14,35 (ἵνα εἰ δυνατόν ἐστιν παρέλθη ἀπ' αὐτοῦ ἡ ὥρα), the passing of the hour for which Jesus prays, and 14,41 (ἦλθεν ἡ ὥρα, ἰδοὺ παραδίδοται ὁ υἱὸς τοῦ ἀνθρώπου εἰς τὰς χεῖρας τῶν ἁμαρτωλῶν.)[93], where he affirms the coming of the hour of the Son of Man's being handed over. This correspondence between the two texts about the hour also indicates the difference between the two situations[94]. If in the first Jesus prays for the removal of the hour in freedom, in the second he no longer prays for this, but announces and accepts his being handed over, the divinely determined destiny. Thus, it demonstrates his having accepted the will of God, especially coming after his formal surrender to it[95]. His further statement: «Rise let us be going; see my betrayer is at hand» (v42), goes even further in disclosing this attitude of acceptance as an established frame of mind by revealing his readiness to face it[96].

1.2.3 The Resoluteness of Jesus' Acceptance (14,49)

Jesus' acceptance of the divine will in 14,36, seen as a frame of mind in 14,41, is revealed in its character of resoluteness in 14,49 which we shall now clarify.

Jesus' attitude of acceptance of the will of God is also displayed by 14,49 where he reacts to the crowd of enemies led by Judas come with swords and clubs to arrest him. He asks if they have come out like this as against a robber to capture him and reminds them that, although day after day he was among them in the temple teaching, they had not seized him, concluding with the saying: «But [this has happened] in order that the Scriptures might be fulfilled.», (ἀλλ' ἵνα πληρωθῶσιν αἱ γραφαί, 14,49).

---

[93] As M. D. HOOKER, *Mark*, 350, points out, this is a theological passive with its idea of the intertwining of the human and the divine agencies. Cf. 1.1. (3).

[94] Cf. W.L. LANE, *Mark*, 522.

[95] Cf. J. GNILKA, *Markusevangelium II*, 263. Similarly, R. PESCH, *Markusevangelium II*, 394 who says: «An der Schwelle zur Verhaftungsszene zeigt der Menschensohnspruch erneut nachdrücklich an, daß Jesus, der sich im Gebet dem Willen des Vaters unterworfen hat, bewußt, in Erfüllung des Willens Gottes, in den Tod geht.». Likewise, W.L. LANE, *Mark*, 522; M. D. HOOKER, *Mark*, 350; S. LÉGASSE, *L'Évangile de Marc II*, 895; C.A. EVANS, *Mark II*, 417.

[96] Cf. W.L. LANE, *Mark*, 522; M. D. HOOKER, *Mark*, 350; R.H. GUNDRY, *Mark*, 858; S. LÉGASSE, *L'Évangile de Marc II*, 895.

The term ἀλλά in the latter clause marks the change of direction from the foregoing considerations and initiates the ἵνα clause[97] expressing the purpose of the happening, the fulfillment of Scripture.

The formulation πληρωθῶσιν αἱ γραφαί, like γέγραπται, is a theological passive and emphasizes that the Scriptures contain the will of God. Jesus sees in this moment the fulfillment of what is expressed in the Scriptures concerning his destiny[98]. Obedience to the divine will expressed in the Scriptures is thus clearly manifested in this saying[99]. The reference to his habitual teaching activity in the temple contained in the periphrastic formulation of the verb in v49 (ἤμην + διδάσκων), during which no one arrested him, despite its offering those who wanted it several occasions for doing so, is meant to suggest that they did not attempt it because it was then not yet the appointed time for the divine will to be fulfilled. They do arrest him now because this time of fulfillment has arrived and so he surrenders to it in obedience. Thus, this statement of Jesus about the fulfillment of the divine will embodied in the Scriptures also clearly demonstrates his attitude of full acceptance of it. Coming immediately after his formal acceptance of his destiny in the preceding prayer (14,36), which is additionally revealed as a frame of mind in 14,41, this further points to the resolute character of that acceptance[100].

---

[97] Most scholars take this as an ellipsis. Thus, R.H. GUNDRY, *Mark*, 880, holds that: «It is better to fill in an ellipsis (but [this has happened] in order that the scriptures would be fulfilled) than to reject a normally telic ἵνα in favor of an abnormally imperatival ἵνα ("but let the Scriptures be fulfilled")». Similarly, J. GNILKA, *Markusevangelium II*, 271; R. PESCH, *Markusevangelium II*, 401; S. LÉGASSE, *L'Évangile de Marc II*, 907. On this basis R.H. GUNDRY, *Ibid.*, 861, further comments that a strongly adversative ἀλλά in the verse and this ellipsis accentuate the fulfillment of the Scriptures. See also, C.A. EVANS, *Mark II*, 426.

[98] Cf. M. D. HOOKER, *Mark*, 352; R. PESCH, *Markusevangelium II*, 401; W.L. LANE, *Mark*, 526, adds that, while the reference to Scripture calls to mind Is 53,12, «he was numbered with the transgressors», in the light of v50, which reports the flight of all the disciples, it recalls 14,27 where Jesus quoted Zech 13,7. Similarly, J. GNILKA, *Markusevangelium II*, 271, who thinks the reference to 14,27 likely, with the flight of the disciples (v50) included in its scope. For a different view, see. S. LÉGASSE, *L'Évangile de Marc II*, 907, who considers this a global reference.

[99] Cf. S. LÉGASSE, *L'Évangile de Marc II*, 907.

[100] C.A. EVANS, *Mark II*, 426, aptly comments on this statement: «Jesus is unfazed; his time in prayer has prepared him for this moment».

Concluding Summary

While in his prayer in Gethsemane Jesus, acknowledging God's almighty power, requests his Father to spare him the bitter destiny of the Passion, he does so with complete acceptance of his eventual will (14,36). It thus manifests his explicitly obedient acceptance of the Passion as the will of God. Following this, in 14,41-42 at the end of his prayer he announces the arrival of the hour of his being handed over, the divinely-determined destiny, manifesting his concurrence with it which is further underlined by his readiness to meet his betrayer, thus revealing his acceptance as an established frame of mind. Lastly, in 14,49 Jesus manifests this attitude of acceptance yet again, when he comments on the manner of his arrest at this point as being in fulfillment of the Scriptures, that is, as per the will of God embodied in them. In the context of his explicit obedience to God's will in the prayer in Gethsemane in 14,36, and the revelation of this acceptance as an established frame of mind in 14,41, this statement of Jesus reveals the resolute character of that acceptance. These texts thus unequivocally confirm that Jesus explicitly and formally accepts his Passion as the will of God for him, and thus reaches the second step in the fulfillment of the commandment to love God.

1.3 Jesus Lives his Passion as the Will of God (Chs 14-15)

After having seen how Jesus accepts his Passion as the will of God for him, we shall now see how he lives it out as the Will of God in his Passion, which is the final step in his fulfillment of the commandment to love God. Although it is possible to show this by analyzing each scene in the Passion, we shall concentrate on demonstrating it in global terms.

In this perspective, it is best illustrated by the two prayers that ring the Passion Narrative namely, 14,36 and 15,34.

The former is the high-point of Jesus' agonized prayer in Gethsemane where, as we just saw, he accepts the Passion as the will of God for him in explicit terms. It contains all the elements of profound reverential trust in God, and filial obedience. Thus, Jesus confesses God's almighty power and his ability to deliver him. Based on this, he makes his confident request to God to free him from the bitter destiny that looms large before him, with an obedient acceptance of the Father's final will concerning that request (14,36). This prayer is thus defined by trust and obedience to God's will[101].

In 15,34, at the end of the Passion, the gospel also gives us a prayer of the dying Jesus, this time in the words of Ps 22,1. Jesus here prays: «My God , My God, Why hast thou forsaken me?». He uses the opening words of this lamentation Psalm to express the deep anguish and absence of God that he experiences. But even in the thick of this negativity[102] he not only turns to God in prayer, but addresses him emphatically as *his* God ('Ο θεός μου ὁ θεός μου, [*bis*])[103], underscoring his unbreakable personal relation to him. Jesus thus clings to God as *his* God articulating his profound trust in *his* God whose absence he experiences in his death[104]. It thus reveals in a powerful way Jesus' tenacious trust in God to whom he commits his life even in this hour of seeming abandonment[105]. As such, it is an expression of Jesus' trustful obedience to God's will in this context of ultimate crisis. Like 14,36 this situation too thus reveals Jesus' profound attachment to God and obedient surrender to him in his Passion[106].

It is also instructive to compare the two texts in their temporality. 14,36 which says: «....yet not what I will, but thou wilt», (ἀλλ' οὐ τί ἐγὼ θέλω ἀλλὰ τί σύ), is couched in the immediate future and thus looks forward to the fulfillment of the will of God, with its language of explicit acceptance[107]. 15,34, on the other hand, is cast in the aorist (cf.

---

[101] For details on this see, 1.2.

[102] The negativity itself, despite its utter desolation, is not without its significance for the messianic mission of Jesus. As S. LÉGASSE, *L'Évangile de Marc II*, 973, contends: «Mais cette absence fait aussi partie de la mission tracée pour Jésus dans les Ecritures: par cet appel et la détresse elle-même qui l'inspire, Jésus réalise, ici encore, le programme messianique défini dans le psaume.»

[103] The use of ὁ θεός in 15,34 is nominative only in form but its function is vocative. 'Ο θεός μου ὁ θεός μου,, is, thus, a direct address to God. Cf. M. ZERWICK, *Biblical Greek*, 11, # 33; 34. See also, Ch III, n.82.

[104] The address of Jesus, therefore, retains his profound trust in God. As S. LÉGASSE, *L'Évangile de Marc II*, 973, comments: «Le «pourquoi», ici comme en d'autres passages psalmiques [n.17. Ps 2,1; 10,1; 74,1.11; 80,13; 88,15], n'est pas une demande d'explication mais traduit une plainte chez celui qui, tout en demeurant fidèle a` son Dieu, déplore son absence et lui reproche son inaction.». Similarly, J. GNILKA, *Markusevangelium II*, 321-322. Likewise, C.A. EVANS, *Mark II*, 507. See also Ch III, n.83.

[105] For a critical evaluation of scholarly opinion on Jesus' reaction here, Ch III, n.83.

[106] For more details on these two scenes and their complementary character see, Ch III, 2.2.3. c) (2).

[107] Cf. W.L. LANE, *Mark*, 518; J. GNILKA, *Markusevangelium II*, 261; M. D. HOOKER, *Mark*, 349; R.H. GUNDRY, *Mark*, 854-855.

ἐγκατέλιπές με). The past tense points to the act that has been real-ized[108]. It thus marks the end of a process and underlines the accom-plishment of Jesus' obedience in the Passion, his fulfillment of the will of God[109]. By their complementing temporality, these texts thus bold-face Jesus' explicit acceptance of the will of God and entry into the process of its fulfillment (14,36), on the one hand, and his accom-plishment of this process (15,34), on the other. Together, they define his fulfillment of the will of God in the living out of his Passion.

By placing these prayers in the beginning and at the end of the Pas-sion, and thus providing it with an inclusion defined by them, the gos-pel characterizes the Passion as a process determined by the same spirit of trustful obedience in which Jesus fulfills the will of God.

Moreover, in so far as these are both prayers of Jesus, this inclusion defines the entire Passion as an act of prayer qualified by the same spirit. The gospel thus presents Jesus as fulfilling the will of God in the Passion in a profound spirit of trustful obedience to God. In so far as he thus fulfills the will of God in the Passion, Jesus fulfills the command-ment to love God.

2. Jesus' Passion as Love of Neighbor

After having seen Jesus' fulfillment of the commandment to love God in the Passion, we shall now proceed to investigate how he fulfills the commandment to love the neighbor in it. For this, we shall dwell on 10,45 and 14,24 where the Passion as understood above, that is, as re-vealed, accepted, and lived as the will of God, is revealed in regard to its significance for people namely, as a service of liberation (10,45) and as a way to communion (14,24).

2.1 The Passion as Service of Liberation (10,45)

We shall first consider the significance of the Passion vis-à-vis oth-ers revealed in 10,45 as service of liberation. It will consist in seeing it as involving a mission as well as a total, effective, and universal love of people.

---

[108] Cf. E.P. GOULD, Mark, 294.

[109] Cf. W.L. LANE, Mark, 572-573; J. GNILKA, Markusevangelium II, 321-322; M.D. HOOKER, Mark, 375.

(1) The Mission, God's Will (ἦλθεν)

10,45, in disclosing the significance of the Passion as seen above as revealed, accepted, and lived out, characterizes it first as a mission[110]. This is implied in the statement that the Son of Man has «come..» (ἦλθεν..)[111]. It is part of this programmatic statement about the mission of Jesus. The «coming» is the result of being sent by God on a mission[112]. This becomes apparent in the gospel in 11,10 where Jesus is acclaimed in his triumphal entry into Jerusalem by the people as [Εὐλογημένος] ὁ ἐρχόμενος ἐν ὀνόματι κυρίου·, «[Blessed is] he who comes in the name of the Lord!». The characterization ὁ ἐρχόμενος which is a depiction of the Messiah, underlines Jesus' coming as a mission from ὁ κύριος, (God), and realized in obedience to him as his representative. He is «the one who comes» (ὁ ἐρχόμενος) because he is sent by the κύριος to accomplish a mission (ἐν ὀνόματι κυρίου). Both his coming and the accomplishment of the mission are thus acts of obedience to the κύριος from whom both originate. This meaning is latent as an essential aspect of his coming and mission in the use of ἦλθεν for the Messiah even where it occurs without the explicit qualifier ἐν ὀνόματι κυρίου[113]. This is also corroborated indirectly by the

---

[110] Mk 10,45 belongs to a small group of sayings of Jesus which express the purpose of his coming. These are introduced sometimes with the subject Son of Man, at other times with «I», and in a few cases they are in the interrogative form. With the subject «Son of Man they occur in Mk 10,45 (Mt 20.28), in Lk 19,10 and in the variants to Lk 9,56 and Mt 18,11; and with «I» in Mk 2,17 (Mt 9,13; Lk 5,32); Mt 5,17; Mt 10,34 (Lk 12,51); Lk 12,49. In the interrogative form they appear in Mk 1,24 (Lk 4,34; cf. Mt 8,29).

These are often programmatic statements about the mission of Jesus. In the majority of instances, they have an antithetic form. The first part of it spells out the mission in negative terms (e.g. οὐκ ἦλθεν διακονηθῆναι) namely, what it decidedly does not consist in. The second introduces the purpose of the mission with ἀλλά in positive terms (e.g. ἀλλὰ διακονῆσαι). This formulation puts in relief the actual purpose of the mission in unambiguous terms. Cf. J. GNILKA, *Markusevangelium II*, 103. V. TAYLOR, *Mark*, 444, adds that the formulation is Semitic. Similarly, R. PESCH, *Markusevangelium I*, 167. Likewise, C.S. MANN, *Mark*, 414.

[111] Cf. W.L. LANE, *Mark*, 383; R. PESCH, *Markusevangelium II*, 162; S. LÉGASSE, *L'Évangile de Marc II*, 640.

[112] The coming involved frequently has rather the sense of appearing, or coming before the public. In this sense, it is especially used of the Messiah (Lk 3,16; Jn 4,25; 7,27.31), who for this reason, on the basis of passages like Ps 117,26; Hab 2,3; Da 7,13, is called ὁ ἐρχόμενος (Mt 11,3; Lk 7,19f.; Hb 10,37) [Hab 2,3], or ὁ ἐρχόμενος ἐν ὀνόματι κυρίου (Mt 21,9; 23,39; Mk 11,9; Lk 13,35; 19,38; Jn 12,13), *BAGD*, 310-311.

[113] Cf. n.112.

motif in Jn of Jesus having come as the one sent by the Father (cf. Jn 16,28). Mk 10,45 thus qualifies the coming and mission of Jesus as the will of God, and hence it also characterizes the Passion and death of Jesus for others which is their culmination as his fulfillment of the will of God.

(2) Total Love (δοῦναι τὴν ψυχὴν αὐτοῦ, 10,45)

While the term ἦλθεν in 10,45 expresses the whole career of Jesus, in particular his Passion, as the fulfillment of the will of God, its remaining elements define the nature of this mission. This is essentially characterized as service (cf. διακονῆσαι) to the point of giving his life (10,45b). Given the antithetic form of 10,45[114], the first part of it spells out the mission in negative terms (οὐκ ἦλθεν διακονηθῆναι ἀλλὰ-- διακονῆσαι) namely, what his mission is not. The ἀλλά, however, accentuates the force of the negation and introduces the purpose of the mission in positive terms (ἀλλὰ διακονῆσαι). The antithetic formulation puts in relief the actual purpose of the mission of the Son of Man in all clarity as service (διακονῆσαι). V45b develops the positive statement further and interprets what the διακονῆσαι consists in namely, in the giving of his life as a ransom for many (καὶ δοῦναι τὴν ψυχὴν -- αὐτοῦ λύτρον ἀντὶ πολλῶν)[115].

Thus the characterization of Jesus' mission, qualified as service, is defined as the «giving of his life» (δοῦναι τὴν ψυχὴν αὐτοῦ). Although τὴν ψυχὴν can have a reflexive meaning following Semitic idiom in which the reflexive relationship is expressed by means of the term נֶפֶשׁ, «soul»[116], its primary meaning is one's «earthly life»[117] and the phrase (δοῦναι τὴν ψυχὴν αὐτοῦ) points to Jesus' laying down his life in the Passion as in Jn 10,17-20. Although as an interpretation of διακονῆσαι the giving of his life refers to the whole of Jesus' career spending it in

---

[114] From the perspective of literary structure, the terms οὐκ and ἀλλά in the phrase οὐκ ἦλθεν διακονηθῆναι ἀλλὰ διακονῆσαι present a sharp contrast. According to M. ZERWICK, Markus-Stil, 122, the οὐκ-ἀλλά contrast is a peculiarity of Markan style and is found in the gospel 29x. The formula guarantees the intended contrast, as the author thinks of this contrast already with the first negative member which merely serves to introduce the positive second member, making the contrast very sharp and the stress on the positive all the more impressive. In this connection, see also n.1, to see its nature as a duality structure.

[115] The infinitives involved here are final infinitives defining the purpose of the Son of Man's coming (ἦλθεν), M. ZERWICK-M. GROSVENOR, A Grammatical Analysis, 143. Also, BDF, 197, # 390.

[116] Cf. BDF, 148, # 283, (4).

[117] Cf. BAGD, 893.

service for others, it reaches its culmination in the Passion in the literal giving of his life for them[118].

The term διακονῆσαι emphasizes the person-oriented character of the service in question as distinct from δουλεύειν which has the nuance of «slaving» or service under subjugation[119]. Such service of Jesus (διακονῆσαι) extends to the point of giving his very life. The term δοῦναι, although it means to grant or bestow, has in the present combination with τὴν ψυχήν the meaning of giving oneself up or sacrificing oneself[120]. It thus underlines its total and wholistic character. Nothing is held back and the very life is given in its entirety for the benefit of others[121]. This characterizes Jesus' Passion as total person-oriented service.

(3) Effective Love (λύτρον, 10,45)

The qualification of Jesus' mission, defined as total person-oriented service by the giving of his life in the Passion, is further characterized as λύτρον ἀντὶ πολλῶν (10,45b). The term λύτρον means price of release, ransom, especially the ransom money for the manumission of slaves[122]. To give up one's life as λύτρον ἀντὶ πολλῶν thus means to give up one's life as a ransom for many (10,45)[123]. The ransom that Jesus pays with his total self-offering for the sake of the many is thus for their effective liberation. The pre-supposition is that they are slaves who are unable to save themselves. «The many» are in a situation of slavery to sin and death, and are in enmity with God and hence they cannot effect their own liberation. They need a liberator who is able to free them. Jesus gives up his life, sacrifices himself, in total love as the ransom for the many from their hopeless situation of alienation, and thus brings them liberation. The total love of Jesus in his self-offering

---

[118] In this connection see also n.1.

[119] Cf. Ch III, 2.2.5 b) (2);. K. STOCK, Boten, 140.

[120] Cf. BAGD, 193; R. PESCH, Markusevangelium II, 163-164; S. LÉGASSE, L'Évangile de Marc II, 640-641.

[121] As K. STOCK, Boten, 143, observes: «Damit wird ausgesagt, wie weit der Dienst des Menschensohnes geht. Er kennt keine Grenzen, denn er setzt das eigene Leben ein.».

[122] Cf. V. TAYLOR, Mark, 444; C.S. MANN, Mark, 415; J. GNILKA, Markusevangeium II, 104.

[123] Cf. BAGD, 482. In this context, V. TAYLOR, Mark, 444-445 clarifies that the phrase ἀντί thus goes with λύτρον and not with δοῦναι. Similarly, W.L. LANE, Mark, 383, stresses its substitutionary nature. Likewise, C.S. MANN, Mark, 415; R. PESCH, Markusevangelium II, 164; J. GNILKA, Markusevangelium II, 104; R.H. GUNDRY, Mark, 581; S. LÉGASSE, L'Évangile de Marc II, 641; C.A. EVANS, Mark II, 121.

is thus also effective love. Hence, in so far as the Passion of Jesus brings about this liberation, it is effective love of the many.

(4) It is Universal Love (ἀντὶ πολλῶν, 10,45)

The total self-offering of Jesus in the Passion which is effective love, is also universal love. This is so because the liberation he achieves is of the many (ἀντὶ πολλῶν, 10,45). While the term ἀντί, as mentioned, has this substitutionary sense in v45, πολλοί has the meaning here of «many» denoting persons[124] and is a Semitism. It is not opposed to «all» but denotes «all» (who are many)[125]. That it involves «all» is supported by the expression of the same thought in 1Tim 2,6 which uses πάντων in place of πολλῶν (cf. ... ἀντίλυτρον ὑπὲρ πάντων)[126]. It is also aided by the equation between οἱ πολλοὶ in Rom 5,15 and πάντας in Rom 5,18[127]. Support for this inclusive meaning is found also in Jn. Thus when Jn 6,51 says: «...and the bread which I shall give for the life of the world is my flesh», the term «world» (κόσμος) includes all human beings (cf. 3,16). Hence, the phrase ἀντὶ πολλῶν as a unit means for or on behalf of all human beings and has a universal significance. It thus qualifies the liberating service of Jesus in the Passion as having a universal character[128]. It has liberated all human beings from slavery to sin and death and from alienation from God (Mk 10,45). It is thus universal love.

---

[124] It is often used without the article (Mt 7,22; 8,11; 12,15; 20,28; 24,5a; 26,28; Mk 2,2; 3,10) as here, *BAGD*, 688.

[125] Cf. M. ZERWICK-M. GROSVENOR, *A Grammatical Analysis*, 143. Similarly, M. D. HOOKER, *Mark*, 249. Likewise, W.L. LANE, *Mark*, 384, who adds that here the sacrifice of the one is contrasted with those for whom it is made. Also, R.H. GUNDRY, *Mark*, 842, who, following, E.C. MALONEY, *Semitic Interference*, 139-42, adds that: [it] «offers a Semitic substitute for «all» and describes «all» as «many» rather than delimiting «many» as fewer than «all» human beings (as in 1Tim 2,6).». In similar vein, LÉGASSE, *L'Évangile de Marc II*, 871, who pointedly observes that the proclamation of the gospel to all the nations (13,10) is based on this inclusive understanding.

[126] Cf. J. GNILKA, *Markusevangelium II*, 104. Also, C.A. EVANS, *Mark II*, 124, who considers this to be a hellenizing adaptation.

[127] In this connection see, E.C. MALONEY, *Semitic Interference*, n.332, who considers the equation as being due to direct or indirect interference of Hebrew, the reference being to Is 53,12e and 11c, where (ה)רבים is used inclusively in Hebrew and (οἱ)πολλοὶ in *The Old Greek version of the Hebrew Bible*.

[128] Cf. A. STOCK, *Method and Message*, 283. Similarly, W.L. LANE, *Mark*, 383. Likewise, J. GNILKA, *Markusevangelium II*, 104.

Concluding Summary

Mk 10,45 interprets the coming and mission of Jesus as being in obedience to the will of God and, in so far as his Passion and death for others is their culmination, it characterizes the latter as his fulfillment of the will of God. But this mission is a mission of service which culminates in the Passion and death. In interpreting the meaning of this service, the statement conceives it as the total giving of his life (10,45b) for the liberation of all human beings. In so far as it is the total giving of his life for all, it is total love of people. But in so far as it brings about the liberation of all human beings from sin, death and alienation from God, it is total, effective and universal love. The text thus interprets the Passion as Jesus' fulfillment of the commandment to love the neighbor, revealing its significance as a service of liberation. He has accordingly loved all human beings by the giving of his life. Indeed, the fact that Jesus has given his very life for doing so means that he has loved all, not just «as himself» only, but «as more than himself»[129].

2.2 Passion as Way to Communion (14,24, [in 14,22-25])

After having seen how Jesus fulfills the commandment to love the neighbor in the Passion, revealed in regard to its significance for people as a service of liberation in 10,45, we shall now see the same as revealed in its meaning for them in 14,24 as a way to communion. This will consist in showing the Passion as a way to such communion with Jesus, with God, and close by highlighting its universal import.

(1) Communion with Jesus: Bread Eaten, Wine Drunk- Life and Joy

While 10,45 highlights the significance of the Passion for others in negative terms as effective of universal liberation of all from slavery to sin, death and alienation from God, 14,24 (within 14,22-26) dwells on its positive effects of communion. One of these is communion with Jesus which we shall take up first for consideration.

The context of 14,24 is the Last Supper, celebrated as the Passover meal, the memorial of Israel's foundational liberation. This in itself marks it as a joyful fellowship celebration for Jesus and the Twelve. Jesus' celebration of it with his disciples also emphasizes its character as a celebration of fellowship with him.

---

[129] It is in line with this understanding that *Didache*, II, 7, makes the demand: «[...] ἀγαπήσεις ὑπὲρ τὴν ψυχήν σου».

But the narrative also clearly highlights the meal as the farewell meal of Jesus[130]. This is underlined by two references, one in the beginning (v18) and the other at the end (v25) of the meal. Thus, v18 which as part of vv17-21 belongs to the narrative of the Last Supper, states that «as they were at table eating (καὶ ἀνακειμένων αὐτῶν καὶ ἐσθιόντων) Jesus said: «Truly, I say to you one of you will betray me, one who is eating with me». Similarly, at the end of the meal Jesus says in v25: «Truly I say to you I shall not drink again of the fruit of the vine until that day when I drink it new in the kingdom of God» (v25). While the references to their being at table and eating in the former and to Jesus' not drinking of the fruit of the wine and of his drinking of it anew (καινόν) in the Kingdom of God all strongly underline the meal fellowship, both these verses also create an atmosphere of farewell. Thus the first, by predicting his betrayal by one of he Twelve, refers to his arrest, trial, Passion and death, and thus casts their shadow on the meal which has started[131] and transforms the latter into a farewell meal before Jesus' impending Passion. The second, by announcing the end of the meal fellowships of the kind they are enjoying now, also refers to the looming Passion and imparts its somber hue to the meal[132].

The announcement by Jesus of his betrayal by one of the Twelve (v18) which hints at his Passion and death, besides rendering the Last Supper a farewell meal, also brings the two ἀμήν-sayings (vv18.25) closer together and qualifies the second of these, promising Jesus' enjoying the eschatological banquet (v25), as a reality clearly lying beyond his death. While the farewell meal is not the end of their meal-fellowship, death must intervene before the promised new banquet in the Kingdom of God takes place. The latter banquet is definitively new (καινόν) and involves a radical transformation of the present one[133]. Even this promise, though it assures continuity to their fellowship, implies that it lies beyond Jesus' Passion and death. In so far as the promise of the new banquet implies the death of Jesus, it also reinforces the situation as a somber farewell meal[134]. Both these sayings ring the narrative of the Last Supper (14,17-21 + 14,22-26) and thus function as an inclusion to it. Hence, with their references to the meal,

---

[130] Cf. S. LÉGASSE, L'Évangile de Marc II, 867.

[131] Cf. R.H. GUNDRY, Mark, 827.

[132] Cf. R. PESCH, Markusevangelium II, 360-361.

[133] Καινόν has this nuance of radical, essentially superior newness, BAGD, 394, as opposed to νέον which, denotes passing, temporal newness, Ibid., 536.

[134] Cf. W.L. LANE, Mark, 508.

underlined as farewell meal, they decidedly characterize the Last Supper as a farewell fellowship meal of Jesus with the Twelve.

In this context of the farewell fellowship meal Jesus «[...] took bread, and blessed and broke it and gave it to them...,v22)». These steps of Jesus' taking, blessing, and breaking the bread and giving it to the disciples, mentioned carefully in the order expected of the head of the family in a Passover meal, underscore meal fellowship. As bread is a life-sustaining reality, these acts expressing its sharing articulate this fellowship celebration[135] as a celebration of life which also produces joy.

But Jesus' final statement which follow the giving of the bread: «Take this is my body» (Λάβετε, τοῦτό ἐστιν τὸ σῶμά μου, v22) actually transforms this bread into a farewell gift to his disciples. This creative step in the giving of the bread as his body, as himself, makes the meal fellowship a unique one, wherein he not only participates but donates himself to them in the form of a farewell gift[136], in which form he would remain with them[137].

Similarly, in v23 we are told that «he took a cup and when he had given thanks he gave to them, and they all drank of it.» Not only the steps of taking the cup, giving thanks, and giving to them but the observation that *all* drank of it (καὶ ἔπιον ἐξ αὐτοῦ πάντες), highlight once again the celebration as a common fellowship[138]. As wine is the symbol of joy shared on special occasions[139], its sharing and drinking together define this fellowship as a joyful one. The context of the

---

[135] Cf. M.D. HOOKER, *Mark*, 340, who points out that it is particularly highlighted by the command «take» (Λάβετε,), since «by sharing the bread, they share in fellowship together». Likewise, R.H. GUNDRY, *Mark*, 841; J. GNILKA, *Markusevangelium II*, 244.

[136] Cf. A. STOCK, *Method and Message*, 358-359; J. GNILKA, *Markusevangelium II*, 244; R. PESCH, *Markusevangelium II*, 357, who adds that the gift of the bread with the words of interpretation that refer so emphatically to his person as messianic self-interpretation, imparts participation with him as the Messiah; ID. *Abendmahl*, 92. For a different view see, C.A. EVANS, *Mark II*, 390-391.

[137] Cf. W.L. LANE, *Mark*, 506.

[138] Cf. A. STOCK, *Method and Message*, 359. Similarly, M.D. HOOKER, *Mark*, 342, who pertinently observes that: «To share someone's cup is to have close fellowship with them.». Likewise, C.A. EVANS, *Mark II*, 392, who thinks that this sharing on the part of the Twelve, given their symbolic significance, underlines the communal dimension which is part of Jesus' stress on the restoration of Israel. Also, R.H. GUNDRY, *Mark*, 841, who adds, that the statement «they all drank of the cup» parallels the command to take the bread.

[139] Cf. M.D. HOOKER, *Mark*, 340.

Passover, however, accentuates this joy in a singular manner as the sacred remembrance of their historic and foundational liberation.

But, as in the case of the bread, Jesus' words in v24: «This is my blood of the covenant, which is poured out for many», (Τοῦτό ἐστιν τὸ αἷμά μου τῆς διαθήκης τὸ ἐκχυννόμενον ὑπὲρ πολλῶν), creatively transforms this wine into his blood, himself, and converts it also into his farewell gift to the disciples, thus taking the fellowship into a uniquely new and unheard of level[140].

In v25 Jesus goes further. While he announces at this point the end of the type of meal-fellowships hitherto celebrated with them, he promises that he would drink of the fruit of the wine anew (καινόν) beyond his death in the Kingdom of God. The term καινόν here, as seen above, emphasizes the radical eschatological newness[141] of the promised banquet. Although Mk does not explicitly state that Jesus would do this in the company of the disciples, as does Mt who adds the phrase μεθ' ὑμῶν in his parallel text (26,29), this can be safely assumed, as Jesus makes this announcement in the context of a strongly-accented farewell fellowship meal with them[142] and also because he does not assert the contrary, that he would celebrate this banquet alone. Hence this statement must be construed as his promise of their new and transformed fellowship in the fulfillment of the Kingdom of God beyond Jesus' death[143]. As such, it takes this fellowship into a qualitatively new and permanent level.

But in so far as the Last Supper is a farewell fellowship meal foreshadowing and interpreting the meaning of Jesus' self-offering (14,24), the fellowship it celebrates and promises is one created by his Passion. The bread broken and given symbolizes his body broken in the Passion, and the blood given to be drunk is his blood poured out in it. Hence, participation in this farewell fellowship meal is sharing in his symboli-

---

[140] R. PESCH, *Markusevangelium II*, 360, points out that this sharing of the wine with the words of interpretation also mediates fellowship with the Messiah, and a participation in the New Covenant based on it.

[141] Cf. n.133. See also, W.L. LANE, *Mark*, 508, who adds that «in this context newness is the mark of the redeemed world and the time of ultimate redemption [...]».

[142] A. STOCK, *Method and Message*, 362. Similarly, S. LÉGASSE, *L'Évangile de Marc II*, 872.

[143] As A. STOCK, *Method and Message*, 361-362, puts it: «Without his death the kingdom would not come, yet beyond death there will be a fulfillment in which there will be no place for fasting or mourning. Coupled to the prediction of separation and death is a confident 'until' that bridges the chasm of death.». Similarly, W.L. LANE, *Mark*, 508. Likewise, R. PESCH, *Abendmahl*, 101, who adds that: «Jesu Todesprophetie hat ihre Spitze in seiner Auferstehungsgewißheit».

cally anticipated Passion and death. Such a participation creates fellowship with Jesus and unique communion with him.

(2) Communion with God (14,24)

Apart from creating communion with Jesus in a unique fellowship, the Passion of Jesus also establishes communion with God. This is involved in Jesus' interpretation of the farewell gift of his blood given as drink to his disciples. This gift, which symbolically anticipates his death, is interpreted in regard to its meaning by his statement: «This is my blood of the covenant which is poured out for many» (14,24). It has thus a twofold qualification: (a) «my blood of the covenant»; (b) «poured out for many». Both these designations of the blood of Jesus point to establishment of community with God. We shall first take up the phrase, «my blood of the covenant», for consideration and see how it creates such community.

The phase, «blood of the covenant», is firmly rooted in the biblical tradition. We shall first clarify both these terms before we deal with the phrase itself.

For the OT blood (αἷμα) is the bearer of life, and hence is sacred. To shed blood is to destroy the bearer of life, and therefore life itself. Hence αἷμα signifies «outpoured blood», «violently destroyed life», «death» or «murder»[144]. Following this, blood is spoken of in the NT in relation to the death of Christ. Yet the focus is not on Christ's material blood, but on his shed blood as the life violently taken from him. The «blood of Christ» thus becomes a graphic phrase for the death of Christ in its soteriological significance[145]. The reference to the shedding of Jesus' blood in a sacrificial sense also has a metaphorical meaning, representing the self-offering, the obedience to God, which Christ demonstrated in his Passion (Phil 2,8; Rom 5,19; Hb 5,8)[146].

The term διαθήκη, covenant, on the other hand, is the Greek (LXX) rendering of the Hebrew term ברית. It signifies not so much a pact or contract which is stipulated between two parties as a solemn, definite and determined act made *unilaterally*, but in relation to another person or a group of persons. Hence it means assurance, obligation, testament,

---

[144] Cf. J. BEHM, «αἷμα», «αἱματεκχυσία», *TDNT*, I, 173. Thus αἷμα is used to refer to the killing of Jesus (Mt 27,4.24; Act 5,28) and of the prophets, saints and witnesses of Jesus (Mt 23,30.35; Lk 11,50f.; Rev 16,6; 17,6; 18,24; 19,2).
[145] Cf. J. BEHM, «αἷμα», «αἱματεκχυσία», *TDNT*, I, 174.
[146] Cf. J. BEHM, «αἷμα», «αἱματεκχυσία», *TDNT*, I, 175.

will or oath[147]. The phrase, τὸ αἷμά μου τῆς διαθήκης, thus expresses the fact that the shedding of the blood of Jesus is the pledge and seal of the definitive, indestructible and eschatological self-obligation (cf. ἡ καινή in Lk 22,20) of God in relation to his people. It reassures definitively that God would never abandon them. Thus, it guarantees God's permanent, unchangeable, and definitive faithfulness to his people.

The phrase seems to be an allusion to Exod 24,8 where a sprinkling of blood was used in the context of the ratification of the Covenant at Sinai. The text of Exod 24,8 says: «And Moses took the blood and threw it upon the people and said:...ἰδοὺ τὸ αἷμα τῆς διαθήκης ἧς διέθετο κύριος πρὸς ὑμᾶς περὶ πάντων τῶν λόγων τούτων, «Behold the blood of the covenant (obligation) which the Lord has made with you in accordance with all these words». In this case, the ordinance (διαθήκη) consists in «all these words», that is, in the Law which God has given to Israel (cf. Exod 24,3-7)[148]. The sprinkling of the people with the blood, seals the promise of the people that they bind themselves to fulfill all the commandments of the Lord (Exod 24,3.7)[149].

There is a parallel in this OT text (Exod 24,8) to the blood of the Covenant spoken of in Mk 14,24. But in the case of the pouring out of Jesus' blood, what it confirms is not a promise of the people but of God. By willing that Jesus should undergo Passion and death (Mk 8,31; 9,31; 10,33; cf. 14,36), God covenants with his people, that is, obligates himself to them with the promise that he would be immutably and forever their God and seals this in the shedding of Jesus' blood[150]. The latter thus seals the promise of God, his self-obligation, to remain always the God of his people[151].

But in this divine covenanting and establishing of the new divine order Jesus has a central role, in so far as he accepts this divine plan[152] and undergoes the divinely-willed Passion and death[153]. It is his obedience to the will of God that brings about the accomplishment of the new covenant. On the one hand, this obedience is the expression of his unqualified love of God[154] and, on the other, in so far as it involves the giving of his life for the realization of the plan of God for the benefit of

---

[147] Cf. E. KUTSCH, «בְּרִית», «Verpflichtung», THAT, I, 339-351; BAGD, 183.
[148] Cf. B.S. CHILDS, Exodus, 505.506; J.I. DURHAM, Exodus, 343.
[149] Cf. B.S. CHILDS, Exodus, 505.506; J.I. DURHAM, Exodus, 343.
[150] Cf. A. STOCK, Method and Message, 360.; R. PESCH, Abendmahl, 95
[151] Cf. W.L. LANE, Mark, 507; R. PESCH, Markusevangelium II, 358.
[152] Cf. 1.2.
[153] Cf. 1.3.
[154] Cf. 1.2; 1.3.

the people, it involves his profound love of them[155]. Thus, in so far as Jesus makes possible the realization of the new covenant by God in his blood he is singularly involved in this divine act. This seems to be also underlined in Jesus' qualifying the gift of the cup, the symbolic anticipation of his death, as «*my* blood of the covenant» (cf. τὸ αἷμά μου τῆς διαθήκης, 14,24).

In sum, the phrase τὸ αἷμά μου τῆς διαθήκης in 14,24 means that the violent death of Christ, his life-offering in obedience to God and love of people, establishes and assures the validity of the new divine order[156]. Just as the old divine order of Sinai was sealed and inaugurated by blood (Hb 9,18f cf. Exod 24,8, דם־הברית), so the new order is established and set in force by the blood of Christ[157]. It thus means that through the Passion of Jesus, at once an act of obedience to God and love of people, God brings about a new and indestructible communion with people[158]. The Passion thus creates community between God and people by God's action through Jesus' obedience to God and love of human beings.

The second qualification of the blood of Jesus, «poured out for many» (τὸ ἐκχυννόμενον ὑπὲρ πολλῶν, 14,24) emphasizes the creation of community with God in another way. The term ἐκχυννόμενον, a passive participle, has the meaning of «poured out», also in the cultic sense and is used in relation to Jesus' death[159]. In the passive, when used of blood, it means «to be shed»[160]. Though a present participle, in gospel usage it stands for the future participle[161]. In this sense it points to the Passion and death of Jesus where this «being poured out» would actually take place. God has determined the blood of Jesus, so poured out in his death in obedience to him and for the sake of the people, to be the means of liberation of all human beings[162]. It liberates all from bondage to sin, death and alienation from God, and thus reconciles them to him. The phrase thus emphasizes the creation of community with God

---

[155] Cf. 2.1, especially, 2.1 (2); 2.1 (3); 2.1 (4).

[156] Cf. J. GNILKA, *Markusevangelium II*, 245.

[157] Cf. J. BEHM, «αἷμα», «αἱματεκχυσία», *TDNT*, I, 174.; S. LÉGASSE, *L'Évangile de Marc II*, 870-871; R PESCH, *Abendmahl*, 95.

[158] Cf. W.L. LANE, *Mark*, 507; R. PESCH, *Markusevangelium II*, 359.362.

[159] Cf. C.A. EVANS, *Mark II*, 394, who adds that it recalls the language of sacrificial atonement and that it probably reflects Is 53,12 in Hebrew or Aramaic.

[160] Cf. *BAGD*, 247; M. ZERWICK-M. GROSVENOR, *A Grammatical Analysis*, 155-56. R.H. GUNDRY, *Mark*, 842, adds that it implies violent death; Likewise, J. GNILKA, *Markusevangelium II*, 245; R. PESCH, *Markusevangelium II*, 358.

[161] Cf. M. ZERWICK, *Biblical Greek*, 95-96, # 282; 283.

[162] Cf. W.L. LANE, *Mark*, 507.

by the Passion of Jesus effected at once by God's action and Jesus' obedience to God and love of people.

(3) Universal Significance (ὑπὲρ πολλῶν, 14,24)

In underlining the communion with God which the Passion of Jesus creates, 14,24 also affirms its universal significance. This is expressed by the phrase ὑπὲρ πολλῶν which states that the pouring out of Jesus' blood is «for many». The term, ὑπέρ, though generally meaning «in favor of», not rarely also covers the meaning of «in place of»[163]. Both meanings are involved here. Jesus' death is both for the benefit of the many and in their stead, that is, it is also substitutionary, as they themselves could not effect it on their own.

As we saw above analyzing 10,45, the term πολλοί is a Semitism not opposed to «all» but denoting «all» (who are many)[164]. That the πολλοί is inclusive and involves «all» is supported, as already referred to: by the expression of the same thought in 1Tim 2,6 which uses πάντων for the purpose in place of πολλῶν; in the equation between οἱ πολλοί in Rom 5,15 and πάντας in Rom 5,18; and also in Jn's use of the term «world» (κόσμος) in Jn 6,51[165]. The phrase τὸ ἐκχυννόμενον ὑπὲρ πολλῶν, qualifying the blood of Jesus as an interpretation of his Passion, thus denotes its universal redemptive significance[166]. It has a radical impact on all human beings, liberating them from slavery to sin, death and alienation from God, an effect which they could not have achieved on their own. As such it is the expression of Jesus' extreme love of all human beings.

Concluding Summary

14,24 reveals Jesus' fulfillment of the commandment to love the neighbor in the Passion in regard to its significance for people as a way to communion, with Jesus, with God, and also as having a universal import, thus in positive terms. The text is placed in the Passover context of the Last Supper. The latter has the nature of a fellowship meal wherein Jesus and the disciples celebrate the memorial of Israel's

---

[163] Cf. M. ZERWICK, *Biblical Greek*, 30, # 91.

[164] Cf. n.125. Also, LÉGASSE, *L'Évangile de Marc II*, 871. For a different view see, R. PESCH, *Markusevangelium II*, 359-360, who sees it as referring to the totality of Israel, although, *Ibid.*, 363, he grants that the macro-text of the gospel sees its impact extending to all human beings.

[165] Cf. 2.1 (4).

[166] Cf. J. GNILKA, *Markusevangelium II*, 246.

foundational liberation but, in so far as in this context Jesus refers to his impending Passion, this fellowship meal assumes the character of a farewell fellowship meal. In this context, he gives his body and blood as food and drink to his disciples, and thus makes of himself a farewell gift to them expressing his profound love for them, which transforms the fellowship celebrated into a unique one, more so because he also promises in this context a transformed eschatological meal fellowship which lies beyond his death. But, in so far as this giving of himself anticipates his salvific death and interprets its significance for them, this farewell fellowship meal involves also a participation in the Passion. The text thus interprets the Passion as creating such communion with Jesus.

On the other hand, 14,24 also reveals the Passion as effecting communion with God. This is involved in its characterization of the blood of Jesus by the phrases «my blood of the covenant», and «poured out for many». The first refers to God's effecting by the death of Jesus the New Covenant, pledging his eternal and irrevocable faithfulness to his people, and thus bringing about the new divine order, and in this way establishing new communion with them, an act in which Jesus also has a central role in so far as he makes possible its realization by his conscious obedience to the plan of God meant for the benefit of the people which thus similtaneously expresses his profound love of God and love of people. The qualification «poured out for many», on the other hand, makes out that God has determined the blood of Jesus, so poured out in his death in obedience to him, to be the means of liberation of all human beings from bondage to sin, death and alienation from him and so reconciles them to him, an act in which Jesus exercises a capital role by his obedient acceptance and living out of the Passion, thus manifesting at once his profound love of God and love of people. Hence, it also emphasizes the creation of community with God by the Passion of Jesus. Besides, the term ὑπὲρ πολλῶν in this context underlines the universal extent and depth of this communion, in so far as it depicts the death of Jesus as both for all human beings and in their stead. Together, these phrases in 14,24 express the nature and depth of the communion with God created by the Passion of Jesus and thus reveal the significance of his fulfillment of the commandment to love the neighbor in it.

2.3 Consequence of Jesus' Fulfillment of the Love Commandment

After having seen how Jesus fulfills the two love commandments in his Passion, we shall now discuss its consequence. This will first consider its import as an act of the Beloved Son, and then ponder its portent for the disciples as his instruction by example.

(1) Act of the Beloved Son

We have seen in the above consideration, how Jesus has fulfilled the love commandment in his Passion. However, the unique identity of Jesus imparts to this fulfillment a singular character. We shall first consider this question.

Our study of the love commandment in Mk revealed that the gospel clearly affirms Jesus' divine identity as the «Beloved Son», as the new and definitive revelation of God given by God himself[167]. Jesus thus stands on a unique personal relation to God as Son to Father[168]. This identity of Jesus as the «Beloved Son» qualifies his fulfillment of the love commandment in the Passion in a singular manner. On account of this it has a unique nature and dignity. As the unique act of the Beloved Son who is on par with God and shares in his attributes[169] Jesus' fulfillment of the love commandment is unique, once-for-all and unrepeatable.

Thus Jesus' obedience to the will of God, despite its being a true human act, is the obedience of the «Beloved Son» to the *Abba,* his dear Father (14,36) which is consequently complete and unblemished as no other is or can be. Despite his appalling humiliation and his experience of Godforsakenness in the Passion (15,34), his obedience to the will of his Father remains perfect and integral. This fact is highlighted by the two prayers that provide an inclusion to the Passion (14,36; 15,34) and by this define it as an act of integral trustful obedience in the midst of terrible suffering and the absence of God[170].

Similarly, Jesus' fulfillment of the commandment to love the neighbor in the Passion as interpreted by both 10,45 and 14,24 involves a uniqueness which is all its own. Thus, when these texts depict the Passion as λύτρον ἀντὶ πολλῶν/ τὸ ἐκχυννόμενον ὑπὲρ πολλῶν respectively, they point to an act of the «Beloved Son» which is proper to him alone. It has a liberating universal effect on all human beings because of his singular reality as the «Beloved Son»[171].

---

[167] Cf. Ch III, 2.2.4 a) (2); 2.2.4 b) (2); 2.2.4 c) (2).
[168] In this connection see, Ch III, n.55; n.127; n.129.
[169] Cf. Ch III, 2.2.3 b); Ch III, 2.2.3 c); Ch III, 2.2.3 d).
[170] Cf. 1.3
[171] Cf. W.L. LANE, *Mark,* 383.

It is not only unique but also once-for-all because of Jesus' identity. It is so perfect and complete that it is both unrepeatable and inimitable in a univocal sense (cf. Hb 9,12). Jesus' fulfillment of the love commandment thus has these singular attributes by reason of his identity as the Beloved Son.

(2) Analogical Following (καὶ γάρ, 10,45)

Although Jesus' fulfillment of the love commandment in the Passion has unique qualities which cannot be reproduced, yet the gospel does demand its following as his instruction by example (cf. καὶ γάρ, 10,45). We shall, in the following treatment, clarify in what manner this is possible.

This issue is elucidated in 10,45 which, as we saw in Ch III discussing both the object of love of neighbor[172] and its modality in the gospel[173], comes as a concluding validation of Jesus' instruction to the Twelve in 10,42-45 following their quarrel over first places (10,35-41) which erupts immediately after the third Passion prediction (10,33-34) on their way to Jerusalem (10,33). Jesus in this teaching, emphasizing the absolute necessity of person-oriented service of all for greatness in his community, grounds it in the life-pattern of the Son of Man who has come on a mission of service to the point of laying down his life for the liberation of all (v45)[174]. They must serve all human beings in this way because the Son of Man serves all of them in this radical manner to the point of giving his life for them[175].

This is underlined by the phrase καὶ γάρ..with its validating character[176]. The formulation gives the behavior of Jesus as the reason for that which is demanded of the disciples and at the same time grounds this demand. In this sense 10,45 can be rendered either as «because also the Son of Man» or «because even the Son of Man», with the second underlining that the Twelve are *a fortiori* obligated to service[177].

This is the only place in Mk where the Son of Man is proposed to the Twelve as an example and the reason for this, as we have already observed in passing[178], is that they are now participants with him on

---

[172] Cf. Ch III, 2.2.5 b) (2).

[173] Cf. Ch III, 2.2.5 c) (2).

[174] For details on this instruction see, Ch III, 2.2.5 b) (2); 2.2.5 c) (2).

[175] For further clarification on the nature of the service of the Son of Man see, Ch III, n.232.

[176] Cf. Ch III, n.233.

[177] Cf. K. STOCK, *Boten*, 141-142; R.H. GUNDRY, *Mark*, 581.

[178] Cf. Ch III, 2.2.5 b) (2); 2.2.5 c) (2).

his way, the way to the Passion (cf. 8,34 + ἀναβαίνομεν, 10,33)[179], where he would give his life as a ransom for many (v45). Being thus associated with him, it is incumbent on the disciples to be on the side of Jesus and to follow his example[180]. It has thus the character of imitation of the Son of Man and his life-pattern in consequence of their discipleship.

Although this validation in 10,45 is in fact true of the whole career of Jesus defined by service (διακονῆσαι), it points specifically to the Passion as its culmination where Jesus offers his life for the liberation of all[181].

This becomes even clearer from this statement's connection to the Passion prediction in 10,33-34 in its wider context. The link between them is provided by the Son of Man statements found in 10,33 and 10,45. These statements in the beginning (10,33) and at the end (10,45) of this section draw the whole section 10,33-45 together into a unity. Because of this 10,45 not only validates the demand made to the Twelve but also interprets the meaning of the Passion prediction of 10,33-34. This is so because it explicitly deals with the Son of Man's mission of service to the point of giving his life as λύτρον ἀντὶ πολλῶν and thereby concludes 10,32-45[182]. As the conclusion of this whole section, v45 thus profoundly interprets the meaning of Jesus' Passion[183].

The nature of 10,45 as the interpretation of the Passion, which, as we saw above, is Jesus' fulfillment of the two love commandments, entails that the disciples' obligation in following Jesus' example (καὶ

---

[179] Cf. Ch III, n.234. Also, H.B. SWETE, *Saint Mark*, 240; W.L. LANE, *Mark*, 385; A. STOCK, *Method and Message*, 283; J. GNILKA, *Markusevangelium II*, 103-104; R. PESCH, *Markusevangelium II*, 163. Likewise, R.H. GUNDRY, *Mark*, 581, who adds that the authority of the Son of Man reinforces the motivation on the part of the disciples. Similarly, LÉGASSE, *L'Évangile de Marc II*, 639-640.

[180] Cf. K. STOCK, *Boten*, 143-144. Similarly, H.B. SWETE, *Saint Mark*, 240; W.L. LANE, *Mark*, 385; A. STOCK, *Method and Message*, 283; J. GNILKA, *Markusevangelium II*, 103-104; R. PESCH, *Markusevangelium II*, 163; M. D. HOOKER, *Mark*, 247-248; R.H. GUNDRY, *Mark*, 581; LÉGASSE, *L'Évangile de Marc II*, 639-640.

[181] Cf. H.B. SWETE, *Saint Mark*, 240. J. GNILKA, *Markusevangelium II*, 103. See also, n.1.

[182] Cf. K. STOCK, *Boten*, 142. Similarly, J. GNILKA, *Markusevangelium II*, 98; Likewise, R. PESCH, *Markusevangelium II*, 150; S. LÉGASSE, *L'Évangile de Marc II*, 631-632. K.G. REPLOH, *Markus-Lehrer der Gemeinde*, 167. See also, A. STOCK, *Method and Message*, 284.

[183] Cf. K. STOCK, *Boten*, 142.

γὰρ..) is actually the obligation of following him in his fulfillment of
these commandments.

As disciples they are thus obligated to follow him in his radical
obedience to God in concurring with and fulfilling God's will, even if
this cannot match the obedience of the Beloved Son to his Father
(14,36). Similarly, they must serve all human beings, rendering person-
oriented service to them to the point of giving their lives for them like
the Son of Man, even though their service is of a different quality than
that of the Son of Man. Because of their association with Jesus and
their participation in his way (cf. ἀναβαίνομεν, 10,33) both are an obligation on them in line with their call to follow him (8,34f).

Nevertheless, the phrase «ransom for many» (λύτρον ἀντὶ πολλῶν),
as we have already noted elsewhere[184], indicates an area which is reserved to Jesus alone as the «Beloved Son»[185]. It points to the unique,
once-for-all and unrepeatable redemptive act of Jesus and the disciples
cannot follow him in this. Yet, both their obedience and their person-
oriented service of giving of life, though not taken in a univocal sense
to that of Jesus, can have an analogically similar effect as this once-for-
all deed of Jesus[186].

Concluding Summary

Jesus' fulfillment of the two love commandments in his Passion has
consequences: (1) in itself as an act of the Beloved Son with his unique
identity; (2) for the disciples as his instruction by example. Because of
Jesus' unique identity as the Beloved Son, revealed in the gospel by
God the Father himself (9,7), his fulfillment of the love commandment
have unique attributes. It is not only unique but also once-for-all, and is
so perfect and complete that it is both unrepeatable and inimitable in a
univocal sense. Nevertheless, the gospel does demand its following as
his instruction by example (cf. καὶ γάρ, 10,45). This verse as the conclusion of 10,32-45 comes as the validating statement of the instruction
which precedes it and in fact also profoundly interprets the Passion
prediction in 10,33-34. It demands from the disciples the following of

---

[184] Cf. Ch III, n.248.

[185] Cf. Also, W.L. LANE, *Mark,* 385, who states: «This painful and glorious destiny of the Son of Man is something unique to his mission and in a definite sense is in-
communicable: only he can accomplish this service.». Similarly, H.B. SWETE, *Saint
Mark,* 240. Likewise, J. GNILKA, *Markusevangelium II,* 103-104.

[186] Cf. Ch III, n.248. See also Jn 10,11-18; 15,12-13 and 1Jn 3,16 where too the
life-offering of Jesus and of the disciples are connected and, as the most capital deed of
Jesus, is shown to be binding on the disciples. Cf. K. STOCK, *Boten,* 143, n.426.

the supreme example of the Son of Man's person-oriented service to the point of giving his life for all, which is actually the demand to imitate his fulfillment of the two love commandments in the Passion. Although it has unique attributes which cannot be reproduced, it is incumbent on the disciples to follow it analogically by virtue of their participation in his way, and in line with their call to follow him (8,34f). This will also have an analogical effect as the unique and once-for-all salvific act of Jesus.

3. General Conclusion

Following our investigation in Ch III of the teaching of Jesus in 12,28-34 on the love commandment, we have studied in this concluding chapter, the question as to how Jesus himself has lived the two commandments in his Passion, the high point of his life and ministry. Taking up the question of Jesus' observance of the commandment to love God, which in the gospel, following its OT sense, means to do the will of God, we investigated how Jesus does the will of God in the Passion, and thus fulfills this commandment. We covered this in three steps: Jesus' revelation of the Passion as the will of God, his acceptance of it as the will of God, and his living it out as the will of God.

Under the first heading, we studied the texts in the gospel in which Jesus reveals the Passion as a divine necessity for him, and hence as the will of God for him. While this is most fundamentally seen in the concept of δεῖ in 8,31, the same revelation is made in the other Passion predictions (9,31; 10,33f), in the theological passives in (9,31; 10,33), and outside them (14,41), in the γέγραπται texts (9,12; 9,13; 14,21; 14,27) that speak of its scriptural necessity, and finally in the contrast between the τὰ τοῦ θεοῦ and the τὰ τῶν ἀνθρώπων in 8,33. This rich diversity of texts manifested Jesus as unequivocally revealing the Passion as the determined will of God for him and implicitly accepting it.

Under the second, we investigated: 14,36, which concerns Jesus' explicit and formal acceptance of the will of God in obedient surrender during his prayer in Gethsemane; 14,41-42 which reveals this acceptance as an established frame of mind at the end of his prayer; and 14,49, which manifests the resolute character of this acceptance in the context of his arrest. These texts and contexts showed how in this step Jesus goes beyond revealing the Passion as the will of God to its explicit and unambiguous personal appropriation.

Under the third, we studied how Jesus lives out the Will of God in his Passion as the final step in his fulfillment of the commandment to love God. Leaving details, we approached the question in global terms and found that in this perspective, it is best illustrated by the two prayers, (14,36 and 15,34), which ring the Passion Narrative and provide an inclusion to it, and thus define it by their spirit characterized by trustful obedience to the divine will and surrender to it in the midst of the experience of the absence of God and dreadful suffering, which thus demonstrates Jesus' living out the Passion as the will of God.

Turning to investigate Jesus' fulfillment of the commandment to love the neighbor, we focused on 10,45 and 14,24 where the Passion as understood above, that is, as revealed, accepted and lived as the will of God, is further revealed in regard to its significance for people, that is, as a service of liberation (10,45) and as a way to communion (14,24).

Considering the first, we found that it consists in seeing it as involving a mission as well as a total, effective, and universal love of people.

Thus, according to 10,45, the coming and mission of Jesus is in obedience to the will of God, and reaches its climax in the Passion. But this mission is a mission of service which culminates in his Passion and death. The statement interprets the meaning of this service as the total giving of his life (10,45b) for the liberation of all human beings. But, in so far as it brings about their liberation from sin, death and alienation from God, it is total, effective and universal love. It thus interprets the Passion as Jesus' fulfillment of the commandment to love the neighbor, revealing its significance as a service of liberation.

Correspondingly, we saw the Passion as revealed in its meaning for the people in 14,24 as a way to communion, and found that it consists in seeing it as a way to such communion with Jesus, with God, and having a universal import.

In dealing with this text, we saw its Passover meal context, revealing the latter as a fellowship meal wherein Jesus and the disciples celebrate the memorial of Israel's foundational liberation but, in so far as in this context Jesus refers to his impending Passion, this fellowship meal assuming the character of a farewell fellowship meal. In this context, Jesus' gesture of giving his body and blood as food and drink to his disciples and in this way making of himself a farewell gift of love to them, transforms the fellowship celebrated into a singular one, all the more so because he also promises at this point a transformed eschatological meal fellowship with them beyond his death (14,25). But, in so far as this giving of himself anticipates his salvific death and interprets its significance for them, this farewell fellowship meal involves a participation in the Passion which creates communion with Jesus.

Additionally, we saw how 14,24 reveals the Passion as effecting communion with God by its characterization of the blood of Jesus by the phrases: «my blood of the covenant», and «poured out for many». The first points to God's effecting by the death of Jesus the New Covenant, pledging his eternal and irrevocable faithfulness to his people and thus bringing about the new divine order and establishing new communion with them, an act in which Jesus has a central role in so far as he makes possible its realization by his obedient acceptance of the plan of God which simultaneously expresses his profound love of God and people. The second, «poured out for many», on the other hand, affirms that God has determined the blood of Jesus, so poured out in his death in obedience to him, to be the means of liberation of all human beings from bondage to sin, death and alienation from him and thus reconciles them to himself where too Jesus has a centrality in so far as he makes it possible by his obedient acceptance of death expressing his extreme love of God and people. This also thus emphasizes the creation of community with God by the Passion of Jesus. Finally, the term ὑπέρ πολλῶν in this context underlines the universal extent and depth of this communion, in so far as it characterizes the death of Jesus as a substitutionary death for all. In this manner 14,24 expresses the nature and depth of the communion with God created by the Passion, and thus reveals the significance of Jesus' fulfillment of the commandment to love the neighbor in it.

After having seen how Jesus fulfills the two love commandments in his Passion, we discussed its two-fold consequence: its import as an act of the Beloved Son and its significance for the disciples as his instruction by example.

The first showed that because of Jesus' unique identity as the Beloved Son (9,7), his fulfillment of these commandments is unique and once-for-all, with the result that it is both unrepeatable and inimitable in a univocal sense. Despite this, however, the gospel requires from the disciples in 10,45 (cf. καὶ γὰρ...,) the analogical following of the supreme example of the Son of Man's person-oriented service to the point of giving his life for all, which is actually the demand to imitate his fulfillment of the two love commandments in the Passion. This is incumbent on them because of their participation in Jesus' way (10,33) and their call to follow him (8,34f) and will have an analogical effect as the unique and once-for-all act of Jesus.

Thus, these texts not only demonstrate Jesus' fulfillment of the two love commandments and interpret its significance for all human beings, but also point to the way the disciples can, and should, follow him in fulfilling these commandments.

However, considering the question of the disciples' obligation to follow Jesus in this regard within the wider context of our discussion in the previous chapter, it would seem, that the succeeding considerations must also be added to what has been said.

Thus, such obligation to follow, in this context, would also involve the fulfillment of the Father's fundamental demand to listen to Jesus (9,7), and Jesus' demands based on this: to understand (8,17.21), to follow (8,34f), to lose one's life for him and the gospel (8,35-36), and to not to be ashamed (8,38) of him. This seems to follow from the gospel's integrated understanding of the love commandment we have seen in Ch III which fully incorporates the reality of Jesus in its conception of the commandment to love God, just as its interpretation widens the OT understanding of the commandment to love the neighbor to include all human beings and their humble, person-oriented service. Thus, in their fulfillment of these commandments, the disciples must also combine these wider aspects of them in the gospel to fully correspond to the Kingdom of God understanding of them which it embodies.

FINAL CONCLUSION

At the end of our investigation of the love commandment we shall, in conclusion, briefly restate our findings, see them within a global vision, and formulate their consequences.

1. A brief Summary of the Findings

We shall begin by giving a succinct summary of the findings of our research in the order in which it was carried out. We conducted our study of the love commandment (12,28-34) in Two Parts. Part I: «The Old Testament Meaning and Context of the Love Commandment (Deut 6,4-5 and Lev 19,18)», comprising Ch I, «The Commandment to Love God: Deuteronomy 6,4-5» and Ch II, «The Commandment to Love the Neighbor: Leviticus 19,18», dwelt on its OT meaning and background in the books of Deuteronomy and Leviticus, a study which enabled us to get a clear picture of these based on the more important recent studies on them.

Thus, the study of the commandment to love God (Deut 6,4-5) in its OT context in Ch I showed that it has a structure involving an address, the formula of monotheistic confession and the commandment to love God exclusively based on it[1]. It clarified the address form שמע ישראל to be a didactic formula which expresses an invitation to listen with an attitude of obedience[2], and the confessional formula to be a monotheistic proclamation which understands the uniqueness of God in exclusive terms[3]. The ו-*conversive* formulation of the commandment which follows the monotheistic proclamation (Deut 6,5) reveals it to be the consequence of it: it is because the Lord God is unique that he should be loved with a whole-hearted devotion[4].

The exegesis of the commandment clarified the love demanded to be a theological concept, meaning the inner holistic orientation of the human person to God based on his/her deliberate decision which con-

---

[1] Ch I, 2.
[2] Ch I, 3.1
[3] Ch I, 3.2
[4] Ch I, 3.3

cretizes itself in the observance of God's commandments[5], while the tripartite formula of the modality of love underlines the holistic character of this love[6]. A consideration of its wider contexts revealed that it has the character of a central commandment in summary form, and thus has a pivotal role in Deuteronomy[7].

The study of the commandment to love the neighbor (Lev 19,18) in Ch II, commenced with an explanation of the structure of Lev 19,17-18 which is a unity offering a contrast structure of 4 prohibitions and two positive general commands[8]. Lev 19,18 itself, though in ו-conversive form, has an adversative formulation, emphasizing that, instead of taking vengeance against an offending brother and nursing a grudge against him, one must love him as oneself[9]. The exegesis revealed the nature of the love commanded to be an interior sentiment expressed in caring deeds such as fraternal correction[10], and the object of love to be רע, a fellow-Israelite and covenant brother who, in the context, is an offending person, an enemy[11]. The modality of love, «as yourself», (כמוך), on the other hand, has an adverbial meaning of «as one loves one's own self», expressing a measure or standard instead of a motivation, and stressing deeds rather than sentiments[12]. While the extension of the commandment to love in v34 to the גר implies the full integration of the resident-alien within the covenant community with all his legal rights[13], the concluding divine self-introductory formula emphasizes, on the one hand, that the commandment rests on the authority of God, and on the other, that the love commanded is a theological love that involves an imitation of God's own attitude[14]. The discussion of the commandment's contexts showed that it (v18) has an apex position both in its immediate and mediate contexts as the high point of the holiness proposed to Israel, clarifying that it is by loving the offending brother, one's enemy, that Israel best fulfills its call to imitate God's holiness[15].

---

[5] Cf. Ch I, 3.3.1, especially 3.3.1 d)
[6] Cf. Ch I, 3.3.2
[7] Cf. Ch I, 4.
[8] Ch II, 2. especially 2.1
[9] Ch II, 2.2
[10] Ch II, 3.1
[11] Ch II, 3.2
[12] Ch II, 3.3
[13] Ch II, 3.4
[14] Ch II, 3.5
[15] Ch II, 4.

Part II: «The Love Commandment in Mark», studied these commandments in Two Chapters: Ch III, «The Love Commandment Pericope: Text in Context» and «The Fulfillment of the Love Commandment in the Passion of Jesus». The first, Ch III, represents the gospel's theoretical interpretation of the two love commandments and the second, Ch IV, Jesus' living it out, his instruction by example. Together, they complete the gospel's total interpretation of these commandments.

Thus Ch III first briefly considered the preliminary questions of introduction, the pericope's structure, and form[16]. In regard to the last, it was found to have a *sui generis* character manifesting a new form which has been identified as *Dialoggespräch* based on the data within the pericope which are not reducible to any known form[17].

This was followed by the exegesis of the pericope, with special emphasis on the text of the commandments, so as to bring out its meaning in context, with careful attention paid to the commandments' vocabulary within the gospel[18]. It revealed that, while the commandments retain their basic OT meaning, they also acquire distinctive Markan specificities, creating a two-level meaning. While the gospel confirms the OT understanding of the two love commandments, in an integral reading it also contains another dimension of meaning which widens this horizon[19].

Thus, for instance, our study of the monotheistic confession as part of the first commandment, like Deut 6,4, on the one hand emphasizes Israel's call to listen, God as Lord, and the relational character of God. On the other, it extends all these affirmations to Jesus and supplies further prerogatives to God and to him, such as forgiveness of sins and goodness, thus producing a wholistic conception of it as commandment, wherein the reality of Jesus coheres integrally in the reality of the Lord God whose acceptance also forms part of this commandment, in view of the command «to listen» at the beginning (12,29)[20].

But Markan specificities are also found at the first level of the pericope *vis-à-vis* the OT texts which include their definition as commandments, their clear hierarchical gradation into the first and the second commandments, their unity-in-difference character within this gradation and the commandments' summary role in relation to all oth-

---

[16] Ch III, 1.

[17] Ch III, 1.3.2

[18] Ch III, 2.

[19] For a systematic, relatively short presentation of these see, Ch III, 2.5

[20] Cf. 2.2.3, in particular 2.2.3 e)

ers (12,29.31) which clearly transcend the OT conception of both Deut 6,4-5 and Lev 19,18, despite their dominant positions in their original contexts[21].

On the other hand, the two-level meaning goes beyond the interpretation of the monotheistic confession to the entirety of the two love commandments. Thus, in the commandment to love God integrally (12,30) this extension is seen in the content of love[22], the modality of love[23] and the object of love[24].

Similarly, the two-level meaning is seen also in the case of the commandment to love the neighbor. While the gospel concurs with its OT meaning in so far as its wording remains the same, an integral reading reveals that the latter enriches it in regard to its status[25], object[26] and modality[27]. Besides, as the concluding confirmation of Jesus clarifies, the two levels of meanings are found integrated in the gospel[28].

While the two love commandments in their integral reading express the above meaning, the dialogal interaction of the scribe (12,32-34) shows that it enthusiastically affirms Jesus' definition of them in their first level of meaning in the pericope. Their characteristic accents of monotheistic emphasis, reasonableness and superordination of love over cult, distinctive of a Jewish frame-of-reference, attempt to affirm and integrate Jesus' definition in the latter[29]. But, as it is an endeavor to provide a Jewish validation of the two love commandments, their integral meaning does not form part of it, as this lies beyond its compass.

Although Jesus' reaction to the scribe's comments is strikingly positive (v34a) and underlines his agreement with his dialogue-partner's understanding of his definition to a large extent[30], his concluding comment «You are not far from the Kingdom of God» (v34b) reveals that, while the agreement is considerable, it is not total, and contains a hint of insufficiency which delicately invites him to go be-

---

[21] Cf. Ch III, 2.2.2; 2.2.6
[22] Cf. Ch III, 2.2.4 a) (2)
[23] Cf. Ch III, 2.2.4 b) (2)
[24] Cf. Ch III, 2.2.4 c) (2)
[25] Cf. Ch III, 2.2.5 a)
[26] Cf. Ch III, 2.2.5 b)
[27] Cf. Ch III, 2.2.5 c)
[28] Cf. Ch III, 2.2.6
[29] Cf. Ch III, 2.3
[30] Cf. Ch III, 2.4.1

yond his position to discover its full meaning to actually belong to the Kingdom of God[31].

We found the solution to his insufficiency offered in the question of the identity of the Messiah (12,35-37) which Jesus raises following his comment, which critiques the inadequacy of the scribal interpretation of the issue and reveals the Messiah's transcendent origin in so far as it is this recognition that he must accept as a precondition to belong to the Kingdom[32]. This recognition indicates how the unique Lordship of the Lord, God confessed in the first commandment (12,29b), integrates the reality of Jesus the Messiah by virtue of his relationship of descent from him (12,35-37). It secures for the scribe belongingness to the Kingdom, because this integral conception of the Lordship of the Lord God corresponds to the Kingdom of God-understanding of the two love commandments the gospel holds[33]. For the same reason, we found that this key revelation also underlines the correctness of the integral meaning of the two love commandments, as the latter depends on and flow from the former. It thus implicitly points to the other aspects of the integral meaning of these commandments as forming part of their Kingdom of God-understanding[34]. By consequence, the invitation to recognize the former as a precondition to belong to the Kingdom, indirectly implies an openness to the recognition and acceptance of the latter as well[35].

In this context of the clarification of the theoretical aspect of the Markan interpretation of the love commandment, Ch IV, «The Fulfillment of the Love Commandment in the Passion of Jesus», dwelt on the practical aspect, his instruction by example, and showed as to how Jesus himself has lived these two commandments in his Passion, the high point of his life and ministry. As regards Jesus' fulfillment of the commandment to love God, which in the gospel means to do the will of God, we saw how Jesus accomplishes this in the Passion and thus fulfills this commandment, covering this in three steps: Jesus' revelation of the Passion as the will of God with implicit acceptance[36]; his formal and explicit acceptance of it as the will of God[37], and his living it out

---

[31] Cf. Ch III, 2.4.2, (1)
[32] Cf. Ch III, 2.4.2
[33] Cf. K. KERTELGE, «Das Doppelgebot», 321-322. Also, Ch III, n.363.
[34] Cf. K. KERTELGE, «Das Doppelgebot», 321-322. Also, Ch III, n.363.
[35] Ch III, 2.5 (5)
[36] Cf. Ch IV, 1.1
[37] Cf. Ch IV, 1.2

as the will of God[38]. The Investigation of Jesus' fulfillment of the commandment to love the neighbor[39] focused on 10,45 and 14,24, where the Passion as understood above, that is, as revealed, accepted and lived as the will of God, is further revealed in regard to its significance for people, that is, as a service of liberation (10,45), and as a way to communion (14,24).

Considering the first, we found that it involves a mission as well as a total, effective, and universal love of people[40]. Correspondingly, we saw the Passion as revealed in its meaning for the people in 14,24, as a way to communion, and found that it involves seeing it as a way to such communion with Jesus, with God, and as having a universal import[41].

Following this, we discussed the two-fold consequence of Jesus' fulfillment of the love commandment: (1) as an act of the Beloved Son (9,7); and (2) in its significance for the disciples as his instruction by example[42]. It showed that, although because of Jesus' singular identity as the Beloved Son his fulfillment of the love commandment is not only unique but also once-for-all and inimitable in a univocal sense, the disciples must follow it analogically by virtue of their participation in Jesus' way and their call to follow him (8,34f), with an analogical effect to the unique act of Jesus[43].

2. The Christological Nature of Markan Specificities

After having presented the main findings of our research succinctly, we shall now see them within a global, unifying vision.

The brief summary of the findings shows that, compared to the OT conception, the Markan newness of the two love commandments, both theoretical and practical, comes from their relationship to Jesus. Thus, as we saw, Mk accomplishes the integral understanding of the monotheistic confession by consistently extending its application to Jesus in regard to the prerogatives involved, both found in the OT and those specific to the gospel. Similarly, he reaches the integral interpretation of the commandment to love God by incorporating the reality of Jesus in regard to the content of love, the modality of love, and the object of

---

[38] Cf. Ch IV, 1.3
[39] Cf. Ch IV, 2.
[40] Cf. Ch IV, 2.1
[41] Cf. Ch IV, 2.2
[42] Cf. Ch IV, 2.3
[43] Cf. Ch IV, 2.3 (1); 2.3 (2)

love along with their full OT conceptions. Likewise, the integral meaning of the commandment to love the neighbor is created on the basis of Jesus' explicit definition, teaching and example. Even the Markan specificities found at the first level of the pericope *vis-à-vis* the OT texts are also wholly dependent on the person of Jesus and his authoritative definition.

In similar vein, the fulfillment of the two love commandments in the Passion of Jesus has its specifically unique nature and consequences because of the singular reality of the person of Jesus as the Beloved Son (9,7). Finally, the disciples are obligated to analogically follow the supreme example of the Son of Man because of his unique transcendent identity and their association with him (cf. καὶ γὰρ.., 10,45) following his call to follow (8,33f). This consistent connection of the Markan specificities with the person of Jesus clarifies them as being profoundly christological.

Thus, Jesus' unique divine reality as the Beloved Son and his consequent authoritative interpretation give the love commandment depth and extension. By reason of his unique identity, his living out the two love commandments gives them unique fulfillment (10,45; 14,24). Similarly, it is his singular reality and the disciples' connection with him and his way that provide the motivation for following his example. They can realize these commandments only by following his supreme example and in communion with him (cf. ἀναβαίνομεν, 10,33). Thus, undoubtedly the Markan interpretation of the Love Commandment is throughly defined by the gospel's Christology at every point.

3. The Consequences

After having seen the deeply christological nature of the Markan specificities of the two love commandments which unifies them within a global vision, we shall draw its consequences.

(1) Because of the crucial role of the person of Jesus in the transformation of the two love commandments both in their theoretical interpretation and in their unique fulfillment, it could be affirmed that for the gospel the person of Jesus is their ultimate hermeneusis. He both gives them singular depth and extension and fulfills them uniquely and paradigmatically. Jesus thus becomes in the gospel their measure and fullness of interpretation.

(2) Given the uniqueness of Jesus' fulfillment of the two love commandments which is once-for-all and inimitable in a univocal sense, it can be followed only analogically[44].

(3) Nevertheless, this task of imitating the supreme once-for-all example of Jesus is incumbent on the disciples (cf. καὶ γάρ, 10,45) because of their response to his absolute call to follow, and their consequent association with him and his way (cf. ἀναβαίνομεν, 10,33)[45].

(4) The gospel thus offers us the two love commandments' unique christological interpretation, their unsurpassable model, and the *raison d'être* for their realization in an analogical sense.

(5) Since, as per 10,45 and 14,24, Jesus has liberated all human beings from bondage to sin, death, and alienation from God and established community with God and with himself[46], he has thus enabled them to analogically follow his example and to respond effectively to realize the two love commandments based on their obligation as disciples (cf. καὶ γάρ, 10,45) to follow him.

(6) This obligation to follow, seen in the wider context of our discussion in Ch III, also involves, on the part of the disciples, the obedience to the Father's fundamental demand to listen to Jesus (9,7), and Jesus' demands based on this: to understand (8,17.21), to follow (8,34f), to lose one's life for him and the gospel (8,35-36), and to not to be ashamed of him (8,38). This follows from the gospel's integrated understanding of the two love commandments which fully incorporates the reality of Jesus in its conception of the first commandment, just as its interpretation enlarges the OT understanding of the commandment to love the neighbor to include all human beings and their humble, person-oriented service. It thus entails that, in their fulfillment of the two love commandments, the disciples must also integrate these wider aspects of the commandments in the gospel to fully correspond to their Kingdom of God-understanding which it embodies.

---

[44] Cf. Ch IV, 2.3 (1)
[45] Cf. Ch IV, 2.3 (2)
[46] Cf. Ch IV, 2.1; 2.2

(7) In regard to the *Dialoggespräch* involved in the pericope, as we saw in the concluding discussion of Ch III, it is precisely this christological fullness of meaning the total gospel holds, that the dialogue partner's conception of it lacks, despite its richness and characteristic Jewish emphases[47]. Hence, in the context of the dialogue, it is the recognition and acceptance of its essential characteristic namely, that Jesus forms part of and integrates into the reality of the Lord God and his Lordship, and openness to the rest, both at the theoretical and the practical levels, that the scribe needs in order to fill his lack to belong to the Kingdom of God (12,34b)[48].

(8) In view of this, as we also saw in the conclusion to Ch III, the gospel's christological interpretation of the two love commandments in their totality is actually their Kingdom of God-understanding[49]. This is the reason why the recognition and acceptance of its essential element, (that Jesus forms part of and integrates into the reality of the Lord God and his Lordship), is the precondition to belong to the Kingdom, with openness to the rest being implied in the recognition and acceptance of this key element[50].

---

[47] Cf. Ch III, 2.4.2 (1)
[48] Cf. Ch III, 5.2 (5)
[49] Cf. K. KERTELGE, «Das Doppelgebot», 321-322. Also, Ch III, n.363 and 395.
[50] Cf. Ch III, 5.2 (5)

ABBREVIATIONS

AASF. DHL	Annales Academiae Scientiarum Fennicae. Dissertationes Humanarum Litterarum
ABD	D.N. FREEDMAN, ed., *The Anchor Bible Dictionary*, I-VI, New York 1992.
AnBib	Analecta Biblica
AncB	Anchor Bible
ATD	Das Alte Testament Deutsch
BAGD	W. BAUER-W.F. ARNDT- F.W. GINGRICH- F. DANKER, *A Greek - English Lexicon of the New Testament & Other Early Christian Literature*, Chicago-London 1979.
BDF	F. BLASS-A.DEBRUNNER-R.W. FUNK, *A Greek Grammar of the New Testament and Other Early Christian Literature*, Chicago-London 1961.
BEThL	Bibliotheca ephemeridum theologicarum Lovaniensium
Bib	*Biblica*
BZNW	Beihefte zur Zeitschrift für die neutestamentliche Wissenschaft
BZAW	Beihefte zur Zeitschrift für die alttestamentliche Wissenschaft
CBQ	The Catholic Biblical Quarterly
CBQ.MS	Catholic Biblical Quarterly Monograph Series
cf.	confer
CGTC	Cambridge Greek Testament commentaries
Ch/Chs	Chapter/Chapters
ed.	editor/editors
EDNT	H. BALZ-G. SCHNEIDER, ed., *Exegetical Dictionary of the New Testament*, I-III, Grand Rapids 1990-1993.
EKK	Evangelisch-Katholischer Kommentar zum Neuen Testament

esp.	especially
ET	*Expository Times*
etc.	et cetera
f/ff.	and the following
FRLANT	Forschungen zur Religion und Literatur des Alten und Neuen Testamentes
Fs.	Festschrift
FZPhTh	Freiburger Zeitschrift für Philosophie und Theologie
HAT	Handbuch zum Alten Testament
HNT	Handbuch zum Neuen Testament
HThK	Herders theologischer Kommentar zum Neuen Testament
ibid.	*ibidem*
ICC	International Critical Commentary
ID.	Idem
Interp.	*Interpretation*
JNES	Journal of Near Eastern Studies
JTS	Journal of Theological Studies
JSNT.S	Journal for the Study of the New Testament, Supplement Series
Le Div	Lectio Divina
LXX	Septuagint
MSSNTS	Monograph Series Society for New Testament Studies
MT	Masoretic Text
n.	footnote number
NCB	New Century Bible Commentary
NEB-NT	Die Neue Echter Bibel, Neues Testament
NIC - NT	New International Commentary on the New Testament
NIC - OT	New International Commentary on the Old Testament
NJBC	The New Jerome Biblical Commentary, R.E. Brown, S.S.; J.A.Fitzmyer, S.J.; R.E. Murphy, O.Carm., New Jersey 1990.
NJPS	*The New Jewish Publication Society of America, Translations to the Holy Scriptures,* According to the Traditional Hebrew Text. The Jewish Publication Society, Philadelphia - New York - Jerusalem 1988.

NT	New Testament
NT	*Novum Testamentum*
NTD	Das Neue Testament Deutsch
NTS	*New Testament Studies*
OBO	Orbis Biblicus et Orientalis
OT	Old Testament
par.	parallel/parallels
RNT	Regensburger Neues Testament
RSV	Revised Standard Version
SBA	Stuttgarter biblische Aufsatzbände
SBL.DS	Society of Biblical Literature, Dissertation Series
SBL.SS	Society of Biblical Literature, Semeia Studies
SBM	Stuttgarter biblische Monographien
Str-B	H. STRACK - P. BILLERBECK, *Kommentar zum Neuen Testament aus Talmud und Midrasch*, I-VI, München 1965.
STAT	Soumalaisen Tiedeakatemian Toimituksia
TDNT	*Theological Dictionary of the New Testament*
THAT	JENNI, E.-WESTERMANN, C., *Theo logisches Handwörterbuch zum Alten Testament*, 1-2, München 1971-1976.
ThHK	Theologischer Handkommentar zum Neuen Testament
THNT	Theologischer Handkommentar zum Neuen Testament
tr.	translator
trans.	translation
ThW	Theologische Wissenschaft
TWAT	BOTTERWECK,G.J.-RINGGREN, H. -FABRY, H-J, *Theologisches Wörterbuch zum Alten Testament*, 1-8., Stuttgart 1984.
v./vv	verse/verses
VD	*Verbum Domini*
WBC	World Biblical Commentary
WMANT	Wissenschaftliche Monographien zum Alten und Neuen Te stament
WUNT	Wissenschaftliche Untersuchungen zum Neuen Testament
x	Symbol for «times»

BIBLIOGRAPHY

1. Commentaries

ACHTEMEIER, *Mark*, Philadelphia 1975.

ANDERSEN, F.I. - FREEDMAN, D.N., *Amos*, AncB 24A, Garden City 1989.

ANDERSEN, F.I. - FREEDMAN, D.N., *Hosea*, AncB 24, Garden City 1980.

BRAULIK, G., *Deuteronomium (1-16,17)*, Würzburg 1986.

CHILDS, B.S., *The Book of Exodus, A Critical, Theological Commentary*, Philadelphia, 1974.

CHRISTENSEN. D.L., *Deuteronomy 1-11*, WBC 6A, Dallas 1991.

CRAIGIE, P.C., *Psalms 1-50*, WBC 19, Waco 1983.

CRAIGIE, P.C - KELLEY, P.H - DRINKARD, J.F. - JR., *Jeremiah 1-25*, WBC 24, Dallas 1991.

CRANFIELD, C.E.B., *The Gospel According to Mark*, CGTC, Cambridge 1959.

CRAWFORD, T.H., *The Book of Proverbs*, ICC, Edinburgh 1963[2].

DRIVER, S.R., *A Critical and Exegetical Commentary on Deuteronomy*, ICC Edinburgh 1902.

DURHAM, J.I., *Exodus*, WBC 3, Waco 1987

EVANS, C.A., *Mark, 8,27-16,20*, WBC 34B, Nashville 2001.

ERNST, J., *Das Evangelium nach Markus*, RNT, Regensburg 1981.

FITZMYER, J.A., *The Gospel According to Luke*, (X-XXIV), AncB 28A, New York 1985.

GERSTENBERGER, E.S., *Das dritte Buch Mose: Leviticus*. ATD 6, Göttingen 1993.

GNILKA, J., *Das Evangelium nach Markus* EKK II/1,2, Zürich 1978-1979.

GNILKA, J., *Das Matthäusevangelium*, HThK, II/2, Freiburg 1988.

GOULD, E.P., A *Critical and Exegetical Commentary of the Gospel According to St. Mark*, ICC, Edinburgh 1907[4].

GRUNDMANN, W., *Das Evangelium nach Markus*, ThHK, Berlin 1965[3]

GUELICH, R.A., *Mark 1,1-8,26*, WBC 34A, Dallas 1989.

GUNDRY, R.H., *Mark, A Commentary on His Apology for the Cross*, Grand Rapids 1993.

HARRINGTON, W., *Mark*, Wilmington 1979.

HAUCK, F., *Das Evangelium des Markus, (Synoptiker I)*, THNT 2, Leipzig 1931.

HARTLEY, J.E., *Leviticus*, WBC 4, Dallas 1992.

HOOKER, M.D., *The Gospel According to Saint Mark*, London 1991.

HUBY, J., *L'Évangile selon Saint Marc*, Paris 1961.

KERTELGE, K., *Markusevangelium*, NEB-NT 2, Würzburg 1994

KNABENBAUER, J., *Evangelium secundum S. Marcum*, Parisiis 1894.

LAGRANGE, M.J., *L'Évangile selon Saint Marc*, Paris 1929[4].

LANE, W.L., *The Gospel According to Mark*, NICNT, Grand Rapids 1982[2].

LÉGASSE, S., *L' Évangile de Marc*, I-II, LD Commentaires 5, Paris 1997.

LEVINE, B.A., *The Leviticus*, JPSTC, Philadelphia 1989.

LOHMEYER, E., *Das Evangelium des Markus*, Göttingen 1967[17].

LÜHRMANN, D., *Das Markusevangelium*, HNT 3, Tübingen 1987.

MANN, C.S., *Mark*, AncB 27, Garden City 1986.

MARCUS, J., *Mark 1-8*, AncB 27, New York 1999.

MEYERS, C.L. - MEYERS E.M., *Zechariah 9-14*, AncB 25c, New York 1993.

MILGROM, J., *Leviticus*, III/1,2,3. AncB 3,3A,3B, New York - London 1991-2000-20001.

MILLER, P.D., *Deuteronomy*, Interpretation XIII, Louisville 1990.

NINEHAM, D.E., *The Gospel of St. Mark*, Middlesex 1963[1].

NOTH, M., *Leviticus*, tr. Anderson, J. E., London 1965.

PENNA, A., *Deuteronomio*, Roma 1976.

PESCH, R., *Das Markusevangelium*, HThK, II/1,2, Freiburg 1980[3]-1977.

RADERMAKERS, J., *La bonne nouvelle de Jésus selon saint Marc*, Bruxelles 1974.

SCHNACKENBURG, R., *Das Evangelium nach Markus*, II/2, Düsseldorf 1988[4].

SCHNIEWIND, J., *Das Evangelium nach Markus*, Göttingen 1952.

SCHÜRMANN, H., *Das Lukasevangelium*, HThK 3, II/2a, Freiburg 1993.

SCHWEIZER, E., *Das Evangelium nach Markus* NTD 1, Göttingen 1983[6].

SISTI, A., *Marco*, Roma 1974[3].

SMITH, R.L., *Micah-Malachi*, WBC 32, Waco 1984.

SWETE, H.B., *The Gospel according to St. Mark*, London 1908[2].

TATE, M.E., *Psalms 51-100*, WBC 20, Dallas 1990.

TAYLOR, V., *The Gospel according to St. Mark*, London 1953.

VAN IERSEL, B.M.F., *Mark: A Reader-Response Commentary*, tr. W.H. Bisseheroux, JSNT.S 164, Sheffield 1998.

WATTS, J.D., *Isaiah 1-33*, WBC 24, Waco 1985.

WEINFELD, M., *Deuteronomy, 1-11*, AncB 5, New York 1991.

WEISS, B., *Das Marcusevangelium und seine Synoptischen Parallelen*, Berlin 1872

————, *Die Evangelien des Markus und Lukas*, Göttingen 1901[9].

WELLHAUSEN, J., *Das Evangelium Marci*, Berlin 1909[2].

WENHAM, G.J., *The Book of Leviticus*, NICOT XIII, Grand Rapids 1979.

WOHLENBERG, G., *Das Evangelium des Markus*, Leipzig 1930[3].

2. Books and Articles

ALAND, K., *Synopsis of the Four Gospels*, Stuttgart 1989[9].

ALBERTZ, M., *Die synoptischen Streitgespräche. Ein Beitrag zur Formengeschichte des Urchristentums*, Berlin 1921.

ALBERTZ, R., *A History of Israelite Religion in The Old Testament Period*, Vol. I, London 1994.

AMBROZIC, A.M., *The Hidden Kingdom. A Redaction-Critical Study of the References to the Kingdom of God in Mark's Gospel*, CBQMS 2, Washington 1972.

BALZ, H. - SCHNEIDER, G., ed. *Exegetical Dictionary of the New Testament*, I-III, Grand Rapids 1990-1993.

BARBIERO, G., *L' asino del nemico*, AnBib 128, Roma 1991.

BARR, J., «'Abbā Isn't Daddy», JTS 39 (1988) 28-47.

BAUER, W.-GINGRICH, F.W.-DANKER, F.W., *A Greek-English Lexicon of the New Testament and Other Early Christian Literature*, Chicago-London 1979[2].

BAUMGÄRTEL, F., «Καρδία», *TDNT* III, 605-607.

BEHM, J., «αἷμα», «αἱματεκχυσία», *TDNT* I, 172-177.

BERGER, K., *Die Gesetzesauslegung Jesu. Ihr historischer Hintergrund im Judentum und im Alten Testament. Teil I: Markus und Parallelen*, WMANT 40, Neukirchen 1972.

————, *Formgeschichte des Neuen Testaments*, Heidelberg 1984.

BIHLMEYER, K., *Die Apostolischen Väter*, Neubearbeitung der Funkschen Ausgabe von Karl Bihlmeyer. Erster Teil: Didache, Barnabas, Klemens I und II, Ignatius, Polykarp, Papias, Quadratus, Diognetbrief, Tübingen 1924.

BLASS, F. - DEBRUNNER, A.- FUNK, R.W., *A Greek Grammar of the New Testament and Other Early Christian Literature*, Chicago-London 1961.

BORNKAMM, G., «Das Doppelgebot der Liebe», in Fs. Rudolf Bultmann, BZNW 21, Berlin 1954, 85-93.

BOTTERWECK, G. J.- RINGGREN, H.-FABRY, H.J., *Theologisches Wörterbuch zum Alten Testament* ,1-8, Stuttgart 1973-1995.

BRAULIK, G., «Das Deuteronomium und die Geburt des Monotheismus», in *Studien zur Theologie des Deuteronomium*, SBA 2, Stuttgart 1988.

BROADHEAD, E.K., *Teaching with Authority: Miracles and Christology in the Gospel of Mark,* Sheffield 1992.

BROWN, R.E., *The Death of the Messiah,* From Gethsemane to the Grave, A Commentary on the Passion Narratives in the Four Gospels, Vol I, London 1994.

BULTMANN, R., *Die Geschichte der synoptischen Tradition,* Göttingen 1931².

BULTMANN, R., *Die Geschichte der synoptischen Tradition, Ergänzungsheft,* bearbeitet von G.Theißen und Ph.Vielhauer, Göttingen 1971⁴.

BURCHARD, C., «Das doppelte Liebesgebot in der frühen christlichen Überlieferung», in *Der Ruf Jesu und die Antwort der Gemeinde.* Fs. J. Jeremias, Göttingen 1970, 39-62.

CHOLEWINSKI, A., *Heiligkeitsgesetz und Deuteronomium,* AnBib 66, Rome 1976.

COLLINS, R.F., «Commandment», *ABD* I, 1097-1099.

COLPE, C., «ὁ υἱὸς τοῦ ἀνθρώπου», *TDNT* VIII, 400-476.

COOK, J.G., *The Structure and Persuasive Power of Mark: A Linguistic Approach,* SBL.SS 28, Atlanta 1995.

DE JONGE, M., ed. *Testamenta XII Patriarcharum,* Pseudepigrapha Veteris Testamenti Graece 1, Leiden 1964.

dE lA POTTERIE, I., «De Compositione evangelii Marci», *VD* 44 (1966)135-141

DIEZINGER, W., «Zum Liebesgebot Mk XII, 28-34 und Par», *NT* 20 (1978) 81-83.

ECKART, O., *Theologische Ethik des Alten Testaments,* ThW3.2, Stuttgart 1994.

EGGER, W., *Methodenlehre zum Neuen Testament. Einführung in linguistische und historisch-kritische Methoden,* Freiburg 1987.

EHRLICH, A.B. *Miqra ki-Pheschuto,* Berlin 1900.

JENNI, E.-WESTERMANN, C., *Theologisches Handwörterbuch zum Alten Testament,* 1-2, München 1971-1976.

FABRY, H.-J., «לֵב», «לֵבָב», *TWAT,* IV, 413-451.

FITZMYER, J.A., «*ABBA* and Jesus' Relation to God» in *`A Cause de L' Évangile,* Fs. P. Jaques Dupont, Le Div 123, Paris 1985, 15-38.

————, «Κύριος», *EDNT* II, 328-331.

FRANCE, A.T., *Jesus and the Old Testament,* London 1971.

FREEDMAN, D.N., ed. *The Anchor Bible Dictionary,* I-VI, New York 1992.

FULLER, R.H., «The Double Commandment of Love: A Test Case for the Criteria of Authenticity», in *Essays on the Love Commandment,* Fuller, R.H., ed. Philadelphia 1978, 41-56.

FURNISH, V.P., *The Love Command in the New Testament,* New York 1972.

GORDON, C.H. «His Name is "One"», JNES 29 (1970) 198-199.

GRUNDMANN, W., «Ἰσχύω», *TDNT* III, 397-402.

———, «δεῖ», *TDNT* II, 21-25.

HAYS, R.B., *The Moral Vision of the New Testament*, A Contemporary Introduction to New Testament Ethics, San Francisco 1996

JACOB, E., «Ψυχη'», *TDNT* IX, 608-631.

JEREMIAS, J., *ABBA*: Studien zur neutestamentlichen Theologie und Zeitgeschichte, Göttingen 1966.

JOÜON, P., *Grammaire del'hébreu biblique, Édition photomécanique corrigée* (1965), Institut Biblique Pontifical, Rome 1923.

KERTELGE, K., «Das Doppelgebot der Liebe im Markusevangelium.» in: ʾA *Cause de L'Évangile*, Fs. P. Jaques Dupont, Le Div 123, Paris 1985, 303-322.

KIILUNEN, J., *Das Doppelgebot der Liebe in synoptischer Sicht. Ein redaktionskritischer Versuch über Mk 12,28-34 und die Parallelen* STAT 250, Helsinki 1989.

KITTEL, G. - FRIEDRICH, G., ed. *Theological Dictionary of the New Testament*, I-IX, Grand Rapids 1964-1976.

KITTEL, G., «Αββα», *TDNT* I, 5-6.

KUTHIRAKKATTEL, S., *The Beginning of Jesus' Ministry According to Mark's Gospel (1,14-3,6): A Redaction Critical Study*, An Bib 123, Roma 1990.

KUTSCH, E., *Verheißung und Gesetz. Untersuchungen zum sogenannten «Bund» im Alten Testament*. BZAW 131, Berlin-New York 1973.

———, «בְּרִית», «Verpflichtung», *THAT* I, 339-351.

LIMBECK, M., «ἐντολή» *EDNT* I, 459-460.

LOHFINK, N., *Das Hauptgebot*, AnBib, Rome 1963.

———, «Gott im Buch Deuteronomium», in *La Notion biblique de Dieu: Le Dieu de la Bible et le Dieu des philosophes*, Coppens, J., ed. BEThL 41, Louvain 1976, 101-126.

———, *Great Themes of the Old Testament*, tr. R. Walls, Edinburgh 1982.

MALINA, A., «*Non Come Gli Scribi» (Mc 1,22) Studio del loro ruolo nel Vangelo di Marco: Estratto della tesi di dottorato nella Facoltà Biblica del PIB*, Roma, Pontificio Istituto Biblico, 2001.

MALONEY, E.C., *Semitic Interference in Marcan Syntax, SBL.DS 51*, Chico 1981.

MATHYS, H.P., *Liebe deinen Nächsten wie dich selbst. Untersuchungenzum alttestamentlichen Gebot der Nächstenliebe (Lev. 19,18)*, OBO 71, Göttingen 1986.

MCBRIDE, S.D., «The Yoke of the Kingdom. An Exposition of Deuteronomy 6,4-5», *Interp* 27 (1973) 273-306.

MEIER, J.P., «Jesus», NJBC, (78), 1316-1328.

METZGER, B., *A Textual Commentary on the Greek New Testament*, Stuttgart 1994[2]

MINETTE DE TILLESSE, G., *Le Secret Messianique dans l' Évangile de Marc*, Lec Div 47, Paris 1968.

MORGENTHALER, R., *Statistik des neutestamentlichen Wortschatzes*, Zürich-Frankfurt 1982[3].

MOULTON, W.F. - GEDEN, A.S. - MOULTON, H.S., ed. *A Concordance to the Greek Testament*, Edinburgh 1978[5].

MUDISO MBA MUNDLA, J.D., *Jesus und die Führer Israels. Studien zu den sog. Jerusalemer Streitgesprächen*, Münster 1984.

NESTLE - ALAND., *Novum Testamentum Graece*, Stuttgart 1995[27.]

NEIRYNCK, F., *Duality in Mark, Contributions to the Study of the MarkanRedaction*, BEThL 31, Leuven 1988[2].

NEUDECKER, R., «"And You Shall Love Your Neighbor as Yourself - I Am the Lord" (Lev 19,18) in Jewish Interpretation.», Bib 73 (1992) 496-517.

NISSEN, A., *Gott und der Nächste im antiken Judentum. Untersuchungen zum Doppelgebot der Liebe*, WUNT 15, Tübingen 1974.

PERRIN, N., *What is Redaction Criticism?*, Philadelphia 1969,

PESCH, R., *Abendmahl und Jesu Todesverständnis*, Quaestiones Disputatae, 80, Freiburg 1978.

PIPER. J., *'Love your Enemies.' Jesus' Love Command in the Synoptic Gospels and in the Early Christian Paraenesis*, MSSNTS 38, Cambridge - London 1979.

RAHLFS, A., *Septuaginta*, I, II, Stuttgart 1962[7.]

REISER, M., *Syntax und Stil des Markusevangeliums im Licht der hellenistischen Volksliteratur*, WUNT 2, Tübingen 1984.

REPLOH, K.G., *Markus-Lehrer der Gemeinde: Eine redaktionsgeschichtliche Studie zu den Jüngerperikopen des Markusevangeliums* SBM 9, Stuttgart 1969.

RHOADS, D. - MICHIE, D., *Mark as Story: An Introduction to the Narrative of a Gospel*, Philadelphia 1982.

SARIOLA, H., *Markus und das Gesetz. Eine redaktionskritische Untersuchung*, AASF. DHL 56, Helsinki 1990.

SCHELBERT, G., «Abba, Vater! Stand der Frage», *FZPhTh* 40 (1993) 257-281.

SCHNEIDER, G., «ἀγάπη», *EDNT* I, 8-12.

SCHRENK, G., «ἐντολή», *TDNT* II, 545-556.

———, «θέλω», *TDNT* III, 44-54.

SCHULLER, E.M., «The Psalm of 4Q 372 1. Within the Context of Second Temple Prayer, *CBQ* 54 (1992) 67-79».

SPICQ, C., *Agape dans le NT*, I-III, analyse des textes par C. Spicq, Études Bibliques, Paris 1958-1959.

STOCK, A., *The Method and Message of Mark*, Wilmington 1989.

STOCK, K., *Boten aus dem Mit-Ihm-Sein. Das Verhältnis zwischen Jesus und den Zwölf nach Markus*, An Bib 70, Rome 1975.

————, «Gliederung und Zusammenhang in Mk 11-12», *Bib* 59 (1978) 481-515.

STRACK, H.L. - BILLERBECK, P., *Kommentar zum neuen Testament aus Talmud und Midrasch*, I-IV, München 1954-1961[2].

SUHL, A., *Die Funktion der alttestamentlichen Zitate und Anspielungen im Markusevangelium*, Gütersloh 1966.

THOMAS, K.J., «Liturgical Citations in the Synoptics», *NTS* 22 (1975-76)205-214.

TOLBERT, M. A., *Sowing the Gospel. Mark's World in Literary-Historical Perspective*, Minneapolis 1989.

WEINFELD, M., *Deuteronomy and the Deuteronomic School*, Oxford 1972.

WEISS, W., «Eine neue Lehre in Vollmacht». *Die Streit-und Schulgespräche des Markus- Evangeliums*, BZNW 53, Berlin-New York 1989.

WESTERMANN, C., «נֶפֶשׁ», «Seele», *THAT*, II, 71-96.

ZERWICK, M., *Untersuchungen zum Markus-Stil*, Romae 1937.

————, *Biblical Greek*, tr. J. Smith, Rome 1963.

ZERWICK, M. - GROSVENOR, M., *A Grammatical Analysis of the Greek New Testament*, Roma 1996[5].

ZOBEL, K., *Prophetie und Deuteronomium. Die Rezeption prophetischer Theologie durch das Deuteronomium*, BZAW 119, Berlin 1992.

AUTHOR INDEX

SCRIPTURAL INDEX

Finito di stampare
nel mese di Giugno 2003

presso la tipografia
"Giovanni Olivieri" di E. Montefoschi
00187 Roma • Via dell'Archetto, 10, 11, 12
Tel. 06 6792327 • E-mail: tip.olivieri@libero.it